FUNDAMENTALS OF
ENGLISH
GRAMMAR

Second Edition

WORKBOOK

FUNDAMENTALS OF
ENGLISH GRAMMAR
Second Edition

WORKBOOK

Betty Schrampfer Azar
Donald A. Azar

PRENTICE HALL REGENTS
Upper Saddle River, New Jersey 07458

Publisher: *Tina B. Carver*
Managing Editor, Production: *Sylvia Moore*
Editorial/Production Supervisor: *Janet Johnston*
Editorial Assistants: *Shelley Hartle, Athena Foley*
Buyer and Scheduler: *Ray Keating*
Illustrator: *Don Martinetti*
Cover Supervisor: *Marianne Frasco*
Cover Designer: *Joel Mitnick Design*
Interior Designer: *Ros Herion Freese*

Printed in the United States of America
10

ISBN   0-13-347097-0

ISBN 0-13-347071-7 (VOL. A)
ISBN 0-13-347089-X (VOL. B)

PRENTICE-HALL INTERNATIONAL (UK) LIMITED, *LONDON*
PRENTICE-HALL OF AUSTRALIA PTY. LIMITED, *SYDNEY*
PRENTICE-HALL CANADA INC., *TORONTO*
PRENTICE-HALL HISPANOAMERICANA, S.A., *MEXICO*
PRENTICE-HALL OF INDIA PRIVATE LIMITED, *NEW DELHI*
PRENTICE-HALL OF JAPAN, INC., *TOKYO*
PEARSON EDUCATION ASIA PTE. LTD., *SINGAPORE*
EDITORA PRENTICE-HALL DO BRASIL, LTDA., *RIO DE JANEIRO*

To Immee, Amelia Azar

Contents

Chapter 1   PRESENT TIME

Chapter 2 PAST TIME

Chapter 3 FUTURE TIME

Chapter 4   NOUNS AND PRONOUNS

Chapter 5   MODAL AUXILIARIES

Chapter 6 QUESTIONS

Chapter 7 THE PRESENT PERFECT AND THE PAST PERFECT

Chapter 8 COUNT/NONCOUNT NOUNS AND ARTICLES

Chapter 9   CONNECTING IDEAS

Chapter 10   GERUNDS AND INFINITIVES

Chapter 11   THE PASSIVE

Chapter 12   ADJECTIVE CLAUSES

Chapter 13 COMPARISONS

Chapter 14 NOUN CLAUSES

Chapter 15 QUOTED SPEECH AND REPORTED SPEECH

Chapter 16 USING WISH; USING *IF*

Preface

This *Workbook* consists of exercises to accompany *Fundamentals of English Grammar (2nd edition)*, a developmental skills text for mid-level ESL/EFL students. The exercises are designated SELFSTUDY (answers given) or GUIDED STUDY (answers not given). The SELFSTUDY practices are intended for students to use independently. The answers are in a separate, detachable *Answer Key* booklet at the back of this book. The GUIDED STUDY practices may be selected by the teacher for additional classwork, homework, or individualized instruction. Answers to the GUIDED STUDY practices, as well as suggestions for using the *Workbook,* can be found in the *Teacher's Guide.*

Many of the initial practices in each unit are tightly controlled and deliberate, intended to clarify form and meaning. Control is then loosened as the manipulative and clarifying practices lead to others that promote free, creative use of the target structures. The *Workbook* also contains suggestions for writing and various group activities such as games and discussions.

ACKNOWLEDGMENTS

I am grateful to the many people who enable me to pursue the work I love. I am especially indebted to my husband, mainstay, and co-author, Don, who kept me afloat through the recent illness and loss of my much loved mother and provided the support system in which our work together could continue and prosper.

I am also greatly indebted to Shelley Hartle, our editorial assistant, without whom it would have been impossible to keep to production schedule. Though still new to the team, she adapted quickly and handled everything with aplomb, from proofing galleys and compiling indexes to tending the ducks when we had to be away.

Many thanks to Janet Johnston, our production editor, who kept everything running smoothly on her end and was wonderfully supportive and understanding. Thanks similarly go to Sylvia Moore, managing editor. Special thanks also go to Tina Carver, publisher, who has been consistently supportive not only as a friend but as a top-notch publishing professional whose sound judgment I highly respect.

My appreciation goes, too, to Ray Adame, Barbara Barysh, Nancy Baxer, Eric Bredenberg, Karen Chiang, Athena Foley, Norman Harris, Terry Jennings, Gordon Johnson, Ray Keating, Andy Martin, Don Martinetti, Gil Muller, Ed Perez, Jack Ross, Jerry Smith, and Ed Stanford. In addition, my gratitude goes to Joy Edwards, Barbara Matthies, and R.T. Steltz. Chelsea Azar has been splendid. Finally, I am lovingly grateful to my father for his continuing support and involvement in my endeavors. Many of his ideas and suggestions are reflected in the text.

BETTY SCHRAMPFER AZAR

Once again, I begin by expressing my gratitude to Betty for her continued patience and guidance, and for the same incredible expertise that she brings to all phases of this project. Much of this was accomplished during a difficult time. Her ability and persistence got the book out. I continue to marvel and to learn.

I want to thank my father-in-law, Bill Schrampfer, for numerous handwritten ideas for topics and sentences. His agile mind provided much fodder. Inspiration appeared from many sources, R.T. Steltz, Tom Hemba, and my uncle Elias George among them, as well as Fred Lockyear, Gary Althen and other colleagues whose brains I often pick without knowing why until I start putting sentences down.

And special thanks still go to Chelsea Azar. She continues to endure our commitment to these projects and always provides joy and support.

DONALD A. AZAR

CHAPTER 1
Present Time

◇ **PRACTICE 1—SELFSTUDY:** Interview questions and answers.

Directions: Complete the sentences with appropriate words.

A: Hi. My name _____*is*_____ Kunio.

B: Hi. My _____*name*_____ is Maria. I _____ glad to meet you.

KUNIO: I _____ glad to _____ you, too. Where _____?

MARIA: I _____ from Mexico. Where _____?

KUNIO: I _____ Japan.

MARIA: Where _____ living now?

KUNIO: On Fifth Avenue in _____ apartment. And you?

MARIA: I _____ living in a dorm.

KUNIO: _____ your field of study?

MARIA: Business. After I study English, I _____ going to attend the School of Business Administration. How _____ you? _____ your major?

KUNIO: Chemistry.

MARIA: _____ you like to do in your free time? _____ you have any hobbies?

KUNIO: I _____ to swim. How _____ you?

MARIA: I read a lot and I _____ stamps from all over the world.

KUNIO: Really? _____ you like some stamps from Japan?

MARIA: Sure! That would be great! Thanks.

KUNIO: I have _____ write your full name on the board when I introduce _____ to the class. _____ do you spell your name?

MARIA: My first _____ is Maria. M-A-R-I-A. My last _____ is Lopez. L-O-P-E-Z.

KUNIO: My _____ name is Kunio. K-U-N-I-O. My _____ name is

Akiwa. A-K-I-W-A.

MARIA: Kunio Akiwa. _____ that right?

KUNIO: Yes, it _____. It's been nice talking with you.

MARIA: I enjoyed it, too.

◇ **PRACTICE 2—GUIDED STUDY: Introducing yourself.**

Directions: Write answers to the questions. Use your own paper.

1. What is your name?
2. Where are you from?
3. Where are you living?
4. Why are you here (in this city)?
   a. Are you a student? If so, what is your major field of study?
   b. Do you work? If so, what is your job?
   c. Do you have another reason for being here?
5. What do you like to do in your free time?
6. What is your favorite season of the year? Why?
7. What are your three favorite books?
8. Describe your first day at this school.

◇ **PRACTICE 3—GUIDED STUDY: Present verbs. (Charts 1–1 → 1–3)**

Directions: All of the following sentences contain mistakes. Find the mistakes and rewrite each
sentence correctly.

Example: I no like cold weather. → ***I don't like cold weather.***

1. I no living at home right now.

2. I be living in this city.

3. Student at this school.

4. I am study English.

5. I am not knowing my teacher's name.

6. (*supply name*) teach our English class.

7. She/He* expect us to be in class on time.

8. We always are coming to class on time.

9. Tom does he going to school?

10. Tom no go to school.

11. My sister don't have a job.

12. Does Sara has a job?

_____

*Choose the appropriate pronoun for your teacher, *he* or *she*.

13. Does you have a job?

14. Is Canada does it be north of the United States?

15. I never to go to my office on Saturday.

16. Ahmed, Toshi, Ji, Ingrid, and Pedro eats lunch together every day.

◇ **PRACTICE 4—SELFSTUDY:**   Present verbs. (Charts 1–1 → 1–3)

Directions: Use the given verb to complete the sentence that follows. Use the SIMPLE PRESENT or the PRESENT PROGRESSIVE.

1. *sit*   I _____*am sitting*_____ at my desk right now.

2. *read*   I _____ the second sentence in this exercise.

3. *look*   I _____ at sentence 3 now.

4. *write* Now I _____ the right completion for this sentence.

5. *do*   I _____ a grammar exercise.

6. *sit*   I usually _____*sit*_____ at my desk when I do my homework. And right

   now I _____*am sitting*_____ at my desk to do this exercise.

7. *read*   I often _____ the newspaper, but right now I

   _____ a sentence in my grammar workbook.

8. *look*   I _____ at the newspaper every day. But right now I

   _____ at my grammar workbook.

9. *write* When I do exercises in this workbook, I _____ the answers in my

   book and then I check them in the *Answer Key*.* Right now I _____

   an answer in the book.

10. *do*   I _____ grammar exercises every day. Right now I

   _____ Practice 4 in this workbook.

◇ **PRACTICE 5—SELFSTUDY:**   Forms of the simple present. (Chart 1–1)

Directions: Review the basic forms of the SIMPLE PRESENT TENSE by completing the sentences with the correct form of the verb "SPEAK."

***PART I*: STATEMENT FORMS**

1. I (*speak*) _____*speak*_____ English.

2. They (*speak*) _____ English.

3. He (*speak*) _____ English.

4. You (*speak*) _____ English.

5. She (*speak*) _____ English.

---

*The *Answer Key* to the selfstudy practices is in the back of this book.

PART II: NEGATIVE FORMS

1. I (speak, not) _____*do not (don't) speak*_____ your language.

2. They (speak, not) _____ English.

3. He (speak, not) _____ English.

4. You (speak, not) _____ English.

5. She (speak, not) _____ English.

PART III: QUESTION FORMS

1. (you, speak) _____*Do you speak*_____ English?

2. (they, speak) _____ English?

3. (he, speak) _____ English?

4. (we, speak) _____ English?

5. (she, speak) _____ English?

◇ **PRACTICE 6—SELFSTUDY: Simple present. (Charts 1–1 → 1–3)**

Directions: Write **-S/-ES** in the blanks where necessary and make any other needed changes in the verb. If the verb does not need **-S/-ES**, put a slash (/) in the blank.

1. Alan like_**s**_ to play soccer.

2. My son watch_**es**_ too much TV.

3. Rita do_**es**_n't like _/_ coffee.

4. Monkeys climb_____ trees.

5. Do_____ you like_____ to climb trees?

6. Do_____ Paul like_____ to cook?

7. Alex like_____ to dance

8. Mike wash_____ his own clothes.

9. Rita go_____ to school at seven.

10. Bees make_____ honey.

11. A bee visit_____ many flowers in one day.

12. Tina get_____ her work done on time.

13. Tina and Pat get_____ their work done.

14. Do_____ Bill get_____ his work done?

15. Eric do_____n't get_____ it done on time.

16. David carry_____ a briefcase to work.

17. Janet play_____ tennis every day.

18. A frog catch_____ flies with its tongue.

19. Frogs are small green animals that live_____ near water.

20. A turtle is another animal that live_____ near water.

◇ PRACTICE 7—GUIDED STUDY: Final forms with *-s/-es.* (Charts 1–1 → 1–3)

Directions: Complete the sentences in COLUMN A with the words from COLUMN B.
- Capitalize the first word of the sentence.
- Add final **-S/-ES** to the verb if necessary.
- Add a period or question mark at the end of the sentence.

Example: 1. **A star shines in the sky at night.**

COLUMN A	COLUMN B
1. a star	A. cause air pollution
2. a hotel	B. stretch when you pull on it
3. newspaper ink	C. support a huge variety of marine life
4. bees	✔ D. shine in the sky at night
5. do automobiles	E. cause great destruction when it reaches land
6. does physical exercise	F. use its long trunk like a hand to pick things up
7. a rubber band	G. improve your circulation and general health
8. a river	H. stain my hands when I read the paper
9. oceans	I. produce one-fourth of the world's coffee
10. Brazil	J. gather nectar from flowers
11. does an elephant	K. flow downhill
12. a hurricane	L. supply its guests with clean towels

◇ PRACTICE 8—SELFSTUDY: Forms of the present progressive. (Charts 1–1 and 1–2)

Directions: Review the basic forms of the PRESENT PROGRESSIVE by completing the sentences with the correct form of the verb "SPEAK."

PART I: **STATEMENT FORMS**

1. I (*speak*) _____ **am speaking** _____ English right now.

2. They (*speak*) _____ English right now.

3. She (*speak*) _____ English right now.

4. You (*speak*) _____ English right now.

PART II: **NEGATIVE FORMS**

1. I (*speak, not*) _____ **am not speaking** _____ English right now.

2. They (*speak, not*) _____ English right now.

3. He (*speak, not*) _____ English right now.

4. You (*speak, not*) _____ English right now.

PART III: **QUESTION FORMS**

1. (*you, speak*) _____ **Are you speaking** _____ English right now?

2. (*they, speak*) _____ English right now?

3. (*she, speak*) _____ English right now?

4. (*we, speak*) _____ English right now?

◇ **PRACTICE 9—SELFSTUDY: Simple present and present progressive. (Charts 1–1 → 1–3)**

Directions: Complete the sentences with **DO, DOES, IS,** or **ARE**. If no completion is needed, put a slash (/) in the blank.

1. Jack ___**does**___ not work at his father's store.

2. ___**Do**___ you have a job?

3. Kate ___**/**___ works at a restaurant.

4. Tom ___**is**___ working this afternoon.

5. _____ you working today?

6. Emily and Sara _____ working at the ice cream store this summer.

7. _____ Eric planning to get a job this summer?

8. _____ you plan to get a job, too?

9. Denise _____ wears jeans to work every day.

10. She _____ a carpenter.

11. Today she _____ working at the Hills' house.

12. She and her partner Scott _____ building a new porch for Mr. and Mrs. Hill.

13. Denise and Scott usually _____ work together on small construction jobs.

14. A turtle _____ lays eggs.

15. _____ snakes lay eggs?

16. _____ a lizard lay eggs?

17. _____ a lizard a reptile?

18. _____ turtles and snakes reptiles?

19. Turtles, snakes, and lizards _____ all reptiles.

20. Almost all reptiles _____ lay eggs.

21. Reptiles _____ cold-blooded.

22. Their body temperature _____ the same as the temperature of their surroundings.

◇ **PRACTICE 10—GUIDED STUDY: Simple present and present progressive. (Charts 1–1 → 1–3)**

Directions: Complete the sentences with **DO, DOES, IS,** or **ARE**. If no completion is needed, put a slash (/) in the blank.

1. A mosquito _____ flying around Sam's head.

2. Mosquitoes _____ pests.

3. They _____ bother people and animals.

4. _____ a male mosquito bite?

5. No, male mosquitoes _____ not bite.

6. Only female mosquitoes _____ bite animals and people.

7. A female mosquito _____ lays 1,000 to 3,000 eggs in her lifetime.

8. How long _____ mosquitoes live?

9. A female mosquito _____ lives for 30 days.

10. A male mosquito _____ not live as long as a female.

11. How long _____ a male mosquito live?

12. It _____ dies after 10 to 20 days.

13. Hillary _____ wearing mosquito repellent.

14. The mosquito repellent _____ smells bad, but it _____ works.

15. The mosquito repellent _____ effective.

16. Mosquitoes _____ stay away from people who _____ wearing mosquito repellent.

17. _____ you ever wear mosquito repellent?

18. _____ mosquito repellent work?

◇ PRACTICE 11—SELFSTUDY: Frequency adverbs. (Charts 1–1 and 1–2)

Directions: Complete each sentence with an appropriate FREQUENCY ADVERB* from the list.

always   *usually*   *often*   *sometimes*   *seldom*   *rarely*   *never*

1. I see one or two movies every week.   → I _____ **often** _____ go to the movies.

2. I let my roommate borrow my car one time last year.

   → I _____ **rarely** _____ let my roommate borrow my car.

3. Maria eats cereal for breakfast seven days a week.

   → Maria _____ eats cereal for breakfast.

4. Four out of five visitors to the museum stay for three hours or longer.

   → Museum visitors _____ stay for at least three hours.

5. We occasionally have quizzes in Dr. Jacobs's history class.

   → Dr. Jacobs _____ gives quizzes in history class.

_____
*See Chart 7–8 for more information about frequency adverbs.

6. If the teacher is on time, the class begins at 8:00 A.M. Once in a while, the teacher is a few

   mintues late.   → The class _____ begins at 8:00 A.M.

7. The train from Chicago has been late ninety percent of the time.

   → The train from Chicago is _____ on time.

8. In the desert, it rains only two days between May and September every year.

   → It _____ rains there in the summer.

9. James asks me to go the the sailboat races every year, but I don't accept his invitation because
   I think sailboat racing is boring.

   → I _____ go to sailboat races with James.

10. Every time I go to a movie, I buy popcorn.

    → I _____ buy popcorn when I go to a movie.

11. Andy and Jake are friends. They go out to dinner at least three times a week.

    → Andy and Jake _____ go out to dinner with each other.

12. Andy and Jake do business with each other every once in a while. Most of the time they don't
    discuss business when they go out to dinner with each other.

    → They _____ discuss business during dinner.

◇ **PRACTICE 12—GUIDED STUDY: Simple present: frequency adverbs. (Charts 1–1 and 1–2)**

Directions: Make sentences about yourself. Use FREQUENCY ADVERBS with the given ideas.

Example: wear sandals in the summer
        → *I usually wear sandals in the summer.*
Example: read poetry in my spare time
        → *I rarely read poetry in my spare time.*

FREQUENCY ADVERBS:

   always   usually   often   sometimes   seldom   rarely   never

1. wear a suit to class

2. go to sleep at ten-thirty

3. read mystery stories before I go to sleep

4. hand in my school assignments on time

5. listen to the radio in the morning

6. speak to strangers at a bus stop

7. believe the things I read in newspapers

8. call a friend if I feel lonely or homesick

9. wear a hat when the weather is chilly

10. have chocolate ice cream for dessert

◇ **PRACTICE 13—SELFSTUDY:** Present progressive. (Charts 1–1 and 1–2)

Directions: Use the PRESENT PROGRESSIVE to identify the actions in the pictures.

He is swimming.
He's doing the crawl.

1. _____

2. _____

3. _____

4. _____

5. _____

6. _____

7. _____

8. _____

◇ **PRACTICE 14—GUIDED STUDY:** Present verbs. (Charts 1-1 and 1-2)

Directions: Use the PRESENT PROGRESSIVE to identify the actions in the pictures.

1. _____

2. _____

3. _____

4. _____

5. _____

6. _____

7. _____

8. _____

◇ **PRACTICE 15—SELFSTUDY:** Simple present and present progressive. (Charts 1–1 → 1–4)

Directions: Complete the sentences with the SIMPLE PRESENT or PRESENT PROGRESSIVE form of the verbs in the list. Each verb is used only one time.

belong	need	see	✔take
bite	play	shine	understand
drive	prefer	sing	watch
look	rain	✔snow	write

1. Look outside! It _____**is snowing**_____. Everything is beautiful and all white.

2. My father _____**takes**_____ the 8:15 train into the city every weekday morning.

3. On Tuesdays and Thursdays, I walk to work for the exercise. Every Monday, Wednesday, and

   Friday, I _____ my car to work.

4. A: Charlie, can't you hear the telephone? Answer it!

   B: You get it! I _____ my favorite TV show. I don't want to miss

   anything.

5. A: What kind of tea do you like?

   B: Well, I'm drinking black tea, but I _____ green tea.

6. I'm gaining weight around my waist. These pants are too tight. I _____ a larger pair of pants.

7. A: Dinner's ready. Please call the children.

   B: Where are they?

   A: They _____ a game outside in the street.

8. It's night. There's no moon. Emily is outside. She _____ at the sky. She _____ more stars than she can count.

9. Michael has a good voice. Sometimes he _____ with a musical group in town. It's a good way to earn a little extra money.

10. A: Ouch!

   B: What's the matter?

   A: Every time I eat too fast, I _____ my tongue.

11. Alicia always _____ in her diary after dinner.

12. Thank you for your help in algebra. Now I _____ that lesson.

13. This magazine isn't mine. It _____ to Colette.

14. I can see a rainbow because the sun _____ and it _____ at the same time.

◇ **PRACTICE 16—SELFSTUDY:** Present verbs: questions and short answers. (Chart 1–5)

Directions: Complete the questions with **DO**, **DOES**, **IS**, or **ARE**. Then complete both the affirmative and negative short answers.

1. A: ___*Are*___ you leaving now?

   B: Yes, ___*I am*___. OR: No, ___*I'm not*___.

2. A: ___*Do*___ your neighbors know that you are a police officer?

   B: Yes, ___*they do*___. OR: No, ___*they don't*___.

3. A: _____ you follow the same routine every morning?

   B: Yes, _____. OR: No, _____.

4. A: _____ Dr. Jarvis know the name of her new assistant yet?

   B: Yes, _____. OR: No, _____.

5. A: _____ Paul and Beth studying the problem?

   B: Yes, _____. OR: No, _____.

6. A: _____ they understand the problem?

   B: Yes, _____. OR: No, _____.

7. A: _____ Mike reading the paper and watching television at the same time?

   B: Yes, _____. OR: No, _____.

8. A: _____ you listening to me?

    B: Yes, _____. OR: No, _____.

9. A: _____ that building safe?

    B: Yes, _____. OR: No, _____.

10. A: _____ the weather affect* your mood?

    B: Yes, _____. OR: No, _____.

◇ **PRACTICE 17—GUIDED STUDY: Present progressive. (Charts 1–1 and 1–2)**

> Directions: In small groups, pretend to perform actions. One member of the group pretends to do something, and the rest of the group tries to guess what the action is and describe it using the PRESENT PROGRESSIVE.

Example: painting a wall

STUDENT A: (pretends to be painting a wall)

OTHERS: You're conducting an orchestra. (No.)
             Are you washing a window? (No.)
             You're painting a wall. (Yes!)

SUGGESTIONS FOR ACTION:

painting a wall	*playing the piano*
drinking a cup of tea/coffee	*swimming*
petting a dog	*driving a car*
dialing a telephone	*watching a tennis match*
climbing a tree	*pitching a baseball*

---

*The word *affect* is a verb: *The weather **affects** my mood.*
 The word *effect* is a noun: *Warm, sunny weather has **a good effect** on my mood.*

◇ **PRACTICE 18—GUIDED STUDY:** Present progressive. (Charts 1–1 and 1–2)

Direction: Practice the PRESENT PROGRESSIVE in pairs or groups.

FIRST: In a small group of your classmates, pretend to perform any usual, common human activity and describe aloud what you are doing.

Example: I'm standing in front of an unpainted wall. I'm opening a can of paint. Now I'm picking up a paintbrush. I'm dipping the brush in a can of paint. I'm lifting the brush. Now I'm painting the wall.

SECOND: Perform the action again while your classmates describe what you are doing.

Example: You're standing in front of an unpainted wall. You're opening a can of paint. Now you're picking up a paintbrush. You're dipping the brush in a can of paint. You're lifting the brush. Now you're painting the wall.

◇ **PRACTICE 19—SELFSTUDY:** Present verbs. (Charts 1–1 → 1–5)

Directions: Use either the SIMPLE PRESENT or the PRESENT PROGRESSIVE of the verbs in parentheses.

1. It (*be*) _____**is**_____ a cool autumn day. The wind (*blow*) _____**is blowing**_____,
   and the leaves (*fall*) _____**are falling**_____ to the ground.

2. My roommate (*eat*) _____ breakfast at exactly seven o'clock every morning. I
   usually (*eat, not*) _____ breakfast at all. What time (*eat, you*)
   _____ in the morning?

3. A: (*shop, you*) _____ at this store every week?

   B: No. I _____. I (*shop, usually*) _____ at the store
   near my apartment.

   A: Why (*shop, you*) _____ here now?

   B: I (*try*) _____ to find something special for my father's birthday.

4. A: Flowers! Flowers for sale! Yes sir!
   Can I help you?

   B: I'll take those—the yellow ones.

   A: Here you are, mister. Are they for
   a special occasion?

   B: I (*buy*) _____
   them for my wife. I (*buy*)
   _____ her flowers
   on the first day of every month.

5. A: I like to read. How about you? (*read, you*) _____ a lot?

   B: Yes, I _____. I (*read*) _____ at least one novel each week,

   and I (*subscribe*) _____ to several magazines. And I always (*look*)

   _____ at the newspaper during breakfast.

6. A: Knock, knock! Anybody home? Hey, Bill! Hi! It's me. Where are you?

   B: I (*be*) _____ in the bedroom!

   A: What are you doing?*

   B: I (*try*) _____ to sleep!

   A: Oh. Sorry. I won't bother you. Tom, shhh. Bill (*rest*) _____.

7. Before you begin to study, you should ask yourself two questions. First, "Why (*study, I*)

   _____ this subject right now?" Second, "What (*want, I*)

   _____ to learn about this topic?" Students (*need*) _____

   to understand the purpose of their study.

8. In cold climates, many trees (*lose*) _____ their leaves in winter. They (*rest*)

   _____ for several months. Then they (*grow*) _____ new leaves

   and flowers in the spring. Some trees (*keep*) _____ their leaves during the

   winter and (*stay*) _____ green all year long. In some regions of the earth, trees

   (*grow, not*) _____ at all. For example, some desert areas (*have, not*)

   _____ any trees. (*grow, trees*) _____ on all of the

   continents in the world?**

◇ **PRACTICE 20—GUIDED STUDY: Present verbs. (Charts 1–1 → 1–4)**

Directions: Use either the SIMPLE PRESENT or the PRESENT PROGRESSIVE of the verbs in parentheses.

1. Ann is a painter. She (*go*) _____ to the opening of every new art show in the

   city. She (*like*) _____ to see the latest work of other artists. Right now she

   (*prepare*) _____ for her own show of her new paintings next month.

2. A: What book (*read, you*) _____?

   B: It's about Spain. I (*think*) _____ you would enjoy it.

   A: I (*see*) _____ sailing ships on the cover.

   B: Yes. It (*be*) _____ about Spanish explorations in the 17th century.

3. A: I (*leave*) _____ now. (*want, you*) _____ to go

   with me into town?

   B: No, thanks. I can't. I (*wait*) _____ for my sister to call from the

   airport so that I can pick her up.

---

*In rapid, informal spoken English, *What are you doing* can sound like "**Whatc**ha do-un?"
**No trees grow in Antarctica.

4. I work for an agricultural equipment company called Ballco. Right now, Ballco (*try*)

_____ to establish business contacts throughout South America. At the

present time, our sales manager (*travel*) _____ in Brazil and (*talk*)

_____ to potential customers. He (*know*) _____ both

Spanish and Portuguese.

5. A: Does the earth turn around and around?

B: Yes, Jimmy. The earth (*spin*) _____ around and around on its axis as it

circles the sun. The earth (*spin*) _____ rapidly at this very moment.

A: I (*feel, not*) _____ anything. (*try, you*) _____

to fool me?

B: Of course not! (*think, you, really*) _____ that the earth isn't

moving?

A: I guess so. Yes. I can't see it move. Yes. It isn't moving.

B: (*believe, you*) _____ only those things that you can see? Look at

the trees out the window. All of them (*grow*) _____ at this very

moment, but you can't see the growth. They (*get*) _____ bigger and

bigger with every second that passes. You can't see the trees grow, and you can't feel the

earth spin, but both events (*take*) _____ place at this moment while

you and I (*speak*) _____.

A: Really? How do you know?

6. A: Look at Della! Where (*go, she*) _____ and why (*walk, she*)

_____ so fast?

B: She (*rush*) _____ to a meeting with the company vice-president.

Every morning at this time, she (*submit*) _____ a report on the

previous day's activities and (*present*) _____ the daily

recommendations.

A: But I (*hear, usually*) _____ the daily recommendations from the

president himself at the ten o'clock staff meetings.

B: Every day, the vice-president (*rewrite*) _____ Della's comments and (*take*)

_____ them to the president. At every ten o'clock meeting, the president

simply (*read*) _____ the same recommendations that Della stayed up

working on the night before, and he (*act*) _____ like he's been up for hours

comtemplating those ideas.

A: Well, I'll be darned! That (*seem, not*) _____ fair!

B: It (*be, not*) _____. But that's the way it works.

◇ **PRACTICE 21—GUIDED STUDY:** Present verbs. (Charts 1–1 → 1–4)

Directions: Change the verb tenses. Use the same verb, but change other words in the sentence to make the meaning of the new verb tense clear.

PART I: Change the italicized verb from the SIMPLE PRESENT to the PRESENT PROGRESSIVE. Change other words to make the meaning of the new verb tense clear.

Example: Jane *walks* to work almost every day.
→ *Right now it's 7:45 in the morning, and Jane* **is walking** *to work.*

1. I *study* English every day.
2. The sun *shines* from morning until night every day.
3. The earth *rotates* on its axis.
4. Dr. Li *talks* to high school students all over the country about the dangers of drugs.
5. When Ted is tired, he *sleeps* wherever he is.

PART II: Change the *italicized* verb from the PRESENT PROGRESSIVE to the SIMPLE PRESENT. Change other words to make the meaning of the new verb tense clear.

Example: Right now, Luigi's team *is winning* the soccer game by a score of one to nothing.
→ *Luigi's team always* **wins** *a lot of soccer games during the year.*

6. Sue and her husband aren't home. They *are traveling* in South America.
7. Listen. Sam *is playing* the piano.
8. We don't have class today because our physics professor *is running* in a marathon this afternoon.
9. My friend Adam *is wearing* jeans today.
10. I*'m doing* a grammar exercise.

◇ **PRACTICE 22—GUIDED STUDY:** Present verbs. (Charts 1–1 → 1–4)

Directions: Complete the sentences in your own words, using the SIMPLE PRESENT or the PRESENT PROGRESSIVE form of a verb, whichever is appropriate.

Example: . . . every day before . . . .
→ *My brother George eats a large breakfast every day before he leaves for work.*

1. . . . usually . . . before . . . .
2. . . . always . . . when . . . .
3. . . . every Wednesday afternoon.
4. . . . at this very moment.
5. . . . every other day or so.
6. Why . . . right now?
7. How often . . . ?
8. . . . sometimes . . . after . . . .
9. . . . rarely . . . when . . . .
10. At the present time, ...

◇ PRACTICE 23—SELFSTUDY: Prepositions. (Chapter 1)

Directions: Complete the sentences with appropriate PREPOSITIONS.*

1. My eight-year-old son Mark is afraid ____*of*____ thunder and lightning.

2. My mother really likes my friend Ahmed because he is always so polite _____ her.

3. Fifty miles is equal _____ eighty kilometers.

4. A: How do I get to your house?

   B: Are you familiar _____ the big red barn on Coles Road? My house is just past that
   and on the left.

   A: Oh, sure. I know where it is.

5. It's so hot! I'm thirsty _____ a big glass of ice water.

6. My boss was nice _____ me after I made that mistake, but I could tell she wasn't pleased.

7. Are you angry _____ me?

8. A: Harry, try some of this pasta. It's delicious.

   B: No, thanks. My plate is already full _____ food.

9. Four council members were absent _____ the meeting last night.

10. A: Why are you so friendly with Mr. Parsons? He's always so mean to everybody.

    B: He's always been very kind _____ me, so I have no reason to treat him otherwise.

11. My sister is so mad _____ me. She won't even speak to me.

12. Is everybody ready _____ dinner? Let's eat before the food gets cold.

---

*See Appendix 1 for a list of preposition combinations.

CHAPTER **2**
Past Time

◇ **PRACTICE 1—SELFSTUDY:** Simple past. (Charts 2–1 → 2–3)

Directions: Change the sentences to PAST TIME. Use a SIMPLE PAST verb. Choose *yesterday* or *last*.

PRESENT	PAST
every day	*yesterday*
every morning	*yesterday morning*
every afternoon	*yesterday afternoon*
every night	*last night*
every week	*last week*
every Monday, Tuesday, etc.	*last Monday, Tuesday, etc.*
every month	*last month*
every year	*last year*

1. I **walk** to my office **every morning**.

   → I _____*walked*_____ to my office ⟨*yesterday*,⟩ *last* morning.

2. I **talk** to my parents on the phone **every week**.

   → I _____*talked*_____ to my parents on the phone *yesterday*, ⟨*last*⟩ week.

3. The post office **opens** at eight o'clock **every morning**.

   → The post office _____ at eight o'clock *yesterday*, *last* morning.

4. Mrs. Hall **goes** to the fruit market **every Monday**.

   → Mrs. Hall _____ to the fruit market *yesterday*, *last* Monday.

5. The company executives **meet** at nine o'clock **every Friday morning**.

   → The executives _____ at nine o'clock *yesterday*, *last* Friday morning.

6. I **make** my own lunch and **take** it to work with me **every morning**.

   → *Yesterday*, *Last* morning, I _____ my own lunch and _____ it to work with me.

7. Mr. Clark **pays** his rent on time **every month**.

   → Mr. Clark _____ his rent on time *yesterday*, *last* month.

8. The baby *falls* asleep at three o'clock *every* afternoon.

   → *Yesterday*, *Last* afternoon, the baby _____ asleep at three o'clock.

9. The last bus to downtown **leaves** at ten o'clock **every night**.

   → The last bus to downtown _____ at ten o'clock *yesterday*, *last* night.

◇ **PRACTICE 2—SELFSTUDY:** Simple past: regular and irregular verbs. (Charts 2–1 → 2–4)

Directions: Write the SIMPLE PAST form of the given verbs.

1. start	*started*	13. sing	
2. go	*went*	14. explore	
3. see		15. ask	
4. stand		16. bring	
5. arrive		17. break	
6. win		18. eat	
7. have		19. watch	
8. make		20. build	
9. finish		21. take	
10. feel		22. pay	
11. fall		23. leave	
12. hear		24. wear	

◇ **PRACTICE 3—SELFSTUDY:** Simple past forms. (Charts 2–1 → 2–4)

Directions: Use the given words to make questions and give answers.

1. *you/answer*

A: _____ ***Did you answer*** _____ the question?

B: Yes, _____ ***I did*** _____ . _____ ***I answered*** _____ the question. OR:

No, _____ ***I didn't*** _____ . _____ ***I didn't answer*** _____ the question.

2. *he/see*

A: _____ the fireworks?

B: Yes, _____ . _____ the fireworks. OR:

No, _____ . _____ the fireworks.

3. *they/watch*

A: _____ the game?

B: Yes, _____ . _____ the game. OR:

No, _____ . _____ the game.

4. *you/understand*

A: _____ the lecture?

B: Yes, _____ . _____ the lecture. OR:

No, _____ . _____ the lecture.

5. *you/be*

A: _____ at home last night?

B: Yes, _____ . _____ at home last night. OR:

No, _____ . _____ at home last night.

◇ **PRACTICE 4—SELFSTUDY: Simple past: regular and irregular verbs. (Charts 2–1 → 2–4)**

Directions: Complete the sentences by using the SIMPLE PAST of the verbs below. Use each verb only one time.

call	hold	sell	swim
fight	jump	✔shake	teach
freeze	ride	stay	think

1. Paul ____**shook**____ the bottle of soda so hard that it sprayed all over his clothes.

2. Carol didn't want to go on vacation with us, so she _____ home alone all week.

3. Since I hurt my knee, I can't go jogging. Yesterday, I _____ in the pool for an hour instead.

4. I was terrified just standing over the pool on the high diving board. Finally, I took a deep breath, held my nose, and _____ into the water.

5. The climber, who was fearful of falling, _____ the rope tightly with both hands.

6. Johnny pushed Alan, and the two boys _____ for a few minutes. Neither boy was hurt.

7. Before Louise started her own company, she _____ chemistry at the university.

8. It was extremely cold last night, and the water we put out for the cat _____ solid.

9. Before I made my decision, I _____ about it for a long, long time.

10. John _____ your house three times to ask you to go to the movie with us, but there was no answer, so we went ahead without you.

11. My car wouldn't start this morning, so I _____ my bicycle to work.

12. I needed money to pay my tuition at the university, so I _____ my motorcycle to my cousin.

◇ **PRACTICE 5—GUIDED STUDY: Simple past: regular and irregular verbs. (Charts 2–1 → 2–4)**

Directions: Complete the sentences by using the SIMPLE PAST of the verbs below. Use each verb only one time.

ask	dig	play	spend
build	forgive	quit	steal
choose	lose	✔ring	talk

1. The phone ____**rang**____ eight times before anybody answered it.

2. Oh my gosh! Call the police! Someone _____ my car!

3. The architectural firm that I work for designed this building. My brother's construction company _____ it. It took them two years to complete it.

4. The children _____ baseball until dark and didn't want to stop for dinner.

5. After I gave a large bone to each of my three dogs, they went to separate corners of the backyard and _____ holes to bury their bones.

6. A: Why isn't Bill here for the meeting? He's supposed to give the weekly report.

   B: I _____ to him last night on the phone, and he said he'd be here.

7. After looking at all the chairs in the furniture store, I finally _____ the red one. It was a difficult decision.

8. A: How are you getting along in your relationship with Carla?

   B: Not bad. Last night I _____ her again to marry me, and she said "maybe."

9. The players are depressed because they _____ the game last weekend. Next time they'll play better.

10. A: How can you take a three-month vacation? What about your job?

    B: I won't be going back to that job ever again. I _____ yesterday.

11. I can't afford a new car because I _____ all my money on new furniture for my apartment.

12. A: Is Elizabeth still angry with you?

    B: No, she _____ me for what I did, and she's speaking to me again.

◇ **PRACTICE 6—SELFSTUDY: Simple past: irregular verbs. (Charts 2–1 → 2–4)**

Directions: Complete the sentences with the SIMPLE PAST of any of the verbs in Chart 2–4.

1. I _____*swept*_____ the kitchen floor with a broom.

2. A bird _____ into our apartment through an open window.

3. I _____ the bird in my hands and put it back outside.

4. My father _____ me how to make furniture.

5. It got so cold last night that the water in the pond _____.

6. When I heard about Sue's problem, I _____ sorry for her.

7. Alex _____ a map for us to show us how to get to the museum.

8. A few minutes ago, I _____ on the radio about a bad plane accident.

9. Joe had an accident. He _____ off the roof and _____ his leg.

10. Sam _____ the race. He ran the fastest.

11. Ted _____ his car to Alaska last summer.

12. The soldiers _____ the battle through the night and into the morning.

13. I used to have a camera, but I _____ it because I needed the money.

14. Jane didn't want anyone to find her diary, so she _____ it in a shoe box in her closet.

15. There was a cool breeze last night. I opened the window, but Colette got cold and _____ it.

16. Rita _____ faster than anyone else in the 100-meter dash.

17. None of the other runners was ever in front of Rita during the race. She _____ all of the other runners in the race from start to finish.

18. Greg is a penny pincher. I was very surprised when he _____ for my dinner.

19. Frank was really thirsty. He _____ four glasses of water.

20. Karen had to decide between a blue raincoat and a tan one. She finally _____ the blue one.

21. Ann _____ a beautiful dress to the wedding reception.

22. My pen ran out of ink, so Sam _____ me an extra one he had.

◇ **PRACTICE 7—GUIDED STUDY: Simple past: irregular verbs. (Charts 2–1 → 2–4)**

Directions: Complete the sentences with the SIMPLE PAST of any of the verbs in Chart 2–4.

1. We _____ at the new restaurant last night. The food wasn't very good.

2. Jason _____ an excellent job of glueing the broken vase together.

3. The sun _____ at 6:21 this morning.

4. My wife gave me a painting for my birthday. I _____ it on a wall in my office.

5. Laurie has circles under her eyes because she _____ only two hours last night. She was studying for her final exams.

6. John is a good carpenter. He _____ the house in which he and his family live.

7. Matt lost his watch. He looked everywhere for it. Finally, he _____ it in the washing machine as he was removing the wet clothes to put them into the dryer. He had washed his watch, but it was still ticking.

8. Joy was barefoot. She stepped on a piece of broken glass and _____ her foot.

9. Danny and I are old friends. We _____ each other in 1975.

10. My friend told me that he had a singing dog. When the dog _____ to sing, I _____ my hands over my ears and _____ the room.

11. My friend _____ a note and passed it to me in class.

12. I didn't want anyone else to see the note, so I _____ it into tiny pieces and _____ it in the wastebasket.

13. My mother _____ all the letters I wrote to her while I was in England. She didn't throw any away.

14. The student with the highest grade point average _____ a speech at the graduation ceremony. She _____ about her hopes for the future of the world.

15. No, I didn't buy these tomatoes. I _____ them in a pot on the balcony outside my apartment.

16. Paul was in a hurry to get to class this morning. He _____ to comb his hair.

17. Last week I _____ an interesting book about the volcanoes in Iceland.

18. When Erica and I were introduced to each other, we _____ hands.

19. Mike is in jail because he _____ a car.

20. The fish I caught was too small. I carefully returned it to the water. It quickly _____ away.

21. I _____ the doorbell for a long time, but no one came to the door.

22. Amanda _____ a lie. I didn't believe her because I _____ the truth.

23. Steve _____ the campfire with only one match. Then he _____ on the fire to make it burn.

◇ **PRACTICE 8—GUIDED STUDY:** Regular verbs: pronunciation of -*ed* endings. (Chart 2–3)

Directions: Practice pronouncing final **-ED** by saying the words in the list aloud.

PRONUNCIATION NOTES: Final **-ed** has three different pronunciations: /t/, /d/, and /əd/.

- Final **-ed** is pronounced /t/ after most voiceless sounds. Voiceless sounds are made by pushing air through your mouth; no sound comes from your throat. Examples of voiceless sounds: /p/, /k/, /f/, /s/, /sh/, /ch/. Pronunciation: *stopped* = *stop* + /t/ (''stopt''); *talked* = *talk* + /t/ (''talkt'').
- Final **-ed** is pronounced /d/ after most voiced sounds. Voiced sounds come from your throat. If you touch your neck when you make a voiced sound, you can feel your voice box vibrate. Your voice box produces voiced sounds. Examples of voiced sounds: /b/, /v/, /n/, and all vowel sounds. Pronunciation: *robbed* = *rob* + /d/ (''robd''); *lived* = *live* + /d/ (''livd'').
- Final **-ed** is pronounced /əd/ after words that end in ''t'' or ''d.'' /əd/ adds a whole syllable to a word. Pronunciation: *wanted* = *want* + /əd/ (''want-ud''); *needed* = *need* + /əd/ (''need-ud'').

1. stopped = *stop* + /**t**/
2. robbed = *rob* + /**d**/
3. wanted = *want* + /**əd**/
4. talked = *talk* + /**t**/
5. lived = *live* + /**d**/
6. needed = *need* + /**əd**/
7. passed = *pass* + /**t**/*
8. pushed = *push* + /**t**/
9. watched = *watch* + /**t**/
10. thanked = *thank* + /**t**/
11. finished = *finish* + /**t**/
12. dreamed = *dream* + /**d**/
13. killed = *kill* + /**d**/
14. turned = *turn* + /**d**/
15. played = *play* + /**d**/
16. continued = *continue* + /**d**/
17. repeated = *repeat* + /**əd**/
18. waited = *wait* + /**əd**/
19. added = *add* + /**əd**/
20. decided = *decide* + /**əd**/

◇ PRACTICE 9—GUIDED STUDY: Regular verbs: pronunciation of *-ed* endings. (Chart 2–3)

Directions: Practice pronouncing final **-ED** by reading the sentences aloud.

1. I **watched** TV. Jean **listened** to the radio. Nick **waited** for the mail.
   watch/t/   listen/d/   wait/əd/

2. I **tasted** the soup. It **seemed** too salty.
   taste/əd/   seem/d/

3. James **planned** for his future. He **saved** money and **started** his own business.
   plan/d/   save/d/   start/əd/

4. I **asked** a question. Joe **answered** it. Then he **repeated** the answer for Ted.
   ask/t/   answer/d/   repeat/əd/

5. I **stared** at the sculpture for a long time. Finally, I **touched** it.
   stare/d/   touch/t/

6. Mary **prepared** a long report for her boss. She **completed** it late last night.
   prepare/d/   complete/əd/

7. After Dick **parked** the car, I **jumped** out and **opened** the door for my mother.
   park/t/   jump/d/   open/d/

8. After I **finished** reading Rod's poem, I **called** him and we **talked** for an hour.
   finish/t/   call/d/   talk/t/

9. Earlier today, I **cleaned** my apartment.
   clean/d/

10. I **washed** the windows, **waxed** the wood floor, and **vacuumed** the carpet.
    wash/t/   wax/t/   vacuum/d/

11. I **expected** to hear from Dr. Li about a scholarship.
    expect/əd/

12. I **crossed** my fingers and **hoped** for good news.
    cross/t/   hope/d/

13. I **poured** water into the glass and **filled** it to the top. I **offered** it to Sara.

14. Tim **dropped** the book. I **picked** it up and **dusted** it off with my hand.

15. She **handed** us the tests at the beginning of class and **collected** them at the end.

16. I **guessed** at most of the answers. I **realized** I should have **studied** harder.

---

*The words "passed" and "past" have the same pronunciation.

Directions: Complete the chart. Refer to Chart 2–5 if necessary.

END OF VERB	DOUBLE THE CONSONANT?	SIMPLE FORM	-ING	-ED
-e	**NO**	excite	**exciting**	**excited**
Two Consonants		exist		
Two Vowels + One Consonant		shout		
One Vowel + One Consonant		ONE-SYLLABLE VERBS pat		
		TWO-SYLLABLE VERBS (STRESS ON **FIRST** SYLLABLE) visit		
		TWO-SYLLABLE VERBS (STRESS ON **SECOND** SYLLABLE) admit		
-y		pray pry		
-ie		tie		

◇ PRACTICE 11—SELFSTUDY: Spelling of -ing. (Chart 2–5)

Directions: Write one "t" or two "t's" in the blanks to spell the **-ing** verb correctly. Then write the simple form of the verb in each sentence.

SIMPLE FORM

1. I'm wai__*t*__ing for a phone call.   1. _____**wait**_____

2. I'm pa__*tt*__ing my dog's head.   2. _____**pat**_____

3. I'm bi____ing my nails because I'm nervous.   3. _____

4. I'm si____ing in a comfortable chair.   4. _____

5. I'm wri____ing in my book.   5. _____

6. I'm figh____ing the urge to have some chocolate ice cream.   6. _____

7. I'm wai____ing to see if I'm really hungry.   7. _____

8. I'm ge____ing up from my chair now.   8. _____

9. I'm star____ing to walk to the refrigerator.   9. _____

10. I'm permi____ing myself to have some ice cream.   10. _____

11. I'm lif____ing the spoon to my mouth.   11. _____

12. I'm ea____ing the ice cream now.   12. _____

13. I'm tas____ing it. It tastes good.   13. _____

14. I'm also cu____ing a piece of cake.   14. _____

15. I'm mee___ing my sister at the airport tomorrow.

15. _____

16. She's visi___ing me for a few days. I'll save some cake and ice cream for her.

16. _____

◇ **PRACTICE 12—SELFSTUDY:** Simple present vs. simple past. (Charts 2–1 → 2–4)

Directions: Use the SIMPLE PRESENT or the SIMPLE PAST form of the verb in parentheses, whichever is appropriate.

1. A: *(hear, you)* _____**Did you hear**_____ the thunder last night?

   B: No, I _____**didn't**_____. I *(hear, not)* _____**didn't hear**_____ anything all night. I

   (be) _____**was**_____ asleep.

2. A: Listen! *(hear, you)* _____**Do you hear**_____ a siren in the distance?

   B: No, I _____**don't**_____. I *(hear, not)* _____**don't hear**_____ anything at all.

3. A: *(build, you)* _____ that bookshelf?

   B: No, I _____. My uncle *(build)* _____ it for me.

4. A: *(be, a fish)* _____ slippery to hold?

   B: Yes, _____. It can slip right out of your hand.

   A: How about frogs? *(be, they)* _____ slippery?

   B: Yes, _____.

   A: What about snakes?

   B: I *(know, not)* _____. I've never touched a snake.

5. A: I *(want)* _____ to go to the mall this afternoon and *(look)* _____

   for a new bathing suit. *(want, you)* _____ to go with me?

   B: I can't. I *(have)* _____ an appointment with my English teacher. Besides, I

   (buy) _____ a new bathing suit last year. I *(need, not)* _____

   a new one this year.

6. I *(offer)* _____ to help my older neighbor carry her groceries into her house

   every time I see her return from the store. She *(be)* _____ always very

   grateful. Yesterday, she *(offer)* _____ to pay me for helping her, but of course I

   (accept, not) _____ the offer.

7. Last Monday night, I (*take*) _____ my sister and her husband to my favorite

restaurant for dinner and (*find*) _____ the doors locked. I (*know, not*)

_____ it then, but my favorite restaurant (*be, not*) _____

open on Mondays. We (*want, not*) _____ to eat anywhere else, so we (*go*)

_____ back to my house. I (*make*) _____ a salad and (*heat*)

_____ some soup. Everyone (*seem*) _____ satisfied even

though I (*be, not*) _____ a wonderful cook.

8. My daughter is twenty-one years old. She (*like*) _____ to travel. My wife and

I (*worry*) _____ about her a little when she (*be*) _____ away

from home, but we also (*trust*) _____ her judgment.

    Last year, after she (*graduate*) _____ from college, she (*go*) _____

to Europe with two of her friends. They (*travel, not*) _____

by train or by car. Instead, they (*rent*) _____ motor scooters and slowly (*ride*)

_____ through each country they visited.

    While she (*be*) _____ away, my wife and I (*worry*) _____

about her safety. We (*be*) _____ very happy when we (*see*) _____

her smiling face at the airport and (*know*) _____ that she was finally safe at

home.

◇ **PRACTICE 13—SELFSTUDY: Past progressive. (Charts 2–6 and 2–7)**

Directions: Complete the sentences by using the PAST PROGRESSIVE of the verbs below. Use each
verb only one time.

answer	count	look	✔stand
begin	drive	melt	walk
climb	eat	sing	

1. Fortunately, I didn't get wet because I _____ ***was standing*** _____ under a large tree

when it began to rain.

2. I saw Ted at the student cafeteria at lunch time. He _____ a

sandwich.

3. Mr. Cook asked an interesting question. The professor _____ Mr.

Cook's question when Mr. Gray rudely interrupted.

4. Robert didn't answer the phone when Sara called. He _S_____ his

favorite song in the shower and didn't hear the phone ring.

5. A: I saw a whale!

   B: Really? Neat! When?

   A: This morning. I _____ on the beach when I heard a sudden

     "whoosh!" It was the spout of a huge gray whale.

6. Three people _____ the east side of the mountain when the avalanche occurred. All three died.

7. A: Were you on time for the play last night?

   B: I drove as fast as I could. The play _____* just as we walked in the door of the theater.

8. Robert came in while I _____ the money from the day's receipts. I completely lost track and had to start all over again.

9. It was difficult to ski because the temperature was rising and the snow _____.

10. A: What do you think was the cause of your accident?

    B: I know what caused it. Paul _____ at the scenery while he _____ the car. He simply didn't see the other car pull out from the right.

◇ **PRACTICE 14—GUIDED STUDY:** Present progressive and past progressive.
(Charts 1–2, 2–6, and 2–7)

Directions: Complete the dialogues by making up answers to the questions. Use the PRESENT PROGRESSIVE or the PAST PROGRESSIVE of the verb in parentheses.

1. A: Why were you at the airport so late last night?

   B: I _**was waiting for my brother's plane.**_ _____ (wait)

2. A: Hi, Eric. I didn't expect to run into you at the airport. Why are you here today?

   B: I _**'m waiting for my brother's plane.**_ _____ (wait)

3. A: Ted saw you around nine yesterday morning. Were you on your way to work when he saw you?

   B: No, I _____ (walk)

4. A: Hi, Greg. How are you this morning? Are you on your way to work?

   B: No, I _____ (walk)

5. A: Why are you laughing? What's so funny?

   B: We _____ (watch)

6. A: Why were you and your friends laughing so loudly a little while ago?

   B: We _____ (watch)

7. A: Where are Ann and Rob? I haven't seen them for a couple of weeks. Are they in town?

   B: No, they _____ (travel)

8. A: Where were Ann and Rob when you got back from your trip? Were they in town?

   B: No, they _____ (travel)

_____
*Spelling note: There are **three n's** in the word *beginning*.

9. A: What was I saying when the phone interrupted me? I lost my train of thought.

   B: You _____ (describe)

10. A: What's Marilyn talking about?

   B: She _____ (describe)

◇ **PRACTICE 15—SELFSTUDY: Past time using time clauses. (Charts 2–1 → 2–8)**

Directions: Combine the two sentences in any order, using the time expression in parentheses.

1. The doorbell rang. I was climbing the stairs. (*while*)
   → *While I was climbing the stairs, the doorbell rang.* OR:
   → *The doorbell rang while I was climbing the stairs.*
2. I gave Alan his pay. He finished his chores. (*after*)
3. The firefighters checked the ashes one last time. They went home. (*before*)
4. Mr. Novak stopped by our table at the restaurant. I introduced him to my wife. (*when*)
5. The kitten was sitting on the roof. An eagle flew over the house. (*while*)
6. My father was listening to a baseball game on the radio. He was watching a basketball game on television. (*while*)

◇ **PRACTICE 16—SELFSTUDY: Simple past vs. past progressive. (Charts 2–1 → 2–8)**

Directions: Complete the sentences with the SIMPLE PAST or the PAST PROGRESSIVE form of the verb in parentheses.

1. It (*begin*) _____**began**_____ to rain while Amanda and I (*walk*) _____**were**_____ _____**walking**_____ to school.

2. While I (*wash*) _____ dishes, I (*drop*) _____ a plate and (*break*) _____ it.

3. I (*hit*) _____ my thumb while I (*use*) _____ the hammer. Ouch!

4. While I (*walk*) _____ under an apple tree, an apple (*fall*) _____ and (*hit*) _____ me on the head.

5. Last month, both my brother and my next-door neighbor were in Thailand, and neither one of them (*know*) _____ that the other was there. While they (*attend*) _____ my daughter's wedding reception last weekend, my neighbor (*mention*) _____ her trip, and my brother was very surprised. It seems that they (*be*) _____ in Bangkok for three days at exactly the same time and (*stay*) _____ in hotels that were only a few blocks away from each other.

6. While I (*look*) _____ at the computer screen, I (*start*) _____ to feel a little dizzy, so I (*take*) _____ a break. While I (*take*) _____ a short break outdoors and (*enjoy*) _____ the warmth of the sun on my face, an elderly gentleman (*come*) _____ up to me

and (ask) _____ for directions to the public library. After I (tell)

_____ him how to get there, he (thank) _____ me and

(go) _____ on his way. Soon a big cloud (come) _____ and

(cover) _____ the sun, so I (go) _____ back inside to work.

◇ **PRACTICE 17—GUIDED STUDY: Simple past vs. past progressive. (Charts 2-1 → 2-8)**

Directions.   Complete the sentences with the SIMPLE PAST or the PAST PROGRESSIVE of the verbs in parentheses.

Late yesterday afternoon while I (*1. prepare*) _____ dinner, the doorbell

(*2. ring*) _____. I (*3. put*) _____ everything down and (*4. rush*)

_____ to answer it. I (*5. open*) _____ the door and (*6. smile*)

_____ at the stranger standing in my doorway. He (*7. hold*) _____

a small vacuum cleaner. While he (*8. tell*) _____ me about this wonderful

vacuum cleaner that he wanted to sell to me, the phone (*9. ring*) _____. I

(*10. excuse*) _____ myself and (*11. reach*) _____ for the phone. While

I (*12. try*) _____ to talk on the phone and listen to the vacuum cleaner

salesman at the same time, my young son (*13. run*) _____ up to me to tell me about

the cat. The cat (*14. try*) _____ to catch a big fish in my husband's prized

aquarium. The fish (*15. swim*) _____ on the bottom to avoid the cat's paw.

I (*16. say*) _____ goodbye to the vacuum salesman and (*17. shut*)

_____ the door. I (*18. say*) _____ goodbye to the person on the

phone and (*19. hang*) _____ up. I (*20. yell*) _____ at the cat and

(21. shoo)* _____ her away from the fish. Then I (22. sat) _____

down in an easy chair and (23. catch) _____ my breath. While I (24. sit)

_____ there, the doorbell (25. ring) _____ again. Then the

phone (26. ring) _____. Then my son said, "Mom! Mom! The dog is in the

refrigerator!" I (27. move, not) _____. "What's next?" I said to myself.

◇ **PRACTICE 18—GUIDED STUDY: Present and past verbs. (Chapters 1 and 2)**

Directions: Complete the sentences with the SIMPLE PRESENT, PRESENT PROGRESSIVE, SIMPLE PAST, or PAST PROGRESSIVE.

PART I:

SITUATION: Right now Toshi (1. sit) _____ **is sitting** _____ at his desk. He (2. write)

_____ in his grammar workbook. His roommate, Oscar, (3. sit)

_____ at his desk, but he (4. study, not) _____. He

(5. stare) _____ out the window. Toshi (6. want) _____ to

know what Oscar (7. look) _____ at. Here is their dialogue:

TOSHI: Oscar, what (8. you, look) _____ at?

OSCAR: I (9. watch) _____ the bicyclists. They are very skillful. I

(10. know, not) _____ how to ride a bike, so I (11. admire)

_____ anyone who can. Come over to the window. Look at that guy

in the blue shirt. He (12. steer) _____ his bike with one hand while

he (13. drink) _____ a Coke with his other. And all the while, he

(14. weave) _____ in and out of the heavy street traffic and the

pedestrian traffic. He (15. seem) _____ fearless.

TOSHI: Riding a bike (16. be, not) _____ as hard as it (17. look) _____.

I'll teach you to ride a bicycle if you'd like.

OSCAR: Really? Great.

TOSHI: How come you don't know how to ride a bike?**

OSCAR: I never (18. have) _____ a bike when I (19. be) _____ a

kid. My family (20. be) _____ too poor. One time I (21. try)

_____ to learn on the bike of one of my friends, but the other kids all

(22. laugh) _____ at me. I never (23. try) _____ again

because I (24. be) _____ too embarrassed. But I'd love to learn now!

When can we start?

_____

*"Shoo! Shoo!" means "Go away! Leave!" When the woman *shooed* the cat, that means she said "Shoo! Shoo!" and made the cat leave.

**"How come?" means "Why?" For example, "How come you don't know how to ride a bike?" means "Why don't you know how to ride a bike?"

PART II:

Yesterday Toshi (*25. sit*) _____ **was sitting** _____ at his desk and (*26. write*) _____ in his grammar workbook. His roommate, Oscar, (*27. sit*) _____ at his desk, but he (*28. study, not*) _____. He (*29. stare*) _____ out the window. He (*30. watch*) _____ bicyclists on the street below.

Toshi (*31. walk*) _____ over to the window. Oscar (*32. point*) _____ out one bicyclist in particular. This bicyclist (*33. steer*) _____ with one hand while he (*34. drink*) _____ a Coke with the other. And all the while, he (*35. weave*) _____ in and out of the heavy traffic. To Oscar, the bicyclist (*36. seem*) _____ fearless.

Oscar never (*37. learn*) _____ how to ride a bike when he (*38. be*) _____ a kid, so Toshi (*39. offer*) _____ to teach him how. Oscar (*40. accept*) _____ gladly.

◇ **PRACTICE 19—SELFSTUDY: Past habit with *used to*. (Chart 2–9)**

Directions: Using the given information, complete the sentences. Use USED TO.

1. When James was young, he hated school. Now he likes school.

   → James _____ **used to hate school** _____.

2. When I was young, I thought that people over forty were very old.

   → I _____ that people over forty were very old.

3. Ann was a secretary for many years, but now she owns her own business.

   → Ann _____, but now she owns her own business.

4. Rebecca had a rat as a pet when she was ten. The rat died, and she hasn't had another rat as a pet since that time.

   → Rebecca _____ as a pet.

5. Before Adam got married, he went bowling five times a week.

   → Adam _____ five times a week.

6. A long time ago, we raised chickens in our yard.

   → We _____ in our yard.

7. When we raised our own chickens, we had fresh eggs every morning.

   → We _____ every morning when we raised our own chickens.

8. When Ben was a child, he often crawled under his bed and put his hands over his ears when he heard thunder.

   → Ben _____ and _____ _____ when he heard thunder.

◇ **PRACTICE 20—GUIDED STUDY: Past habit with *used to*. (Chart 2–9)**

Directions: Combine the given ideas into a sentence with "**USED TO . . . , BUT NOW . . . .**"

1. Years ago, I smoked two packs of cigarettes a day. Now, I don't smoke at all.
   → *I used to smoke two packs a day, but now I don't smoke at all.*
2. Amanda always stayed up late when she was a student. When she got a job after she graduated, she had to go to bed early.
   → *Amanda used to stay up late, but now she goes to bed early.*
3. My neighbor Bill drove his car to work every day last year. Now, he rides the bus.
4. At the beginning of the semester, Eric worked hard. Now, he is too busy with his social life.
5. Millions of years ago, dinosaurs ruled the world. Millions of years ago, they also became extinct.
6. The Allens had a large house when their children lived at home, but they moved to a small three-room apartment after the children grew up and left home.
7. Susan ate a balanced diet when she was a child. Now she's a teenager and eats a lot of junk food.
8. When I was a child, I didn't stay up late. Now, I'm up late every night because I have to study a lot.
9. Hiroki never wore cowboy boots when he lived in Japan. When he moved to Texas, he started wearing cowboy boots every day.
10. When I was a kid, I didn't have a job in the summer. I went swimming every day during the summer. Now I have to go to work, so I can go swimming only on weekends.

◇ **PRACTICE 21—GUIDED STUDY: Past habit with *used to*. (Chart 2–9)**

Directions: Write about or discuss in small groups the following topics. Use **USED TO**. Try to think of at least two or three differences for each topic.

1. Compare past and present means of transportation.
   (e.g., *People used to take long trips across the Atlantic by ship, but now they fly from one continent to another in a few hours.*)
2. Compare past and present clothing.
   (e.g., *Shoes used to have buttons, but now they don't.*)
3. Compare your grandparents' lives when they were teenagers to the lives of teenagers today.
   (e.g., *My grandparents didn't use to watch rented movies on TV with their friends, but today teenagers often watch movies together for entertainment.*)
4. Compare past and present beliefs.
   (e.g., *Some people used to believe the moon was made of cheese, but now we know that the moon is not made of cheese.*)

◇ **PRACTICE 22—GUIDED STUDY: Verb tense review. (Chapters 1 and 2)**

Directions: Complete the sentences with the verbs in parentheses. Use the SIMPLE PAST, SIMPLE PRESENT, or PAST PROGRESSIVE.

(1) Once upon a time, a king and his three daughters (*live*) _____**lived**_____ in a castle in a faraway land. One day while the king (*think*) __**was thinking**__ about his daughters, he (*have*) _____**had**_____ an idea. He (*form*) _____**formed**_____ a plan for finding husbands for them.

(2) When it (come) _____**came**_____ time for the three daughters to marry, the king (announce) _____**announced**_____ his plan. He said, "I'm going to take three jewels to the center of the village. The young men (meet) _____**meet** *_____ at the fountain there every day. The three young men who find the jewels will become my daughters' husbands."

(3) The next day, the king (choose) _____ three jewels—an emerald, a ruby, and a diamond—and (take) _____ them into the village. He (hold) _____ them in his hand and (walk) _____ among the young men. First he (drop) _____ the emerald, then the ruby, and then the diamond. A handsome man (pick) _____ up the emerald. Then a wealthy prince (spot) _____ the ruby and (bend) _____ down to pick it up. The king (be) _____ very pleased.

(4) But then a frog (hop) _____ toward the diamond and (pick) _____ it up. The frog (bring) _____ the diamond to the king and said, "I (be) _____ the Frog Prince. I claim your third daughter as my wife."

(5) When the king (tell) _____ Tina, his third daughter, about the Frog Prince, she (refuse) _____ to marry him. When the people of the land (hear) _____ the news about the frog and the princess, they (laugh) _____ and (laugh) _____. "Have you heard the news?" the people (say) _____ to each other. "Princess Tina is going to marry a frog!"

(6) Tina (feel) _____ terrible. "I (be) _____ the unluckiest person in the world," she (sob) _____. She (believe) _____ no

---

*The simple present is used here because the story is giving the king's exact words in a quotation. Notice that quotation marks (" . . . ") are used. See Chart 15–1 for more information about quotations.

one (*love*) _____ her and her father (*understand, not*) _____ her. She (*hide*) _____ from her friends and (*keep*) _____ her pain in her heart. Every day she (*grow*) _____ sadder and sadder. Her two sisters (*have*) _____ grand weddings. Their wedding bells (*ring*) _____ with joy across the land.

(7) Eventually, Tina (*leave*) _____ the castle. She (*run*) _____ away from her family and (*go*) _____ to live by herself in a small cottage in the woods. She (*eat*) _____ simple food, (*drink*) _____ water from the lake, (*cut*) _____ her own firewood, (*wash*) _____ her own clothes, (*sweep*) _____ the floor, (*make*) _____ her own bed, and (*take*) _____ care of all her own needs. But she (*be*) _____ very lonely and unhappy.

(8) One day Tina (*go*) _____ swimming. The water (*be*) _____ deep and cold. Tina (*swim*) _____ for a long time and (*become*) _____ very tired. While she (*swim*) _____ back toward the shore, she (*lose*) _____ the desire to live. She (*quit*) _____ trying to swim to safety. She (*drown*) _____ when the frog suddenly (*appear*) _____ and, with all his strength, (*push*) _____ Tina to land. He (*save*) _____ her life.

(9) "Why (*save, you*) _____ my life, Frog?"

"Because you (*be*) _____ very young and you (*have*) _____ a lot to live for."

"No, I (*do, not*) _____," said the princess. "I (*be*) _____ the most miserable person in the whole universe."

(10) "Let's talk about it," (*say*) _____ the frog, and they (*begin*) _____

to talk. Tina and the Frog Prince (*sit*) _____ together for hours and hours. Frog

(*listen*) _____ and (*understand*) _____. He (*tell*)

_____ her about himself and his own unhappiness and loneliness. They (*share*)

_____ their minds and hearts. Day after day, they (*spend*) _____

hours with each other. They (*talk*) _____, (*laugh*) _____, (*play*)

_____, and (*work*) _____ together.

    (11) One day while they (*sit*) _____ near the lake, Tina (*bend*)

_____ down and, with great affection, (*kiss*) _____ the frog on his

forehead. Suddenly the frog (*turn*) _____ into a man. He (*take*) _____

Tina in his arms and said, "You (*save*) _____ me with your kiss. Outside, I (*look*)

_____ like a frog. But you (*see*) _____ inside and (*find*)

_____ the real me. Now I (*be*) _____ free. An evil wizard turned

me into a frog until I found the love of a woman with a truly good heart." When Tina (*see*)

_____ through outside appearances, she (*find*) _____ true love.

    (12) Tina and the prince (*return*)

_____ to the castle and (*get*)

_____ married. Her two sisters, she

discovered, (*be*) _____ very

unhappy. The handsome husband (*ignore*)

_____ his wife and (*talk, not*)

_____ to her. The wealthy

husband (*make*) _____ fun of his wife

and (*give*) _____ her orders all the

time. But Tina and her frog prince (*live*)

_____ happily ever after.

◇ PRACTICE 23—GUIDED STUDY: Past time. (Chapter 2)

Directions: In a small group, make up a story that happens in past time.

FIRST: One member of the group should begin the story, then the next student continues the story, and then the next ones until the story is finished.

SECOND: One member of the group should repeat the whole story orally while the others listen.

THIRD: The group should discuss any changes they want to make in the story.

FOURTH: Then each member of the group should write this story; in other words, each member of the group should write **the same story**.

Story suggestions:

1. A creative story about fictional people and events.
   Possible beginning: *One day a person named Joe decided he had a boring life, so he decided to do something new and different every day for the rest of his life.   The next morning was a Monday. Joe got up and left his apartment . . . .*

2. An inventive tale about people and talking animals.
   Possible beginning: *Once upon a time, a bear named Jane and a crow named Frank became friends.   They got tired of their lives in the wilderness, so they decided to go to a city . . . .*

3. A humorous story about a fictional student in your class who constantly has bad luck.
   Possible beginning: *There is a student named . . . in our class who always seems to have bad luck.   One day he wanted to sharpen his pencil, but he forgot what he was doing.   The pencil got shorter and shorter.   Then finally (. . .)'s finger was in the pencil sharpener.   He sharpened his finger to a point before he realized what he was doing.   Now he has one finger that is pointed at the end . . . .*

4. A murder mystery with various suspects.
   Possible beginning: *On a dark and stormy night, Mr. Fox lit a candle and took his money box from its hiding place.   He unlocked it and slowly counted each gold coin.   He didn't hear footsteps coming up the stairs.   The door creaked open . . . .*

◇ PRACTICE 24—GUIDED STUDY: Past time. (Chapter 2)

Directions: With your classmates, write a story that happens in the past.   Each student should write one paragraph of three to five sentences at a time.   One student begins the story.   Then he or she passes the paper on to another student, who will then write a paragraph and pass the paper on—until everyone in the class has had a chance to write a paragraph.   Use the story suggestions in Practice 23 above or make up your own story beginning.

◇ PRACTICE 25—SELFSTUDY: Prepositions of time. (Chart 2–10)

Directions: Complete the sentences with appropriate PREPOSITIONS.

1. Jack goes shopping ___*on*___ Saturdays.

2. Elaine and I had a light lunch _____ noon, and then we played tennis _____ the afternoon.

3. A: Hi, John.   It's good to see you again.   When I saw you _____ December, you were working at the department store.   Are you still working there?

   B: No.   I quit _____ January 1st.   _____ present, I'm working at Joe's Music Shop. _____ the future, I hope to have my own music store.

4. _____ 1988, we moved to this city. We arrived _____ night and couldn't find our new house. We got a hotel room and found the house _____ the morning.

5. I like to visit friends _____ the evening. I don't like to stay home by myself _____ night.

6. Excuse me. Are you busy _____ the moment?

7. A: When did you and your family go to New York?

   B: _____ 1990.

   A: _____ the spring or fall?

   B: We arrived _____ June 15 and left _____ the 21st.

8. What are the most important events that occurred _____ the nineteenth century?

◇ PRACTICE 26—SELFSTUDY: Prepositions. (Chapters 1 and 2)

Directions: Complete the sentences with appropriate PREPOSITIONS.

1. Richard got mad ___*at*___ me when I asked him to get up early ___*in*___ the morning.

2. I'm ready _____ a change and a better job. I'll choose more carefully _____ the future.

3. A: Are you prepared to answer all questions for the court?

   B: Yes, I am.

   A: Where were you _____ February 3, 1991, _____ exactly 8:12 P.M.?

   B: I was having dinner with friends.

   A: Don't you usually work _____ the evening?

   B: I was absent _____ work. I was angry _____ a co-worker and didn't go to work that day. I left my friends _____ midnight.

   A: No more questions for this witness, Your Honor.

4. A: Are you familiar _____ the new musical play downtown?

   B: I'm told it's very good. We're going to see it _____ the summer.

5. A: What do you do _____ Sunday afternoons?

   B: I go to the amusement park with my family almost every Sunday.

   A: Oh. Isn't the park full _____ people _____ Sundays? I hate crowds.

   B: It's not so bad _____ the early afternoon. It gets worse later in the day.

6. My son was afraid _____ dogs _____ the past, but now he's asking me to get him one.

CHAPTER 3
Future Time

◇ **PRACTICE 1—SELFSTUDY:** Present, past, and future. (Chapters 1, 2, and 3)

Directions: Complete the sentences with the given verbs. Use:
a. the SIMPLE PRESENT
b. the SIMPLE PAST, and
c. **BE GOING TO/WILL.**

1. *arrive*
   a. Joe _____***arrives***_____ on time **every day**.
   b. Joe _____***arrived***_____ on time **yesterday**.
   c. Joe _____***is going to arrive***_____ on time **tomorrow**. OR:
      Joe _____***will arrive***_____ on time **tomorrow**.

2. *arrive?*
   a. _____ Joe _____ on time **every day**?
   b. _***Did***_ Joe _____***arrive***_____ on time **yesterday**?
   c. _____ Joe _____ on time **tomorrow**? OR:
      _____ Joe _____ on time **tomorrow**?

3. *arrive, not*
   a. Mike _____ on time **every day**.
   b. Mike _____ on time **yesterday**.
   c. Mike _____***isn't going to be***_____ on time **tomorrow**. OR:
      Mike _____ on time **tomorrow**.

4. *eat*
   a. Ann _____ breakfast **every day**.
   b. Ann _____ breakfast **yesterday**.
   c. Ann _____ breakfast **tomorrow**. OR:
      Ann _____ breakfast **tomorrow**.

5. *eat?*
   a. _____ you _____ breakfast **every day**?
   b. _____ you _____ breakfast **yesterday**?
   c. _____ you _____ breakfast **tomorrow**? OR:
      _____ you _____ breakfast **tomorrow**?

6. *eat, not*
   a. I _____ breakfast **every day**.
   b. I _____ breakfast **yesterday**.
   c. I _____ breakfast **tomorrow**. OR:
      I _____ breakfast **tomorrow**.

◇ PRACTICE 2—SELFSTUDY: Present, past, and future. (Chapters 1, 2, and 3)

Directions: Complete the sentences with forms of the verb in italics. Use the SIMPLE PRESENT, SIMPLE PAST, and **BE GOING TO**.

1. A: I *got* up at five this morning.

   B: Oh? ____**Do**____ you _____*get*_____ up at five every morning?

   A: Yes, I ____**do**____, I _____*get*_____ up at five every morning.

   B: ____**Did**____ you _____*get*_____ up at five yesterday morning?

   A: Yes, I ____**did**____. I _____*got*_____ up at five yesterday morning.

   B: ____**Are**____ you _____*going to get*_____ up at five tomorrow morning?

   A: Yes, I ____**am**____. I _____*'m going to get*_____ up at five tomorrow morning.

2. A: I *studied* last night.

   B: Oh? _____ you _____ every night?

   A: Yes, I _____. I _____ every night.

   B: _____ you _____ last Saturday night?

   A: Yes, I _____. I _____ last Saturday night.

   B: _____ you _____ tomorrow night?

   A: Yes, I _____. I _____ tomorrow night.

◇ PRACTICE 3—GUIDED STUDY: Present, past, and future. (Chapters 1, 2, and 3)

Directions: Write a dialogue by completing the sentences with your own words.

A: I . . . yesterday.
B: Oh? . . . you . . . every day?
A: Yes, I . . . . I . . . every day.
B: . . . you . . . two days ago?
A: Yes, I . . . . I . . . two days ago.
B: . . . you . . . tomorrow?
A: Yes, I . . . . I . . . tomorrow.

◇ PRACTICE 4—SELFSTUDY: *Be going to.* (Chart 3–1)

Directions: Complete the sentences with **BE GOING TO** and the words in parentheses.

1. A: What (*you, do*) _____*are you going to do*_____ this afternoon?

   B: I (*finish*) _____*am going to finish*_____ my report.

2. A: Where (*Ryan, be*) _____ later tonight?

   B: He (*be*) _____ at Kim's house.

3. A: (*you, have*) _____ a hamburger for lunch?

   B: I (*eat, not*) _____ lunch. I don't have enough time.

4. A: (*you, finish*) _____ this exercise soon?

   B: I (*finish*) _____ it in less than a minute.

5. A: When (*you, call*) _____ your sister?

   B: I (*call, not*) _____ her. I (*write*) _____

   _____ her a letter.

6. A: What (*Laura, talk*) _____ about in her speech tonight?

   B: She (*discuss*) _____ the economy of Southeast Asia.

◇ **PRACTICE 5—GUIDED STUDY:** *Be going to.* (Chart 3–1)

Directions: Pair up with a classmate.
STUDENT A: Ask a question using **BE GOING TO** and the given words.
STUDENT B: Answer the question. Use **BE GOING TO**.

Example: what/do next Monday?
STUDENT A: What are you going to do next Monday?
STUDENT B: I'm going to go to my classes as usual.

Example: watch TV tonight?
STUDENT A: Are you going to watch TV tonight?
STUDENT B: Yes, I'm going to watch TV tonight. OR: No, I'm not going to watch TV tonight.

1. where/go after your last class today?
2. have pizza for dinner tonight?
3. what/do this evening?
4. when/visit your family?
5. play soccer with (. . .)* Saturday?
6. what/do this coming Saturday?
7. look for a new place to live soon?
8. where/live next year?

(Change roles: STUDENT A *becomes* STUDENT B *and vice versa.)*

 9. what time/go to bed tonight?
10. what/wear tomorrow?
11. wear your raincoat tomorrow?
12. take a trip sometime this year or next?
13. where/go and what/do?
14. how long/stay at this school?
15. talk to your family soon?
16. when/see your family again?

◇ **PRACTICE 6—GUIDED STUDY:** *Be going to.* (Chart 3–1)

Directions: Use the given words to make sentences with **BE GOING TO**. Use your own ideas. Be
sure to use a form of **BE GOING TO** in each sentence. Notice the various time expressions that are
used to indicate future time.

Example: you/today?
Response: Are you going to eat lunch at McDonald's today?

_____

*The symbol (. . .) means that you should use the name of a person you know.

Example: (. . .)/tonight.
Response: Abdul is going to hang around with his friends tonight.

1. I/in a half an hour.
2. I/after a while.
3. you/today?
4. (. . .)/later today.
5. I/not/tomorrow morning.
6. you/the day after tomorrow?
7. my friends/next Sunday.
8. we/this coming Monday.
9. (. . .)/this week?
10. (. . .) and I/not/this weekend.
11. (. . .) and (. . .)/this year.
12. I/two years from now.
13. my country/in the future.
14. people/in the twenty-first century?

◇ **PRACTICE 7—SELFSTUDY:** *Will.* (Chart 3–2)

Directions: Complete the dialogues. Use WILL.

1. A: (*you, help*) _____**Will you help**_____ me tomorrow?

   B: Yes, _____**I will***_____. OR: No, _____**I won't**_____.

2. A: (*Paul, lend*) _____ us some money?

   B: Yes, _____. OR: No, _____.

3. A: (*Jane, graduate*) _____ this spring?

   B: Yes, _____. OR: No, _____.

4. A: (*her parents, be*) _____ at the ceremony?

   B: Yes, _____. OR: No, _____.

5. A: (*I, benefit*) _____ from this business deal?

   B: Yes, _____. OR: No, _____.

◇ **PRACTICE 8—SELFSTUDY:** *Will probably.* (Chart 3–3)

Directions: Complete the sentences with WILL or WON'T. Also use PROBABLY.

1. The clouds are leaving, and the sun is coming out. It _____**probably won't**_____ rain anymore.

2. The weather is cold today. There's no reason to expect the weather to change. It _____**will probably**_____ be cold tomorrow, too.

3. Sam, Sharon, and Carl worked hard on this project. They _____ turn in the best work. The other students didn't work as hard.

4. Ronald is having a very difficult time in advanced algebra. He didn't understand anything that happened in class today, and he _____ understand tomorrow's class either.

5. Jan skipped lunch today. She _____ eat as soon as she gets home.

_____

*Pronouns are NOT contracted with helping verbs in short answers.
   CORRECT: *Yes, I will.*
   INCORRECT: *Yes, I'll.*

6. I don't like parties. Mike really wants me to come to his birthday party, but I

   _____ go. I'd rather stay home.

7. Conditions in the factory have been very bad for a long time. All of the people who work on

   the assembly line are angry. They _____ vote to go out on strike.

8. We are using up the earth's resources at a rapid rate. We _____

   continue to do so* for years to come.

◇ PRACTICE 9—GUIDED STUDY: *Will probably.* (Chart 3-3)

Directions: For each situation, predict something that **WILL PROBABLY** happen and something that
PROBABLY WON'T happen.

Example: Emily has a test in ten minutes. She didn't study for it at all. (*pass it / fail it*)
Response: She probably won't pass it. She'll probably fail it.

1. It's raining. Greg doesn't have an umbrella. (*get wet / stay outside for a long time*)
2. Mr. Lee works at an aircraft factory. He has a bad cold. (*go to work / stay home today*)
3. Sam didn't sleep at all last night. (*go to bed early tonight / stay up all night again tonight*)
4. Alan has to go to Chicago on business. He hates to fly. (*go by plane / take a bus or a train*)

Use your own words to make predictions with WILL PROBABLY *and* PROBABLY WON'T:

5. (. . .) likes movies. There's a new movie at the local theater.
6. The weather is going to be rainy tomorrow. You like this kind of weather.
7. (. . .) is going to spend five days in New York as a tourist.
8. Many important events are taking place in the world today. What are some of these events?
   Make predictions about them.

◇ PRACTICE 10—GUIDED STUDY: *Be going to* and *will.* (Chart 3-3)

Directions: For each situation, predict the future. Use **WILL** or **BE GOING TO**. Use **PROBABLY** if
you wish. Use the negative if you wish.

Example: people/go to work only four days a week.
   → *People will probably go to work only four days a week.*

1. we/use electric motors in automobiles in the future
2. we/use solar energy to heat buildings in the future
3. clothing styles/change a lot in fifty years
4. today's rock music/popular twenty years from now
5. we/be able to communicate by videophone
6. doctors/be able to replace nearly all vital organs
7. the population of the earth/double in thirty-five years
8. the earth/have enough fresh water to support a population of twelve billion
9. the earth's tropical rain forests/disappear
10. What other predictions can you make about the twenty-first century?

---

*Do so means "do the thing that the speaker/writer just mentioned." In this sentence, do so = use up the earth's
resources at a rapid rate.*

◇ **PRACTICE 11—SELFSTUDY:** *Be going to* vs. *will.* (Chart 3–4)

Directions: Using the given information about SPEAKER B's plans, complete the sentences with either **BE GOING TO** or **WILL.***

1. (SPEAKER B *is planning to listen to the news at six.*)

   A: Why did you turn on the radio?

   B: I ___*'m going to*___ listen to the news at six.

2. (SPEAKER B *didn't have a plan to show the other person how to solve the math problem, but she is glad to do it.*)

   A: I can't figure out this math problem. Do you know how to do it?

   B: Yes. Give me your pencil. I ___*'ll*___ show you how to solve it.

3. (SPEAKER B *has made a plan. He is planning to lie down because he doesn't feel well.*)

   A: What's the matter?

   B: I don't feel well. I _____ lie down for a little while. If anyone calls, tell

   them I'll call back later.

   A: Okay. I hope you feel better.

4. (SPEAKER B *did not plan to take the other person home. He is making the offer spontaneously. He thinks of the idea only after the other person talks about missing his bus.*)

   A: Oh no! I wasn't watching the time. I missed my bus.

   B: That's okay. I _____ give you a ride home.

   A: Hey, thanks!

5. (SPEAKER B *has a plan.*)

   A: Why did you borrow money from the bank?

   B: I _____ buy a new pickup.** I've already picked it out.

6. (SPEAKER B *does not have a plan.*)

   A: Mom, can I have a candy bar?

   B: No, but I _____ buy an apple for you. How does that sound?

   A: Okay, I guess.

7. (SPEAKER B *has already made her plans about what to wear. Then* SPEAKER B *makes a spontaneous offer.*)

   A: I can't figure out what to wear to the Harvest Moon Ball. It's formal, isn't it?

   B: Yes. I _____ wear a floor-length gown.

   A: Maybe I should wear my red gown with the big sleeves. But I think it needs cleaning.

   B: I _____ take it to the cleaner's for you when I go downtown this afternoon

   if you'd like.

   A: Gee, thanks. That'll save me a trip.

───────────────

*Usually **be going to** and **will** are interchangeable: you can use either one of them with little or no difference in meaning. Sometimes, however, they are NOT interchangeable. In this exercise, only one of them is correct, not both. See Chart 3–4.

**A *pickup* is a small truck.

◇ **PRACTICE 12—SELFSTUDY:** *Be going to* vs. *will.* (Chart 3–4)

Directions: Complete the sentences with either **BE GOING TO** or **WILL**.

1. A: Why are you looking for a screwdriver?

   B: One of the kitchen chairs has a loose screw. I _____ fix it.

2. A: The computer printer isn't working again! What am I going to do?

   B: Calm down. Give Tom a call. He _____ fix it for you. It's probably just a loose connection.

3. A: Are you gong to the post office soon?

   B: Yeah. Why?

   A: I need to send this letter today.

   B: I _____ mail it for you.

   A: Thanks.

4. A: Why are you carrying that box?

   B: I _____ mail it to my sister. I'm on my way to the post office.

5. A: Let's meet for a beer after work.

   B: Sounds good to me. I _____ meet you at the Blue Goose Bar at six.

6. A: Can you meet me for a beer after work?

   B: I'd like to, but I can't. I _____ stay at the office until seven tonight.

7. A: It's grandfather's eighty-fifth birthday next Sunday. What _____ you _____ give him for his birthday?

   B: I _____ give him a walking stick that I made myself.

8. A: I have a note for Joe from Rachel. I don't know what to do with it.

   B: Let me have it. I _____ give it to him. He's in my algebra class.

   A: Thanks. But you have to promise not to read it.

◇ **PRACTICE 13—SELFSTUDY:** Time clauses. (Chart 3–5)

Directions: Combine the two sentences in any order, using the time expression in parentheses. Underline the time clause in the sentence you write. Pay special attention to the verb tense you use in the time clause.

1. I'll call Mike tomorrow. I'll tell him the good news. (*when*)
   → ***When I call Mike tomorrow, I'll tell him the good news.***
   OR: ***I'll tell Mike the good news when I call him tomorrow.***
2. Ann will lock all the doors. She will go to bed. (*before*)
3. I'm going to be in London for two days. I'm going to visit the Tate Museum. (*when*)
4. The show will start. The curtain will go up. (*as soon as*)
5. Nick is going to change the oil in his car. He's going to take a bath. (*after*)
6. We'll call you. We'll drive over to pick you up. (*before*)
7. I'll call you. I'll get an answer from the bank about the loan. (*when*)
8. I'll get my paycheck. I'll pay my rent. (*as soon as*)

◇ **PRACTICE 14—SELFSTUDY: Time clauses. (Chart 3–5)**

Directions: Use the given verbs to complete the sentences. Use the SIMPLE PRESENT and **WILL/ WON'T**.

1. *take/read*

   I __*'ll read*__ the textbook before I __**take**__ the final exam.

2. *return/call*

   Mr. Lee _____ his wife as soon as he _____ to the hotel

   tonight.

3. *be, not /come*

   I _____ home tomorrow when the painters _____ to paint my

   apartment. Someone else will have to let them in.

4. *prepare/go*

   Before I _____ to my job interview tomorrow, I _____ a list of

   questions I want to ask about the company.

5. *visit /take*

   When Sandra _____ us this weekend, we _____ her to our

   favorite seafood restaurant.

6. *find /move/graduate*

   Sara _____ out of her parents' house after she _____ from

   school next month and _____ a job.

◇ **PRACTICE 15—SELFSTUDY: *If*-clauses. (Chart 3–5)**

Directions: Use the given verbs to complete the sentences. Use the SIMPLE PRESENT and **WILL/WON'T**.

1. *not go/ be*

   If it __**is**__ cold and rainy tomorrow morning, I __**won't go**__ jogging.

2. *get /pay*

   If I _____ a job soon, I _____ you the money I owe you.

3. *not go/ be*

   The boss _____ very disappointed if you _____ to the meeting

   tomorrow.

4. *stop/tell*

   I _____ taking these pills if Dr. Matthews _____ me it's okay.

5. *get /be /eat*

   If Barbara _____ home on time tonight, we _____ dinner at

   6:30. If she _____ late, dinner _____ late.

◇ **PRACTICE 16—GUIDED STUDY:** Time clauses and *If*-clauses. (Chart 3–5)

Directions: Combine the ideas in the pairs of sentences. Use **WHEN**, **AFTER**, **AS SOON AS**, or **IF**. Pay special attention to verb tenses. Underline the "time clause" or "*if*-clause" in each sentence you write.

Example: I'll see you Sunday afternoon. I'll give you my answer (then).★

Written: When I see you Sunday afternoon, I'll give you my answer.

OR: I'll give you my answer when I see you Sunday afternoon.

1. I'm going to clean up my apartment (first). My friends are going to come over (later).
2. The storm will be over (in an hour or two). I'm going to do some errands (then).
3. (Maybe) you won't learn how to use a computer. (As a result), you will have trouble finding a job.
4. Joe will meet us at the coffee shop. He'll finish his report (soon).
5. Sue will wash and dry the dishes. (Then) she will put them away.
6. They may not leave at seven. (As a result), they won't get to the theater on time.

◇ **PRACTICE 17—SELFSTUDY:** Parallel verbs. (Chart 3–5)

Directions: Underline the first verb in each parallel structure. Circle the word **and**. Then complete the sentence with the PARALLEL FORM OF THE VERB in parentheses.

1. Last night, I was listening to music (and) (*do*) _____**(was) doing**_____ my homework when Kim stopped by.

2. My classmates are going to meet at Danny's (and) (*study*) _____**(are going to) study**_____ together tonight.

3. Tomorrow the sun will rise at 6:34 and (*set*) _____ at 8:59.

4. While Paul was carrying brushes and paint and (*climb*) _____ a ladder, a bird flew down and (*sit*) _____ on his head. Paul dropped the paint and (*spill*) _____ it all over the ground.

5. Next weekend, Nick is going to meet his friends downtown and (*go*) _____ to a soccer game.

6. Anna moves into her apartment on Sunday and (*start*) _____ her new job on Monday.

7. My pen slipped out of my hand and (*fall*) _____ to the floor.

8. I'm getting up early tomorrow morning and (*walk*) _____ to work.

_____

★When you combine the sentences, omit the words in parentheses.

9. When I first arrived in this city and (*start*) _____ going to school here, I knew no one. I was lonely and (*feel*) _____ that I didn't have a friend in the world. One day while I was watching TV alone in my room and (*feel*) _____ sorry for myself, a woman I had met in one of my classes knocked on my door and (*ask*) _____ me if I wanted to accompany her to the student center. That was the beginning of my friendship with Lisa King. Now we see each other every day and usually (*spend*) _____ time talking on the phone, too. This week we're borrowing her brother's car and (*go*) _____ to visit her aunt in the country. Next week we're going to take a bus to Fall City and (*go*) _____ to a football game. I'm really enjoying our friendship.

◇ **PRACTICE 18—SELFSTUDY:** Parallel verbs. (Chart 3–5)

Directions: Complete the sentences with the verbs in parentheses.

1. Fifteen years from now, my wife and I (*retire*) _____**will retire**_____ and (*travel*) _____**(will) travel**_____ all over the world.

2. If I feel tense, I (*close*) _____**close**_____ my eyes and (*think*) _____**think**_____ about nothing at all.

3. A: What is Pete doing in the other room?

   B: He (*watch*) _____ TV and (*study*) _____ for his chemistry exam.

4. Every morning without exception, Mrs. Carter (*take*) _____ her dog for a walk and (*buy*) _____ a newspaper at Charlie's newsstand.

5. Before I (*go*) _____ to your boss and (*tell*) _____ her about your mistake, I want to give you an opportunity to explain it to her yourself.

6. Next month, I (*take*) _____ my vacation and (*forget*) _____ about everything that is connected to my job.

7. Kathy thinks I was the cause of her problems, but I wasn't. Someday she (*discover*) _____ the truth and (*apologize*) _____ to me.

8. Yesterday I (*see*) _____ the man who stole the radio from my car last Friday. I (*run*) _____ after him, (*catch*) _____ him, and (*knock*) _____ him down. A passerby (*go*) _____ to call the police. I (*sit*) _____ on the man while I (*wait*) _____ for them to come. After they (*get*) _____ there and (*understand*) _____ the situation, they (*put*) _____ handcuffs on him and (*take*) _____ him to jail.

◇ **PRACTICE 19—GUIDED STUDY: Past and future. (Chapters 2 and 3)**

Directions: Read Part I. Use the information in Part I to complete Part II with appropriate verbs and tenses. Use **WILL** (not *be going to*) for future time in Part II.

PART I:

(1) Yesterday morning **was** an ordinary morning. I **got** up at 6:30. I **washed** my face and **brushed** my teeth. Then I **put** on my jeans and a sweater. I **went** to the kitchen and **started** the electric coffee maker.

(2) Then I **walked** down my driveway to get the morning newspaper. While I **was walking** to get the paper, I **saw** a deer. It **was eating** the flowers in my garden. After I **watched** the deer for a little while, I **made** some noise to make the deer run away before it **destroyed** my flowers.

(3) As soon as I **got** back to the kitchen, I **poured** myself a cup of coffee and **opened** the morning paper. While I **was reading** the paper, my teenage daughter **came** downstairs. We **talked** about her plans for the day. I **helped** her with her breakfast and **made** a lunch for her to take to school. After we **said** goodbye, I **ate** some fruit and cereal and **finished** reading the paper.

(4) Then I **went** to my office. My office **is** in my home. My office **has** a desk, a computer, a radio, a TV set, a copy machine, and a lot of bookshelves. I **worked** all morning. While I **was working**, the phone **rang** many times. I **talked** to many people. At 11:30, I **went** to the kitchen and **made** a sandwich for lunch. As I said, it **was** an ordinary morning.

PART II:

(1) Tomorrow morning _____**will be**_____ an ordinary morning. I _**'ll get**_____ up at 6:30. I _**'ll wash**_____ my face and _____**brush**_____ my teeth. Then I _____ probably _____ on my jeans and a sweater. I _____ to the kitchen and _____ the electric coffee maker.

(2) Then I _____ down my driveway to get the morning newspaper. If I _____ a deer in my garden, I _____ it for a while and then _____ some noise to chase it away before it _____ my flowers.

(3) As soon as I _____ back to the kitchen, I _____ myself a cup of coffee and _____ the morning paper. While I'm reading the paper, my teenage daughter _____ downstairs. We _____ about her plans for the day. I _____ her with her breakfast and _____ a lunch for her to take to school. After we _____ goodbye, I _____ some fruit and cereal and _____ reading the morning paper.

(4) Then I _____ to my office. My office _____ in my home. My office _____ a desk, a computer, a radio, a TV set, a copy machine, and a lot of bookshelves. I _____ all morning. While I'm working, the phone _____ many times. I _____ to many people. At 11:30, I _____ to the kitchen and _____ a sandwich for lunch. As I said, tomorrow morning _____ an ordinary morning.

Directions: Complete the sentences with the PRESENT PROGRESSIVE. Use the verbs in the list. Use each verb only one time. Notice the future time expressions in italics.

arrive	*leave*	*speak*	*take*
attend	*meet*	*spend*	✓*travel*
get	*see*	*study*	*visit*

1. Kathy _____**is travellng**_____ to Caracas *next month* to attend a conference.

2. A: Are you expecting guests? Your apartment is so neat!

   B: How did you guess? My parents _____ *tomorrow* for a two-day visit.

3. A: Do you have any plans for lunch today?

   B: I _____ Shannon at the Shamrock Cafe *in an hour*. Want to join us?

4. A: I _____ a bicycle for my son for his birthday *next month*. Do you

   know anything about bikes for kids?

   B: Sure. What do you want to know?

5. Amanda likes to take her two children with her on trips whenever she can, but she

   _____ not _____ them with her to El Paso, Texas, *next week*. It's

   strictly a business trip.

6. A: What are your plans for the rest of the year?

   B: I _____ French in Grenoble, France, *this coming summer*. Then I'll be

   back here in school in the fall.

7. A: Why are you packing your suitcase?

   B: I _____ for Los Angeles *in a couple of hours*.

8. A: My regular doctor, Dr. Jordan, _____ a conference in Las Vegas *next*

   week, so I _____ her partner, Dr. Peterson, when I go for my

   appointment *next Friday*.

9. A: Do we have a test in English class tomorrow?

   B: No. Don't you remember? We're going to have a guest lecturer.

   A: Really? Who? Are you sure we don't have a test?

   B: A professor from the Department of Environmental Sciences _____

   to our class tomorrow morning.

   A: Great. That sounds interesting. And it sure beats having a test.

10. A: Why are you looking for your passport?

    B: I need it because I'm leaving for Taipei next Monday.

    A: Oh? How long will you be away?

    B: A week. I _____ the first few days with my brother, who is going to

    school there. After that I _____ some old friends I went to school

    with in Australia several years ago. They've invited me to be their house guest.

    A: Sounds like a great trip. Hope you find your passport.

◇ **PRACTICE 21—SELFSTUDY:** The present progressive to express future time. (Chart 3–7)

Directions: Look at Fred's calendar. Then complete the sentences about Fred's plans for the coming week. Use the PRESENT PROGRESSIVE.

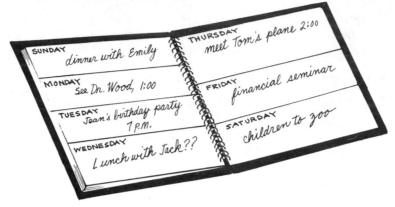

1. Fred _____ ***is eating dinner with Emily*** _____ on Sunday.

2. He _____ on Monday.

3. He _____ on Tuesday.

4. He _____ probably _____ on Wednesday.

5. He _____ on Thursday.

6. He _____ on Friday.

7. He _____ on Saturday.

◇ **PRACTICE 22—GUIDED STUDY:** The present progressive to express future time. (Chart 3–7)

Directions: Make a calendar of **your plans** for the coming week. Then complete the sentences about these plans. Use the PRESENT PROGRESSIVE.

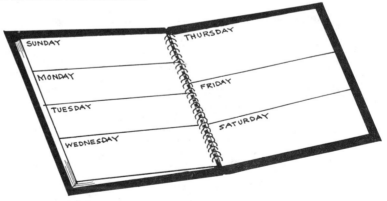

1. I _____ on Sunday.

2. I _____ on Monday.

3. I _____ on Tuesday.

4. I _____ on Wednesday.

5. I _____ on Thursday.

6. I _____ on Friday.

7. I _____ on Saturday.

◇ **PRACTICE 23—GUIDED STUDY:** The present progressive to express future time. (Chart 3–7)

Directions: Think of a place you would like to visit. Pretend you are going to take a trip there this weekend. Pretend you have already made all of your plans. Write a paragraph in which you describe your trip. Use the PRESENT PROGRESSIVE where appropriate.

Example: This coming weekend, my friend Benito and I are taking a trip. We're going to Nashville, Tennessee. Benito likes country music and wants to go to some shows. I don't know anything about country music, but I'm looking forward to going to Nashville. We're leaving Friday afternoon as soon as Benito gets off work. (Etc.)

Possible questions to answer in your paragraph:

1. Where are you going?
2. When are you leaving?
3. Are you traveling alone?
4. How are you getting there?
5. Where are you staying?
6. Who are you visiting, if anyone?
7. How long are you staying there?
8. When are you getting back?

◇ **PRACTICE 24—SELFSTUDY:** The simple present to express future time. (Chart 3–8)

Directions: Use any of the verbs in the list to complete the sentences. Use the SIMPLE PRESENT to express future time.

begin	finish	leave
close	get in	open
end	land	start

1. A: What time ___*does*___ class ___*begin* (OR: *start*)___ tomorrow morning?

   B: It ___*begins* (OR: *starts*)___ at eight o'clock sharp.

2. A: The coffee shop _____ at seven o'clock tomorrow morning. I'll meet you there at 7:15.

   B: Okay. I'll be there.

3. A: What time are you going to go to the airport tonight?

   B: Tom's plane _____ around 7:15, but I think I'll go a little early in case it gets in ahead of schedule.

4. A: What time should we go to the theater tonight?

   B: Around 7:30. The movie _____ at 8:00.

   A: What time _____ it _____?

   B: It's a two-hour movie. It _____ at 10:00.

5. A: What time _____ the dry cleaning shop _____ tonight? If I don't get there in time, I'll have nothing to wear to the banquet tonight.

   B: It _____ at 6:00. I can pick up your dry cleaning for you.

   A: Hey, thanks! That'll really help!

6. A: What's the hurry?

   B: I've got to take a shower, change clothes, and get to the theater fast. The play

   _____ in forty-five minutes, and I don't want to miss the beginning.

◇ **PRACTICE 25—SELFSTUDY:** *Be about to.* (Chart 3–10)

   Directions: Describe the actions that are about to happen in the pictures. Use **BE ABOUT TO**.

1. ***The chimpanzee is about to eat a banana.***

2. _____

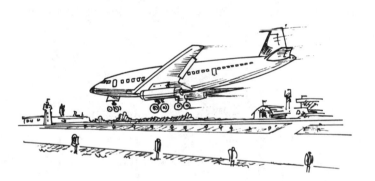

3. _____

4. _____

◇ **PRACTICE 26—SELFSTUDY:** Verb tense review. (Chapters 1, 2 and 3)

   Directions: Complete the sentences with a form of the verb in parentheses.

   1. A: I'll lend you my bike if I (*need, not*) _____ it tomorrow.

      B: Thanks.

   2. A: Everyone in the office (*plan*) _____ to come to the annual company

         picnic tomorrow. (*you, come*) _____?

      B: Of course!

   3. A: How (*you, get, usually*) _____ to work?

      B: I (*take*) _____ the commuter train every morning.

4. A few days ago, Janet (*watch*) _____ a drama on TV when the screen suddenly (*become*) _____ blank and the TV set (*stop*) _____ working. She never (*find*) _____ out how the story ended.

5. A: I (*go*) _____ to a lecture on Shakespeare tomorrow evening. Want to join me?

    B: Nah. Brian and I (*go*) _____ to a movie—*Godzilla Eats the Earth.*

6. A: When's Barbara going to call? We have to leave soon.

    B: She (*call, probably*) _____ any minute. I'm sure she'll call us before we (*go*) _____ out to dinner.

7. A: Look! There (*be*) _____ a police car behind us. Its lights (*flash*) _____.

    B: I (*know*) _____! I (*know*) _____! I (*see*) _____ it!

    A: What (*go*) _____ on? (*you, speed*) _____?

    B: No, I'm not. I (*go*) _____ the speed limit.

    A: Ah, look. The police car (*pass*) _____ us. Whew.

8. Sometime in the next twenty-five years, a spaceship with a human crew (*land*) _____ on Mars. At least, that's what I (*think*) _____.

9. I usually (*ride*) _____ my bicycle to work in the morning, but it (*rain*) _____ when I left my house early this morning, so I (*drive*) _____ my car. After I (*arrive*) _____ at work, I (*discover*) _____ that I had left my briefcase at home.

10. A: How do you like your new job?

    B: I don't start it until tomorrow. I (*give*) _____ you an answer next week.

11. A: What (*you, wear*) _____ to Eric's wedding tomorrow?

    B: My blue dress, I guess. How about you?

    A: I (*plan*) _____ to wear my new outfit. I (*buy*) _____ it just a few days ago. It (*be*) _____ a yellow suit with a white blouse. Just a minute. I (*show*) _____ it to you. Wait right here. I (*get*) _____ it from my closet and (*bring*) _____ it out.

12. A: Where's my blue sweater?

    B: Lizzy (*wear*) _____ it today.

    A: She's what? I (*lend, not*) _____ her my sweater.

    B: Oh? Well, Lizzy (*be*) _____ back soon. You can get your sweater back then.

◇ **PRACTICE 27—SELFSTUDY:** Verb tense review. (Chapters 1, 2, and 3)

Directions: Complete the sentences with a form of the verb in parentheses.

(1) Two hundred and fifty years ago, people (*make*) _____ their own clothes. They (*have, not*) _____ machines for making clothes. There (*be, not*) _____ any clothing factories. People (*wear*) _____ homemade clothes that were sewn by hand.

(2) Today, very few people (*make*) _____ their own clothes. Clothing (*come*) _____ ready-made from factories. People (*buy*) _____ almost all their clothes from stores.

(3) The modern clothing industry (*be*) _____ international. As a result, people from different countries often (*wear*) _____ similar clothes. For example, people in many different countries throughout the world (*wear*) _____ jeans and T-shirts.

(4) However, regional differences in clothing still (*exist*) _____. For instance, people of the Arabian deserts (*wear*) _____ loose, flowing robes to protect themselves from the heat of the sun. In northern Europe, fur hats (*be*) _____ common in the winter.

(5) In the future, there (*be, probably*) _____ fewer and fewer differences in clothing in the world. People throughout the world (*wear*) _____ clothes from the same factories. (*we all, dress*) _____ almost alike in the future? TV shows and movies about the future often (*show*) _____ everybody in a uniform of some kind. What (*you, think*) _____?

◇ **PRACTICE 28—GUIDED STUDY:** Verb tense review. (Chapters 1, 2, and 3)

Directions: Complete the sentences with a form of the verb in parentheses.

Dianne, Sara, and Emily all (*1. go*) _____ to college together twenty years ago. They (*2. have*) _____ a wonderful time and (*3. learn*) _____ a lot. Now, the three of them (*4. work*) _____ at the same insurance company. They (*5. eat*) _____ lunch together every day and sometimes (*6. tell*) _____ stories about their school days.

Yesterday, they (*7. remember*) _____ a funny incident at a special banquet during their sophomore year. At this dinner, they (*8. sit*) _____ at the same table as the president of the university. Everything (*9. go*) _____ along fine, but then disaster (*10. strike*) _____. To make a long story short, Sara (*11. spill*) _____ a serving dish full of spaghetti onto the president.

Sara (*12. be*) _____ terribly embarrassed. She (*13. apologize*) _____ profusely and (*14. leave*) _____ the banquet room in tears.

Now, twenty years later, the three women (*15. remember*) _____ every detail, especially the look on the president's face. When they (*16. tell*) _____that story at lunch yesterday, they (*17. laugh*) _____ until tears streamed down their faces.

The spaghetti incident (*18. be, not*) _____ funny when it happened, but it (*19. be*) _____ funny to the women now. Terrible embarrassments that we suffer when we (*20. be*) _____ young often seem funny when we (*21. be*) _____ older. As we (*22. get*) _____ older, we (*23. get*) _____ more tolerant of our own foibles. Right now you (*24. be*) _____ young. When you (*25. be*) _____ older, you (*26. smile*) _____ with amusement about some of the seemingly terrible and embarrassing things that happen to you as a young adult.

◇ **PRACTICE 29—GUIDED STUDY: Verb tense review. (Chapters 1, 2, and 3)**

Directions: Complete the sentences with a form of the verb in parentheses.

1. This morning, Bob (*comb*) _____ his hair when the comb (*break*) _____. So he (*finish*) _____ combing his hair with his fingers and (*rush*) _____ out the door to class.

2. I'm exhausted! When I (*get*) _____ home tonight, I (*read*) _____ the paper and (*watch*) _____ the news. I (*do, not*) _____ any work around the house.

3. A: My cousin (*have*) _____ a new cat. She now (*have*) _____ four cats.

   B: Why (*she, have*) _____ so many?

   A: To catch the mice in her house.

   B: (*you, have*) _____ any cats?

   A: No, and I (*get, not*) _____ any. I (*have, not*) _____ mice in my house.

4. A: Ouch!

   B: What happened?

   A: I (*cut*) _____ my finger.

   B: It (*bleed*) _____!

   A: I know!

   B: Put pressure on it. I (*get*) _____ some antibiotic and a bandage.

   A: Thanks.

5. A: (*you, take*) _____ the kids to the amusement park tomorrow morning?

   B: Yes. It (*open*) _____ at 10:00. If we (*leave*) _____ here at 9:30, we (*get, probably*) _____ there at 9:55. The kids can be the first ones in the park.

6. A: Your phone (*ring*) _____.

    B: I (*know*) _____.

    A: (*you, answer*) _____ it?

    B: No.

    A: (*you, want*) _____ me to get it?

    B: No thanks.

    A: Why (*you, want, not*) _____ to answer your phone?

    B: I (*expect*) _____ another call from the bill collector. I have a bunch of

        bills I haven't paid. I (*want, not*) _____ to talk to her.

    A: Oh.

7. My grandmother used to say, "If adversity (*destroy, not*) _____ you,

    it will strengthen you." In other words, if you (*learn*) _____ to survive bad

    times and bad luck, you will become a stonger person.

8. A: Peter B. Peas is a piece-by-piece pizza eater.

    B: What (*you, say*) _____?

    A: I (*say*) _____, "Peter B. Peas is a piece-by-piece pizza eater." It (*be*)

        _____ a tongue-twister. How fast can *you* say it?

9. A: Okay, let's all open our fortune cookies.

    B: What (*yours, say*) _____?

    A: Mine says, "An unexpected gift (*add*) _____ to your pleasure."

        Great! (*you, plan*) _____ to give me a gift soon?

    B: Not that I know of. Mine says, "Your trust in a friend (*prove*) _____

        well-founded." Good. I (*like*) _____ having trustworthy friends.

C: This one says, "A smile (*overcome*) _____ a language barrier."
Well, that's good! After this, when I (*understand, not*) _____
people who (*speak*) _____ English to me, I (*smile, just*)
_____ at them!

D: My fortune is this: "Your determination (*make*) _____ you succeed in
everything."

A: Well, it (*look*) _____ like all of us (*have*) _____ good
luck in the future!

10. A: (*the sun, keep*) _____ burning forever, or (*it, burn, eventually*)
_____ itself out?

B: It (*burn, eventually*) _____ itself out, but that
(*happen, not*) _____ for another five or ten billion years.

◇ PRACTICE 30—GUIDED STUDY: Future time. (Chapter 3)

Directions: Do you believe that some people are able to predict the future? Pretend that you have
the ability to see into the future. Choose several people you know (classmates, teachers, family
members, friends) and tell them in writing about their future lives. Discuss such topics as marriage,
children, jobs, contributions to humankind, fame, and exciting adventures. With your words, paint
interesting and fun pictures of their future lives.

◇ PRACTICE 31—SELFSTUDY: Prepositions. (Chapter 3)

Directions: Complete the sentences with appropriate PREPOSITIONS.★

1. What are you laughing _____?

2. I can't stop staring _____ Tom's necktie. The colors are wild!

3. A: I don't believe _____ flying saucers. Do you?

   B: I don't know. I think anything is possible.

4. Ted is going to help me _____ my homework tonight.

5. Do you mind if I apply _____ your job after you quit?

6. I'm traveling _____ Indonesia next week to discuss my new business plan _____ our
contacts in Jakarta.

7. I admire Carmen _____ her courage and honesty in admitting that mistake.

8. A: Where did you get that new car?

   B: I borrowed it _____ my neighbor.

9. A: What are you two arguing _____?

   B: Modern art.

10. A: Where will you go to school next year?

    B: Well, I applied _____ admission at five different universities, but I'm worried that
none of them will accept me.

◇ **PRACTICE 32—SELFSTUDY: Prepositions. (Chapters 1 and 3)**

Directions: Complete the sentences with appropriate PREPOSIITONS.

1. Dan is always nice _____ everyone.

2. A: How long do you need to keep the Spanish book you borrowed _____ me?

   B: I'd like to keep it until I'm ready _____ the exam next week.

3. A: Why weren't you more polite _____ Alan's friend?

   B: Because he kept staring _____ me all evening. He made me nervous.

4. A: We're going to beat you in the soccer game on Saturday.

   B: No way. Two of your players are equal _____ only one of ours.

   A: Oh yeah? We'll see.

5. Stop pouring! My cup is already full _____ coffee.

6. May I please borrow some money _____ you? I'm thirsty _____ an ice-cream soda, and we're walking right by the ice cream shop.

7. A: Do you believe _____ astrology?

   B: I'm really not familiar _____ it.

8. A: Mike, I really admire you _____ your ability to remember names. Will you help me _____ the introductions?

   B: Sure. Ellen, let me introduce you _____ Pat, Andy, Debbie, Nora, Jack, and Kate.

---

*See Appendix 1 for a list of preposition combinations.

CHAPTER 4
Nouns and Pronouns

◇ **PRACTICE 1—SELFSTUDY: Plural nouns. (Charts 4–1 and 4–2)**

Directions: These sentences have many mistakes in the use of nouns. <u>Underline</u> each NOUN. Write the correct PLURAL FORM if necessary. Do not change any of the other words in the sentences.

                            streets   *highways*

1. <u>Chicago</u> has busy ~~<u>street</u>~~ and ~~<u>highway</u>~~.

2. Box have six side.

3. Big city have many problem.

4. Banana grow in hot, humid area.

5. Insect don't have nose.

6. Lamb are the offspring of sheep.

7. Library keep book on shelf.

8. Parent support their child.

9. Indonesia has several active volcano.

10. Baboon are big monkey. They have large head and sharp tooth. They eat leaf, root, insect, and egg.

◇ **PRACTICE 2—SELFSTUDY: Plural nouns. (Chart 4–1)**

Directions: Write the correct SINGULAR or PLURAL form.

SINGULAR	PLURAL	SINGULAR	PLURAL
1. *mouse*	mice	9. duty	_____
2. pocket	*pockets*	10. highway	_____
3. _____	teeth	11. _____	thieves
4. _____	tomatoes	12. belief	_____
5. _____	fish	13. potato	_____
6. _____	women	14. radio	_____
7. branch	_____	15. offspring	_____
8. friend	_____	16. _____	children

SINGULAR	PLURAL	SINGULAR	PLURAL
17. season	_____	21. occurrence	_____
18. custom	_____	22. _____	phenomena
19. business	_____	23. sheep	_____
20. _____	centuries	24. _____	loaves

◇ **PRACTICE 3—GUIDED STUDY:** Plural nouns. (Chart 4–1)

Directions: Practice pronouncing **FINAL -S/-ES** by saying the words in the list aloud.

PRONUNCIATION NOTES: Final *-s/-es* has three different pronunciations: /s/, /z/, and /əz/.

- /s/ is the sound of "s" in "bus." Final *-s* is pronounced /s/ after voiceless sounds: *seats* = *seat* + /s/. (Examples of voiceless sounds are: /t/, /p/, /k/, /f/.)
- /z/ is the sound of "z" in "buzz." Final *-s* is pronounced /z/ after voiced sounds: *seeds* = *seed* + /z/. (Examples of voiced sounds are: /d/, /b/, /r/, /l/, /m/, /n/ and all vowel sounds.)
- /əz/ adds a whole syllable to a plural noun. Final *-es* and *-s* are pronounced /əz/ after *-sh, -ch, -s, -z,* and *-ge/dge* sounds:

wishes = *wish* + /əz/	*sizes* = *size* + /əz/
matches = *match* + /əz/	*pages* = *page* + /əz/
classes = *class* + /əz/	*judges* = *judge* + /əz/

---

1. cats = *cat* + /s/
2. heads = *head* + /z/
3. eyes = *eye* + /z/
4. cars = *car* + /z/
5. backs = *back* + /s/
6. words = *word* + /z/
7. boats = *boat* + /s/
8. lips = *lip* + /s/
9. ribs = *rib* + /z/
10. hills = *hill* + /z/

11. dishes = *dish* + /əz/
12. matches = *match* + /əz/
13. eyelashes = *eyelash* + /əz/
14. edges = *edge* + /əz/
15. pages = *page* + /əz/
16. horses = *horse* + /əz/
17. glasses = *glass* + /əz/
18. places = *place* + /əz/
19. prices = *price* + /əz/
20. prizes = *prize* + /əz/

◇ **PRACTICE 4—GUIDED STUDY:** Plural nouns. (Chart 4–1)

Directions: Practice pronouncing **FINAL -S/-ES** by reading the sentences aloud.

1. Our **classrooms** have **tables**, **chairs**, and **desks**.
   classroom/z/ table/z/ chair/z/ desk/s/

2. **Carrots** and **peas** are **vegetables**.
   carrot/s/ pea/z/ vegetable/z/

3. I was in Alaska for two **weeks** and three **days**.
   week/s/ day/z/

4. **Hospitals**, **businesses**, and **schools** use closed-circuit television.
   hospital/z/ business/ə z/   school/z/

5. There were two **messages** on my answering machine.
         message/ə z/

6. There are many TV **programs** about **doctors**, **detectives**, and **cowboys**.
            program/z/   doctor/z/ detective/z/   cowboy/z/

7. **Insects** don't have **ears**. They have **membranes** that can detect **vibrations**.
   insect/s/   ear/z/   membrane/z/   vibration/z/

8. Modern **tools**, **machines**, and **sources** of power make our **jobs** easier.
      tool/z/ machine/z/   source/ə z/   job/z/

9. **Writers** need to support their **opinions** with **facts** and logical **thoughts**.
   writer/z/   opinion/z/   fact/s/   thought/s/

10. Cotton is used to make **blankets**, **blouses**, **rugs**, **gloves**, and **shirts**.
         blanket/s/ blouse/ə z/ rug/z/ glove/z/   shirt/s/

◇ PRACTICE 5—SELFSTUDY: Subjects, verbs, objects, and prepositions. (Charts 4–2 and 4–3)

Directions: Identify the SUBJECTS (**S**), VERBS (**V**), OBJECTS (**O**), and PREPOSITIONAL PHRASES (**PP**) in the following sentences.

    S   **V**   **O**
1. [Bridges] [cross] [rivers.]
           S   **V**   **PP**
2. [A terrible earthquake] [occurred] [in Turkey.]

3. Airplanes fly above the clouds.

4. Trucks carry large loads.

5. Rivers flow toward the sea.

6. Salespeople treat customers with courtesy.

7. Bacteria can cause diseases.

8. Clouds are floating across the sky.

9. The audience in the theater applauded the performers at the end of the

   show.

10. Helmets protect bicyclists from serious injuries.

◇ PRACTICE 6—SELFSTUDY: Nouns and verbs. (Charts 4–1 → 4–3).

Directions: Some words can be used both as a noun and as a verb. If the word in *italics* is used as a NOUN, circle **n**. If the word in *italics* is used as a VERB, circle **v**. (**n**. = **noun** and **v**. = **verb**).

1. **n.** (**v.**) People *smile* when they're happy.

2. (**n.**) **v.** Mary has a nice *smile* when she's happy.

3. **n.** **v.** Emily likes her *work*.

4. **n.** **v.** Emily and Mike *work* at the cafeteria.

5. **n.** **v.** The semester will *end* next month.

6. **n.** **v.** I'll go on vacation at the *end* of next month.

7. **n.** **v.** The child wrote her *name* on the wall with a crayon.

8. **n.** **v.** People often *name* their children after relatives.

9. **n.** **v.** I rarely add *salt* to my food.

10. **n.** **v.** Some people *salt* their food before they even taste it.

11. **n.** **v.** Kings and queens *rule* their countries.

12. **n.** **v.** We learned a spelling *rule* in grammar class.

13. **n.** **v.** People usually *store* milk in a refrigerator.

14. **n.** **v.** We went to the *store* to buy some milk.

15. **n.** **v.** Airplanes *land* on runways at the airport.

16. **n.** **v.** The ship reached *land* after seventeen days at sea.

17. **n.** **v.** I took a *train* from New York to Boston.

18. **n.** **v.** I *train* my dogs to sit on command.

19. **n.** **v.** Alex *visits* his aunt every week.

20. **n.** **v.** Alex's aunt enjoys his *visits* every week.

21. **n.** **v.** Marilyn killed the *flies* in the kitchen with a fly swatter.

22. **n.** **v.** Marti *flies* her airplane to an island in Canada at least once a month.

◇ **PRACTICE 7—GUIDED STUDY:** Nouns and verbs. (Charts 4–1 → 4–3)

Directions: Use each word in **two** different sentences. Use the word as a NOUN (n.) in the first sentence and as a VERB (v.) in the second sentence. Consult your dictionary if necessary to find out the different uses and meanings of a word.

Example: watch
Written: **n. *I am wearing a <u>watch</u>.***
v. *I <u>watched</u> TV after dinner last night.*

1. snow	4. phone	7. water
2. paint	5. smoke	8. circle
3. tie	6. face	9. mail

Other common words that are used as both nouns and verbs are listed below. Choose several from the list to make additional sentences. Use your dictionary if necessary.

center/centre,* date, experience, fear, fish, garden, mind, place, plant, promise, question, rain, rock, season, sense, shape, shop, star, tip, trip, value

---

*center = American English.
centre = British English.

◇ **PRACTICE 8—SELFSTUDY:** Adjectives. (Chart 4–4)

Directions: All of the following words are adjectives. For each, write an ADJECTIVE that has the OPPOSITE MEANING.

1. new _____*old*_____   13. dangerous _____
2. young _____*old*_____   14. noisy _____
3. cold _____   15. shallow _____
4. fast _____   16. sweet _____
5. sad _____   17. cheap _____
6. good _____   18. dark _____
7. wet _____   19. heavy _____
8. easy _____   20. public _____
9. soft _____   21. left _____
10. wide _____   22. wrong _____
11. clean _____   23. weak _____
12. empty _____   24. long _____

◇ **PRACTICE 9—SELFSTUDY:** Adjectives and nouns. (Chart 4–4)

Directions: Circle each ADJECTIVE. Draw an arrow to the noun it describes.

1. Paul has a (loud) voice.
2. Sugar is (sweet)
3. The students took an easy test.
4. Air is free.
5. We ate some delicious food at a Mexican restaurant.
6. An encyclopedia contains important facts about a wide variety of subjects.
7. The child was sick.
8. The sick child crawled into his warm bed and sipped hot tea.

◇ **PRACTICE 10—GUIDED STUDY:** Adjectives and nouns. (Chart 4–4)

Directions: Add ADJECTIVES to the sentences. Choose **two** of the three adjectives in each list to add to the given sentences.

Example: hard, heavy, strong   A man lifted the box.
→ *A strong man lifted the heavy box.*

1. *beautiful, safe, red*   Roses are flowers.
2. *dark, cold, dry*   Rain fell from the clouds.
3. *empty, wet, hot*   The waiter poured coffee into my cup.
4. *easy, blue, young*   The girl in the dress was looking for a telephone.

5. *quiet, sharp, soft*   Annie sleeps on a bed in a room.

6. *fresh, clear, hungry*   Mrs. Fox gave the children some fruit.

7. *dirty, modern, delicious*   After we finished our dinner, Frank helped me with the dishes.

8. *round, inexperienced, right*   When Tom was getting a haircut, the barber accidentally cut Tom's ear with the scissors.

◇ PRACTICE 11—SELFSTUDY: Nouns as adjectives. (Chart 4–5)

Directions: Use the information in *italics* to complete the sentences. Each completion should have a NOUN THAT IS USED AS AN ADJECTIVE in front of another noun.

1. *Articles in newspapers* are called _____ ***newspaper articles*** _____.

2. *Numbers on pages* are called _____.

3. *Money that is made of paper* is called _____.

4. *Buildings with apartments* are called _____.

5. *Chains for keys* are called _____.

6. *Governments in cities* are called _____.

7. *Ponds for ducks* are called _____.

8. *Pads for shoulders* are called _____.

9. *Knives that people carry in their pockets* are called _____.

10. *Lights that regulate traffic* are called _____.

◇ PRACTICE 12—SELFSTUDY: Nouns. (Charts 4–1 → 4–5)

Directions: These sentences contain many mistakes in noun usage. Make the nouns PLURAL whenever possible and appropriate. Do not change any other words.

           bottles   ***caps***
1. Medicine ~~bottle~~ have childproof ~~cap~~.

2. Airplane seat are narrow and uncomfortable.

3. Science student do laboratory experiment in their class.

4. Housefly are dangerous pest. They carry germ.

5. Computer cannot think. They need human operator.

6. There are approximately 250,000 different kind of flower in the world.

7. Newspaper reporter have high-pressure job.

8. Good telephone manner are important.

9. I bought two theatre ticket for Thursday evening's performance of *A Doll's House*.

10. Our daily life have changed in many way in the past one hundred year. We no longer need to use oil lamp or candle in our house, raise our own chicken, or build daily fire for cooking.

Directions: These sentences contain many mistakes in noun usage. Make the nouns PLURAL whenever possible and appropriate. Do not change any other words.

kinds birds
1. There are around 8,600 ~~kind~~ of ~~bird~~ in the world.

2. Bird hatch from egg.

3. Baby bird stay in their nest for several week or

   month. Their parent feed them until they can fly.

4. People eat chicken egg. Some animal eat bird egg.

5. Fox and snake are natural enemy of bird.

   They eat bird and their egg.

6. Some bird eat only seed and plant. Other bird eat mainly insect and earthworm.

7. Weed are unwanted plant. They prevent farm crop and garden flower from growing properly.

   Bird help farmer by eating weed seed and harmful insect.

8. Rat, rabbit, and mouse can cause huge loss on farm by eating stored crop. Certain big bird

   like hawk help farmer by hunting these animal.

9. The feather of certain kind of bird are used in pillow and mattress. The soft feather from

   goose are often used for pillow. Goose feather are also used in winter jacket.

10. The wing feather from goose were used as pen from the sixth century to the nineteenth

    century, when steel pen were invented.

◇ PRACTICE 14—SELFSTUDY: Personal pronouns. (Chart 4–6)

Directions: Find each PRONOUN. Note how it is used:
- SUBJECT (**S**)
- OBJECT OF A VERB (**O of vb**), or
- OBJECT OF A PREPOSITION (**O of prep**).

        O of vb
1. The teacher helped [me] with the lesson.

  S   **O *of prep***
2. [I] carry a dictionary with [me] at all times.

3. Mr. Fong has a computer. He uses it for many things. It helps him in many ways.

4. Jessica went to Hawaii with Ann and me. We like her, and she likes us. We had a good time with her.

5. Mike had dirty socks. He washed them in the kitchen sink and hung them to dry in front of the window. They dried quickly.

6. Joseph and I are close friends. No bad feelings will ever come between him and me. He and I share a strong bond of friendship.

◇ PRACTICE 15—SELFSTUDY: Personal pronouns. (Chart 4–6)

Directions: Circle each PRONOUN, and draw an arrow to the noun or noun phrase it refers to.

1. [Janet] had [a green apple.] (She) ate (it) after class.

2. Betsy called this morning. John spoke to her.

3. Nick and Rob are at the market. They are buying fresh vegetables.

4. Eric took some phone messages for Karen. They're on a pad of yellow paper in the kitchen.

5. When Louie called, Alice talked to him. He asked her for a date. She accepted.

6. Jane wrote a letter to Mr. and Mrs. Moore. She mailed it to them yesterday. They should get the letter from her on Friday.

◇ PRACTICE 16—SELFSTUDY: Personal pronouns. (Chart 4–6)

Directions: Complete the sentences with **SHE, HE, IT, HER, HIM, THEY,** or **THEM**.

1. I have a grammar book. _____*It*_____ is black.
2. Tom borrowed my books. _____*He*_____ returned _____*them*_____ yesterday.
3. Susan is wearing some new earrings. _____ look good on _____.

4. Don't look directly at the sun. The intensity of its light can injure your eyes. Don't look at _____ directly even if you are wearing sunglasses.

5. Table tennis (also called ping-pong) began in England in the late 1800s. Today _____ is an international sport. My brother and I played _____ a lot when we were teenagers. I beat _____ sometimes, but _____ was a better player and usually won.

6. Do bees sleep at night? Or do _____ work in the hive all night long? You never see _____ after dark. What do _____ do after night falls?

7. The apples were rotten, so we didn't eat _____ even though we were really hungry.

8. The scent of perfume rises. According to one expert, you should put _____ on the soles of your feet.

9. Clean, safe water is fundamental to human health. It is shocking that an estimated 800 million people in the world are still without _____. Unsafe water causes illnesses. _____ contributes to high numbers of deaths in children under five years of age.

10. Magazines are popular. I enjoy reading _____. _____ have news about recent events and discoveries. Recently, I read about "micromachines." _____ are human-made machines that are smaller than a grain of sand. One scientist called _____ "the greatest scientific invention of our time."

◇ PRACTICE 17—SELFSTUDY: Personal pronouns. (Chart 4–6)

Directions: Circle the correct PRONOUN.

1. You can ride with Jennifer and   I, (me.)

2. Did you see Mark?   *He, Him*   was waiting in your office to talk to you.

3. I saw Rob a few minutes ago. I passed Sara and   *he, him*   on the steps of the classroom building.

4. Nick used to work in his father's store, but his father and   *he, him*   had a serious disagreement. Nick left and started his own business.

5. When the doctor came into the room, I asked   *she, her*   a question.

6. The doctor was very helpful.   *She, Her*   answered all of my questions.

7. Prof. Molina left a message for you and   *I, me*.   *He, him*   needs to see   *we, us*.

8. Emily is a good basketball player. I watch Betsy and   *she, her*   carefully during games.   *They, Them*   are the best players.

9. One time my little sister and   *I, me*   were home alone. When our parents returned, they found a valuable vase had been broken.   *They, Them*   blamed   *we, us*   for the broken vase, but in truth the cat had broken   *it, them*.   *We, Us*   got in trouble with   *they, them*   because of the cat.

10. Take these secret documents and destroy   *it, them*.

11. Ron invited Mary and   *I, me*   to have dinner with   *he, him*.

12. Maureen likes movies. Ron and   *she, her*   go to the movies every chance they get.

13. Tom and   *I, me*   both want to marry Ann. She has to choose between   *he and I, him and me*.

◇ PRACTICE 18—SELFSTUDY: Possessive nouns. (Chart 4–7)

Directions: Use the *italicized* noun in the first sentence to write a POSSESSIVE NOUN in the second sentence. Pay special attention to where you put the apostrophe.

1. I have one *friend*. My _____**friend's**_____ name is Paul.

2. I have two *friends*. My _____**friends'**_____ names are Paul and Kevin.

3. I have one *son*. My _____ name is Ryan.

4. I have two *sons*. My _____ names are Ryan and Scott.

5. I have one *baby*. My _____ name is Joy.

6. I have two *babies*. My _____ names are Joy and Erica.

7. I have one *child*. My _____ name is Anna.

8. I have two *children*. My _____ names are Anna and Keith.

9. I know one *person*. This _____ name is Nick.

10. I know several *people*. These _____ names are Nick, Karen and Rita.

11. I have one *teacher*. My _____ name is Ms. West.

12. I have two *teachers*. My _____ names are Ms. West and Mr. Fox.

13. I know a *man*. This _____ name is Alan Burns.

14. I know two *men*. These _____ names are Alan Burns and Joe Lee.

15. We live on the *earth*. The _____ surface is seventy percent water.

◇ PRACTICE 19—SELFSTUDY: Possessive nouns. (Chart 4–7)

Directions: These sentences contain mistakes in the punctuation of possessive nouns. Add APOSTROPHES in the right places.

1. A king's chair is called a throne.

2. Kings' chairs are called thrones.

3. Babies toys are often brightly colored.

4. It's important to make sure a babys toys are safe.

5. Someone called, but because of the static on the phone, I couldn't understand the callers words.

6. A receptionists job is to write down callers names and take messages.

7. Newspapers aren't interested in yesterdays news. They want to report todays events.

8. Each flight has at least two pilots. The pilots seats are in a small area called the cockpit

9. Rain forests cover five percent of the earths surface but have fifty percent of the different species of plants.

10. Mosquitoes wings move incredibly fast.

11. A mosquitos wings move about one thousand times per second. Its wing movement is the sound we hear when a mosquito is humming in our ears.

12. The average pulse of a human being is seventy beats per minute. A cats heart beats one hundred and thirty times per minute. Elephants have slow heartbeats. Did you know that an elephants heart beats only twenty-five times per minute?

13. When we went to the circus, we saw three elephants. All of us enjoyed watching the elephants tricks. Elephants are quite intelligent animals that can be taught to respond to spoken commands.

14. Elephants like to roll in mud. The mud protects the animals bodies from insects and the sun.

15. When we were walking in the woods, we saw an animals footprints on the muddy path.

◇ PRACTICE 20—GUIDED STUDY: Possessive nouns. (Chart 4–7)

Directions: Make the nouns POSSESSIVE if necessary.

1. I met Dan~~'s~~ sister yesterday. **Dan's**

2. I met Dan and his sister yesterday. (no change)

3. I know Jack roommates.

4. I know Jack well. He's a good friend of mine.

5. I have one roommate. My roommate desk is always messy.

6. You have two roommates. Your roommates desks are always neat.

7. Jo Ann and Betty are sisters.

8. Jo Ann is Betty sister. My sister name is Sonya.

9. My name is Richard. I have two sisters. My sisters names are Jo Ann and Betty.

10. There is an old saying: "A woman work is never done."

11. I read a book about the changes in women roles and men roles in modern society.

12. Jupiter is the largest planet in our solar system. We cannot see Jupiter surface from the earth because thick clouds surround the planet.

13. Mercury is the closest planet to the sun. Mercury atmosphere is extremely hot and dry.

14. Mars* surface has some of the same characteristics as the earth surface, but Mars could not support life as we know it on earth. The plants and animals that live on the earth could not live on any of the other planets in our solar system.

15. Venus is sometimes called the earth twin because the two planets are almost the same size. But like Mars, Venus surface is extremely hot and dry.

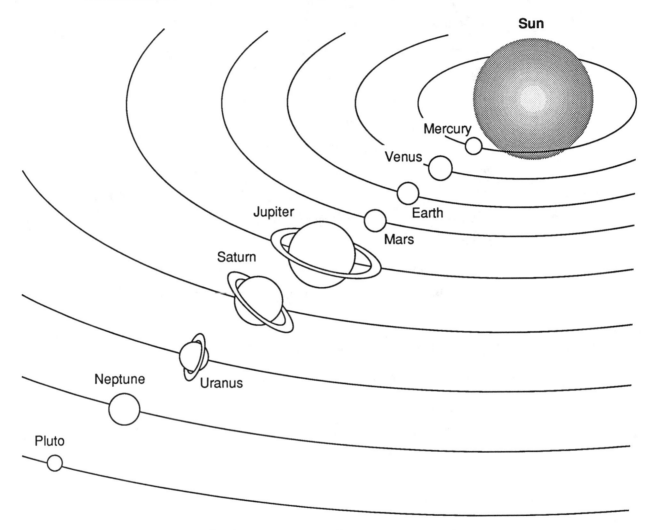

16. The planets English names come from ancient Roman mythology. For example, Mars was the name of the god of war in ancient Rome. Jupiter was the king of the gods. Mercury, who was Jupiter son, was the messenger of the gods. Venus was the goddess of love, beauty, and creativity. Venus son was named Cupid, the god of love and desire.

---

*When a singular noun ends in -s, there are two possible possessive forms, as in the examples below:

SINGULAR NOUN	POSSESSIVE FORMS
James	I know *James'* brother. OR: I know *James's* brother.
Chris	*Chris'* car is red. OR: *Chris's* car is red.
Carlos	*Carlos'* last name is Rivera. OR: *Carlos's* last name is Rivera.

◇ **PRACTICE 21—GUIDED STUDY:** Review of nouns + -s/-es. (Charts 4–1 and 4–7)

Directions: Add **-S/-ES** if necessary. Add an APOSTROPHE to possessive nouns as appropriate.

Examples: **Butterflies**
~~Butterfly~~ are beautiful.

David's
Nick is ~~David~~ brother.

1. Most leaf are green.

2. My mother apartment is small.

3. Potato are good for us.

4. Do bird have teeth?

5. Tom last name is Miller.

6. Two thief stole Mr. Lee car.

7. Mountain are high, and valley are low.

8. A good toy holds a child interest for a long time.

9. Children toy need to be strong and safe.

10. All of the actor name are listed on page six of your program.

11. Teacher are interested in young people idea.

12. Almost all monkey have opposable thumb on not only their hand but also their feet. People have thumb only on their hand.

◇ **PRACTICE 22—SELFSTUDY:** Possessive pronouns and possessive adjectives. (Chart 4–8)

Directions: Complete the sentences with POSSESSIVE PRONOUNS or POSSESSIVE ADJECTIVES that refer to the words in *italics*.

1. A: Can I look at your grammar book?

   B: Why? *You* have _____**your**_____ own* book. *You* have _____**yours**_____, and I have mine.

2. A: Anna wants to look at your grammar book.

   B: Why? *She* has _____ own book. *She* has _____, and I have mine.

3. A: Tom wants to look at your grammar book.

   B: Why? *He* has _____ own book. *He* has _____, and I have mine.

4. A: Tom and I want to look at your grammar book.

   B: Why? *You* have _____ own books. *You* have _____, and I have mine.

5. A: Tom and Anna want to look at our grammar books.

   B: Why? *They* have _____ own books. *We* have _____ own books. *They* have _____, and *we* have _____.

---

*__Own__ frequently follows a possessive adjective: e.g., *my own, your own, their own*. The word __own__ emphasizes that nobody else possesses the exact same thing(s); ownership belongs **only** to me (*my own book*), to you (*your own book*), to them (*their own books*), to us (*our own books*), etc.

◇ **PRACTICE 23—GUIDED STUDY:** Possessive pronouns and possessive adjectives.
(Charts 4–8 and 4–9)

Directions: Complete the sentences with POSSESSIVE PRONOUNS or POSSESSIVE ADJECTIVES that refer to the words in *italics*.

1. *Sara* asked _____**her**_____ mother for permission to go to a movie.

2. I don't need to borrow your bicycle. *Sara* loaned me _____**hers**_____.

3. *Ted and I* are roommates. _____ apartment is small.

4. Brian and Louie have a huge apartment, but *we* don't. _____ is small.

5. *You* can find _____ keys in the top drawer of the desk.

6. The keys in the drawer belong to you. *I* have _____ in _____ pocket. *You* should look in the drawer for _____.

7. *Tom and Paul* talked about _____ experiences in the wilderness areas of Canada. I've had a lot of interesting experiences in the wilderness, but nothing to compare with _____.

8. *I* know Eric well. He is a good friend of _____. *You* know him, too, don't you? Isn't he a friend of _____, too?

9. Omar, *my wife and I* would like to introduce you to a good friend of _____. His name is Dan Lightfeather.

◇ **PRACTICE 24—SELFSTUDY:** Reflexive pronouns. (Chart 4–10)

Directions: Complete the sentences with REFLEXIVE PRONOUNS that refer to the words in italics.

1. *I* enjoyed _____**myself**_____ at Disney World.

2. *Paul* enjoyed _____.

3. *Paul and I* enjoyed _____.

4. Hi, Emily! Did *you* enjoy _____?

5. Hi, Emily and Dan! Did *you* enjoy _____?

6. *Jessica* enjoyed _____.

7. *Jessica and Paul* enjoyed _____.

◇ **PRACTICE 25—SELFSTUDY:** Reflexive pronouns. (Chart 4–10)

Directions: Complete the sentences with the words in the list + REFLEXIVE PRONOUNS. Use any appropriate verb tense.

believe in	*help*	*talk to*
✔*blame*	*introduce*	*teach*
✔*cut*	*kill*	*work for*
feel sorry for	*take care of*	*wish*

1. This accident was my fault. I caused it. I was responsible. In other words, I _____**blamed**_____ _____**myself**_____ for the accident.

2. Be careful with that sharp knife! You _____ **are going to cut yourself** _____ if you're not careful.

3. It was the first day of class. I sat next to another student and started a conversation about the class and the classroom. After we had talked for a few minutes, I said, "My name is Rita Woo." In other words, I _____ to the other student.

4. When I walked into the room, I heard Joe's voice. He was speaking. I looked around, but the only person I saw and heard was Joe. In other words, Joe _____ _____ when I walked into the room.

5. My wife and I have our own business. We don't have a boss. In other words, we _____.

6. Mr. and Mrs. Hall own their own business. No one taught them how to run a business. In other words, they _____ everything they needed to know about running a small business.

7. Mr. Baker committed suicide. In other words, he _____.

8. I climbed to the top of the diving tower and walked to the end of the diving board. Before I dived into the pool, I said "good luck" to myself. In other words, I _____ _____ luck.

9. Rebecca is in bed because she has the flu. She isn't at work. Instead, she's resting at home and drinking plenty of fluids. She is being careful about her health. In other words, she _____.

10. Sometimes we have problems in our lives. Sometimes we fail. But we shouldn't get discouraged and sad. We need to have faith that we can solve our problems and succeed. If we _____, we can accomplish our goals.

11. When I failed to get the new job, I was sad and depressed. In other words, I _____ _____ because I didn't get the job.

12. In a cafeteria, people walk through a section of the restaurant and pick up their food. They are not served by waiters. In other words, in a cafeteria people _____ _____ to the food they want.

◇ PRACTICE 26—SELFSTUDY: Pronouns. (Charts 4–6 → 4–10)

Directions: Circle the correct PRONOUNS.

1. Nick invited *I, me* to go to dinner with *he, him.*

2. Sam and you should be proud of *yourself, yourselves.* The two of you did a good job.

3. The room was almost empty. The only furniture was one table. The table stood by *it, itself* in one corner.

4. The bird returned to *its, it's** nest to feed *its, it's* offspring.

5. Nick has his tennis racket, and Ann has *her, hers, her's.**

6. Where's Eric? I have some good news for Joe and *he, him, his, himself.*

7. Don't listen to Greg. You need to think for *yourself, yourselves*, Jane. It's *you, your, yours* life.

8. We all have *us, our, ours* own ideas about how to live *our, ours, our's** lives.

9. You have your beliefs, and we have *our, ours.*

10. People usually enjoy *themself, themselves, theirselves*** at family gatherings.

11. History repeats *himself, herself, itself.*

12. David didn't need my help. He finished the work by *him, himself, his, his self.*

◇ **PRACTICE 27—GUIDED STUDY:** Pronoun review. (Charts 4–6 → 4–10)

Directions: Complete the sentences with PRONOUNS that refer to the words in *italics*.

1. *Tom* is wearing a bandage on _____**his**_____ arm. _____**He**_____ hurt _____**himself**_____ while _____**he**_____ was repairing the roof. I'll help _____**him**_____ with the roof later.

2. I have *a sister*. _____ name is Kate. _____ and I share a room.

3. *My sister and I* share a room. _____ room is pretty small. _____ have only one desk.

4. Our desk has five drawers. *Kate* puts _____ things in the two drawers on the right.

5. *I* keep _____ stuff in the two drawers on the left. She and _____ share the middle drawer.

6. *Kate* doesn't open my two drawers, and I don't open _____.

7. *I* don't put things in her drawers, and she doesn't put things in _____.

8. *Ms. Lake and Mr. Ramirez* work together at the advertising company. _____ often work on projects by _____, but I work with _____ sometimes. My office is next to _____. _____ office has _____ names on the door, and mine has my name.

9. I have my dictionary, and *Sara* has _____. But *Nick* doesn't have _____.

10. My friend *James* enjoyed _____ at Mike's house yesterday. When I talked to _____ on the phone, _____ told me about _____ day with Mike. _____ and Mike played basketball, ate junk food, and played computer games. I like James a lot. I'm going to spend next Saturday with Mike and _____ at a science fair.

---

*REMINDER: Apostrophes are NOT used with possessive pronouns. Note that *its* = possessive adjective, *it's* = it is. Also note that *her's, your's,* and *our's* are **NOT POSSIBLE** in grammatically correct English.

NOTE: *themself* and *theirselves* are not really words—they are **NOT POSSIBLE in grammatically correct English. Only *themselves* is the correct reflexive pronoun form.

11. *Karen* has a bandage on _____ thumb because _____ accidentally cut

_____ with a hatchet while _____ was cutting wood for _____

fireplace.

12. We don't agree with you. *You* have _____ opinion, and *we* have _____.

◇ **PRACTICE 28—SELFSTUDY:** Singular forms of *other*. (Chart 4–11)

Directions: Complete the sentences with **ANOTHER** or **THE OTHER**.

1. There are two birds in Drawing A. One is an eagle. _____*The other*_____ is a chicken.

2. There are three birds in Drawing B. One is an eagle.

   a. _____ one is a chicken.

   b. _____ bird is a crow.

3. There are many kinds of birds in the world. One kind is an eagle.

   a. _____ kind is a chicken.

   b. _____ kind is a crow.

   c. _____ kind is a sea gull.

   d. What is the name of _____ kind of bird in the world?

4. There are two women in Picture A. One is Ann. _____ is Sara.

5. There are three men in Picture B. One is Alex. _____ one is Mike.

6. In Picture B, Alex and Mike are smiling. _____ man looks sad.

7. There are three men in Picture B. All three have common first names. One is named Alex.

    a. _____ is named David.

    b. The name of _____ one is Mike.

8. There are many common English names for men. Alex is one.

    a. Mike is _____.

    b. David is _____.

    c. John is _____ common name.

    d. Joe is _____.

    e. What is _____ common English name for a man?

◇ **PRACTICE 29—SELFSTUDY:** Plural forms of *other*. (Chart 4–12)

    Directions: Complete the sentences with **THE OTHER, THE OTHERS, OTHER,** or **OTHERS.**

1. There are four birds in the picture. One is an eagle, and another one is a crow.

    _____ birds in the picture are chickens.

2. There are four birds in the picture. One is an eagle, and another one is a crow.

    _____ are chickens.

3. Birds have different eating habits. Some birds eat insects.

    a. _____ birds get their food chiefly from plants.

    b. _____ eat only fish.

    c. _____ hunt small animals like mice and rabbits.

    d. _____ birds prefer dead and rotting flesh.

4. There are five English vowels. One is "a." Another is "e."

    a. What are _____ vowels?

    b. _____ are "i", "o", and "u."

5. There are many consonants in English. The letters "b" and "c" are consonants.

    a. What are some _____ consonants?

    b. Some _____ arc "d", "f", and "g."

6. Some people are tall, and _____ are short. Some people are neither tall nor short.

7. Some people are tall, and _____ people are short.

8. Some animals are huge. _____ are tiny.

9. Some animals are huge. _____ animals are tiny.

10. A: There were ten questions on the test. Seven of them were easy.

    _____ three were really hard.

    B: Any question is easy if you know the answer. Seven of the questions were "easy" for you because you had studied for them. _____ were "hard" only because you hadn't studied for them.

◇ **PRACTICE 30—SELFSTUDY:** Summary forms of *other*. (Charts 4–11 → 4–13)

Directions: Choose the correct completion.

Example: Copper in one kind of metal. Silver is __**A**__.
    A. another   B. the other   C. the others   D. others   E. other

1. Summer is one season. Spring is _____.
    A. another   B. the other   C. the others   D. others   E. other

2. There are four seasons. Summer is one. _____ arc winter, fall and spring.
    A. Another   B. The other   C. The others   D. Others   E. Other

3. What's your favorite season? Some people like spring the best. _____ think fall is the nicest season.
    A. Another   B. The other   C. The others   D. Others   E. Other

4. My eyes are different colors. One eye is gray and _____ is green.
    A. another   B. the other   C. the others   D. others   E. other

5. One color I like a lot is blue. _____ colors that I think are nice are green and yellow. Purple is a pretty color, too.
    A. Another   B. The other   C. The others   D. Others   E. Other

6. There are five letters in the word "fresh." One of the letters is a vowel. _____ are consonants.
    A. Another   B. The other   C. The others   D. Others   E. Other

7. Alex failed his English exam, but his teacher is going to give him _____ chance to pass it.
   A. another B. the other C. the others D. others E. other

8. Some people drink tea in the morning. _____ have coffee. I prefer fruit juice.
   A. Another B. The other C. The others D. Others E. Other

9. There are five digits in the number 20,000. One digit is a 2. _____ digits are all zeroes.
   A. Another B. The other C. The others D. Others E. Other

10. Smith is a common last name in English. _____ common names are Johnson, Jones, and Miller. Others are Anderson, Moore, and Brown.
   A. Another B. The other C. The others D. Others E. Other

◇ PRACTICE 31—GUIDED STUDY: Summary forms of *other*. (Charts 4–11 → 4–13)

Directions: Complete the sentences with your own words. Use a form of OTHER in the blank and underline it.

Example: I have . . . books on my desk. One is . . . , and _____ is/are . . . .
Written: **I have three books on my desk. One is a grammar book, and the others are my dictionary and a science book.**

1. I have two favorite colors. One is . . . , and _____ is . . . .

2. Some students walk to school. _____ . . . .

3. Ted drank . . . , but he was still thirsty, so . . . _____ one.

4. I speak . . . languages. One is . . . , and _____ is/are . . . .

5. Some people . . . , and _____ . . . .

6. I have . . . (sisters, brothers, and/or cousins). One is . . . , and _____ is/are . . . .

7. One of my teachers is . . . . _____ is/are . . . .

8. . . . and . . . are two common names in my country. _____ are . . . .

9. . . . of the students in my class are from . . . . _____ students are from . . . .

10. There are many popular sports in the world. One is . . . . _____ is . . . . _____ are . . . .

◇ PRACTICE 32—SELFSTUDY: Capitalization. (Chart 4–14)

Directions: Add CAPITAL LETTERS where necessary.

1. Do you know *R*obert *J*ones?

2. Do you know my uncle? (*no change*)

3. I like uncle joe and aunt sara.

4. I'd like you to meet my aunt.

5. susan w. miller is a professor.

6. I am in prof. miller's class.

7. The weather is cold in january.

8. The weather is cold in winter.

9. I have three classes on monday.

10. I would like to visit los angeles.

11. It's a large city in california.

12. I like to visit large cities in foreign countries.

13. There are fifty states in the united states of america.

14. It used to take weeks or months to cross an ocean.

15. Today we can fly across the atlantic ocean in hours.

16. I live on a busy street near the local high school.

17. I live on market street near washington high school.

18. We stayed at a very comfortable hotel.

19. We stayed at the hilton hotel in bangkok.

20. Yoko is japanese, but she can also speak german.

◇ PRACTICE 33—SELFSTUDY: Prepositions. (Chapter 4)

Directions: Complete the sentences with appropriate PREPOSITIONS.*

1. How much did you pay ___**for**___ that beautiful table?

2. A: Did you talk _____ the manager _____ returning that dress?

   B: No. She didn't arrive _____ the store while I was there. I waited _____ her for a
   half an hour and then left.

3. I listened _____ you very carefully, but I didn't understand anything you said.

4. When I graduated _____ college, my mother and father told everyone we knew that I had
   graduated.

5. I paid too much _____ this watch. It's not worth it.

6. A: We don't have all day! How long is it going take for someone to wait _____ us? I'm
   hungry.

   B: We just got here. Be patient. Do you have to complain _____ everything?

7. When did you arrive _____ Mexico City?

8. A: This sauce is delicious! What is it?

   B: Well, it consists _____ tomatoes, garlic, olive oil, and lemon juice all blended
   together.

9. There were ten people at the meeting and ten different opinions. No one agreed _____
   anyone else _____ the best way to solve the club's financial problems.

10. I have to complain _____ the manager. Both the food and the service are terrible.

◇ PRACTICE 34—SELFSTUDY: Prepositions. (Chapters 1, 3, and 4)

Directions: Complete the sentences with appropriate PREPOSITIONS.

1. Everyone is talking _____ the explosion in the high school chemistry lab.

2. Carlos was absent _____ class six times last term.

3. Fruit consists mostly _____ water.

_____
*See Appendix 1 for a list of preposition combinations.

4. Our children are very polite _____ adults, but they argue _____ their playmates all the time.

5. Three centimeters is equal _____ approximately one and a half inches.

6. I'm not ready _____ my trip. I haven't packed yet.

7. I borrowed some clothes _____ my best friend.

8. Are you familiar _____ ancient Roman mythology?

9. I discussed my problem _____ my uncle.

10. Someday astronauts will travel _____ another solar system.

11. Jennifer arrived _____ Singapore last Tuesday.

12. Jack's plane arrived _____ the airport in Mexico City two hours ago.

13. I admire you _____ your ability to laugh _____ yourself when you make a silly mistake.

14. A: Why are staring _____ the wall?

    B: I'm not. I'm thinking.

15. A: Are you two arguing _____ each other _____ your in-laws again?

    B: Do you know what his father did?

    C: Oh yeah? Listen _____ what her sister said.

    A: Shh. I don't want to hear any of this. Stop complaining _____ me _____ your relatives. I don't agree _____ either of you.

CHAPTER 5
Modal Auxiliaries

◇ **PRACTICE 1—SELFSTUDY:** *To* with modal auxiliaries. (Chart 5–1)

Directions: Add the word **TO** where necessary. Write Ø if **TO** is not necessary.

1. Mr. Alvarez spilled tea on his shirt. He must _____Ø_____ change clothes before dinner.

2. Mr. Alverez has _____*to*_____ change his shirt before dinner.

3. Everyone should _____ pay attention to local politics.

4. Everyone ought _____ participate in local government.

5. May I _____ borrow your pen?

6. A good book can _____ be a friend for life.

7. Jimmy is yawning and rubbing his eyes. He must _____ be sleepy.

8. You can't _____ open a can without a can opener, can you?

9. I'd like to stay and talk some more, but I've got _____ hurry over to the chemistry building for my next class.

10. A: Should I _____ tell the boss about the accounting error in the report?

    B: You have _____ tell him. That error could _____ get the company in trouble.

    A: I know that I ought _____ be honest about it, but I'm afraid he'll get angry. He might _____ fire me. Would you _____ go with me to see him?

    B: I think you should _____ do this yourself. You can _____ do it. I'm sure the boss will _____ understand.

    A: No, you must _____ go with me. I can't _____ face him alone.

◇ **PRACTICE 2—GUIDED STUDY:** *To* with modal auxiliaries. (Chart 5–1)

Directions: Add the word **TO** where necessary. Write Ø if **TO** is not necessary.

(1) Everyone in my family has _____*to*_____ contribute to keeping order in our house. My parents

(2) assign chores to my brother, George, and me. We must _____Ø_____ do these tasks every day.

(3) Sometimes if one of us is busy and can't _____ do a chore, the other one may _____ take

(4) care of it.

(5) For example, last Friday it was George's turn to wash the dishes after dinner. He couldn't

(6) _____ stay to do it because he had _____ hurry to school for a basketball game. George

(7) asked me, "Will you _____ do the dishes for me, please? I'll _____ do them for you

(8) tomorrow when it's your turn. I've got _____ get to the school for the game." I reluctantly

(9) agreed to do George's chores and washed the dishes after dinner. But then the next night, George

(10) "forgot" that we had traded days. When I reminded him to wash the dishes, he said, "Who?

(11) Me? It's not *my* turn. You have _____ do the dishes tonight. It's *your* turn."

(12) I think I'd better _____ write our agreement down when I take my brother George's

(13) chores, and I ought _____ give him a copy of the agreement. George has a short memory,

(14) especially if he has _____ wash dishes or take out the garbage. I should _____ write

(15) everything down. In fact, I might _____ write out a weekly schedule. Then we could

(16) _____ write our names in and change assignments if necessary. That ought _____ solve

(17) the problem. I must _____ remember to do that.

◇ **PRACTICE 3—SELFSTUDY: Expressing ability. (Chart 5–2)**

Directions: Choose one of the words in parentheses to complete each sentence.

1. A _____*zebra*_____ **can't stretch** its neck to reach the tops of trees. (*giraffe, zebra*)

2. A single _____ **can kill** a thousand mice in a year. (*bee, cat*)

3. _____ **can crush** small trees under their huge feet. (*Rabbits, Elephants*)

4. _____ **can climb** trees with ease. (*Monkeys, Chickens*)

5. Did you know that _____ **can survive** seventeen days without any water at all? (*ducks, camels*)

6. One _____ **can produce** as much as 8,500 lbs. (3,860 kgs) of milk in a year. (*cow, bull*)

7. A person **can sit** on a _____ without hurting it. (*horse, cat*)

8. A _____ **can carry** heavy loads on its back. (*donkey, snake*)

9. A _____ **can stay** high up in the trees for weeks, leaping from branch to branch. (*squirrel, polar bear*)

10. Most _____ **can lift** objects that are ten times heavier than their own bodies. (*people, ants*)

◇ **PRACTICE 4—GUIDED STUDY:** Expressing ability. (Chart 5–2)

Directions: Interview a classmate about each item in the list below, then write a report about your classmate's abilities.

Example: read pages that are upside down?
STUDENT A: (Jose), can you read pages that are upside down?
STUDENT B: Yes, I can. Here, I'll show you.
   OR: No, I can't.
   OR: I don't know. I'll try. Turn your book upside down and I'll try to read it.

PART I: STUDENT A interviews STUDENT B:

1. speak more than two languages?
2. play chess?
3. drive a car?
4. read upside down?
5. play any musical instrument?
6. do card tricks?
7. pat the top of your head up and down with one hand and rub your stomach in a circular motion with the other hand at the same time?

PART II: STUDENT B interviews STUDENT A:

8. fold a piece of paper in half more than six times?
9. draw well—for example, draw a picture of me?
10. cook?
11. walk on your hands?
12. play tennis?
13. use a computer?
14. write legibly with both your right hand and your left hand?

◇ **PRACTICE 5—GUIDED STUDY:** Expressing past ability. (Chart 5–2)

Directions: Complete the sentences with **COULD** or **COULDN'T** and your own words.

Example: A year ago I . . . , but now I can.
Written: ***A year ago I couldn't speak English, but now I can.***

1. When I was a baby, I . . . , but now I can.
2. When I was a child, I . . . , but now I can't.
3. When I was thirteen, I . . . , but I couldn't do the same thing when I was three.
4. Five years ago, I . . . , but now I can't.
5. Last year/month/week, I . . . , but now I can.

◇ **PRACTICE 6—SELFSTUDY:** Expressing ability and possibility. (Charts 5–2 and 5–3)

Directions: Complete the sentences with CAN, CAN'T, MAY, or MAY NOT.

1. I _____ *can* _____ play only one musical instrument: the piano. I _____ *can't* _____ play a guitar.

2. Dark clouds are gathering in the sky. It _____ rain soon.

3. Michael will be your interpreter during your trip to Korea. He _____ speak Korean fluently.

4. One minute John wants to go to the dinner party. The next minute he doesn't want to go. He can't make up his mind. He _____ go to the dinner party tonight, or he _____.

5. You'd better take a book with you to the airport when you go to meet Danny's plane. It _____ be late because of the snowstorm in Denver.

6. A: What channel is the news special on tonight?
   B: I'm not sure. It _____ be on Channel Seven. Try that one first.

7. Alice is a runner. She likes to compete, but two days ago she broke her ankle when she fell. She _____ run in the race tomorrow.

8. A: Do you remember a famous actor named Basil Rathbone? Is he still making movies?
   B: I think he _____ be dead.

Directions: *Complete the sentences with* CAN, CAN'T, MIGHT, *or* MIGHT NOT.

9. Jessica hasn't made up her mind about where to go to school. She _____ *might* _____ or she _____ *might not* _____ attend Duke University. She just doesn't know yet.

10. Ducks _____ swim well, but chickens _____ because they don't have webbed feet.

11. A: What are you going to order?
    B: I dunno.* I _____ have a hamburger or a cheeseburger.

12. A: Carol's in New York now. Is she going to return to school in Chicago in September?
    B: It depends. If she _____ find a job in New York, she'll stay there this fall. Who knows? She _____ stay there through the winter and spring, too. If she likes her job, she _____ want to return to school in Chicago next year at all. We'll have to wait and see.

13. A: Which one of these oranges is sweet? I like only sweet oranges.
    B: How should I know? I _____ tell if an orange is sweet just by looking at it. _____ you? Here. Try this one. It _____ be sweet enough for you. If it isn't, put some sugar on it.

_____
*"I dunno" = informal spoken English for "I don't know."

◇ PRACTICE 7—SELFSTUDY: Meanings of *could*. (Charts 5-2 → 5-4)

Directions: Choose the expression that has the same meaning as the *italicized* verb.

1. Twenty years ago, David *could speak* Arabic fluently. Now he's forgotten a lot.
   Ⓐ was able to speak   B. may/might speak

2. Let's leave for the airport now. Lenny's plane *could arrive* early tonight.
   A. was able to arrive   B. may/might arrive

3. "Where's Alice?"
   "I don't know. She *could be* at the mall."
   A. was able to be   B. may/might be

4. I think I'll take my umbrella. It *could rain* today.
   A. was able to rain   B. may/might rain

5. "What's in this box?"
   "I don't know. It looks like a bottle, but it *could be* a flower vase."
   A. was able to be   B. may/might be

6. When I was a child, we *could swim* in the Duckfoot River, but now it's too polluted.
   Today even the fish get sick.
   A. were able to swim   B. may/might swim

7. "How long will it take you to paint two small rooms?"
   "I'm not sure. If the job isn't complicated, I *could finish* by Thursday."
   A. was able to finish   B. may/might finish

8. When I was a kid, I *could jump* rope really well.
   A. was able to jump   B. may/might jump

◇ PRACTICE 8—GUIDED STUDY: Expressing possibility. (Chart 5-4)

Directions: For each situation, use **COULD** to suggest possible courses of action.

Example: Jack has to go to work early tomorrow. His car is out of gas. His bicycle is broken.
Response: Jack could take the bus to work.
          He could take a gas can to a gas station, fill it up, and carry it home to his car.
          He could try to fix his bicycle.
          He could get up very early and walk to work. Etc.

1. Nancy walked to school today. Now she wants to go home. It's raining hard. She doesn't
   have an umbrella. She doesn't want to get wet.

2. Ann and Carmen want to get some exercise. They have a date to play tennis this morning, but
   the tennis court is covered with snow.

3. Sam just bought a new camera. He has it at home now. He has the instruction manual. It is written in Japanese. He can't read Japanese. He doesn't know how to operate the camera.

4. Dennis likes to travel around the world. He is twenty-two years old. Today he is alone in (*name of a city*). He needs to eat, and he needs to find a place to stay overnight. But while he was asleep on the train last night, someone stole his wallet. He has no money.

◇ **PRACTICE 9—GUIDED STUDY: Expressing possibility. (Charts 5–2 → 5–4)**

Directions: Complete the sentences with your own words.

Example: I could _____ today. (. . .) could _____ too, but we'll probably _____.
Response: **I could** skip class and go to a movie **today.** Pedro **could** come along **too, but we'll probably** go to class just like we're supposed to.

1. Tonight I could _____. Or I might _____. Of course, I may _____. But I'll probably

    _____.

2. Next year, I might _____. But I could _____. I may _____. But I'll probably _____.

3. My friend (. . .) may _____ this weekend, but I'm not sure. He/She might _____.

    He/She could also _____. But he/she'll probably _____.

4. One hundred years from now, _____ may _____. _____ could _____.

    _____ will probably _____.

◇ **PRACTICE 10—SELFSTUDY: Polite questions. (Charts 5–5 and 5–6)**

Directions: Circle the correct completion.

1. A: This desk is too heavy for me. *May,* (*Can*) you help me lift it?

    B: Sure. No problem.

2. A: Ms. Milan, *may, will* I be excused from class early today? I have a doctor's appointment.

    B: Yes. You may leave early. That would be fine.

3. A: I'm having trouble with this word processor. *Would, May* you show me how to set the

    margins one more time?

    B: Of course.

4. A: Andrew, *would, could* I speak to you for a minute?

    B: Sure. What's up?

5. A: I can't meet David's plane tonight. *Can, May* you pick him up?

    B: Sorry. I have to work tonight. Call Uncle Frank. Maybe he can pick David up.

6. A: *Could, May* you please take these letters to the post office before noon?

    B: I'd be happy to, sir. Hmmm. It's almost eleven-thirty. *May, Will* I leave for the post

    office now and then go to lunch early?

    A: That would be fine.

7. A: Marilyn, are you feeling okay? *Would, Can* I get you something?

    B: *May, Will* you get me a glass of water, please?

    A: Right away.

8. A: Darn these medicine bottles! I can't ever get the cap off!

   B: *Would, Could* I open that for you?

   A: Thanks. I'd really appreciate it.

◇ **PRACTICE 11—GUIDED STUDY: Polite questions. (Charts 5–5 und 5–6)**

Directions: Write a dialogue for each situation. The beginning of each dialogue is given.

Example:
   SITUATION: You're in a restaurant. You want the waiter to refill your coffee cup. You catch the waiter's eye and raise your hand slightly. The waiter approaches your table.
   DIALOGUE: *A: Yes? What can I do for you?*

Written: **A: *Yes? What can I do for you?***

   B: *Could I please have some more coffee?*

   A: *Of course. Right away.*

1. SITUATION: You've been waiting in line at a busy bakery. Finally, the person in front of you is getting waited on, and the clerk turns toward you.
   DIALOGUE: *A: Next!*

2. SITUATION: You are at work. You feel sick. Your head is pounding, and you have a slight fever. You really want to go home. You see your boss, Mr. Jenkins, passing by your desk.
   DIALOGUE: *A: Mr. Jenkins?*

3. SITUATION: Your cousin, Willy, is in the next room listening to music. You are talking on the telephone. The music is getting louder and louder. Finally, you can no longer hear your conversation over the phone. You put the phone down and turn toward the door to the next room.
   DIALOGUE: *A: Willy!*

4. SITUATION: The person next to you on the plane has finished reading his newspaper. You would like to read it.
   DIALOGUE: *A: Excuse me.*

5. SITUATION: You see a car on the side of the road with the hood raised and an older man standing next to it. He looks tired and concerned. You pull over and get out of your car to walk over to him.
   DIALOGUE: *A: Do you need some help, sir?*

◇ **PRACTICE 12—SELFSTUDY: Expressing advice. (Chart 5–7)**

Directions: Choose the correct completion.

1. Danny doesn't feel well. He _____ see a doctor.
   A. should   B. ought   C. had

2. Danny doesn't feel well. He _____ better see a doctor.
   A. should   B. ought   C. had

3. Danny doesn't feel well. He _____ to see a doctor.
   A. should   B. ought   C. had

4. It's extremely warm in here. We _____ open some windows.
   A. should   B. ought   C. had

5. It's really cold in here. We _____ to close some windows.
   A. should   B. ought   C. had

6. There's a police car behind us. You _____ better slow down!
   A. should   B. ought   C. had

7. People who use public parks _____ clean up after themselves.
   A. should   B. ought   C. had

8. I have no money left in my bank account. I _____ better stop charging things on my credit card.
   A. should   B. ought   C. had

9. It's going to be a formal dinner and dance. You _____ to change clothes.
   A. should   B. ought   C. had

10. This library book is overdue. I _____ better return it today.
    A. should   B. ought   C. had

◇ PRACTICE 13—GUIDED STUDY: Expressing advice. (Chart 5–7)

Directions: Give advice. Use **SHOULD**, **OUGHT TO**, and **HAD BETTER**.

Example: I forgot my dad's birthday. It was yesterday. I feel terrible about it. What should I do?
Possible responses:
> *You'd better call him on the phone right away.*
> *You should send him a card and a little present.*
> *You ought to write him a long letter and tell him you're sorry.*

1. Sam studies, but he doesn't understand his physics class. It's the middle of the term, and he is failing the course. He needs a science course in order to graduate. What should he do?

2. Dan just discovered that he made dinner plans for tonight with two different people. He is supposed to meet his financée at one restaurant at 7:00, and he is supposed to meet his boss at a different restaurant across town at 8:00. What should he do?

3. The boss wants me to finish my report before I go on vacation, but I probably don't have time. What should I do?

4. I borrowed Karen's favorite book of poems. It was special to her. A note on the inside cover said "To Karen." The poet's signature was at the bottom of the note. Now I can't find the book. I think I lost it. What am I going to do?

◇ PRACTICE 14—SELFSTUDY: Expressing necessity. (Chart 5–8)

Directions: Choose the correct completion.

1. I _____ to wash the dishes after dinner last night. It was my turn.
   A. have   B. has   C. had   D. must

2. Bye! I'm leaving now. I _____ got to take this package to the post office.
   A. have   B. has   C. had   D. must

3. I know you didn't mean what you said. You _____ think before you speak!
   A. have   B. has   C. had   D. must

4. Yesterday everyone in the office _____ to leave the building for a fire drill. I'm glad it wasn't a real fire.
   A. have   B. has   C. had   D. must

5. Janet _____ to take an educational psychology course next semester. It's a required course.
   A. have   B. has   C. had   D. must

6. Pete, Chris, and Anna _____ to stay after class this afternoon. Professor Irwin wants them to help him grade papers.
   A. have   B. has   C. had   D. must

7. Mr. Silva, you _____ not be late today. The vice-president is coming in, and you're the only one who can answer her questions about the new project.
   A. have   B. has   C. had   D. must

8. Last year our town didn't have many tourists because of the oil spill. Business was bad. My wife and I own a small souvenir shop near the ocean. We _____ to borrow money from the bank last month to save our business.
   A. have   B. has   C. had   D. must

◇ PRACTICE 15—GUIDED STUDY: Expressing necessity. (Chart 5–8)

Directions: Use the information in *PART I* to answer the questions in *PART II*. Answer in complete sentences using the verb in *italics*.

PART I: **INFORMATION**

a. Mr. Lin is nearsighted.

b. Carmen's boss just told her that she's going to Rome next month to an important international conference.

c. Gloria's car is in the garage.

d. Jake's parents are going out to play cards with their friends.

e. The students in this class want to improve their English.

f. Professor Clark got the flu.

PART II: **QUESTIONS**

1. Who *has to take* the bus to work and why?
   → *Gloria has to take the bus to work because her car is in the garage.*

2. Who *had to cancel* classes and why?

3. Who *must renew* her passport immediately and why?

4. Who *has to wear* glasses and why?

5. Who's *got to stay* home and babysit his little sister tonight and why?

6. Who *has to study* hard and why?

◇ PRACTICE 16—SELFSTUDY: Expressing necessity, lack of necessity, and prohibition.
                         (Charts 5–8 and 5–9)

Directions: Complete the sentences with **MUST NOT** or **DON'T HAVE TO**.

1. You _____**must not**_____ drive when you are tired. It's dangerous.

2. I live only a few blocks from my office. I _____**don't have to**_____ drive to work.

3. You _____ play loud music late at night. The neighbors will call the police.

4. This box isn't as heavy as it looks. You _____ help me with it. Thanks anyway for offering to help.

5. Susan, you _____ go to the university. Your father and I think you should, but it's your choice.

6. People _____ spend their money foolishly if they want to stay out of financial trouble.

7. My new telephone has a "memory." I _____ look up phone numbers anymore. All I have to do is push a button next to someone's name.

8. When you first meet someone, you _____ ask personal questions. For example, it's not polite to ask a person's age.

9. The nations of the world _____ stop trying to achieve total world peace.

10. My husband and I grow all of our own vegetables in the summer. We _____ buy any vegetables at the market.

◇ PRACTICE 17—SELFSTUDY: Expressing necessity, lack of necessity, and prohibition. (Charts 5–8 and 5–9)

Directions: Complete each sentence with a form of **HAVE TO** or **MUST**. Use the negative if necessary to make a sensible sentence.

1. Smoking in this building is prohibited. You _____*must/have to*_____ extinguish your cigar.

2. Alan's company pays all of his travel expenses. Alan _____*doesn't have to*_____ pay for his own plane ticket to the business conference in Amman, Jordan.

3. Our company provides free advice on the use of our products. You _____ pay us.

4. Charles could get fired if he misses any more morning meetings. He _____ be late today under any circumstances.

5. Everyone here _____ leave immediately! The building is on fire!

6. Lynn _____ attend the meeting tonight because she isn't working on the project that we're going to discuss. We're going to discuss raising money for the new library. Lynn isn't involved in that.

7. The construction company _____ finish the building by the end of the month. That's the date they promised, and they will lose a lot of money if they are late.

8. Please remember, you _____ call my house between three and four this afternoon. That's when the baby sleeps, and my mother will get upset if we wake him up.

◇ PRACTICE 18—GUIDED STUDY: Expressing advice and necessity. (Charts 5–7 → 5–9)

Directions: Use the given information to discuss the situation. Use expressions like **OUGHT TO, HAS TO, COULD, SHOULD, MIGHT, HAS GOT TO, HAD BETTER.**

Example: Carol is just recovering from the flu and tires easily. She's at work today.
Possible responses:
    Carol should go directly home from work and get plenty of rest.
    She ought to talk to her boss about leaving work early today.

She's got to take care of her health.
She must not get too tired.
She doesn't have to stay at work if she doesn't feel well.

1. Sara is fifteen. She doesn't have a driver's license. She's planning to drive her brother's car to her girlfriend's house. Her brother isn't home. Her parents aren't home.

2. Steve is a biology major. Chemistry is a required course for biology majors. Steve doesn't want to take chemistry. He thinks it's boring. He would rather take a course in art history or creative writing.

3. Matt and Amy are eighteen years old. They are students. Matt doesn't have a job. Amy works part-time as a waitress. Matt and Amy met a month ago. They fell in love. They plan to get married next week.

4. Kate invited a friend to her apartment for dinner at 8:00 tonight. Right now it's 7:20, and Kate is unexpectedly in a long and late business meeting with an important client. It takes her 30 minutes to get home from her office. She hasn't had time to shop for food for tonight's dinner.

5. I know a story about a rabbit named Rabbit and a frog named Frog. Rabbit and Frog are good friends, but Rabbit's family doesn't like Frog, and Frog's family doesn't like Rabbit. Rabbit's family says, "You shouldn't be friends with Frog. He's too different from us. He's green and has big eyes. He looks strange. You should stay with your own kind." And Frog's family says, "How can you be friends with Rabbit? He's big and clumsy. He's covered with hair and has funny ears. Don't bring Rabbit to our house. What will the neighbors think?"

◇ **PRACTICE 19—GUIDED STUDY:** Expressing advice and necessity. (Charts 5–7 → 5–9)

Directions: Read the passage, and then give advice either in a discussion group or in writing.

Mr. and Mrs. Holtz don't know what to do about their fourteen-year-old son, Mark. He's very intelligent but has no interest in school or in learning. His grades are getting worse, but he won't do any homework. Sometimes he skips school without permission, and then he writes an excuse for the school and signs his mother's name.

His older sister, Kathy, is a good student and never causes any problems at home. Mark's parents keep asking him why he can't be more like Kathy. Kathy makes fun of Mark's school grades and tells him he's stupid.

All Mark does when he's home is stay in his room and listen to very loud music. Sometimes he doesn't even come downstairs to eat meals with his family. He argues with his parents whenever they ask him to do chores around the house, like taking out the garbage.

Mr. and Mrs. Holtz can't stay calm when they talk to him. Mrs. Holtz is always yelling at her son. She nags him constantly to do his chores, clean up his room, finish his homework, stand up straight, get a haircut, wash his face, and tie his shoes. Mr. Holtz is always making new rules. Some of the rules are unreasonable. For instance, one rule Mr. Holtz made was that his son could not listen to music after five o'clock. Mark often becomes angry and goes up to his room and slams the door shut.

This family needs a lot of advice. Tell them what changes they should make. What should Mr. and Mrs. Holtz do? What shouldn't they do? What about Kathy? What should she do? And what's Mark got to do to change his life for the better?

Use each of the following words at least once in the advice you give:
- a. should
- b. shouldn't
- c. have got to/has got to
- d. had better
- e. ought to
- f. have to/has to
- g. must

◇ PRACTICE 20—SELFSTUDY: Making logical conclusions. (Chart 5–10)

Directions: Complete the following sentences. Use **MUST** or **MUST NOT**.

1. Joe just bought a new car a few weeks ago, and now he's buying a new car for his sister. Joe _____**must**_____ earn a lot of money.

2. I offered Holly something to eat, but she doesn't want anything. She _____**must not**_____ be hungry.

3. My uncle has been working in the hot sun for hours. He's soaked with perspiration. He _____ be thirsty.

4. A: Erica's really bright. She always gets above ninety-five percent (95%) on her math tests.

   B: I'm sure she's bright, but she _____ also study a lot.

5. A: Fido? What's wrong, old boy?

   B: What's the matter with the dog?

   A: He won't eat. He _____ feel well.

6. A: I've called the bank three times, but no one answers the phone. The bank _____ be open today.

   B: It isn't. Today's a holiday, remember?

   A: Oh, of course!

7. A: Listen. Someone is jumping on the floor in the apartment above us. Look. Your chandelier is shaking.

   B: Mr. Silverberg _____ be doing his morning exercises. The same thing happens every morning. Don't worry about it.

◇ **PRACTICE 21—GUIDED STUDY:** Making logical conclusions. (Chart 5–10)

Directions: Make a logical conclusion about each of the following situations. Use **MUST**.

Example: Emily is crying.
Response: *She must be unhappy.*

1. Debbie has a big smile on her face.
2. Steve is coughing and sneezing.
3. Rick is wearing a gold ring on the fourth finger of his left hand.
4. Sam is shivering.
5. Matt just bought three mouse traps.
6. Kate just bought a box of floppy disks.
7. James is sweating.
8. Robert never hands in his homework on time.
9. Rita rents ten movies every week.
10. Marilyn always gets the highest score on every test her class takes.
11. Brian can lift one end of a compact car by himself.

◇ **PRACTICE 22—SELFSTUDY:** Imperative sentences. (Chart 5–11)

Directions: Pretend that someone says the following sentences to **you**. Which verbs give **you** instructions? <u>Underline</u> the IMPERATIVE VERBS.

1. I'll be right back. <u>Wait</u> here.

2. <u>Don't wait</u> for Rebecca. She's not going to come with us.

3. Read pages thirty-nine to fifty-five before class tomorrow.

4. What are you doing? Don't put those magazines in the trash. I haven't read them yet.

5. Come in and have a seat. I'll be right with you.

6.

DON'T CROSS THIS
FIELD UNLESS YOU
CAN DO IT IN
9.9 SECONDS.
THE BULL CAN
DO IT IN 10.

(NO TRESPASSING)

7. Don't just stand there! Do something!

8. A: Call me around eight, okay?

   B: Okay.

9. Here, little Mike. Take this apple to Daddy. That's good. Go ahead. Walk toward Daddy. That's great! Now give him the apple. Wonderful!

10. Capitalize the first word of each sentence. Put a period at the end of a sentence. If the sentence is a question, use a question mark at the end.

◇ PRACTICE 23—GUIDED STUDY: Imperative sentences. (Chart 5-11)

Directions: Pretend that someone says the following sentences to **you**. Which verbs give **you** instructions? <u>Underline</u> the IMPERATIVE VERBS.

1. Here's a number puzzle:

   • Write down the number of the month you were born. (For example, write "2" if you were born in February. Write "3" if you were born in March.)

   • Double it.

   • Add 5.

   • Multiply by 50.

   • Add your age.

   • Subtract 250.

   • In the final number, the last two digits on the right will be your age, and the one or two digits on the left will be the month you were born. (Try it! It works.)

2. Here are some ways to handle stress in your life:

   • Get daily physical exercise.

   • Manage your time efficiently. Don't overload your daily schedule.

   • Take time for yourself. Learn to relax. Read, reflect, listen to music, or just do nothing for a period every day.

   • Don't waste time worrying about things you can't change. Recognize the things that you can't change and accept them.

◇ PRACTICE 24—SELFSTUDY: Making suggestions with *let's* and *why don't*. (Chart 5-12)

Directions: Complete the sentences, using verbs from the list. The verbs may be used more than once.

ask	*fly*	*pick up*	*see*
call	*get*	*play*	*stop*
fill up	*go*	*save*	*take*

1. A: There's a strong wind today. Let's _____*go*_____ to the top of the hill on Cascade Avenue and _____*fly*_____ our kite.

   B: Sounds like fun. Why don't we _____*see*_____ if Louie wants to come with us?

   A: Okay. I'll call him.

2. A: What should we buy Mom for her birthday?

   B: I don't know. Let's _____ her some perfume or something.

   A: I have a better idea. Why don't we _____ her out for dinner and a movie?

3. A: My toe hurts. Let's not _____ dancing tonight.

   B: Okay. Why don't we _____ chess instead?

4. A: Let's _____ a taxi from the airport to the hotel.

   B: Why don't we _____ a bus and _____ ourselves some money?

5. A: We're almost out of gas. Why don't we _____ at a gas station and

           _____ before we drive the rest of the way to the beach?

   B: Okay. Are you hungry? I am. Let's _____ some hamburgers, too.

   A: Great.

6. A: Let's _____ to a movie at the mall tonight.

   B: I've already seen all the good movies there. What else can we do?

   A: Well, Marika has a car. Why don't we _____ her and _____ if she

      wants to drive us into the city to an ice hockey game?

   B: Okay. What's her number?

◇ **PRACTICE 25—GUIDED STUDY:** Making suggestions with *why don't you.* (Chart 5–12)

Directions: Make suggestions using **WHY DON'T YOU.** STUDENT A should state the problem, and then others should offer suggestions.

Example: I'm at a restaurant with some business clients. I left my wallet at home. I don't have enough money to pay the bill. What am I going to do?

STUDENT A: Okay, here's the situation. I'm at a restaurant with some business customers. I sell computer parts. I need these customers. I need to impress my clients. I have to pay for dinner, but I left my wallet at home. I don't have enough money to pay the bill. I'm really embarrassed. What am I going to do?

STUDENT B: Why don't you call your office and ask someone to bring you some money?

STUDENT C: Why don't you borrow the money from one of your customers?

STUDENT D: Why don't you excuse yourself and go home to get your wallet?

STUDENT E: Why don't you have a private discussion with the manager? Arrange to pay the bill later.

1. I feel like doing something interesting and fun tonight. Any suggestions?

2. I need regular physical exercise. What would you suggest?

3. My pants keep slipping down! I'm always pulling them up.

4. An important assignment is due in Professor Black's history class today. I haven't done it. Class starts in an hour. What am I going to do?

5. I've lost the key to my apartment, so I can't get in. My roommate isn't home. He's at a concert. What am I going to do?

6. My friend and I had an argument. We stopped talking to each other. Now I'm sorry about the argument. I want to be friends again. What should I do?

7. I work hard all day long every day. I never take time to relax and enjoy myself. I need some recreation in my life. What do you think I should do?

8. I'm trying to learn English, but I'm making slow progress. What can I do to learn English faster?

◇ PRACTICE 26—SELFSTUDY: Stating preferences. (Chart 5–13)

Directions: Complete the sentences with **PREFER**, **LIKE**, or **WOULD RATHER**.

1. I _____*prefer*_____ cold weather to hot weather.

2. A: What's you favorite fruit?

   B: I _____*like*_____ strawberries better than any other fruit.

3. Mary _____*would rather*_____ save money than enjoy herself.

4. Unfortunately, many children _____ candy to vegetables.

5. A: Why isn't your brother going with us to the movie?

   B: He _____ stay home and read than go out on a Saturday night.

6. A: Does Peter _____ football to baseball?

   B: No. I think he _____ baseball better than football.

   A: Then, why didn't he go to the game yesterday?

   B: Because he _____ watch sports on TV than go to a ball park.

7. I _____ jog in the morning than after work.

8. Heidi enjoys her independence. She is struggling to start her own business, but she

   _____ borrow money from the bank than ask her parents for help.

9. A: Do you want to go to the Japanese restaurant for dinner?

   B: That would be okay, but in truth I _____ Chinese food to Japanese

   food.

   A: Really? I _____ Japanese food better than Chinese food. What shall

   we do?

   B: Let's go to the Italian restaurant.

10. A: Mother, I can't believe you have another cat! Now you have four cats, two dogs, and three

    birds.

    B: I know, dear. I can't help it. I love having animals around.

    A: Honestly, Mother, I sometimes think you _____ animals to people.

    B: Honestly, dear, sometimes I do.

◇ PRACTICE 27—GUIDED STUDY: Stating preferences. (Chart 5–13)

Directions: Give a sentence with the same meaning, using the word(s) in parentheses.

Example: Alex would rather swim than jog. (*prefer*)
Response: Alex prefers swimming to jogging.

Example: My son likes fish better than beef. (*would rather*)
Response: My son would rather eat / have fish than beef.

1. Kim likes salad better than dessert. (*prefer*)
2. In general, Nicole would rather have coffee than tea. (*like*)
3. Bill prefers teaching history to working as a business executive. (*would rather*)
4. When considering a pet, Sam prefers dogs to cats. (*like*)

5. On a long trip, Susie would rather drive than ride in the back seat. (*prefer*)

6. I like studying in a noisy room better than studying in a completely quiet room.
(*would rather*)

7. Alex likes music better than sports. (*would rather*)

◇ **PRACTICE 28—SELFSTUDY: Cumulative review. (Charts 5–1 → 5–13)**

Directions: Each of the following has a short dialogue. Try to imagine a situation in which the dialogue could take place, and then choose the best completion.

Example:
"My horse is sick."
"Oh? What's the matter? You __*B*__ call the vet."
   A. will   B. had better   C. may

1. "Does this pen belong to you?"
"No. It _____ be Susan's. She was sitting at that desk."
   A. must   B. will   C. had better

2. "I need the milk. _____ you get it out of the refrigerator for me?"
"Sure."
   A. May   B. Should   C. Could

3. "Let's go to a movie this evening."
"That sounds like fun, but I can't. I _____ finish a report before I go to bed tonight."
   A. have got to   B. would rather   C. ought to

4. "Hey, Ted. What's up with Ken? Is he upset about something?"
"He's angry because you recommended Ann instead of him for the promotion. You _____ sit down with him and try to explain your reasons. At least that's what I think."
   A. should   B. will   C. can

5. "Does Tom want to go with us to the film festival tonight?"
"No. He _____ go to the wrestling match than the film festival."
   A. could   B. would rather   C. prefers

6. "I did it! I did it! I got my driver's license!"
"Congratulations, Michelle. I'm really proud of you."
"Thanks, Dad. Now _____ I have the car tonight? Please, please!"
"No. You're not ready for that quite yet."
   A. will   B. should   C. may

7. "I just tripped on your carpet and almost fell! There's a hole in it. You _____ fix that before someone gets hurt."
"Yes, Uncle Ben. I should. I will. I'm sorry. Are you all right?"
   A. can   B. ought to   C. may

8. "Are you going to the conference in Atlanta next month?"
"I _____. It's sort of 'iffy' right now. I've applied for travel money, but who knows what my supervisor will do."
   A. will   B. have to   C. might

9. "What shall we do after the meeting this evening?"
"_____ pick Jan up and all go out to dinner together."
   A. Why don't   B. Let's   C. Should

10. "There's a mistake in this report."
"Really? You _____ tell Erica before she gives it to Ms. Allen."
   A. had better   B. may   C. would rather

11. "Have you seen my denim jacket? I _____ find it."
    "Look in the hall closet."
    A. may not   B. won't   C. can't

12. "_____ you hand me that book, please? I can't reach it."
    "Sure. Here it is."
    A. Would   B. Should   C. Must

13. "Bye, Mom! I'm going to go play soccer with my friends."
    "Wait a minute, young man! You _____ do your chores first."
    A. must not   B. must   C. would rather

14. "What do you like the most about your promotion?"
    "I _____ get up at 5:30 in the morning anymore. I can sleep until 7:00."
    A. must not   B. would rather   C. don't have to

15. "Do you think that Scott will quit his job?"
    "I don't know. He _____. He's very angry. We'll just have to wait and see."
    A. must   B. may   C. will

◇ **PRACTICE 29—GUIDED STUDY:** Cumulative review. (Charts 5–1 → 5–13)

Directions: Each of the following has a short dialogue. Try to imagine a situation in which the dialogue could take place, and then choose the best completion.

Example:
    "My horse is sick."
    "Oh? What's the matter? You __*B*__ call the vet."
    A. will   B. had better   C. may

1. "Do you have a minute? I need to talk to you."
   "I _____ leave here in ten minutes. Can we make an appointment for another time?"
   A. have to   B. could   C. may

2. "Yes? _____ I help you?"
   "Yes. Do you have these sandals in a size eight?"
   A. Should   B. Can   C. Will

3. "Let's go bowling Saturday afternoon."
   "Bowling? I _____ play golf than go bowling."
   A. had better   B. should   C. would rather

4. "The hotel supplies towels, you know. You _____ pack a towel in your suitcase."
   "This is my bathrobe, not a towel."
   A. don't have to   B. must not   C. couldn't

5. "I heard that Bill was seriously ill."
   "Really? Well, he _____ be sick anymore. He just left for New York on a business trip."
   A. won't   B. must   C. must not

6. "Dianne found a library book on a bench at Central Park. Someone had left it there."
   "She _____ take it to any library in the city. I'm sure they'll be glad to have it back."
   A. will   B. should   C. would rather

7. "Do you understand how this computer program works?"
   "Sort of, but not really. _____ you explain it to me one more time? Thanks."
   A. Could   B. Should   C. Must

8. "Did you climb to the top of the Statue of Liberty when you were in New York?"
   "No, I didn't. My knee was very sore, so I _____ climb all those stairs."
   A. couldn't   B. might not   C. must not

9. "Rick, _____ you work for me this evening? I'll take your shift tomorrow."
   "Sure. I was going to ask you to work for me tomorrow anyway."
      A. would   B. should   C. must

10. "Beth got another speeding ticket yesterday."
    "Oh? That's not good. She _____ be more careful. She'll end up in serious trouble if she gets
    any more."
      A. would rather   B. will   C. ought to

11. "Are you going to take the job transfer when the company moves out of town?"
    "I _____ accept their offer if they are willing to pay all of my moving expenses."
      A. must not   B. might   C. maybe

12. "How are we going to take care of your little brother and go to the concert at the same time?"
    "I have an idea. _____ we take him with us?"
      A. Why don't   B. Let's   C. Will

13. "Are you going to admit your mistake to the boss?"
    "Yes. I _____ tell her about it than have her hear about it from someone else."
      A. can   B. should   C. would rather

14. "Meet me at Tony's at five. Please! I _____ talk to you. It's important."
    "Is something wrong?"
      A. could   B. will   C. have got to

15. "What are you children doing? Stop! You _____ play with sharp knives."
    "What?"
      A. mustn't   B. couldn't   C. don't have to

◇ PRACTICE 30—GUIDED STUDY: Review of auxiliary verbs. (Chapters 1 → 5)

Directions: Complete the sentences with any appropriate auxiliary verb in the list. There may be
more than one possible completion. Also include any words in parentheses.

List of auxiliary verbs:

am	does	is	should
are	did	may	was
can	had better	might	were
could	has to	must	will
do	have to	ought to	would

1. A: Hello?

   B: Hello. This is Gisella Milazzo. __*May (Could/Can)*__ I speak with Ms. Morgan, please?

2. A: Where's the newspaper?

   B: I (*not*) _____*don't*_____ have it. Ask Kevin.

3. A: _____ you rather go downtown today or tomorrow?

   B: Tomorrow.

4. A: _____ Nick going to be at the meeting tomorrow?

   B: I hope so.

5. A: _____ you talk to Amanda yesterday?

   B: Yes. Why?

6. A: _____ I help you, sir?

   B: Yes. _____ you show me the third watch from the left on the top shelf?

   A: Of course.

7. A: I'm sorry. _____ you repeat that? I couldn't hear you because my dog _____ barking.

B: I said, "Why is your dog making all that noise?"

8. A: I don't know whether to turn left or right at the next intersection.

B: I think you _____ pull over and look at the map.

9. A: Hurry up. Kate and Greg _____ waiting for us.

B: I _____ hurrying!

10. A: Andy can't teach his class tonight.

B: He _____ teach tonight! He'll be fired if he doesn't show up.

11. A: Stop! (*not*) _____ touch that pan! It's hot! You'll burn yourself.

B: Relax. I had no intention of touching it.

12. A: What _____ you carrying? _____ you want some help?

B: It's a heavy box of books. _____ you open the door for me, please?

13. A: Hello?

B: Hello. _____ I please speak to Sandra Wilson?

A: I'm sorry. There's no one here by that name. You _____ have the wrong number.

14. A: Stop! You (*not*) _____ pick those flowers! It's against the law to pick flowers in a national park.

B: Really? I didn't know that.

15. A: Everyone _____ work toward cleaning up the environment.

B: I agree. Life on earth (*not*) _____

survive if we continue to poison the

land, water, and air.

◇ **PRACTICE 31—GUIDED STUDY: Cumulative review. (Chapter 5)**

Directions: Following is a passage for you to read. The topic is the process of writing a composition. Read the passage through completely to get the main ideas. Then read it again slowly and choose from the words in *italics*. Which completions seem best to you? Why? Discuss your choices.

Writing a Composition

(1)   "What? Not another composition! I hate writing compositions. I'm not good at it." Do you ever complain about having to write compositions in English class? A lot of students do. You *may, cannot* find it difficult and time-consuming, but you are learning a useful skill. The ability to write clearly *is, must be* important. It *can, must* affect your success in school and in your job. You *may, can* learn to write effectively by practicing. Preparing compositions is one of the best ways to learn the skill of writing clearly.

(2)   The first step in writing a composition is to choose a subject that interests you. You *maybe, should* write about a subject you already know about or *can, have to* find out about through research. Writers *might, should* never pretend to be experts. For example, if you have never bought a car and are not knowledgeable about automobiles, you *should, should not* choose to write an essay on what to look for when buying a used car—unless, of course, you plan to research the subject in books and magazines and make yourself an expert.   There is one topic about which you are the most knowledgeable expert in the world, and that topic *is, will be* yourself and your experiences. Many of the most interesting and informative compositions are based simply on a writer's personal experience and observations. The questions you should ask yourself when choosing a topic are "Do I have any expertise in this subject?" and if not,   "*Will, Can* I be able to find information about this subject?"

(3)   After you have a topic and have researched it if necessary, start writing down your thoughts. These notes *must not, do not have to* be in any particular order. You *do not have to, could not* worry about grammar at this time. You *can, may* pay special attention to that later.

(4)   Next you *have to, may* organize your thoughts. You *cannot, might not* say everything possible about a subject in one composition. Therefore, you *may, must* carefully choose the ideas and information you want to include. Look over your notes, think hard about your topic, and find a central idea. Answer these questions: "What *am, do* I want my readers to understand? What *is, does* my main idea? How *can, must* I put this idea into one sentence?" Good writing depends on clear thinking. Writers *should, should not* spend more time thinking than actually writing. After you have a clearly formed main idea, choose relevant information from your notes to include in your composition.

(5)   Before you begin to write the actual composition, you *ought to, can* know exactly what you want to say and how you are going to develop your ideas. Many good writers *prepare, prepared* an outline before they start. An outline is like a road map to keep you headed toward your destination without getting lost or sidetracked.

(6)   There *are, ought to be* many ways to begin a composition. For example, you *might, must* begin with a story that leads up to your main idea. Or you *may, ought to* start with a question that you want your reader to think about and then suggest an answer. *Maybe, May be* you *could, have to* introduce your topic by defining a key word. Simply presenting interesting factual information *is, will be* another common way of beginning a composition. Your goals in your first paragraph *is, are* to catch your reader's attention and then state your main idea clearly and concisely. By the end of the first paragraph, your reader *may, should* understand what you are going to cover in the composition.

(7)   If possible, write the entire first draft of your composition in a single sitting. After you have a first draft, the next step is rewriting. Every composition *could, should* go through several drafts. Rewriting is a natural part of the process of writing. You *will, do not have to* find many things that you *can change, changed* and improve when you reread your first draft. As you revise, you *will, should* be careful to include connecting words such as **then**, **next**, **for example**, **after**, and **therefore**. These words connect one idea to another so that your reader will not get lost. Also pay attention to grammar, punctuation, and spelling as you revise and rewrite. Your dictionary *should, can* be next to you.

(8)   Writing *is, may be* a skill. It improves as you gain experience with the process of choosing a subject, jotting down thoughts, organizing them into a first draft, and then rewriting and polishing. At the end of this process, you *should, should not* have a clear and well-written composition.

◇ PRACTICE 32—SELFSTUDY: Prepositions. (Chapter 5; Appendix 1)

Directions: Complete each sentence with the appropriate preposition.

1. A: Why are you so friendly __*with/to*__ George? I thought you didn't like him.

    B: I'm not crazy _____ his attitude toward his work, but I have to encourage him to do the best he can.

2. A: Do you think it's bad that I drink so much coffee every day?

   B: I believe too much of almost anything is bad _____ you.

3. I don't know why they fired me. It certainly isn't clear _____ me.

4. A: Dad, I got ninety-five percent on my algebra exam!

   B: I'm proud _____ you. I knew you could do it.

5. A: You seem to be interested _____ aerobic exercise and jogging.

   B: I think regular physical exercise is good _____ everyone.

6. That sweater is very similar _____ mine. Did you buy it at the mall?

7. Most children are afraid _____ noises in the middle of the night.

8. A: You were up awfully late last night.

   B: I couldn't sleep. I was hungry _____ something sweet, and I couldn't find anything in the kitchen.

9. I have no doubt that I'm doing the right thing. I'm sure _____ it.

10. George Gershwin, an American composer, is most famous _____ *Rhapsody in Blue*, an orchestral piece that combines jazz with classical music.

11. A: Why is Gary avoiding you? Is he angry about something?

    B: I don't know. I'm not aware _____ anything I did that could upset him.

12. A: Who is responsible _____ this dog? He's chewing on my desk!

    B: I'm sorry, sir. She followed me from home. I'll take her outside.

13. My car is a lot like yours, but different _____ Margaret's.

CHAPTER 6
Questions

◇ **PRACTICE 1—SELFSTUDY:** Asking "interview" questions. (Charts 6–1 → 6–13)

Directions: In the following, pretend that you are interviewing a member of your class named Anna. Write your name in line (1), and then complete the dialogue with appropriate QUESTIONS.

(1)   ME: Hi. My name is _____. Our teacher has asked me to interview you so that I can practice asking questions. Could I ask you a few questions about yourself?

     ANNA: Sure.

(2)   ME: Well, first of all, ___*what is your name?*_____

     ANNA: Anna.

(3)   ME: _____

     ANNA: Yes, that's my first name.

(4)   ME: _____

     ANNA: Polanski.

(5)   ME: _____

     ANNA: P-O-L-A-N-S-K-I.

     ME: Let me make sure I have that right. Your first name is Anna, A-N-N-A. And your last name is Polanski, P-O-L-A-N-S-K-I. Right?

     ANNA: That's right.

(6)   ME: _____

     ANNA: Poland.

(7)   ME: _____

     ANNA: Warsaw.

(8)   ME: _____

     ANNA: Two weeks ago.

(9)   ME: _____

     ANNA: Because I wanted to study at this school.

(10) ME: _____

     ANNA: Biochemistry.

(11) ME: _____

     ANNA: I'm going to stay here for four years or until I graduate.

(12) ME: _____

     ANNA: I'm living at my aunt and uncle's house.

(13) ME: _____

ANNA: No. Not far.

(14) ME: _____

ANNA: Six blocks.

(15) ME: _____

ANNA: Sometimes I take the bus, but usually I walk.

(16) ME: You're lucky. I live far away from the school, so it takes me a long time to get here every morning. But that's my only big complaint about living here. Otherwise, I like going to this school a lot. _____

ANNA: Very much.

ME: Well, thanks for the interview. I think I have enough information for the assignment. Nice to meet you.

ANNA: Nice to meet you, too.

◇ PRACTICE 2—SELFSTUDY: Yes/no questions and short answers. (Charts 6–1 and 6–2)

Directions: Complete Speaker A's QUESTIONS with DO, DOES, IS, or ARE. Complete Speaker B's SHORT ANSWERS.

1. A: I need a flashlight. _____*Do*_____ you have one?

   B: No, _____*I don't*_____.

2. A: _____ Alaska in North America?

   B: Yes, _____.

3. A: _____ snakes have legs?

   B: No, _____.

4. A: _____ you going to be in class tomorrow?

   B: Yes, _____.

5. A: _____ aspirin relieve pain?

   B: Yes, _____.

6. A: _____ all snakebites poisonous?

   B: No, _____.

7. A: _____ crocodiles lay eggs?

   B: Yes, _____.

8. A: _____ you doing a grammar exercise?

   B: Yes, _____.

9. A: _____ Africa the largest continent?

   B: No, _____. Asia is.

10. A: _____ ants eat other insects?

    B: Yes, _____.

11. A: Mercury is a liquid metal used in thermometers. _____ mercury have a boiling point?

    B: Yes, _____. It boils at 356.58°C.

◇ PRACTICE 3—SELFSTUDY: Yes/no questions. (Chapters 1, 2, 3, 5, and Chart 6–1)*

Directions: Write the correct QUESTION FORM. The answer to the question is in parentheses.

		helping verb	subject	main verb	rest of sentence
1. SIMPLE PRESENT	A:	*Do*	*you*	*like*	*coffee?*
	B:	Yes, I like coffee.			

		helping verb	subject	main verb	rest of sentence
2. SIMPLE PRESENT	A:				
	B:	Yes, Tom likes coffee.			

		helping verb	subject	main verb	rest of sentence
3. PRESENT PROGRESSIVE	A:				
	B:	Yes, Ann is watching TV.			

		helping verb	subject	main verb	rest of sentence
4. PRESENT PROGRESSIVE	A:				
	B:	Yes, I'm having lunch with Rob.			

		helping verb	subject	main verb	rest of sentence
5. SIMPLE PAST	A:				
	B:	Yes, Sara walked to school.			

		helping verb	subject	main verb	rest of sentence
6. PAST PROGRESSIVE	A:				
	B:	Yes, Ann was taking a nap.			

		helping verb	subject	main verb	rest of sentence
7. SIMPLE FUTURE	A:				
	B:	Yes, Ted will come to the meeting.			

		helping verb	subject	main verb	rest of sentence
8. MODAL: *CAN*	A:				
	B:	Yes, Rita can ride a bicycle.			

		form of *be*	subject	rest of sentence
9. MAIN VERB *BE* SIMPLE PRESENT	A:			
	B:	Yes, Ann is a good artist.		

		form of *be*	subject	rest of sentence
10. MAIN VERB *BE* SIMPLE PAST	A:			
	B:	Yes, I was at the wedding.		

Question forms of tenses and modals can be found in the following charts:
Simple present and present progressive: Chart 1–2
Simple past: Chart 2–2
Past progressive: Chart 2–7
Simple future (*will*): Chart 3–2
Modal *can*: Chart 5–2

◇ **PRACTICE 4—GUIDED STUDY:** Yes/no questions. (Charts 6–1 and 6–2)

Directions: Write dialogues between Speakers A and B. Make up QUESTIONS that will fit with the given idea in B's answer.

Example: B: No, I _____. I'm allergic to them.
Written: **A: Do you like cats (dogs/strawberries/etc.)?**
      B: No, I don't. I'm allergic to them.

Example: B: Yes, we _____. Would you like to come along with us?
Written: **A: Are you and Yoko going to the festival Saturday?**
      B: Yes, we are. Would you like to come along with us?

1. B: No, she _____. It was too expensive.
2. B: Yes, he _____. Yesterday.
3. B: No, I _____. I forgot.
4. B: Yes, we _____. It was delicious.
5. B: Yes, they _____. Don't worry.

6. B: No, I _____. I never learned how to.
7. B: Yes, I _____. What about you?
8. B: Maybe. Let me think about it.
9. B: Probably. She usually does.
10. B: Sure. Sounds like a good idea to me.

◇ **PRACTICE 5—SELFSTUDY:** Yes/no and information questions. (Charts 6–1 and 6–2)

Directions: Complete the dialogues by writing Speaker A's QUESTION. Write Ø if no word is needed in a space.

	(question word)	helping verb	subject	main verb	rest of sentence
1. A:	**Ø**	**Did**	**you**	**hear**	**the news yesterday?**

B: Yes, I did. (I heard the news yesterday.)

	(question word)	helping verb	subject	main verb	rest of sentence
2. A:	**When**	**did**	**you**	**hear**	**the news?**

B: Yesterday. (I heard the news yesterday.)

	(question word)	helping verb	subject	main verb	rest of sentence
3. A:	Ø				

B: Yes, he is. (Eric is reading today's paper.)

	(question word)	helping verb	subject	main verb	rest of sentence
4. A:					Ø

B: Today's paper. (Eric is reading today's paper.)

	(question word)	helping verb	subject	main verb	rest of sentence
5. A:					

B: Yes, I did. (I found my wallet.)

	(question word)	helping verb	subject	main verb	rest of sentence
6. A:					

B: On the floor of the car. (I found my wallet on the floor of the car.)

	(question word)	helping verb	subject	main verb	rest of sentence
7. A:					

B: Because he enjoys the exercise. (Mr. Li walks to work because he enjoys the exercise.)

	(question word)	helping verb	subject	main verb	rest of sentence

8. A: _____ _____ _____ _____ _____
   B: Yes, he does. (Mr. Li walks to work.)

	(question word)	helping verb	subject	main verb	rest of sentence

9. A: _____ _____ _____ _____ _____
   B: Yes, she will. (Ms. Cook will return to her office at one o'clock.)

	(question word)	helping verb	subject	main verb	rest of sentence

10. A: _____ _____ _____ _____ _____
   B: At one o'clock. (Ms. Cook will return to her office at one o'clock.)

	(question word)	form of *be*	subject	rest of sentence

11. A: _____ _____ _____ _____
   B: Yes, it is. (The orange juice is in the refrigerator.)

	(question word)	form of *be*	subject	rest of sentence

12. A: _____ _____ _____ _____
   B: In the refrigerator. (The orange juice is in the refrigerator.)

◇ **PRACTICE 6—SELFSTUDY: Information questions. (Charts 6–1 and 6–2)**

Directions: Make QUESTIONS for the given answers. Use the information in parentheses. Use
WHEN, WHAT TIME, WHERE, or **WHY.** Pay special attention to the word order in the questions.

1. A: _____***What time (When) do the fireworks start***_____ this evening?
   B: 9:30. (The fireworks start at 9:30 this evening.)

2. A: _____ to see the principal?
   B: Because I need to get his signature on this application form. (I'm waiting to see the
   principal because I need to get his signature on this application form.)

3. A: _____ her new job?
   B: Next Monday morning. (Rachel starts her new job next Monday morning.)

4. A: _____ home for work?
   B: Around 6:00. (I usually leave home for work around 6:00.)

5. A: _____ to the meeting?
   B: Because I fell asleep after dinner and didn't wake up until 9:00. (I didn't get to the
   meeting because I fell asleep after dinner and didn't wake up until 9:00.)

6. A: _____ razor blades?
   B: At many different kinds of stores. (You can buy razor blades at many different kinds of
   stores.)

7. A: _____ for home?
   B: Next Saturday. (I'm leaving for home next Saturday.)

8. A: _____ Chinese?
   B: In Germany. (I studied Chinese in Germany.)

   A: _____ Chinese in Germany?
   B: Because there is a good Chinese language school there. (I studied Chinese in Germany
   because there is a good Chinese language school there.)

   A: _____ to China to study Chinese?
   B: Because I had a scholarship to study in Germany. (I didn't go to China to study Chinese
   because I had a scholarship to study in Germany.)

9. A: _____ to finish this project?
   B: Next month. (I expect to finish this project next month.)

10. A: _____?
    B: To Mars. (The spaceship will go to Mars.)

◇ **PRACTICE 7—GUIDED STUDY: Yes/no and information questions. (Charts 6–1 and 6–2)**

Directions.   Create dialogues between Speakers A and B. In each dialogue:
   A: asks a QUESTION.
   B: gives the SHORT ANSWER that is given below, and then gives a LONG ANSWER.

Example: After midnight.
Dialogue: A: What time did you go to bed last night?
            B: After midnight. I went to bed after midnight last night.

1. The day before yesterday.
2. Yes, I do.
3. Because I had to.
4. At 8:30.
5. Yes, he is.
6. In a supermarket.

7. Tomorrow afternoon.
8. A notebook.
9. No, I can't.
10. Because . . . .
11. Yeah, sure. Why not?
12. I don't know. Maybe.

◇ **PRACTICE 8—GUIDED STUDY: Asking for the meaning of a word. (Charts 6–2 and 6–3)**

Directions: Ask your classmates for the meaning of the *italicized* word in each sentence below. If no one knows the meaning, look it up in a dictionary.

   PART I: Ask questions using **"What does . . . mean?"**

1. Captain Cook *explored* many islands in the Pacific Ocean.
   STUDENT A: **What does** "explored" **mean?**
   STUDENT B: "Explored" means "went to a new place and found out about it."
   OR:
   STUDENT A: **What does** "explore" **mean?**
   STUDENT B: "Explore" means "(to) go to a new place and find out about it."*

2. I think Carol's *mad*.
   STUDENT A: **What does** "mad" **mean?**
   STUDENT B: "Mad" can mean "crazy" or "angry."

3. Water is *essential* to all forms of life on earth.

4. Why do soap bubbles *float*?

5. The water on the streets and sidewalks *evaporated* in the morning sun.

6. It's raining. *Perhaps* we should take a taxi.

7. Some fish *bury* themselves in the sand on the ocean bottom and live their entire lives there.

8. He gently put his hand *beneath* the baby's head.

9. I *grabbed* my briefcase and started running for the bus.

10. On the average, how many times a minute do people *blink*?

_____

*Sometimes the infinitive form (*to* + *verb*) is used in definitions of verbs: *"to explore"* means *"to go* to a new place and find out about it."

PART II: Ask for the meaning of nouns.

11. We walked hand in hand through the *orchard*.
    STUDENT A: **What is** an orchard?
    STUDENT B: An orchard is a place where fruit trees grow.
    OR:
    STUDENT A: **What does** ''orchard'' **mean?**
    STUDENT B: ''Orchard'' means ''a place where fruit trees grow.''

12. Sometimes children have *nightmares*.
    STUDENT A: **What are** nightmares?
    STUDENT B: Nightmares are very bad dreams.
    OR:
    STUDENT A: **What does** ''nightmare(s)'' **mean?**
    STUDENT B: ''Nightmare(s)'' means ''very bad dream(s).''

13. Would you like to see the *photographs* from our vacation?

14. While we were eating at the outdoor restaurant, I noticed a *bug* in my soup.

15. Mrs. Hall often wears *pearls*.

16. My daughter is at the university. She wants to be an *archaeologist*.

17. People throughout the world enjoy *fables*.

18. Mark and Olivia went to Hawaii on their *honeymoon*.

19. The *margins* on your composition should be at least one inch wide.*

20. I'm not very good at *small talk*, so I avoid social situations like cocktail parties.

21. If you want to use a computer, you have to learn the *keyboard*.

22. Mr. Weatherbee liked to have *hedges* between his house and his neighbors' houses. He planted the bushes close together so that people couldn't see through them.

◇ PRACTICE 9—GUIDED STUDY: Questions with *why*. (Chart 6–2)

Directions: Create dialogues between Speakers A and B. In each dialogue:
   A: says the sentence in the book.
   B: asks **WHY?** or **WHY NOT?** and then asks the full *why*-question.
   A: makes up an answer to the question.

Example: A: I can't go with you tomorrow.

Dialogue: A: I can't go with you tomorrow.
            B: Why not? Why can't you go with me tomorrow?
            A: Because I have to study for a test.**

1. A: I ate two breakfasts this morning.

2. A: I don't like to ride on airplanes.

3. A: I'm going to sell my guitar.

4. A: I didn't go to bed last night.

5. A: I'm happy today.

6. A: I had to call the police last night.

7. A: I can't explain it to you.

8. A: I'm not speaking to my cousin.

---

*One inch = approximately two and a half centimeters.

**See Chart 9–6 for the use of *because*. ''Because I have to study for a test'' is an adverb clause. It is not a complete sentence. In this dialogue, it is the short answer to a question.

◇ **PRACTICE 10—SELFSTUDY:** Questions with *who*, *who(m)*, and *what*. (Chart 6–3)

Directions: Make questions with **WHO**, **WHO(M)**, and **WHAT**. Write "**S**" if the question word is the subject. Write "**O**" if the question word is the object.

	QUESTION	ANSWER
	S	*S*
1.	*Who knows?*	**Someone** knows.
	O	*O*
2.	*Who(m) did you ask?*	I asked **someone**.
3.	_____	**Someone** knocked on the door.
4.	_____	Sara met **someone**.
5.	_____	**Someone** will help us.
6.	_____	I will ask **someone**.
7.	_____	Eric is talking to **someone** on the phone.
8.	_____	**Someone** is knocking on the door.
9.	_____	**Something** surprised them.
10.	_____	Mike learned **something**.
11.	_____	**Something** will change Ann's mind.
12.	_____	Tina can talk about **something**.

◇ **PRACTICE 11—SELFSTUDY:** *Who, who(m)*, and *what*. (Chart 6–3)

Directions: Complete the dialogues by making QUESTIONS. Use the information in the long answer in parentheses to make the question.

1. A: **Who taught you to play chess?** _____
   B: My mother. (My mother taught me to play chess.)

2. A: _____
   B: A bank robbery. (Robert saw a bank robbery.)

3. A: _____
   B: Robert did. (Robert got a good look at the bank robber.)

4. A: _____
   B: A toy for my brother's children. (I'm making a toy for my brother's children.)

5. A: _____
   B: Joe. (That calculator belongs to Joe.)

6. A: _____
   B: A bag of candy. (I have a bag of candy in my pocket.)

7. A: _____
   B: A mouse. (The cat killed a mouse.)

8. A: _____
   B: Curiosity. (Curiosity killed the cat.)*

_____

Curiosity is the desire to learn about something. "Curiosity killed the cat" is an English saying that means we can get into trouble when we want to know too much about something that doesn't really concern us.

9. A: _____
   B: My father. (I got a letter from my father.)

10. A: _____
    B: My sister. (My sister wrote a note on the envelope.)

11. A: _____
    B: Gravity. (Gravity makes an apple fall to the ground from a tree.)

◇ **PRACTICE 12—SELFSTUDY:** *What* + a form of *do.* (Chart 6–4)

Directions: Use the information in parentheses to make QUESTIONS with **WHAT** + A FORM OF **DO** to complete each dialogue. Use the SAME VERB TENSE OR MODAL that is used in the parentheses.

1. A: ***What is Alex doing?*** _____
   B: Watching a movie on TV. (Alex is watching a movie on TV.)

2. A: ***What should I do if someone calls while you're out?*** _____
   B: Just take a message. (You should take a message if someone calls while I'm out.)

3. A: _____
   B: They explore space. (Astronauts explore space.)

4. A: I spilled some juice on the floor. _____
   B: Wipe it up with a paper towel. (You should wipe it up with a paper towel.)

5. A: _____
   B: Play tennis at Waterfall Park. (I'm going to play tennis at Waterfall Park Saturday morning.)

6. A: _____
   B: I see my doctor. (I see my doctor when I get sick.)

7. A: _____
   B: Carry this suitcase. (You can carry this suitcase to help me.)

8. A: _____
   B: She smiled. (Sara smiled when she heard the good news.)

◇ **PRACTICE 13—GUIDED STUDY:** *What* + a form of *do.* (Chart 6–4)

Directions: Use the information in parentheses to make QUESTIONS with **WHAT** + A FORM OF **DO** to complete each dialogue. Use the SAME VERB TENSE OR MODAL that is used in the parentheses.

1. A: _____
   B: I think she plans to look for a job in hotel management. (Emily is going to look for a job in hotel management after she graduates.)

2. A: _____
   B: Can you make twelve photocopies of this report? (You can make twelve photocopies of this report to help me get ready for the meeting.)

3. A: _____
   B: Ran down the stairs and out of the building. (I ran down the stairs and out of the building when the fire alarm sounded.)

4. A: _____
   B: Let's go to the shopping mall, okay? (I would like to go to the shopping mall after school today.)

5. A: _____
   B: Make this coin stand on edge. (I'm trying to make this coin stand on edge.)

6. A: _____
   B: He needs to hand in all of his homework. (Kevin needs to hand in all of his homework if he wants to pass advanced algebra.)

7. A: _____
   B: He's an airplane mechanic. (Nick repairs airplanes for a living.)

8. A: Did you say something to that man over there? Why does he look angry?
   B: I accidentally ran into him and stepped on his foot.

   A: _____
   B: Said something nasty. (He said something nasty when I bumped into him.)

   A: _____
   B: Apologized. (I apologized.)

   A: Then _____
   B: Walked away without saying a word. (Then he walked away without saying a word.)
   A: What an unpleasant person!
   B: I didn't mean to step on his foot. It was just an accident.

◇ **PRACTICE 14—GUIDED STUDY:** *What* + a form of *do.* (Chart 6–4)

Directions: Create dialogues between Speakers A and B. Speaker A should ask a question that will produce B's given answer. The question should contain **WHAT** + A FORM OF **DO**.

Example: B: Study in the corner of the cafeteria.
Dialogue: A: What are you going to do after class today?
              B: Study in the corner of the cafeteria.

   1. B: Watch TV.
   2. B: Washing his dog.
   3. B: Went home and slept.
   4. B: Writing dialogues.
   5. B: Go to a movie.
   6. B: Get a job on a cruise ship.

◇ **PRACTICE 15—GUIDED STUDY:** *What kind of.* (Chart 6–5)

Directions: Find people who own the following things. Ask them questions using **WHAT KIND OF**.

Example: a camera
First, ask a classmate, friend, or family member: *Do you have a camera?*
If the answer is yes, ask next: *What kind of camera to do you have?*★
Then write the information you have gotten, for example:

→ **Maria has a 35 millimeter Kodak camera.**

1. a camera
2. a TV
3. a bicycle
4. a car
5. a refrigerator
6. a computer
7. a watch
8. a dog
9. a VCR
10. ???

◇ **PRACTICE 16—SELFSTUDY:** *Which* vs. *what.* (Chart 6–6)

Directions: Complete the questions with **WHICH** or **WHAT**.

1. A: This hat comes in brown and in gray. _____*Which*_____ color do you think your husband would prefer?
   B: Gray, I think.

2. A: I've never been to Mrs. Hall's house. _____*What*_____ color is it?
   B: Gray.

3. A: I have two dictionaries. _____ one do you want?
   B: The Arabic–English dictionary.

4. A: Yes, may I help you?
   B: Please.
   A: _____ are you looking for?
   B: An Arabic–English dictionary.
   A: Right over there in the reference section.
   B: Thanks.

5. A: _____ languages do you speak other than your native language?
   B: Italian and English.
   A: _____ of those two languages do you speak more fluently?
   B: English.

6. A: _____ did you get on your last test?
   B: I don't want to tell you. It was really awful.

7. A: _____ job do you think I should take?
   B: The one at the small computer company. That's the best of the three job offers you've had.

8. A: Here's the remote control if you want to watch TV for a while.
   B: Thanks, I think I will.
   A: Push this button to turn it on.

   B: Okay. And _____ button should I push to change channels?

_____

★If the answer is no, ask another question from the list.

◇ **PRACTICE 17—SELFSTUDY:** *Who* vs. *whose.* (Chart 6–7)

Directions: Complete the questions with **WHO** or **WHOSE**.

1. A: _____*Who*_____ is driving to the game tonight?
   B: Heidi is.

2. A: _____*Whose*_____ car are we taking to the game?
   B: Heidi's.

3. A: This notebook is mine. _____ Is that? Is it yours?
   B: No, it's Sara's.

4. A: There's Ms. Adams. _____ is standing next to her?
   B: Mr. Wilson.

5. A: _____ was the first woman doctor in the United States?
   B: Elizabeth Blackwell, in 1849.

6. A: _____ suitcase did you borrow for your trip?
   B: Andy's.

7. A: _____ motorcycle ran into the telephone pole?
   B: Bill's.

8. A: Okay! _____ forgot to put the ice cream back in the freezer?
   B: I don't know. Don't look at me. It wasn't me.

◇ **PRACTICE 18—GUIDED STUDY:** Asking questions. (Charts 6–1 → 6–7)

Directions: Pair up with a classmate.

STUDENT A: Choose any one of the possible answers below and ask a question that would produce that answer.
STUDENT B: Decide which of the answers STUDENT A has in mind and answer his/her question. Pay special attention to the form of STUDENT A's question. Correct any errors.

(If you don't have a classmate to pair up with, write dialogues in which the given phrases are the answers to questions.)

Example:

STUDENT A: What's Maria's favorite color?
STUDENT B: *(Student B reviews the list of possible answers below and chooses the appropriate one.)* Pink.

POSSIBLE ANSWERS

Sure! Thanks!

Call the insurance company.

Next week.

A rat.

George.

Cooking dinner.

Turkey.

Probably.

The teacher's.

Not that one. The other one.

A Panasonic or a Sony.

Pink.

No, a friend of mine gave them to me a few days ago.

◇ **PRACTICE 19—SELFSTUDY:** Using *how.* (Chart 6–8)

Directions: Complete the sentences with any of the words in the given list.

busy	fresh	safe	soon
expensive	hot	serious	well

1. A: How _____*hot*_____ does it get in Chicago in the summer?

   B: Very _____*hot*_____. It can get over 100°. (100°F = 37.8°C)

2. A: How _____ will dinner be ready? I'm really hungry.

   B: In just a few more minutes.

3. A: Look at that beautiful vase! Let's get it.

   B: How _____ is it?

   A: Oh my gosh! Never mind. We can't afford it.

4. A: Sorry to interrupt, Ted, but I need some help. How _____ are you today? Do you have time to read over this report?

   B: Well, I'm always _____, but I'll make time to read it.

5. A: How _____ is Toshi about becoming an astronomer?

   B: He's very _____. He already knows more about the stars and planets than his high school teachers.

6. A: How _____ is a car with an airbag?

   B: Well, there have been bad accidents where both drivers walked away without injuries because of airbags.

7. A: Tomatoes for sale! Hey, lady! Wanna* buy some tomatoes? Tomatoes for sale!

   B: Hmmm. They look pretty good. How _____ are they?

   A: Whaddaya* mean "How _____ are they?" Would I sell something that wasn't _____? They were picked from the field just this morning.

_____

*"Wanna" and "whaddaya" aren't usually written as words. They represent spoken English:
   "wanna" = "want to" (*Wanna buy some tomatoes? = Do you want to buy some tomatoes?*)
   "whaddaya" = "what do you" (*Whaddaya mean? = What do you mean?*).

8. A: Do you know Jack Young?

   B: Yes.

   A: Oh? How _____ do you know him?

   B: Very _____. He's one of my closest friends. Why?

   A: He's applied for a job at my store.

◇ PRACTICE 20—SELFSTUDY: Using *how far* and *how long* (Charts 6–10 and 6–12)

Directions: Complete the questions with **FAR** or **LONG**.

1. A: How _____*far*_____ is it to the nearest police station?
   B: Four blocks.

2. A: How _____*long*_____ does it take you to get to work?
   B: Forty-five minutes.

3. A: How _____ is it to your office from home?
   B: About twenty miles.

4. A: How _____ is it from here to the airport?
   B: Ten kilometers.

5. A: How _____ does it take to get to the airport?
   B: Fifteen minutes.

6. A: How _____ above sea level is Denver, Colorado?
   B: One mile. That's why it's called the Mile High City.

7. A: How _____ does it take to fly from Chicago to Denver?
   B: Around three hours.

8. A: How _____ did it take you to build your own boat?
   B: Four years.

9. A: How _____ did you walk?
   B: Two miles.

10. A: How _____ did you walk?
    B: Two hours.

◇ PRACTICE 21—SELFSTUDY: Using *how*. (Chart 6–8)

Directions: Complete the questions with **OFTEN, FAR, LONG,** or **MANY**.

1. A: How _____*often*_____ do you eat out at a restaurant?
   B: About once a week.

2. A: How _____ did you sleep last night?
   B: Six hours.

3. A: How _____ hours did you sleep last night?
   B: Six.

4. A: How _____ did you walk yesterday?
   B: About four miles.

5. A: How _____ miles did you walk yesterday?
   B: About four.

6. A: How _____ kilometers did you walk yesterday?
   B: About six.

7. A: How _____ did your father teach at the university?
   B: Forty-four years.

8. A: How _____ years did your father teach at the university?
   B: Forty-four.

9. A: How _____ do you play softball in the summer?
   B: Sometimes three or four times a week.

10. A: How _____ times a week do you play softball in the summer?
    B: Sometimes three or four times a week.

11. A: How _____ does it take to get a haircut at Bertha's Beauty Boutique?
    B: Half an hour.

12. A: How _____ do you get a haircut?
    B: About every six weeks, I'd guess.

13. A: How _____ is it from the earth to the moon?
    B: Approximately 239,000 miles or 385,000 kilometers.

14. A: How _____ times a day do you brush your teeth?
    B: At least three.

15. A: How _____ does a snake shed its skin?
    B: From once a year to more than six times a year, depending on the kind of snake.

16. A: How _____ is it from your desk to the door?
    B: I'd say about four regular steps or two giant steps.

17. A: How _____ does it take to get over a cold?
    B: As they say, a cold is three days coming, three days here, and three days going.

◇ PRACTICE 22—GUIDED STUDY: Using *how*. (Charts 6–8 → 6–13)

Directions: Make questions for the given answers. Use **HOW** in each question.

Example: It's very important.
Written: **How important is good health?**

1. Very expensive.

2. I took a taxi.

3. Four hours.

4. He's nineteen.

5. In five minutes.

6. With a knife.

7. Every day.

8. Three blocks.

9. Fine.

10. With two t's.

11. It gets below zero.

12. Her grades are excellent.

◇ **PRACTICE 23—SELFSTUDY:** Cumulative review. (Charts 6–1 → 6–13)

Directions: Using the information in parentheses, make QUESTIONS for the given answers.

1. A: ___*When are you going to buy a new bicycle?*___
   B: Next week. (I'm going to buy a new bicycle next week.)

2. A: ___*How are you going to pay for it?*___
   B: With my credit card. (I'm going to pay for it with my credit card.)

3. A: _____
   B: Ten years. (I had my old bike for ten years.)

4. A: _____
   B: Four or five times a week. (I ride my bike four or five times a week.)

5. A: _____
   B: I usually ride my bike. (I usually get to work by riding my bike.)

6. A: _____
   B: Yes. (I'm going to ride my bike to work tomorrow.)

7. A: _____
   B: I decided I would rather walk. (I didn't ride my bike to work today because I decided I would rather walk.)

8. A: _____
   B: Two weeks ago. (Jason got his new bike two weeks ago.)

9. A: _____
   B: Billy. (Billy broke Jason's new bike.)

10. A: _____
    B: Jason's new bike. (Billy broke Jason's new bike.)

11. A: _____
    B: Jason's new bike. (Jason's new bike is broken.)

12. A: _____
    B: He ran into a brick wall. (Billy broke Jason's bike by running into a brick wall.)

13. A: _____
    B: Yes, it does. (My bike has a comfortable seat.)

14. A: _____
    B: A ten-speed. (I have a ten-speed bicycle.)

15. A: _____
    B: The blue one. (The blue bicycle is mine, not the red one.)

16. A: _____
    B: Inside my apartment. (I keep my bicycle inside my apartment at night.)

17. A: _____
    B: David. (That bike belongs to David.)

18. A: _____
    B: Suzanne's. (I borrowed Suzanne's bike.)

19. A: _____
    B: In the park. (Rita is in the park.)

20. A: _____
    B: Riding her bike. (She's riding her bike.)

21. A: _____
    B: 25 miles. (Rita rode her bike 25 miles* yesterday.)

22. A: _____
    B: B-I-C-Y-C-L-E. (You spell ''bicycle'' B-I-C-Y-C-L-E.)

◇ **PRACTICE 24—GUIDED STUDY: Cumulative review. (Charts 6–1 → 6–13)**

Directions: Complete the dialogues by writing QUESTIONS for the given answers. Use the information in parentheses to form the questions.

1. A: ***When will the clean clothes be dry?*** _____
   B: In about an hour. (The clean clothes will be dry in about an hour.)

2. A: _____
   B: I went to a baseball game. (I went to a baseball game Saturday afternoon.)

3. A: _____
   B: The small paperback. (I bought the small paperback dictionary, not the large one with the hard cover.)

4. A: _____
   B: Four hours. (It took me four hours to clean my apartment before my parents came to visit.)

5. A: _____
   B: Stand on a chair. (You can reach the top shelf by standing on a chair.)

6. A: _____
   B: Whole wheat bread. (I like whole wheat bread the best.)

7. A: _____
   B: Because I was in the middle of dinner with my family. (I didn't answer the phone when it rang because I was in the middle of dinner with my family.)

8. A: _____
   B: Maria and her sister. (I'm going to the show with Maria and her sister.)

_____
*25 miles = 40.225 kilometers.

9. A: _____
   B: Eric. (Eric repaired the radio.)

10. A: _____
    B: It's not bad. It rarely gets below zero. (It rarely gets below zero in my hometown in the winter.)

11. A: _____
    B: He's playing tennis. (Jack is playing tennis.)

12. A: _____
    B: Anna. (He is playing tennis with Anna.)

13. A: _____
    B: Serving the ball. (Anna is serving the ball.)

14. A: _____
    B: A tennis ball. (She is throwing a tennis ball in the air.)

15. A: _____
    B: Rackets. (Anna and Jack are holding rackets.)

16. A: _____
    B: A net. (A net is between them.)

17. A: _____
    B: On a tennis court. (They are on a tennis court.)

18. A: _____
    B: For an hour and a half. (They have been playing for an hour and a half.)

19. A: _____
    B: Jack. (Jack is winning right now.)

20. A: _____
    B: Anna. (Anna won the last game.)

◇ PRACTICE 25—GUIDED STUDY: Cumulative review. (Charts 6–1 → 6–13)

Directions: Make dialogues from the given words. Include both Speaker A and Speaker B.

Example: . . . usually get up?
Written: **A: *What time do you usually get up?***
                B: 6:30.

1. . . . should I meet you?
2. . . . fruit do you like best?
3. . . . is south of the United States?
4. . . . times a week do you . . . ?
5. . . . do tomorrow?
6. . . . is it from . . . to . . . ?

7. . . . killed . . . ?
8. . . . you breathing hard?
9. . . . do for a living?
10. . . . spell "happened"?
11. . . . take to get to our hotel from the airport?
12. . . . didn't you call me when . . . ?

◇ PRACTICE 26—GUIDED STUDY: Cumulative review. (Charts 6–1 → 6–13)

Directions: In small groups (or by yourself), make up questions about some or all of the following topics. What would you like to know about these topics? What are you curious about? Share your questions with your classmates. Maybe some of them can answer some of your questions.

Example: tigers
Questions: How long do tigers usually live? Where do they live? What do they eat? Do they kill and eat people? How big is a tiger? Is it bigger than a lion? Can a tiger climb a tree? Do tigers live alone or in groups? Do they have natural enemies? Are human beings their only enemy? Will tigers become extinct soon? How many tigers are there in the world today? How many tigers were there one hundred years ago?

TOPICS:

1. world geography
2. the universe
3. the weather

4. dinosaurs
5. birds
6. (a topic of your own choosing)

◇ PRACTICE 27—GUIDED STUDY: *What about* and *how about*. (Chart 6–14)

Directions: Complete the dialogues with your own words.

1. A: _____?

    B: Nine or nine-thirty.

    A: That's too late for me. How about _____?

    B: Okay.

2. A: _____?

    B: No, Tuesday's not good for me.

    A: Then what about _____?

    B: Okay. That's fine.

3. A: There's room in the car for one more person. Do you think _____ would like

    to go to _____ with us?

    B: _____ can't go with us because _____.

    A: Then how about _____?

    B: _____.

4. A: Do you like fish?

   B: Yes, very much. How about _____?

   A: Yes, I like fish a lot. In fact, I think I'll order fish for dinner tonight. That sounds good.

      What about _____?

   B: No, I think I'll have _____.

◇ **PRACTICE 28—SELFSTUDY:** Tag questions. (Chart 6–15)

    Directions: Complete the TAG QUESTIONS with the correct verb.

  1. SIMPLE PRESENT

    a. You **like** strong coffee, _____*don't*_____ you?

    b. David **goes** to Ames High School, _____ he?

    c. Kate and Sara **live** on Tree Road, _____ they?

    d. Jane **has** the keys to the storeroom, _____ she?

    e. Jane**'s** in her office, _____ she?

    f. You**'re** a member of this class, _____ you?

    g. Jack **doesn't** have a car, _____ he?

    h. Ann **isn't** from California, _____ she?

  2. SIMPLE PAST

    a. Paul **went** to Florida, _____ he?

    b. You **didn't talk** to the boss, _____ you?

    c. Tom's parents **weren't** at home, _____ they?

    d. That **was** Pat's idea, _____ it?

  3. PRESENT PROGRESSIVE, *BE GOING TO*, and PAST PROGRESSIVE

    a. You**'re studying** hard, _____ you?

    b. Tom **isn't working** at the bank, _____ he?

    c. It **isn't going to rain** today, _____ it?

    d. Susan and Kevin **were waiting** for us, _____ they?

    e. It **wasn't raining**, _____ it?

  4. MODAL AUXILIARIES

    a. You **can answer** these questions, _____ you?

    b. Kate **won't tell** anyone our secret, _____ she?

    c. Sam **should come** to the meeting, _____ he?

    d. Alice **would like** to come with us, _____ she?

    e. I **don't have to come** to the meeting, _____ I?

    f. Steve **had to leave** early, _____ he?

◇ PRACTICE 29—SELFSTUDY: Tag questions. (Chart 6–15)

Directions: Add TAG QUESTIONS.

1. Mr. Adams was born in England, _____*wasn't he*_____?

2. Flies can fly upside down, _____?

3. All birds lay eggs, _____?

4. Mike isn't married, _____?

5. You would rather have a roommate than live alone, _____?

6. These gloves are yours, _____?

7. That's Brian's algebra book, _____?

8. Fire can't melt a diamond, _____?

9. You should call your mom today, _____?

10. Ms. Boxlight will be here tomorrow, _____?

11. Tony Wah lives in Los Angeles, _____?

12. You didn't forget to finish your homework, _____?

13. Tomorrow isn't a holiday, _____?

14. I don't have to be at the meeting, _____?

15. This isn't your book, _____?

16. Jack and Elizabeth were in class yesterday, _____?

17. Jennifer won't be here for dinner tonight, _____?

18. Lightning can kill swimmers when it strikes water. It kills the fish in the water, too,

_____?

◇ PRACTICE 30—GUIDED STUDY: Tag questions. (Chart 6–15)

Directions: Make sentences with TAG QUESTIONS. Your sentences should express your opinion. In the example, the speaker believes that Li is a common name in China.

Example: I think that Li (is/isn't) a common name in China.
Question: Li is a common name in China, isn't it?

1. I think that Athens (is/isn't) the capital of Italy.

2. I think that Athens (is/isn't) the capital of Greece.

3. I think that plants (can/can't) grow in deserts.

4. I think that deserts (are/aren't) complete wastelands.

5. I think that cactuses (thrive/don't thrive) in deserts.

6. I think that dinosaurs (weighed/didn't weigh) more than elephants.

7. I think that blue whales (are/aren't) larger than dinosaurs.

8. I think that whales (lay/don't lay) eggs.

9. I think that turtles (lay/don't lay) eggs.

10. I think that Abraham Lincoln (was/wasn't) the first president of the United States.

11. I think that we (will/won't) have a test on Chapter 6.

12. I think that . . . .

◇ PRACTICE 31—GUIDED STUDY: Asking questions. (Chapter 6)

Directions: Pair up with a classmate or any other partner. Together create a long dialogue for the given situation. One of you is Speaker A and the other is Speaker B. The beginning of the dialogue is given.

1. SITUATION: The dialogue takes place on the telephone.
   Speaker A: You are a travel agent.
   Speaker B: You want to take a trip.

   DIALOGUE: A: *Hello, Worldwide Travel Agency. May I help you?*
   B: *Yes, I need to make arrangements to go to (think of a place) . . . .*
   A: *Etc.*
   B: *Etc.*

2. SITUATION: The dialogue takes place at a police station.
   Speaker A: You are a police officer.
   Speaker B: You are the suspect of a crime.

   DIALOGUE: A: *Where were you at eleven o'clock on Tuesday night, the 16th of this month?*
   B: *I'm not sure I remember. Why do you want to know, Officer?*
   Etc.

3. SITUATION: The dialogue takes place in an office.
   Speaker A: You are the owner of a small company.
   Speaker B: You are interviewing for a job in Speaker A's company.

   DIALOGUE: A: *Come in, come in. I'm (. . .). Glad to meet you.*
   B: *How do you do? I'm (. . .). I'm pleased to meet you.*
   A: *Have a seat, (. . .).*
   B: *Thank you.*
   A: *So you're interested in working at (make up the name of a company)?*
   Etc.

◇ PRACTICE 32—SELFSTUDY: Prepositions. (Chapter 6; Appendix 1)

Directions: Complete each sentence with the appropriate preposition.

1. Ask Ann to help you. She knows something ___*about*___ geometry.

2. Something's the matter _____ Dan. He's crying.

3. Do whatever you want. It doesn't matter _____ me.

4. Look _____ those clouds. It's going to rain.

5. Are you looking forward _____ your trip to Israel?

6. A: Does this watch belong _____ you?

   B: Yes. Where did you find it? I searched _____ it everywhere.

7. I woke up frightened after I dreamed _____ falling off the roof of a building.

8. Tomorrow I'm going to ask my father _____ a ride to school.

9. Tomorrow I'm going to ask my father _____ his work. I don't know much

   _____ his new job, and I want to ask him about it.

10. Please empty that bowl of fruit and separate the fresh apples _____ the old apples.

CHAPTER 7
The Present Perfect and the Past Perfect

◇ **PRACTICE 1—SELFSTUDY:** Forms of the present perfect. (Charts 7–1 → 7–3)

Directions: Complete the dialogues with the given verbs and any words in parentheses. Use the PRESENT PERFECT.

1. *eat* A: (*you, ever*) _____***Have you ever eaten***_____ pepperoni pizza?

   B: Yes, I ___***have***___. I ___***have eaten***___ pepperoni pizza many times. OR:

   No, I ___***haven't***___. I (*never*) ___***have never eaten***___ pepperoni pizza.

2. *talk* A: (*you, ever*) _____ to a famous person?

   B: Yes, I _____. I _____ to a lot of famous people. OR:

   No, I _____. I (*never*) _____ to a famous person.

3. *rent* A: (*Erica, ever*) _____ a car?

   B: Yes, she _____. She _____ a car many times. OR:

   No, she _____. She (*never*) _____ a car.

4. *see* A: (*you, ever*) _____ a shooting star?

   B: Yes, I _____. I _____ a lot of shooting stars. OR:

   No, I _____. I (*never*) _____ a shooting star.

5. *catch* A: (*Joe, ever*) _____ a big fish?

   B: Yes, he _____. He _____ lots of big fish. OR:

   No, he _____. He (*never*) _____ a big fish.

6. *have* A: (*you, ever*) _____ a bad sunburn?

   B: Yes, I _____. I _____ a bad sunburn several times. OR:

   No, I _____. I (*never*) _____ a bad sunburn.

◇ **PRACTICE 2—SELFSTUDY: The present perfect. (Charts 7–1 → 7–3)**

Directions: Complete the sentences with the PRESENT PERFECT of the verbs in the list and any words in parentheses. Use each verb only one time.

eat	look	save	✔use
give	play	sleep	wear
improve	rise	speak	win

1. People _____ *have used* _____ sheep's wool to make clothing for centuries.

2. The night is over. It's daytime now. The sun _____.

3. I (*never*) _____ golf, but I'd like to. It looks like fun.

4. Our team is great. They _____ all of their games so far this year. They haven't lost a single game.

5. Amy must be mad at me. She (*not*) _____ one word to me all evening. I wonder what I did to make her angry.

6. The cat must be sick. He (*not*) _____ any food for two days. We'd better call the vet.

7. Our teacher _____ us a lot of tests and quizzes since the beginning of the term.

8. We put a little money in our savings account every month. We want to buy a car, but we (*not*) _____ enough money yet. We'll have enough in a few more months.

9. (*you, ever*) _____ outdoors for an entire night? I mean without a tent, with nothing between you and the stars?

10. My aunt puts on a wig whenever she goes out, but I (*never*) _____ a wig in my whole life.

11. Paul's health _____ a lot since he started eating the right kinds of food, exercising regularly, and handling the stress in his life. He's never felt better.

12. I can't find my keys. I _____ everywhere—in all my pockets, in my briefcase, in my desk. They're gone.

◇ **PRACTICE 3—SELFSTUDY: The present perfect vs. the simple past. (Chart 7–4)**

Directions: Complete the sentences with the SIMPLE PAST or the PRESENT PERFECT.

1. A: When are you going to call Jane?

   B: I (*call, already*) ____ *have already called* ____ her. I (*call*) ____ *called* ____ her a half an hour ago.

2. A: When are you going to begin working at the candy store?

   B: I (*begin, already*) _____ working there. I (*begin*) _____ yesterday morning.

3. A: Are you going to eat lunch soon?

   B: I (*eat, already*) _____. I (*eat*) _____ lunch an

   hour ago.

4. A: When are you going to get a new computer?

   B: I (*buy, already*) _____ one. I (*buy*) _____ it

   last week.

5. A: When is Steve going to leave for the concert?

   B: He (*leave, already*) _____. He (*leave*) _____

   an hour ago.

6. A: Will you please lock the door?

   B: I (*lock, already*) _____ it. I (*lock*) _____ it

   when I got home.

◇ **PRACTICE 4—SELFSTUDY: Irregular verbs. (Charts 2–3, 2–4, and 7–4)**

Directions: This is a review of IRREGULAR VERBS. Complete the sentences with the SIMPLE PAST and the PRESENT PERFECT of the given verbs.

1. *begin*   I _____**began**_____ a new diet and exercise program last week. I

   _____**have begun**_____ lots of new diet and exercise programs in my lifetime.

2. *bend*   I _____ down to pick up my young son from his crib this morning.

   I _____ down to pick him up many times since he was born.

3. *broadcast* The radio _____ news about the terrible earthquake in Iran

   last week. The radio _____ news about Iran every day

   since the earthquake occurred.

4. *catch*   I _____ a cold last week. I _____ a lot of

   colds in my lifetime.

5. *come*   A tourist _____ into Mr. Nasser's jewelry store after lunch. A lot of

   tourists _____ into his store since he opened it last year.

6. *cut*   I _____ some flowers from my garden yesterday. I

   _____ lots of flowers from my garden so far this summer.

7. *dig*   The workers _____ a hole to fix the leak in the water pipe. They

   _____ many holes to fix water leaks since the earthquake.

8. *draw*   The artist _____ a picture of a sunset yesterday. She

   _____ many pictures of sunsets in her lifetime.

9. *feed*   I _____ birds at the park yesterday. I _____

   birds at the park every day since I lost my job.

10. *fight*   We _____ a war last year. We _____ several

    wars since we became an independent country.

11. *forget* I _____ to turn off the stove after dinner. I _____ to turn off the stove a lot of times in my lifetime.

12. *hide* The children _____ in the basement yesterday. They _____ in the basement often since they discovered a secret place there.

13. *hit* The baseball player _____ the ball out of the stadium yesterday. He _____ a lot of homeruns since he joined our team.

14. *hold* My husband _____ the door open for me when we entered the restaurant. He _____ a door open for me many times since we met each other.

15. *keep* During the discussion yesterday, I _____ my opinion to myself. I _____ my opinions to myself a lot of times in my lifetime.

16. *lead* Mary _____ the group discussion at the conference. She _____ group discussions many times since she started going to conferences.

17. *lose* Eddie _____ money at the racetrack yesterday. He _____ money at the racetrack lots of times in his lifetime.

18. *meet* I _____ two new people in my class yesterday. I _____ a lot of new people since I started going to school here.

19. *ride* I _____ the bus to work yesterday. I _____ the bus to work many times since I got a job downtown.

20. *ring* The doorbell _____ a few minutes ago. The doorbell _____ three times so far today.

21. *see*   I _____ a good movie yesterday. I _____ a lot

of good movies in my lifetime.

22. *steal*   The fox _____ a chicken from the farmer's yard last night. The fox

_____ three chickens so far this month.

23. *stick*   I _____ a stamp on the corner of the envelope. I _____

_____ lots of stamps on envelopes in my lifetime.

24. *sweep*   I _____ the floor of my apartment yesterday. I _____

_____ the floor of my apartment lots of times since I moved in.

25. *take*   I _____ a test yesterday. I _____ lots of tests

in my life as a student.

26. *upset*   The Smith children _____ Mr. Jordan when they broke his

window. Because they are careless and noisy, they _____ Mr.

Jordan many times since they moved in next door.

27. *withdraw*   I _____ some money from my bank account yesterday. I

_____ more than three hundred dollars from my bank

account so far this month.

28. *write*   I _____ a letter to a friend last night. I _____

lots of letters to my friends in my lifetime.

◇ **PRACTICE 5—GUIDED STUDY:** Irregular verbs. (Charts 2–3, 2–4, and 7–4)

Directions: This is a review of IRREGULAR VERBS. Complete the sentences with the SIMPLE PAST or
the PRESENT PERFECT of the given verbs.

1. *go*   a. I _____***have gone***_____ to every play at the local theater so far this year.

b. My whole family _____***went***_____ to the play last weekend.

2. *give*   a. Jane _____***gave***_____ me a ride home from work today.

b. (*she, ever*) _____***Has she ever given***_____ you a ride home since she started

working in your department?

3. *fall*   a. I _____ down many times in my lifetime, but never hard

enough to really hurt myself or break a bone.

b. Mike _____ down many times during football practice

yesterday.

4. *break*   a. (*you, ever*) _____ a bone in your body?

b. I _____ my leg when I was ten years old. I jumped off the

roof of my house.

5. *shake*   a. In my entire lifetime, I (*never*) _____ hands with a famous

movie star.

b. In 1990, I _____ hands with a famous soccer player.

6. *hear*   a. I _____ you practicing your trumpet late last night.

           b. In fact, I _____ you practicing every night for two weeks.

7. *fly*   a. Mike is a commercial airline pilot. Yesterday he _____ from Tokyo to Los Angeles.

           b. Mike _____ to many places in the world since he became a pilot.

8. *wear*   a. Carol really likes her new leather jacket. She _____ it every day since she bought it.

           b. She _____ her new leather jacket to the opera last night.

9. *build*   a. (*you, ever*) _____ a piece of furniture?

           b. My daughter _____ a table in her woodworking class at the high school last year.

10. *teach*   a. Ms. Kent _____ math at the local high school since 1982.

           b. She _____ in Hungary last year on an exchange program.

11. *find*   a. In your lifetime, (*you, ever*) _____ something really valuable?

           b. My sister _____ a very expensive diamond ring in the park last year.

12. *drive*   a. After I took Danny to school, I _____ straight to work.

           b. I'm an experienced driver, but I (*never*) _____ a bus or a big truck.

13. *sing*　　a. I _____ a duet with my mother at the art benefit last night.

　　　　　　b. We _____ together ever since I was a small child.

14. *run*　　a. I (*never*) _____ in a marathon race, and I don't intend to.

　　　　　　b. I'm out of breath because I _____ all the way over here.

15. *tell*　　a. Last night, my brother _____ me a secret.

　　　　　　b. He _____ me lots of secrets in his lifetime.

16. *stand*　　a. When I visited the U.N. last summer, I _____ in the main gallery and felt a great sense of history.

　　　　　　b. Many great world leaders _____ there over the years.

17. *spend*　　a. I _____ all of my money at the mall yesterday.

　　　　　　b. I don't have my rent money this month. I (*already*) _____ it on other things.

18. *make*　　a. I consider myself fortunate because I _____ many good friends in my lifetime.

　　　　　　b. I _____ a terrible mistake last night. I forgot that my friend had invited me to his apartment for dinner.

19. *rise*　　a. The price of flour _____ a lot since 1990.

　　　　　　b. When his name was announced, Jack _____ from his seat and walked to the podium to receive his award.

20. *feel*　　a. I _____ terrible yesterday, so I stayed in bed.

　　　　　　b. I _____ terrible for a week now. I'd better see a doctor.

◇ **PRACTICE 6—SELFSTUDY:** *Since* vs. *for.* (Chart 7–5)

　　Directions: Complete the sentences with **SINCE** or **FOR**.

　　1. David has worked for the power company ____*since*____ 1990.

　　2. His brother has worked for the power company ____*for*____ five years.

　　3. I have known Peter Gow _____ September.

　　4. I've known his sister _____ three months.

　　5. Jonas has walked with a limp _____ many years.

　　6. He's had a bad leg _____ he was in the war.

　　7. Rachel hasn't been in class _____ last Tuesday.

　　8. She hasn't been in class _____ three days.

　　9. I've had a toothache _____ yesterday morning.

　　10. I've had this toothache _____ thirty-six hours.

　　11. My vision has improved _____ I got new reading glasses.

　　12. I've had a cold _____ almost a week.

　　13. Jake hasn't worked _____ last summer when the factory closed down.

　　14. I attended Jefferson Elementary School _____ six years.

◇ **PRACTICE 7—SELFSTUDY:** Sentences with *since*-clauses. (Chart 7–5)

Directions: Complete the sentences with the words in parentheses.

1. I (know) _____**have known**_____ Mark Miller since we (be) _____**were**_____ in college.

2. Jeremy (change) _____ his major three times since he (start) _____ school.

3. Ever since* I (be) _____ a child, I (be) _____ afraid of snakes.

4. I can't wait to get home to my own bed. I (sleep, not) _____ well since I (leave) _____ home three days ago.

5. Ever since Danny (meet) _____ Nicole, he (be, not) _____ able to think about anything or anyone else. He's in love.

6. Otto (have) _____ a lot of problems with his car ever since he (buy) _____ it. It's a lemon.

7. A: What (you, eat) _____ since you (get) _____ up this morning?

   B: I (eat) _____ a banana and some yogurt. That's all.

8. I'm eighteen. I have a job and am in school. My life is going okay now, but I (have) _____ a miserable home life when I (be) _____ a young child. Ever since I (leave) _____ home at the age of fifteen, I (take) _____ care of myself. I (have) _____ some hard times, but I (learn) _____ how to stand on my own two feet.

◇ **PRACTICE 8—GUIDED STUDY:** *Since* vs. *for.* (Chart 7–5)

Directions: Write sentences *about yourself* using **SINCE**, **FOR**, or **NEVER** with the PRESENT PERFECT.

Example: have (a particular kind of watch)
Written: **I've had my Seiko quartz watch for two years. OR:**
         I've had my Seiko quartz watch since my eighteenth birthday.

Example: smoke cigars/cigarettes/a pipe
Written: **I've never smoked cigarettes. OR:**
         I've smoked cigarettes since I was seventeen.

1. know (a particular person)
2. live in (this city)
3. study English
4. be in this class/at this school/with this company
5. have long hair/short hair/a mustache
6. wear glasses/contact lenses
7. have (a particular article of clothing)
8. be interested in (a particular subject)
9. be married
10. have a driver's license

_____

Ever since has the same meaning as *since.*

◇ PRACTICE 9—GUIDED STUDY: Verb tense review. (Chapters 1, 2, 3, and 7)

Directions: Following is a conversation between two people: Ann and Ben. Complete the sentences with the words in parentheses.

(1) BEN: I (*need*) _____**need**_____ to earn some extra money for my school expenses. Got any ideas?

(2) ANN: (*you, have, ever*) _____ a job at a restaurant?

(3) BEN: Yes, I _____**have**_____. I (*work*) _____ at several restaurants since I (*start*) _____ going to college.

ANN: When was the last time you worked at a restaurant?

(4) BEN: I (*have*) _____ a job as a dishwasher last fall.

ANN: Where?

BEN: At the Bistro Cafe.

(5) ANN: How long (*you, work*) _____ there?

BEN: For two months.

(6) ANN: (*you, enjoy*) _____ your job as a dishwasher at the Bistro?

(7) BEN: No, I _____. It (*be*) _____ hard work for low pay.

(8) ANN: Where (*you, work*) _____ right now?

(9) BEN: I (*have, not*) _____ a job right now.

(10) ANN: (*you, want*) _____ a part-time or full-time job?

(11) BEN: I (*plan*) _____ to look for a part-time job, maybe twenty hours a week.

(12) ANN: I (*go*) _____ to Al's Place tomorrow to see about a job. The restaurant (*look*) _____ for help. Why don't you come along with me?

(13) BEN: Thanks. I think I (*do*) _____ that. I (*look, never*) _____ _____ for a job at Al's Place before. Maybe the pay will be better than at the Bistro.

(14) ANN: I (*know, not*) _____. We (*find*) _____ out when we (*go*) _____ there tomorrow.

◇ PRACTICE 10—SELFSTUDY: The present perfect progressive. (Charts 7–6 and 7–7)

Directions: Use the given information to complete the dialogues between Speaker A and Speaker B. Use the PRESENT PERFECT PROGRESSIVE.

1. Eric is studying. He started to **study** at seven o'clock. It is now nine o'clock.

A: How long _____**has Eric been studying**_____?

B: He _**'s been studying**_____ for _____**two hours**_____.

2. Kathy is working at the computer. She began to **work** at the computer at two o'clock. It is now three o'clock.

A: How long _____**has Kathy been working at the computer**_____?

B: She _**'s been working**_____ since _____**two o'clock**_____.

3. It began to **rain** two days ago. It is still raining.

   A: How long _____?

   B: It _____ for _____.

4. Liz is reading. She began to **read** at ten o'clock. It is now ten-thirty.

   A: How long _____?

   B: She_____ for _____.

5. Boris began to **study** English in 1990. He is still studying English.

   A: How long _____?

   B: He_____ since _____.

6. Three months ago, Nicole started to **work** at the Silk Road Clothing Store.

   A: How long _____?

   B: She_____ for _____.

7. Ms. Rice started to **teach** at this school in September 1992.

   A: How long _____?

   B: She_____ since _____.

8. Mr. Fisher is **driving** a Chevy. He bought it twelve years ago.

   A: How long _____?

   B: He _____ for _____.

9. Mrs. Taylor is **waiting** to see her doctor. She arrived at the waiting room at two o'clock. It is now three-thirty.

   A: How long _____?

   B: She_____ for _____.

10. Ted and Erica started to **play** tennis at two o'clock. It's now four-thirty.

   A: How long _____?

   B: They_____ since _____.

◇ PRACTICE 11—SELFSTUDY: The present perfect progressive. (Charts 7–6 and 7–7)

Directions: Choose the correct verb form.

1. Where have you been? I __**B**__ for you for over an hour!
   A. am waiting   B. have been waiting

2. I'm exhausted! I _____ for the last eight hours without a break.
   A. am working   B. have been working

3. Shhh! Susan _____. Let's not make any noise. We don't want to wake her up.
   A. is sleeping   B. has been sleeping

4. Annie, go upstairs and wake your brother up. He _____ for over ten hours. He has chores to do.
   A. is sleeping   B. has been sleeping

5. Erin has never gone camping. She _____ in a tent.
   A. has never slept   B. has never been sleeping

6. This is a great shirt! I _____ it at least a dozen times, and it still looks like new.
    A. have washed   B. have been washing

7. Aren't you about finished with the dishes? You _____ dishes for thirty minutes or more. How long can it take to wash dishes?
    A. have washed   B. have been washing

8. We _____ to the Steak House restaurant many times. The food is excellent.
    A. have gone   B. have been going

◇ PRACTICE 12—GUIDED STUDY: Verb tenses. (Charts 7–2 → 7–7)

Directions: Make sentences about your life using the given time expressions. Use the SIMPLE PAST, PRESENT PERFECT, or PRESENT PERFECT PROGRESSIVE.

Example: for the last two weeks
Written: **I've had a cold for the last two weeks.**

1. since I was a child
2. for a long time
3. two years ago
4. so far today
5. many times in my lifetime

6. never
7. since last Tuesday
8. for a number of years*
9. a week ago today
10. for the last ten minutes

◇ PRACTICE 13—GUIDED STUDY: Verb forms. (Chapters 1, 2, 3, and 7)

Directions: Complete the sentences with the words in parentheses.

Dear Adam,

(1)   Hi! How are you? Remember me? Just a joke! I (*write, not*) _____

(2) to you for at least six months, but that's not long enough for you to forget me! I think about

(3) writing to you often, but I (*be, not*) _____ a good correspondent for the

(4) last few months. You (*hear, not*) _____ from me for such a long time

(5) because I (*be*) _____ really busy. For the last few months, I (*work*)

(6) _____ full-time at a shoe store and (*go*) _____ to school

(7) at the local community college to study business and computers. When I (*write*) _____

(8) to you six months ago—last April, I think—I (*go*) _____ to the university

(9) full-time and (*study*) _____ anthropology. A lot of things (*happen*)

(10) _____ since then.

(11)   At the end of the spring semester last June, my grades (*be*) _____ terrible. As

(12) a result, I (*lose*) _____ my scholarship and my parents' support. I really (*mess*)

(13) _____ up when I (*get*) _____ those bad grades. When I (*show*)

(14) _____ my grade report to my parents, they (*refuse*) _____ to help

(15) me with my living expenses at school anymore. They (*feel*) _____ that I was

(16) wasting my time and their money, so they (*tell*) _____ me to get a job. So last

———————————
a number of years = many years.

(17) June, I (*start*) _____ working at a shoe store: Imperial Shoes at Southcenter Mall.

(18) It (*be, not*) _____ a bad job, but it (*be, not*) _____ wonderful

(19) either. Every day, I (*fetch*) _____ shoes from the back room for people to try on,

(20) boxes and boxes of shoes, all day long.

(21) I (*meet*) _____ some pretty weird people since I (*start*) _____

(22) this job. A couple of weeks ago, a middle-aged man (*come*) _____ into the store.

(23) He (*want*) _____ to try on some black leather loafers. I (*bring*) _____

(24) the loafers, and he (*put*) _____ them on. While he (*walk*) _____

(25) around to see if they fit okay, he (*pull*) _____ from his pocket a little white

(26) mouse with pink eyes and (*start*) _____ talking to it. He (*look*) _____

(27) right at the mouse and (*say*) _____, "George, (*you, like*) _____

(28) this pair of shoes?" When the mouse (*twitch*) _____ its nose, the man (*say*)

(29) _____, "Yes, so do I." Then he (*turn*) _____ to me and (*say*)

(30) _____, "We'll take them." Can you believe that!?

(31) Most of the people I meet are nice—and normal. My favorite customers (*be*) _____

(32) people who (*know*) _____ what they want when they (*enter*) _____

(33) the store. They (*come*) _____ in, (*point*) _____ at one pair of shoes,

(34) politely (*tell*) _____ me their size, (*try*) _____ the shoes on, and

(35) then (*buy*) _____ them, just like that. They (*agonize, not*) _____

(36) _____ for a long time over which pair to buy.

(37) I (*learn*) _____ one important thing from working at the shoe

(38) store: I (*want, not*) _____ to sell shoes as a career. I (*need*)

(39) _____ a good education that (*prepare*) _____ me for a job that I can

(40) enjoy for the rest of my life. And even though I love studying anthropology, I (*decide*)

(41) _____ that a degree in business and computers will provide the best

(42) career opportunities.

(43) I (*want, always*) _____ to be independent, and now I (*be*)

(44) _____. I (*have*) _____ to pay every penny of my tuition and living

(45) expenses now. Ever since I (*lose*) _____ my scholarship and (*make*)

(46) _____ my parents mad, I (*be*) _____ completely on my own.

(47) I'm glad to report that my grades at present (*be*) _____ excellent, and right now I

(48) (*enjoy, really*) _____ my work with computers. In the future, I (*continue*)

(49) _____ to take courses in anthropology whenever I can fit them into my

(50) schedule, and I (*study*) _____ anthropology on my own for the rest of

(51) my life, but I (*pursue*) _____ a career in business. Maybe there is some

(52) way I can combine anthropology, business, and computers. Who knows?

(53) There, I (*tell*) _____ you everything I can think of that is at all

(54) important in my life at the moment. I think I (*grow*) _____ up a lot during

(55) the last six months. I (*understand*) _____ that my education is

(56) important. Losing my scholarship (*make*) _____ my life more difficult, but I

(57) (*feel*) _____ that I (*take, finally*) _____ charge of

(58) my life. It's a good feeling.

(59)   Please write. I'd love to hear from you.

(60)   Jessica

◇ PRACTICE 14—GUIDED STUDY: Verb forms. (Charts 7–4 and 7–5)

Directions: Think of a friend you haven't spoken to or written to since the beginning of this term. Write this friend a letter about your activities from the start of this school term to the present time. Begin your letter as follows:

> Dear (. . .),
>   I'm sorry I haven't written for such a long time. Lots of things have happened since I last wrote to you.

◇ PRACTICE 15—SELFSTUDY: Midsentence adverbs. (Chart 7–8)

PART I: Placement of MIDSENTENCE ADVERBS IN STATEMENTS.

Directions: *Choose the correct place to add* ALWAYS *to the following sentences.*

1. Kate _____**Ø**_____ is _____**always**_____ late.

2. Mike _____**always**_____ finishes _____**Ø**_____ his work on time.

3. Gina _____ finished _____ her work early.

4. Nick _____ will _____ *finish* his work on time.

5. Rick _____ has _____ *helped* me with my work.

6. Bill _____ helped _____ me with my work.

7. They _____ are _____ helpful.

8. They _____ help _____ me when I need it.

9. They _____ have _____ *helped* me.

10. Sara _____ can _____ *help* you if you ask her to.

Directions: *Choose the correct place to add* USUALLY *to the following sentences.*

11. They _____ are _____ very helpful.

12. They _____ help _____ me when I need it.

13. They _____ have _____ *helped* me.

14. Sara _____ can _____ *help* you if you ask her to.

PART II: Placement of MIDSENTENCE ADVERBS in QUESTIONS.

Directions: *Choose the correct place to add* USUALLY *to the following sentences.*

15. *Do* _____ you _____ *work* hard?

16. *Is* _____ Mike _____ at home in the evenings?

17. *Did* _____ your mom _____ *read* to you at bedtime?

18. *Were* _____ you _____ in bed by nine?

19. *Can* _____ students _____ *understand* Prof. Milano's lectures?

Directions: *Choose the correct place to add* **EVER** *to the following sentences.*

20. *Do* _____ you _____ *work* hard?

21. *Is* _____ Mike _____ at home in the evenings?

22. *Did* _____ your mom _____ *read* to you at bedtime?

23. *Were* _____ you _____ in bed by nine?

24. *Can* _____ students _____ *understand* Prof. Milano's lectures?

PART III: Placement of MIDSENTENCE ADVERBS in NEGATIVE SENTENCES.

Directions: *Choose the correct place to add* **PROBABLY** *to the following sentences.*

25. Janet _____ *won't* _____ *attend* a meeting.

26. Frank _____ *isn't* _____ in his office.

27. Emily _____ *doesn't* _____ *know* the answer.

28. Brian _____ *hasn't* _____ *finished* his homework yet.

Directions: *Choose the correct place to add* **EVER** *to the following sentences.*

29. Janet _____ *won't* _____ *give* me a straight answer.

30. Frank _____ *isn't* _____ in his office.

Directions: *Choose the correct place to add* **ALWAYS** *to the following sentences.*

31. Emily _____ *doesn't* _____ *know* the right answer in class.

32. Brian _____ *hasn't* _____ *finished* his homework on time.

◇ **PRACTICE 16—GUIDED STUDY:** Frequency adverbs. (Chart 7–8)

Directions: Choose the appropriate FREQUENCY ADVERB to give a sentence with the same meaning. Put the frequency adverb in the correct place.

1. Alice drives to work every day without exception. (*always, generally*)

    → Alice _____**always drives**_____ to work.

2. Jake is tired all of the time. (*always, frequently*)

    → Jake _____**is always**_____ tired.

3. Scott goes swimming at the beach only once a year. (*sometimes, rarely*)

    → Scott _____ swimming at the beach.

4. Have you met David French at any time in your life? (*just, ever*)

    → Have you _____ David French?

5. Karen isn't late for work at any time. (*generally, never*)

    → Karen _____ late for work.

6. Eric is late for work about once a month. (*usually, sometimes*)

    → Eric _____ late for work.

7. Danny is absent from a lot of classes because of illness. (*occasionally, frequently*)

→ Danny _____ absent because of illness.

8. Kathy is a happy, optimistic person most of the time. (*generally, always*)

→ Kathy _____ a happy, optimistic person.

9. It seems to me that very, very few of my wishes come true. (*seldom, occasionally*)

→ My wishes _____ true.

10. Polar bears are huge white bears that live along the northern coasts of Canada, Greenland, and Russia. For the most part, polar bears hunt seals for food. (*generally, rarely*)

→ Polar bears _____ seals for food.

11. Very few polar bears have ever killed a human being. (*often, rarely*)

→ Polar bears _____ human beings.

12. Human beings have killed large numbers of polar bears for their pelts. (*frequently, always*)

→ Human beings _____ polar bears for their pelts.

13. Wild polar bears can live to be thirty-three years old. Polar bears in captivity in zoos may live a little longer. (*usually, seldom*)

→ Polar bears _____ past thirty-five years of age.

◇ **PRACTICE 17—SELFSTUDY:** *Already, still, yet, anymore.* (Chart 7–9)

Directions: Choose the correct completion.

1. I haven't finished my composition yet. I'm __**B**__ working on it.
   A. already　　　　　B. still　　　　　C. yet　　　　　D. anymore

2. *Top Rock Videos* used to be my favorite TV show, but I stopped watching it a couple of years ago. I don't watch it _____.
   A. already　　　　　B. still　　　　　C. yet　　　　　D. anymore

3. I don't have to take any more math classes. I've _____ taken all the required courses.
   A. already　　　　　B. still　　　　　C. yet　　　　　D. anymore

4. I used to nearly choke on an airplane because of all the smoke in the cabin. But smoking is now forbidden by law on all domestic flights. You can't smoke in an airplane _____.

    A. already   B. still   C. yet   D. anymore

5. I'm not quite ready to leave. I haven't finished packing my suitcase _____.

    A. already   B. still   C. yet   D. anymore

6. "Don't you have a class at two?"
"Yeah, why?"
"Look at your watch."
"Oh my gosh, it's _____ past two! Bye!"

    A. already   B. still   C. yet   D. anymore

7. Don't sit there! I painted that chair yesterday and the paint isn't completely dry _____.

    A. already   B. still   C. yet   D. anymore

8. 1448 South 45th Street is Joe's old address. He doesn't live there _____.

    A. already   B. still   C. yet   D. anymore

9. Mr. Wood is eighty-eight years old, but he _____ goes into his office every day.

    A. already   B. still   C. yet   D. anymore

10. "Are you going to drive to Woodville with us for the street festival Saturday?"
"I don't know. I might. I haven't made up my mind _____."

    A. already   B. still   C. yet   D. anymore

◇ **PRACTICE 18—GUIDED STUDY:** Adverb placement. (Charts 7–8 and 7–9)

Directions: Complete the sentences with your own words.

Example: I . . . not . . . because I've already . . . .

Possible responses:

        I'm not *hungry* **because I've already** *eaten.*
        I'm not *going to go to the movie* **because I've already** *seen it.*
        I don't *have to take the English test* **because I've already** *taken it.*

1. I used to . . . , but . . . anymore.
2. I can't . . . because I haven't . . . yet.
3. Are . . . still . . . ?
4. . . . because I've already . . . .
5. She didn't . . . because she probably hasn't . . . .
6. I still . . . , but . . . yet.
7. Dan doesn't . . . because he has already . . . .
8. I can . . . because I've finally . . . .
9. Ann . . . ago. She still . . . .
10. I don't . . . anymore, but . . . still . . . .

◇ **PRACTICE 19—SELFSTUDY:** The past perfect. (Chart 7–10)

Directions: Identify which action took place first (**1st**) in the past and which action took place second (**2nd**).

1. The tennis player **jumped** in the air for joy. She **had won** the match.

    a. __**1st**__ The tennis player won the match.

    b. __**2nd**__ The tennis player jumped in the air.

2. Before I went to bed, I **checked** the front door. My roommate **had** already **locked** it.

    a. ___*2nd*___ I checked the door.

    b. ___*1st*___ My roommate locked the door.

3. I **looked** for Bob, but he **had left** the building.

    a. _____ Bob left the building.

    b. _____ I looked for Bob.

4. I **laughed** when I saw my son. He **had emptied** a bowl of noodles on top of his head.

    a. _____ I laughed.

    b. _____ My son emptied a bowl of noodles on his head.

5. Oliver **arrived** at the airport on time, but he couldn't get on the plane. He **had left** his ticket at home.

    a. _____ Oliver left his ticket at home.

    b. _____ Oliver arrived at the airport.

6. I **handed** Betsy today's newspaper, but she didn't want it. She **had read** it during her lunch hour.

    a. _____ I handed Betsy the newspaper.

    b. _____ Betsy read the newspaper.

7. After Carl arrived in New York, he **called** his mother. He **had promised** to call her as soon as he got in.

    a. _____ Carl made a promise to his mother.

    b. _____ Carl called his mother.

8. Stella was alone in a strange city. She walked down the avenue slowly, looking in shop windows. Suddenly, she **turned** her head and **looked** behind her. Someone **had called** her name.

    a. _____ Stella turned her head and looked behind her.

    b. _____ Someone called her name.

◇ PRACTICE 20—SELFSTUDY: The present perfect vs. the past perfect. (Chart 7–10)

Directions: Complete the sentences with the PRESENT PERFECT or the PAST PERFECT form of the verb in parentheses.

1. A: Oh no! We're too late. The train (leave, already) _____ *has already left* _____.

   B: That's okay. We'll catch the next train to Athens.

2. Last Thursday, we went to the station to catch a train to Athens, but we were too late. The train (leave, already) _____ *had already left* _____.

3. A: Go back to sleep. It's only six o'clock in the morning.

   B: I am not sleepy. I (sleep, already) _____ for seven hours. I'm going to get up.

4. I woke up at six, but I couldn't get back to sleep. I wasn't sleepy. I (sleep, already) _____ for seven hours.

5. A: I'll introduce you to Professor Newton at the meeting tonight.

   B: You don't need to. I (meet, already) _____ him.

6. Jack offered to introduce me to Professor Newton, but it wasn't necessary. I (meet, already) _____ him.

7. A: Do you want to go to the movie tonight?

   B: What are you going to see?

   A: *Distant Drums.*

   B: I (see, already) _____ it. Thanks anyway.

8. I didn't go to the movie with Erin last Tuesday night. I (see, already) _____ it.

9. A: Jane? Jane! Is that you? How are you? I haven't seen you for ages!

   B: Excuse me? Are you talking to me?

   A: Oh. You're not Jane. I'm sorry. It is clear that I (make) _____ a mistake. Please excuse me.

10. Yesterday I approached a stranger who looked like Jane Moore and started talking to her. But she wasn't Jane. It was clear that I (make) _____ a mistake. I was really embarrassed.

◇ PRACTICE 21—SELFSTUDY: The past progressive vs. the past perfect. (Chart 7–10)

Directions: Choose the correct completion.

1. Amanda didn't need to study the multiplication tables in fifth grade. She __*B*__ them.
   A. was learning   B. had already learned

2. I enjoyed visiting Tommy's class. It was an arithmetic class. The students __*A*__ their multiplication tables.
   A. were learning   B. had already learned

3. While I _____ up the mountain, I got tired. But I didn't stop until I reached the top.
   A. was walking   B. had walked

4. I was very tired when I got to the top of the mountain. I _____ a long distance.
       A. was walking   B. had walked

5. I knocked. No one answered. I turned the handle and pulled sharply on the door, but it did not open. Someone _____ it.
       A. was locking   B. had locked

6. "Where were you when the earthquake occurred?"
   "In my office. I _____ to my assistant. We were working on a report."
       A. was talking   B. had already talked

7. "Ahmed's house was destroyed in the earthquake."
   "I know! It's lucky that he and his family _____ for his parents' home before the earthquake struck."
       A. were leaving   B. had already left

8. We drove two hundred miles to see the circus in Kansas City. When we got there, we couldn't find the circus. It had left town. We _____ all the way to Kansas City for nothing.
       A. were driving   B. had driven

◇ **PRACTICE 22—SELFSTUDY:** **The present perfect, past progressive, and past perfect. (Chart 7–10)**

Directions: Complete the sentences with the correct forms of the words in parentheses. Use the PRESENT PERFECT, PAST PROGRESSIVE, or PAST PERFECT.

1. When I went to bed, I turned on the radio. While I (*sleep*) _____, somebody turned it off.

2. You're from Jakarta? I (*be, never*) _____ there. I'd like to go there someday.

3. I started to tell Rodney the news, but he stopped me. He (*already, hear*) _____ _____ it.

4. When Gina went to bed, it was snowing. It (*snow, still*) _____ when she woke up in the morning.

5. Rita called me on the phone to tell me the good news. She (*pass*) _____ _____ her final exam in English.

6. I couldn't think. The people around me (*make*) _____ too much noise. Finally, I gave up and left to try to find a quiet place to work.

7. Are you still waiting for David? (*he, come, not*) _____ yet? He's really late, isn't he?

8. Otto was in the hospital last week. He (*be, never*) _____ a patient in a hospital before. It was a new experience for him.

9. A couple of weeks ago Mr. Fox, our office manager, surprised all of us. When he walked into the office, he (*wear*) _____ a bright red jacket. Everyone stopped and stared. Mr. Fox is a conservative dresser. Before that time, he (*wear, never*) _____ anything but a blue or gray suit. And he (*wear, not*) _____ that jacket again since that time. He wore it only once.

◇ **PRACTICE 23—SELFSTUDY: Verb tense review. (Chapters 1, 2, 3, and 7)**

Directions: Choose the correct completion.

1. My mother began to drive cars when she was fourteen. Now she is eighty-nine, and she still drives. She _____ cars for seventy-five years.
   A. has been driving   B. drives   C. drove   D. was driving

2. In every culture, people _____ jewelry since prehistoric times.
   A. wear   B. wore   C. have worn   D. had worn

3. It's hard for many young people to find jobs today. As a result, many young adults in their twenties and even early thirties _____ with their parents.
   A. have still lived   B. are still living   C. still lived   D. were still living

4. Australian koala bears are interesting animals. They _____ practically their entire lives in trees without ever coming down to the ground.
   A. are spending
   B. have been spending
   C. spent
   D. spend

5. If you continue to work hard and try your best, I _____ you. But if you stop working, I'm through.
   A. will help   B. am helping   C. help   D. have helped

6. It's raining hard. It _____ an hour ago and _____ yet.
   A. starts . . . doesn't stop   C. has started . . . didn't stop
   B. started . . . hasn't stopped   D. was starting . . . isn't stopping

7. Alex's bags are almost ready for his trip. He _____ for Syria later this afternoon.
   A. leave   B. left   C. has left   D. is leaving

8. I heard a slight noise, so I walked to the front door to investigate. I looked down at the floor and saw a piece of paper. Someone _____ a note under the door to my apartment.
   A. has pushed   B. is pushing   C. had pushed   D. pushed

9. I walked slowly through the market. People _____ all kinds of fruits and vegetables. I studied the prices carefully before I decided what to buy.
   A. have sold   B. sell   C. had sold   D. were selling

10. The first advertisement on radio was broadcast in 1922. Since that time, companies _____ tens of billions of dollars to advertise their products on radio and television.
   A. are spending   B. have spent   C. spent   D. spend

◇ **PRACTICE 24—GUIDED STUDY: Verb tense review. (Chapters 1, 2, 3, and 7)**

Directions: Choose the correct completion.

1. Were you at the race yesterday? I _____ you there.
   A. haven't seen   B. didn't see   C. wasn't seeing   D. don't see

2. Nicky, please don't interrupt me. I _____ to Grandma on the phone. Go play with your trucks.
   A. talk   B. have talked   C. am talking   D. have been talking

3. Now listen carefully. When Aunt Martha _____ tomorrow, give her a big hug.
   A. arrives   B. will arrive   C. arrived   D. is going to arrive

4. I _____ my glasses three times so far this year. One time I dropped them on a cement floor. Another time I sat on them. And this time I stepped on them.
    A. broke   B. was breaking   C. have broken   D. have been breaking

5. Kate reached to the floor and picked up her glasses. They were broken. She _____ on them.
    A. stepped   B. had stepped   C. was stepping   D. has stepped

6. Sarah gets angry easily. She _____ a bad temper ever since she was a child.
    A. has   B. will have   C. had   D. has had

7. Now, whenever Sarah starts to lose her temper, she _____ a deep breath and _____ to ten.
    A. takes . . . counts   C. took . . . counted
    B. has taken . . . counted   D. is taking . . . counting

8. I unlocked my door and walked into my apartment. I was surprised to see my nephew there. He _____ in the middle of the front room. He _____ in through an open window in the bathroom. I demanded to know why he was in my apartment.
    A. stood . . . was coming   C. was standing . . . came
    B. stood . . . came   D. was standing . . . had come

9. Ever since I told Ted about my illness, he _____ me. Why are people like that?
    A. is avoiding   B. avoided   C. avoids   D. has been avoiding

10. The phone rang, so I _____ it up and _____ hello.
    A. picked . . . had said   C. was picking . . . said
    B. picked . . . said   D. was picking . . . had said

◇ **PRACTICE 25—SELFSTUDY: Prepositions. (Chapter 7; Appendix 1)**

Directions: Complete each sentence with the appropriate preposition.

1. Please don't argue. I insist ___**on**___ lending you the money for your vacation.

2. That thin coat you're wearing won't protect you _____ the bitter, cold wind.

3. A: What's the matter? Don't you approve _____ my behavior?

   B: No, I don't. I think you are rude.

4. A: Can I depend _____ you to pick up my mother at the airport tomorrow?

   B: Of course you can!

5. A: The police arrested a thief in my uncle's store yesterday.

   B: What's going to happen _____ him? Will he go to jail?

6. My friend Ken apologized _____ me _____ forgetting to pick me up in his car after the movie last night. I forgave him _____ leaving me outside the theater in the rain, but I'm not going to rely _____ him for transportation in the future.

7. A: Thank you _____ helping me move to my new apartment last weekend.

   B: You're welcome.

8. It isn't fair to compare Mr. Carlson _____ Ms. Anders. They're both good teachers, but they have different teaching methods.

9. I've had a bad cold for a week and just can't get rid _____ it.

10. Excuse me _____ interrupting you, but I have a call on the other line. Could I get back to you in a second?

CHAPTER **8**
Count/Noncount Nouns and Articles

◇ **PRACTICE 1—SELFSTUDY:** Count and noncount nouns. (Charts 8–1 and 8–2)

Directions: Identify count and noncount nouns.
- Write the word **ONE** in the blank if possible.
  NOTE: *One* is a number. It is used with singular count nouns.
- If it is not correct to use the word *one*, write a slash (/) in the blank.
  NOTE: *One* cannot be used with noncount nouns. A *noncount noun* is called a "noncount noun" because you can't "count" it with numbers *one, two, three*, etc.

1. I have ____/____ **furniture** in my apartment.	*furniture* →	count	(noncount)
2. I have ___*one*___ **table** in my apartment.	*table* →	(count)	noncount
3. Rita is wearing _____ **ring** on her left hand.	*ring* →	count	noncount
4. Rita is wearing _____ **jewelry** on her left hand.	*jewelry* →	count	noncount
5. I have _____ **homework** to do tonight.	*homework* →	count	noncount
6. I have _____ **assignment** to do.	*assignment* →	count	noncount
7. I have _____ **job** to finish.	*job* →	count	noncount
8. I have _____ **work** to do.	*work* →	count	noncount
9. I asked _____ **question**.	*question* →	count	noncount
10. I was looking for _____ **information**.	*information* →	count	noncount
11. I learned _____ new **word** today.	*word* →	count	noncount
12. I learn _____ new **vocabulary** every day.	*vocabulary* →	count	noncount

◇ **PRACTICE 2—SELFSTUDY:** Count and noncount nouns: *a/an* and *some*.
(Charts 8–1 and 8–2)

Directions: Complete the sentences with **A/AN** (for count nouns) or **SOME** (for noncount nouns).

1. I bought ___*some*___ **furniture** for my apartment.
2. I bought _____*a*_____ **table** for my apartment.
3. Rita is wearing _____ **ring** on her left hand.
4. Rita is wearing _____ **jewelry** on her left hand.
5. I have _____ **homework** to do tonight.
6. I have _____ **assignment** to do.
7. I have _____ **job** to finish.
8. I have _____ **work** to do.

9. I asked _____ **question**.

10. I was looking for _____ **information**.

11. I learned _____ new **word** today.

12. I learn _____ new **vocabulary** every day.

◇ PRACTICE 3—SELFSTUDY: Count and noncount nouns: adding *-s*. (Charts 8–1 and 8–2)

Directions: Add *-s* if possible. Otherwise, write a slash (/) in the blank.

1. I bought **some furniture** _/_ for my apartment.

2. I bought **some table**____ for my apartment.

3. Rita is wearing **some ring** ____ on her left hand.

4. Rita is wearing **some jewelry**____ on her left hand.

5. I have **some homework** ____ to do tonight.

6. I have **some assignment**____ to do.

7. I have **some job**____ to finish.

8. I have **some work** ____ to do.

9. I asked **some question** ____.

10. I was looking for **some information** ____.

11. I learned **some new word** ____ today.

12. I learn **some new vocabulary**____ every day.

◇ PRACTICE 4—SELFSTUDY: Count and noncount nouns: using *two*. (Charts 8-1 and 8-2)

Directions: Change **SOME** to **TWO** if possible. Otherwise, write nothing.

1. I bought **some furniture** for my apartment. (*no change*)

2. I bought ~~some~~ *two* **tables** for my apartment.

3. Rita is wearing **some rings** on her left hand.

4. Rita is wearing **some jewelry** on her left hand.

5. I have **some homework** to do tonight.

6. I have **some assignments** to do.

7. I have **some jobs** to finish.

8. I have **some work** to do.

9. I asked **some questions**.

10. I was looking for **some information**.

11. I learned **some new words** today.

12. I learn **some new vocabulary** every day.

◇ **PRACTICE 5—SELFSTUDY:** Count and noncount nouns: using *a lot of.* (Charts 8–1 and 8–2)

Directions: Change **SOME** to **A LOT OF** if possible. Otherwise, write nothing.

a lot of
1. I bought ~~some~~ **furniture** for my apartment.

a lot of
2. I bought ~~some~~ **tables** for my apartment.

3. Rita is wearing **some rings** on her left hand.

4. Rita is wearing **some jewelry** on her left hand.

5. I have **some homework** to do tonight.

6. I have **some assignments** to do.

7. I have **some jobs** to finish.

8. I have **some work** to do.

9. I asked **some questions**.

10. I was looking for **some information**.

11. I learned **some** new **words** today.

12. I learn **some** new **vocabulary** every day.

◇ **PRACTICE 6—SELFSTUDY:** Count and noncount nouns: using *too many* and *too much.* (Charts 8–1 and 8–2)

Directions: Complete the sentences with **MANY** or **MUCH**.

1. I bought too ___*much*___ **furniture** for my apartment.

2. I bought too ___*many*___ **tables** for my apartment.

3. Rita is wearing too _____ **rings** on her left hand.

4. Rita is wearing too _____ **jewelry** on her left hand.

5. I can't go to a movie tonight. I have too _____

   homework to do.

6. I have too _____ **assignments** to do.
   I can't finish all of them.

7. I have too _____ **jobs** to finish. I can't do all of them.

8. I have too _____ **work** to do. I can't finish all of it.

9. The child asked too _____ **questions**. I couldn't answer all of them.

10. I can't remember everything I read in the encyclopedia. There is too _____

    information for me to remember all of it.

11. Sam's writing is wordy. He uses too _____ **words** when he writes.

12. The teacher asked us to learn too _____ new **vocabulary**. I couldn't remember all the

    new words.

◇ **PRACTICE 7—SELFSTUDY:** Count and noncount nouns: using *a few* and *a little*.
(Charts 8–1 and 8–2)

Directions: Complete the sentences with **A FEW** or **A LITTLE**.

1. I bought _____*a little*_____ **furniture** for my apartment.
2. I bought _____*a few*_____ **tables** for my apartment.
3. Rita is wearing _____ **rings** on her left hand.
4. Rita is wearing _____ **jewelry** on her left hand.
5. I have _____ **homework** to do tonight.
6. I have _____ **assignments** to do.
7. I have _____ **jobs** to finish.
8. I have _____ **work** to do.
9. I asked _____ **questions**.
10. I was looking for _____ **information**.
11. I learned _____ new **words** today.
12. I learn _____ new **vocabulary** every day.

◇ **PRACTICE 8—SELFSTUDY:** *A* vs. *an*: singular count nouns. (Charts 8–1 and 8–2)

Directions: Write **A** or **AN** in the blanks.

1. _____ game		13. _____ eye
2. _____ rock		14. _____ new car
3. _____ store		15. _____ old car
4. _____ army		16. _____ used car
5. _____ egg		17. _____ uncle
6. _____ island		18. _____ house
7. _____ ocean		19. _____ honest mistake
8. _____ umbrella		20. _____ hospital
9. _____ university*		21. _____ hand
10. _____ horse		22. _____ aunt
11. _____ hour**		23. _____ ant
12. _____ star		24. _____ neighbor

A university, a unit, a uniform, a union: these nouns begin with a consonant sound, so *a* (not *an*) is used. *An uncle, an umbrella, an umpire, an urge*: these nouns begin with a vowel sound, so *an* (not *a*) is used.

**If the "h" is silent, *an* is used: *an hour, an honor, an honest person*. Usually the "h" is pronounced and *a* is used: *a holiday, a hotel, a hero, a high point, a home*, etc.

◇ **PRACTICE 9—SELFSTUDY:** *A/an* vs. *some*. (Charts 8–1 → 8–3)

Directions: Complete the sentences with **SOME** or **A/AN**.

1. I wrote _____*a*_____ **letter**.
2. I got _____*some*_____ **mail**.
3. We bought _____ **equipment** for our camping trip.
4. You need _____ **tool** to cut wood.
5. I ate _____ **food**.
6. I had _____ **apple**.
7. I wore _____ old **clothing**.
8. I wore _____ old **shirt**.
9. Jim asked me for _____ **advice**.
10. I gave Jim _____ **suggestion**.
11. I read _____ interesting **story** in the paper.
12. The paper has _____ interesting **news** today.
13. I read _____ **poem** after dinner.
14. I read _____ **poetry** after dinner.
15. I know _____ **song** from India.
16. I know _____ Indian **music**.
17. I learned _____ new **idiom**.
18. I learned _____ new **slang**.

◇ **PRACTICE 10—SELFSTUDY:** Count and noncount nouns. (Charts 8–1 → 8–3)

Directions: Add final **-S/-ES** if possible. Otherwise, write a slash (/) in the blank.

1. I'm learning a lot of **grammar**_/_.
2. We're studying count and noncount **noun** _s_.
3. Olga knows several **language**____.
4. Olga has learned a lot of **English** ____.
5. Sara doesn't like to wear **makeup**____.
6. We enjoyed the **scenery**____ in the countryside.
7. Colorado has high **mountain** ____.
8. City streets usually have a lot of **traffic**____.
9. The streets are full of **automobile**____.
10. I had **sand** ____ in my shoes from walking on the beach.
11. The air was full of **dust** ____ from the wind storm.
12. Florida is famous for its white sand **beach** ____.
13. I've learned a lot of **slang** ____ from my new friends.
14. I made a lot of **mistake**____ on my last composition.
15. I have some important **information** ____ for you.

16. I have some important **fact**____ for you.

17. My favorite team has won a lot of **game**____ this year.

18. Thailand and India have a lot of hot **weather**____.

19. We heard a lot of **thunder**____ during the storm.

20. I drink a lot of **water**____ when the weather is hot.

21. Both of my **parent** ____ have very good **health** ____.

22. A **circle**____ has 360 **degree**____.

23. **Professor**____ have a lot of **knowledge**____ about their fields of study.

24. Everyone in my **family**____ wished me a lot a **luck** ____.

25. I thanked my two **neighbor**____ for their **help**____.

26. Sometimes **factory**____* cause **pollution** ____.

27. Parents take **pride** ____ in the success of their **children** ____.**

28. I admire **people**____ who use their **intelligence**____ to the fullest extent.

◇ **PRACTICE 11—GUIDED STUDY: Count and noncount nouns. (Chart 4–1 and 8–1 → 8–3)**

Directions: Add final -**S**/-**ES** as necessary. Do not make any other changes. The number in parentheses at the end of each section is the number of nouns that need final -*s/-es*.

1. ~~Plant~~ *Plants* are the oldest living ~~thing~~ *things* on earth. (2) = (2 nouns need final -*s/-es*)

2. Scientist divide living thing into two group: plant and animal. Generally speaking, plant stay in one place, but animal move around. (7)

3. Flower, grass, and tree grow every place where people live. Plant also grow in desert, in ocean, on mountaintop, and in polar region. (7)

4. Plant are useful to people. We eat them. We use them for clothing. We build house from them. Plant are also important to our health. We get many kind of beneficial drug from plant. In addition, plant provide beauty and enjoyment to all our life. (8)

5. Crop are plant that people grow for food. Nature can ruin crop. Bad weather—such as too much rain or too little rain—can destroy field of corn or wheat. Natural disaster such as flood and storm have caused farmer many problem since people first began to grow their own food. (9)

6. Food is a necessity for all living thing. All animal and plant need to eat. Most plant take what they need through their root and their leaf. The majority of insect live solely on plant. Many bird have a diet of worm and insect. Reptile eat small animal, egg, and insect. (15)

---

*See Chart 4–1 for variations in the spelling of words with a final -*s*.
**Some nouns have irregular plurals. See Chart 4–1.

◇ PRACTICE 12—GUIDED STUDY: Count and noncount nouns. (Charts 8–1 → 8–3)

Directions: Choose one or more of the given topics. MAKE A LIST of the things you see. Use expressions of quantity when appropriate.

Example: I'm sitting in my office. These are the things I see:
- *two windows*
- *three desk lamps*
- *a lot of books—around 200 books about English grammar*
- *office equipment—a Macintosh computer, a printer, a photocopy machine*
- *typical office supplies—a stapler, paper clips, pens, pencils, a ruler, disks*
- *some photographs—three pictures of my daughter, one of my husband, one of my parents, two photos of my editors, and several pictures of good friends*
- *Etc.*

1. Sit in any room of your choosing. List the things you see (including things other people are wearing if you wish).
2. Look out a window. List the things and people you see.
3. Go to a place outdoors (a park, a zoo, a city street) and list what you see.
4. Travel in your imagination to a room you lived in when you were a child. List everything you can remember about that room.

◇ PRACTICE 13—SELFSTUDY: *How many* and *how much*. (Charts 8–1 → 8–3; 4–1; and 6–2)

Directions: Complete the questions with MANY or MUCH. Add final -S/-ES if necessary to make a noun plural. (Some of the count nouns have irregular plural forms.) If a verb is needed, choose the correct one from the parentheses. If final -S/-ES is not necessary, put a slash (/) in the blank.

1. How ___*many*___ letter__*s*__ (is, (are)) there in the English alphabet?[1]
2. How ___*much*___ mail ___/___ did you get yesterday?
3. How ___*many*___ man _*men*_ (has, (have)) a full beard at least once in their life?
4. How ___*many*___ family _*ies*_ (is, (are)) there in your apartment building?
5. How _____ word _____ (is, are) there in this sentence?
6. How _____ sentence_____ (is, are) there in this exercise?
7. How _____ chalk_____ (is, are) there in the classroom?
8. How _____ English _____ does Stefan know?
9. How _____ English **literature**_____ have you studied?
10. How _____ English **word** _____ do you know?
11. How _____ **gasoline**_____ does it take to fill the tank in your car?

    (*British*: How _____ **petrol** _____ does it take to fill the tank?)
12. How _____ **homework** _____ did the teacher assign?
13. How _____ **grandchild** _____ does Mrs. Cunningham have?
14. How _____ **page**_____ (is, are) there in this book?
15. How _____ **library**_____ (is, are) there in the U.S.?[2]

---

[1]Answer: twenty-six (26) = There are twenty-six letters in the English alphabet.
[2]Answer: approximately fifteen thousand (15,000).

16. How _____ **bone**_____ (*is, are*) there in the human body?[3]

17. How _____ **tooth** _____ does the average person have?[4]

18. How _____ **water**_____ do you drink every day?

19. How _____ **cup** _____ of tea do you usually drink in an average day?

20. How _____ **tea** _____ do you usually drink in an average day?

21. How _____ **glass** _____ of water do you drink every day?

22. How _____ **fun** _____ did you have at the amusement park?

23. How _____ **education** _____ does Ms. Martinez have?

24. How _____ **soap** _____ should I use in the dishwasher?

25. How _____ **island** _____ (*is, are*) there in Indonesia?[5]

26. How _____ **people**_____ (*was, were*) there on earth 2,000 years ago?[6]

27. How _____ **human being** _____ (*is are*) there in the world today?[7]

28. How _____ **people**_____ will there be by the year 2030?[8]

29. How _____ **zero** _____ (*is, are*) there in a billion?[9]

30. How _____ **butterfly**_____ can you see in one hour on a summer day in a flower garden?

◇ **PRACTICE 14—SELFSTUDY:** *A few* vs. *a little.* (Charts 8–1 → 8–3)

Directions: Complete the sentences with **A FEW** or **A LITTLE**. Add a final **-S** to the noun if necessary. Otherwise, write a slash (/) in the blank.

1. Let's listen to _____*a little*_____ **music** _/_ during dinner.

2. Let's sing _____*a few*_____ **song** _s_ around the campfire.

3. We all need _____ **help**___ at times.

4. Ingrid is from Sweden, but she knows _____ **English**___.

5. I need _____ more **apple**___ to make a pie.

6. I like _____ **honey**___ in my coffee.

7. I have a problem. Could you give me _____ **advice**___ ?

8. I need _____ **suggestion** ___.

9. He asked _____ **question** ___.

10. We talked to _____ **people**___ on the plane.

11. Please give me _____ more **minute**___.

12. Ann opened the curtains to let in _____ **light** ___ from outdoors.

13. I have _____ **homework** ___ to do tonight.

[3]Answer: two hundred and six (206).
[4]Answer: thirty-two (32).
[5]Answer: more than thirteen thousand seven hundred (13,700).
[6]Answer: approximately two hundred and fifty million (250,000,000).
[7]Answer: around six billion (6,000,000,000).
[8]Answer: estimated at more than twelve billion (12,000,000,000).
[9]Answer: nine (9).

◇ **PRACTICE 15—SELFSTUDY:** *How many* and *how much.* (Charts 8–1 → 8–4; 4–1; and 6–2)

Directions: Make questions with **HOW MANY** or **HOW MUCH**. Use the information in parentheses to form Speaker A's question.

1. A: How *How many children do the Millers have?*
   B: Three. (The Millers have three children.)

2. A: How *How much money does Jake make?*
   B: A lot. (Jake makes a lot of money.)

3. A: How _____
   B: Eleven. (There are eleven players on a soccer team.)

4. A: How _____
   B: Just a little. (I have just a little homework tonight.)

5. A: How _____
   B: 5,280. (There are 5,280 feet in a mile.)*

6. A: How _____
   B: 1,000. (There are 1,000 meters/metres in a kilometer/kilometre.)

7. A: How _____
   B: Three. (I took three suitcases on the plane to Florida.)

8. A: How _____
   B: A lot. (I took a lot of suntan oil with me.)

9. A: How _____
   B: Two pairs. (I took two pairs of sandals.)

10. A: How _____
    B: One tube. (I took one tube of toothpaste.)

11. A: How _____
    B: Just a short time, only two hours. (The flight took two hours.)

12. A: How _____
    B: Three. (I've been in Florida three times.)

13. A: How _____
    B: A lot. (There are a lot of apples in the two baskets.)

14. A: How _____
    B: A lot. (There is a lot of fruit in the two baskets.)

_____
*1 foot = 30 centimeters/centimetres; 1 mile = 1.6 kilometers/kilometres.

◇ PRACTICE 16—SELFSTUDY: Units of measure with noncount nouns. (Chart 8–5)

Directions: What units of measure are usually used with the following nouns? More than one unit of measure can be used with some of the nouns.

PART I: You are going to the store. What are you going to buy? Choose from these units of measure:

bag   bottle   box   can (tin)*   jar

1. a ___can/jar___ of olives
2. a ___box___ of breakfast cereal
3. a _____ of mineral water
4. a _____ of jam or jelly
5. a _____ of tuna fish
6. a _____ of crackers
7. a _____ of soup
8. a _____ of sugar
9. a _____ of wine
10. a _____ of corn
11. a _____ of peas
12. a _____ of flour
13. a _____ of soda pop**
14. a _____ of paint

PART II: You are hungry and thirsty. What are you going to have? Choose from these units of measure:

bowl   cup   glass   piece   slice

15. a ___cup/glass___ of green tea
16. a ___bowl___ of breakfast cereal
17. a _____ of cantaloupe
18. a _____ of bread
19. a _____ of apple pie
20. a _____ of orange juice
21. a _____ of soup
22. a _____ of candy
23. a _____ of beer
24. a _____ of noodles
25. a _____ of mineral water
26. a _____ of popcorn
27. a _____ of cheese on a cracker
28. a _____ of rice
29. a _____ of strawberries and ice cream

◇ PRACTICE 17—GUIDED STUDY: Units of measure with noncount nouns. (Chart 8–5)

Directions: What units of measure are usually used with the following nouns? More than one unit of measure can be used with some of the nouns.

You are going to the store. What are you going to buy? Choose from these units of measure:

bag   bottle   box   can (tin)   jar

1. a _____ of pickles
2. a _____ of aspirin
3. a _____ of laundry detergent
4. a _____ of instant coffee
5. a _____ of sardines
6. a _____ of sugar
7. a _____ of peanut butter
8. a _____ of soy sauce
9. a _____ of uncooked noodles
10. a _____ of refried beans

---

*a can = a tin in British English.

**Soda pop refers to sweet carbonated beverages (also called "soft drinks"). This kind of drink is called "soda" in some parts of the United States, but "pop" in other parts of the country.

◇ PRACTICE 18—GUIDED STUDY: *How many* and *how much.*
                              (Charts 8–1 → 8–3; 4–1; and 6–2)

Directions: Pair up with another student.

PART I: Pretend you are going on a trip. Make a list of ten or so things you are going to take. Exchange your list with your partner. Using your partner's list, ask **HOW MANY** or **HOW MUCH** of each item she/he is going to take on her/his trip.

Example: STUDENT A's list: **suitcases, money, a passport, shoes** (etc.)
STUDENT B: How many suitcases are you going to take?
STUDENT A: Two.
STUDENT B: How much money?
STUDENT A: Three hundred dollars.
STUDENT B: How many passports?
STUDENT A: Just one, of course.
STUDENT B: How many pairs of shoes?
STUDENT A: Etc.

PART II: Look at the shopping list.
STUDENT A: Ask your partner **HOW MANY** or **HOW MUCH** of each item he/she is going to buy.
STUDENT B: Make up a reasonable answer.

SHOPPING LIST
coffee
chicken or steak
potatoes
rice
shoes
toothpaste
bath soap
light bulbs
notebook paper
(rolls of) film
bread
mustard

PART III: Pretend you are going on a shopping trip. Make a list of ten or so things you are going to buy. Exchange your list with your partner. Using your partner's list, ask questions using **HOW MANY, HOW MUCH, WHAT KIND OF,** or any other question that occurs to you.

◇ PRACTICE 19—GUIDED STUDY: Count and noncount nouns. (Charts 8–1 → 8–3)

Directions: In several paragraphs, describe the perfect meal. Use your imagination. If you use the name of a dish that your reader is probably unfamiliar with, describe it in parentheses.

Example:
        I'm going to imagine for you the perfect meal. I am on a terrace high on a hillside in Nepal. When I look out, I see snow-capped mountains in the distance. The valley below is hazy and beautiful. I'm with my friends Olga and Roberto. The table has a white tablecloth and a vase of blue flowers. I'm going to eat all of my favorite kinds of food.
        First the waiter is going to bring escargots. (Escargots are snails cooked in butter and seasoned with garlic and other herbs). Etc.

◇ **PRACTICE 20—SELFSTUDY: Noncount abstractions. (Chart 8-3)**

Directions: Complete the sentence in COLUMN A with words from COLUMN B. The completed sentences will be common sayings in English.

COLUMN A

1. Ignorance is __D__
2. Honesty is _____
3. Time is _____
4. Laughter is _____
5. Beauty is _____
6. Knowledge is _____
7. Experience is _____

COLUMN B

A. the best teacher.
B. the best medicine.
C. power.
✔D. bliss.*
E. in the eye of the beholder.
F. money.
G. the best policy.

◇ **PRACTICE 21—GUIDED STUDY: Noncount abstractions. (Chart 8-3)**

Directions: In groups (or by yourself), complete the lists with ABSTRACT NOUNS.

a. Name six good qualities you admire in a person.

1. ____*patience*____   4. _____
2. _____   5. _____
3. _____   6. _____

b. Name five bad qualities people can have.

1. ____*greed*____   4. _____
2. _____   5. _____
3. _____

c. What conditions, goals, and values is it important for a country to have?

1. ____*prosperity*____   4. _____
2. _____   5. _____
3. _____

d. Certain bad conditions exist in the world. What are they?

1. ____*hunger*____   4. _____
2. _____   5. _____
3. _____

After you finish the lists, answer this question: How many of the nouns in your lists can be made plural with a final -s/-es? Add -s/-es to the nouns if possible.

_____

*"Ignorance is bliss" is a saying. It means: If you know about problems, you have to worry about them and solve them. If you don't know about problems, you can avoid them and be happy (*bliss* = *happiness*). Many people do not believe that this saying is true. What do you think?

◇ **PRACTICE 22—SELFSTUDY:** Using *a* or *ø* for generalizations. (Chart 8-6)

Directions: Write **A** or **Ø** in the blank before each singular noun. Then write a sentence with the plural form of the noun if possible.

SINGULAR SUBJECTS	PLURAL SUBJECTS
1. __A__ bird has feathers.	1. ____ *Birds have feathers.*
2. __Ø__ corn is nutritious.	2. ____ *(none possible)*
3. ____ milk is white.	3. _____
4. ____ flower is beautiful.	4. _____
5. ____ water is a clear liquid.	5. _____
6. ____ horse is strong.	6. _____
7. ____ jewelry is expensive.	7. _____
8. ____ honey comes from bees.	8. _____
9. ____ shirt has sleeves.	9. _____
10. ____ soap produces bubbles.	10. _____

◇ **PRACTICE 23—SELFSTUDY:** Using *a* or *some*. (Chart 8-6)

Directions: Write **A** or **SOME** in the blank before each singular noun. Then write a sentence with the plural form of the noun if possible.

SINGULAR OBJECTS	PLURAL OBJECTS
1. I saw ___*a*___ bird.	1. ____ *I saw some birds.*
2. I ate ___*some*___ corn.	2. ____ *(none possible)*
3. Would you like _____ milk?	3. _____
4. I picked _____ flower.	4. _____
5. I drank _____ water.	5. _____
6. I fed grass to _____ horse.	6. _____
7. Pat is wearing _____ jewelry.	7. _____
8. I bought _____ honey.	8. _____
9. Tom bought _____ new shirt.	9. _____
10. I need _____ soap to wash the dishes.	10. _____

◇ **PRACTICE 24—SELFSTUDY:** *A/an* vs. *the*: singular count nouns. (Chart 8-6)

Directions: Complete the sentences with **A/AN** or **THE**.

1. A: ___*A*___ dog makes a good pet.

   B: I agree.

2. A: Did you feed ___*the*___ dog?

   B: Yes, I did.

3. A: Let's listen to _____ radio.

   B: Okay. I'll turn it on.

4. A: Does your car have _____ radio?

   B: Yes, and _____ tape player.

5. My dorm room has _____ desk, _____ bed, _____ chest of drawers, and two chairs.

6. A: Jessica, where's the stapler?

   B: On _____ desk. If it's not there, look in _____ top drawer.

7. A: Sara, put your bike in _____ basement before dark.

   B: Okay, Dad.

8. Our apartment building has _____ basement. Sara keeps her bike there at night.

9. Every sentence has _____ subject and _____ verb.

10. Look at this sentence: *Jack lives in Miami*. What is _____ subject and what is _____ verb?

11. A: I can't see you at four. I'll be in _____ meeting then. How about four-thirty?

    B: Fine.

12. A: What time does _____ meeting start Tuesday?

    B: Eight.

13. Jack's car ran out of gas. He had to walk _____ long distance to find _____ telephone and call his brother for help.

14. _____ distance from _____ sun to _____ earth is 93,000,000 miles.

15. A: Jake, _____ telephone is ringing. Can you get it?

    B: Sure.

16. A: I have _____ question.

    B: Okay. What do you want to know?

17. A: Ms. Ming, you have to help me!

    B: Calm down. What's _____ problem?

18. A: I wrote _____ poem. Would you like to read it?

    B: Sure. What's it about?

19. A: Was _____ lecture interesting?

    B: Yes. _____ speaker gave _____ interesting talk.

20. A: Where should we go for _____ cup of coffee after class?

    B: Let's go to _____ cafe around _____ corner from the First National Bank.

◇ **PRACTICE 25 —SELFSTUDY:** ø vs. *the*: plural count nouns and noncount nouns. (Chart 8–6)

Directions: Write Ø or **THE** in the blanks.

1. A: _____Ø_____ dogs make good pets.

    B: I agree.

2. A: Did you feed _____*the*_____ dogs?

    B: Yes, I did.

3. A: _____Ø_____ fruit is good for you.

    B: I agree.

4. A: _____*The*_____ fruit in this bowl is ripe.

    B: Good. I think I'll have a piece.

5. As every parent knows, _____ children require a lot of time and attention.

6. A: Frank, where are _____ children?

    B: Next door at the Jacksons.

7. _____ paper is made from _____ trees or other plants.

8. _____ paper in my notebook is lined.

9. A: Mom, please pass _____ potatoes.

    B: Here you are. Anything else? Want some more chicken, too?

10. _____ potatoes are _____ vegetables.

11. _____ nurses are trained to care for sick and injured people.

12. When I was in Memorial Hospital, _____ nurses were wonderful.

13. _____ frogs are _____ small animals without _____ tails that live on

    land or in water. _____ turtles also live on land or in water, but they have

    _____ tails and _____ hard shells.

14. A: Nicole, what are those animals doing in here!?

    B: We're playing. _____ frogs belong to Jason. _____ turtles are mine.

15. There are many kinds of _____ books. We use _____ textbooks and _____ workbooks in school. We use _____ dictionaries and _____ encyclopedias for reference. For _____ entertainment, we read _____ novels and _____ poetry.

16. _____ books on this desk are mine.

17. All of our food comes from _____ plants. Some food, such as _____ fruit and _____ vegetables, comes directly from _____ plants. Other food, such as _____ meat, comes indirectly from _____ plants.

18. I'm not very good at keeping houseplants alive. _____ plants in my apartment have to be tough. They survive in spite of me.

19. A: What do you want to be when you grow up?

    B: _____ engineer.

    A: Really? Why?

    B: Because _____ engineers build _____ bridges.

    A: That's right. And where do they build bridges?

    B: Across _____ rivers, across _____ valleys, across _____ highways, across _____ railroad tracks, and across _____ other places I can't think of right now.

20. There was a bad earthquake in my city. I couldn't drive from my side of the city to the other side because _____ bridges across the river were unsafe. All of them had been damaged in the quake.

◇ **PRACTICE 26—SELFSTUDY:**   Using *the* for second mention. (Chart 8–6)

Directions: Write A/AN, SOME, or THE in the blanks.

1. I had ____*a*____ banana and ____*an*____ apple. I gave ____*the*____ banana to Mary. I ate ____*the*____ apple.

2. I had ___*some*___ bananas and ___*some*___ apples. I gave ____*the*____ bananas to Mary. I ate ____*the*____ apples.

3. I drank ___*some*___ coffee and ___*some*___ milk. ___*The*___ coffee was hot. _____ milk was cold.

4. I have _____ desk and _____ bed in my room. _____ desk is hard. _____ bed is hard, too, even though it's supposed to be soft.

5. I forgot to bring my things with me to class yesterday, so I borrowed _____ pen and _____ paper from Joe. I returned _____ pen, but I used _____ paper for my homework.

6. I bought _____ bag of flour and _____ sugar to make _____ cookies. _____ sugar was okay, but I had to return _____ flour. When I opened _____ flour, I found _____ little bugs in it. I took it back to the people at the store and showed them _____ little bugs. They gave me _____ new bag of flour. _____ new bag didn't have any bugs in it.

7. Yesterday while I was walking to work, I saw _____ birds in _____ tree. I also saw _____ cat under _____ tree. _____ birds didn't pay any attention to _____ cat, but _____ cat was watching _____ birds intently.

8. Once upon a time, _____ princess fell in love with _____ prince. _____ princess wanted to marry _____ prince, who lived in a distant land. She summoned _____ messenger to take _____ things to _____ prince to show him her love. _____ messenger took _____ jewels and _____ robe made of yellow and red silk to _____ prince. _____ princess anxiously awaited _____ messenger's return. She hoped that _____ prince would send her _____ tokens of his love. But when _____ messenger returned, he brought back _____ jewels and _____ beautiful silk robe that _____ princess had sent. Why? Why? she wondered. Then _____ messenger told her: _____ prince already had _____ wife.

◇ **PRACTICE 27—GUIDED STUDY:** Using *the* for second mention. (Chart 8–6)

Directions: Write **A/AN**, **SOME**, or **THE** in the blanks.

(1)   One day last month while I was driving through the countryside, I saw _____ man

(2) and _____ truck next to _____ covered bridge. _____ bridge crossed

(3) _____ small river. I stopped and asked _____ man, "What's the matter? Can I be

(4) of help?"

(5)   "Well," said _____ man, "my truck is about a half inch* too tall. Or _____

(6) top of _____ bridge is a half inch too short. Either way, my truck won't fit under

(7) _____ bridge."

(8)   "Hmmm. There must be _____ solution to this problem," I said.

(9)   "I don't know. I guess I'll have to turn around and take another route."

(10)   After a few moments of thought, I said, "Aha! I have _____ solution!"

(11)   "What is it?" said _____ man.

(12)   "Let a little air out of your tires. Then _____ truck won't be too tall and you can

(13) cross _____ bridge over _____ river."

(14)   "Hey, that's _____ great idea. Let's try it!" So _____ man let a little air out

(15) of _____ tires and was able to cross _____ river and be on his way.

◇ **PRACTICE 28—SELFSTUDY:** Summary: *A/an* vs. ø vs. *the*. (Chart 8–6)

Directions: Write **A/AN**, **Ø**, or **THE** in the blanks.

1. A: What would you like for breakfast?

    B: _____*An*_____ egg and some toast.

    A: How would you like _____*the*_____ egg?

    B: Fried, sunny side up.

———————
*One-half inch = 1.27 centimeters.

2. _____Ø_____ eggs are nutritious.

3. It is _____ scientific fact: _____ steam rises when _____ water boils.

4. A: I'm looking for _____ tape player. Where is it?

   B: It's on one of _____ shelves next to my desk.

   A: Ah! There it is. Thanks.

   B: You're welcome.

   A: Hmmm. I don't think it works. Maybe _____ batteries are dead.

5. _____ chalk is _____ necessity in a classroom.

6. A: Where'd _____ plumber go? _____ sink's still leaking!

   B: Relax. He went to shut off _____ water supply to _____ house. He'll fix
   _____ leak when he gets back.

7. _____ water is essential to human life, but don't drink _____ water in the Flat
   River. It'll kill you! _____ pollution in that river is terrible.

8. A: How did you get here? Did you walk?

   B: No, I took _____ taxi.

9. A: We're ready to go, kids. Get in _____ car.

   B: Just _____ minute! We forgot something.

   A: Marge, can you get _____ kids in _____ car, please?

   B: Just _____ minute, Harry. They're coming.

10. _____ newspapers are _____ important source of _____ information.

11. _____ sun is _____ star. We need _____ sun for _____ heat,
    _____ light, and _____ energy.

12. _____ ducks are my favorite farm animals.

13. A: Where's _____ letter I wrote to Ted?

    B: It's gone. _____ strong wind blew it on _____ floor, and _____ dog
    tore it up. I threw _____ scraps in _____ wastebasket.

14. _____ efficient transportation system is _____ essential part of a healthy
    economy.

15. A: Did you set _____ alarm?

    B: Yes.

    A: Did you lock _____ door?

    B: Yes.

    A: Did you check _____ stove?

    B: Yes.

    A: Did you close all _____ windows?

    B: Yes.

    A: Then let's turn out _____ lights.

    B: Goodnight, dear.

16. Karen is _____ exceptionally talented person.

17. A: Can I have some money, Dad?

B: What for?

A: I want to go to the movies with my friends and hang around the mall.

B: What you need is a job! _____ money doesn't grow on _____ trees, you know.

18. A doctor cures _____ sick people. _____ farmer grows _____ crops. _____ architect designs _____ buildings. _____ artist creates _____ new ways of looking at _____ world and _____ life.

19. _____ earthquakes are _____ relatively rare events in central Africa.

20. My city experienced _____ earthquake recently. I was riding my bicycle when _____ earthquake occurred. _____ ground beneath me trembled so hard that it shook me off my bike.

◇ **PRACTICE 29—GUIDED STUDY:** Summary: *A/an* vs. *ø* vs. *the.* (Chart 8–6)

Directions: Complete the sentences with **A/AN**, **Ø**, or **THE**.

1. _____ good food keeps us healthy and adds _____ pleasure to our lives.

2. A: What is your favorite food?

B: _____ ice cream—it's cold, sweet, and smooth.

3. _____ pizza originated in Italy. It is a pie with _____ cheese, _____ tomatoes, and other things on top. _____ "pizza" is _____ Italian word for _____ "pie."

4. A: Hey, Nick. Pass _____ pizza. I want another piece.

B: There're only two pieces left. You take _____ big piece, and I'll take _____ small one.

5. We had _____ steamed rice, _____ fish, and _____ vegetables for lunch yesterday. _____ rice was cooked just right. _____ fish was very tasty. _____ vegetables were fresh.

6. A: Well, are you ready to leave?

   B: Let me take just one last sip of coffee. I've really enjoyed this meal.

   A: I agree. _____ food was excellent—especially _____ fish. And _____ service was exceptionally good. Let's leave _____ waitress _____ good tip.

   B: I usually tip around fifteen percent, sometimes eighteen percent.

7. Only one of _____ continents in _____ world is uninhabited. Which one?

8. Last week, I took _____ easy exam. It was in my economics class. I had _____ right answers for all of _____ questions on _____ exam. My score was 100%.

9. Generally speaking, anyone who goes to _____ job interview should wear _____ nice clothes.

10. A mouse has _____ long, thin, almost hairless tail. _____ rats also have _____ long, skinny tails.

11. Years ago, people used _____ wood or _____ coal for _____ heat, but now most people use _____ gas, _____ oil, or _____ electricity.

12. _____ good book is _____ friend for _____ life.

13. _____ gold is _____ excellent conductor of _____ electricity. It is used in many of the electrical circuits on _____ spaceship.

14. A: Where's Alice?

    B: She's in _____ kitchen making _____ sandwich.

15. In ancient times, people did not use _____ coins for money. Instead they used _____ shells, _____ beads, or _____ salt. The first coins were made around 2600 years ago. Today, most money is made from _____ paper.

16. Ted, pass _____ salt, please. And _____ pepper. Thanks.

17. _____ different countries have _____ different geography. Italy is located on _____ peninsula. Japan is _____ island nation.

18. There are some wonderful small markets in my neighborhood. You can always get _____ fresh fish at Mr. Rico's fish market.

19. A: I saw _____ good program on TV last night.

    B: Oh? What was it?

    A: It was _____ documentary about wildlife in Alaska. It was really interesting. Did you see it, too?

    B: No, I watched _____ old movie. It wasn't very good. I wish I'd known about _____ documentary. I would have watched it.

20. _____ modern people, just like their ancestors, are curious about _____ universe. Where did _____ moon come from? Does _____ life exist on other planets? What is _____ star? How large is _____ universe? How long will _____ sun continue to burn?

◇ **PRACTICE 30—SELFSTUDY:** Object pronouns: *one* vs. *it*. (Charts 8–7 and 8–8)

Directions: Complete the sentences with **ONE** or **IT**.

1. A: Do you need a pen?
   B: No. I already have _____ *one* _____.

2. A: Where is my pen?
   B: Mike has _____ *it* _____.

3. A: Do you have a car?
   B: No. I don't have enough money to get _____.

4. A: Does Erica like her new car?
   B: Does she like _____? She loves _____!

5. A: Do you have a bicycle?
   B: Yes.
   A: Can I use _____ this afternoon?

6. A: Does Tom have a bicycle?
   B: No, but I think Eric has _____.

7. A: Do you see an empty table?
   B: Yes. I see _____ over there in the corner.

8. A: This table is empty.
   B: Let's take _____.

9. A: Do you have a dictionary?
   B: No, but I think Yoko has _____.

10. A: Where's my dictionary?
    B: I don't know. I haven't seen _____.

◇ **PRACTICE 31—GUIDED STUDY:** Object pronouns: *one* vs. *it*. (Charts 8–7 and 8–8)

Directions: Complete the sentences with **ONE** or **IT**.

1. A: Where's my pencil?
   B: Jason has _____.

2. A: I need a pencil.
   B: Jason has an extra _____. Ask him.

3. I don't have a small calculator. I need to buy _____ for my math class.

4. A: Do you have a small calculator?
   B: Yes.
   A: May I borrow _____ for a minute?

5. A: Are you going to take a sandwich along with you for lunch?
   B: No. I'll get _____ at the deli around the corner from the office.

6. I made a sandwich for James's lunch, but he forgot to take _____ to school.

7. Westville Hospital is the name of our new hospital. We built _____ two years ago.

8. Our village doesn't have a hospital. We hope to build _____ in the next five years.

9. When I moved into my new apartment, I wanted to hang my paintings on the wall. I didn't have a hammer, so I went to the hardware store and bought _____.

10. My friend Ralph helped me hang my paintings on the wall. When I handed him the hammer, he dropped _____ on his toe.

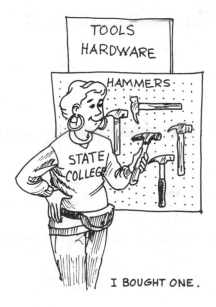

I BOUGHT ONE.

RALPH DROPPED IT.

◇ PRACTICE 32—SELFSTUDY: *Some/any* vs. *it/them*. (Charts 8-7 and 8-8)

Directions: Select the appropriate completion from the *italicized* words.

1. A: Where did you get all of this new furniture?

   B: I bought   *some*, (*it*.)

2. A: Does Jones Department Store sell bedroom furniture?

   B: No, but you can find   *some*, *it*   at Charlie's Bargain Warehouse.

3. A: What are you eating?

   B: Cheese. Would you like   *some*, *it*? There's plenty.

4. A: Here's the cheese you wanted me to buy.

   B: Thanks. Put   *some*, *it*   in the refrigerator, please.

5. A: Where did you get these magazines?

   B: I got   *some*, *them*   at the newstand on Pyle Street.

6. A: Do you read a lot of magazines?

   B: Not usually, but I often pick   *some*, *them*   up at the airport before I get on a flight. I always read magazines when I fly.

7. A: How about some hot tea?

   B: Thanks, but I don't want   *any*, *it*   right now.

8. A: Here's some hot tea. Would you like some sugar or lemon?

   B: No, but I'd like to put a little milk in   *some*, *it*.

◇ **PRACTICE 33—GUIDED STUDY:** *Some/any* vs. *it/them.* (Charts 8–7 and 8–8)

Directions: Select the appropriate completion from the *italicized* words.

1. A: Where are the scissors—the ones with the orange handles?

   B: I put *some, it, them* in the top drawer.

2. A: Do you have any scissors?

   B: No, but I think Aunt Ella has *some, it, them.* Ask her.

3. A: Do you have any dog shampoo?

   B: No, but I think Aunt Ella has *some, it, them.* Ask her.

4. A: What are those?

   B: What do you mean? They're scissors, of course.

   A: Where did you get *some, it, them*?

   B: I borrowed *some, it, them* from Aunt Ella.

5. A: What's that?

   B: It's shampoo especially for dogs. It kills fleas.

   A: Where did you get *some, it, them*?

   B: I borrowed *some, it, them* from Aunt Ella. My dog has fleas. I'm going to give her a bath and kill *some, it, them.*

   A: Look at the label. Read *some, it, them.* What does it say?

   B: It says "Flea Shampoo" on the label.

   A: That means you're supposed to give the fleas a bath, not the dog!

   B: Oh sure! Ha-ha. Stop joking around and help me give the dog a bath.

6. A: I'm going to the post office this afternoon.

   B: Really? Could you take these letters with you and mail *some, it, them* for me? Thanks.

7. A: Is the mail here?

   B: Yes.

   A: Did I get *any, it, them*?

8. A: Take this letter and give *some, it, them* to Alison.

B: Okay.

9. A: Could you save those newspapers for me? I'd like to read *some, it, them* later.

B: Sure.

A: I especially want to read the local paper. Be sure to save *some, it, them* for me.

B: Don't worry.

10. A: Does your son Kevin like to read books?

B: He hasn't read *any, it, them* in a long time.

A: Maybe you should buy *some, it, them* for him. Children like to have their own books.

B: I bought him a book for his last birthday. He never read *some, it, them*.

◇ **PRACTICE 34—SELFSTUDY: Prepositions. (Chapter 8; Appendix1)**

Directions: Complete each sentence with the appropriate preposition.

1. The twins may look alike, but Robby's behavior is very different ____*from*____ Tim's.

2. I'm sorry _____ my behavior last night. I was pretty upset and was just feeling

sorry _____ myself. I didn't mean anything I said.

3. I spoke _____ my brother _____ your problem, and he said that there

was nothing he could do to help you.

4. All right, children, here is your math problem: add ten _____ twelve, subtract two

_____ that total; divide ten _____ that answer; and multiply the result

_____ five. What is the final answer?

5. I feel pretty good about my final examination in English. I'm hoping _____ a good

grade, and I'm anxious to get my paper back.

6. Please try to concentrate _____ my explanation. I can't repeat it.

7. A: Did you hear _____ the plans to build a new hotel in the middle of town? It's

wonderful!

B: Yes, I heard, but I disagree _____ you. I think it's terrible! It means the town

will be full of tourists all the time.

8. A: Have you heard _____ your friend in Thailand recently?

B: Yes. She's having a difficult time. She's not accustomed _____ hot weather.

9. A: I must tell you _____ a crazy thing that happened last night. Have you heard?

B: What? What happened?

A: A hundred monkeys escaped _____ the zoo.

B: You've got to be kidding! How did that happen?

Directions: Complete each sentence with the appropriate preposition.

1. I'm ready _____ the test. I studied hard.

2. It's important for you to believe _____ your own abilities. Tell yourself, "I can do it!"

3. _____ the past, people traveled from Europe _____ North and South America only by boat.

4. I applied _____ a job at a florist's. I like to arrange flowers.

5. I will not discuss this _____ you. It's private information.

6. It's not polite to laugh _____ other people's mistakes.

7. Carol's house is full _____ people. Is she having a party?

8. Listen _____ me!

9. Jack arrived _____ the bus stop just after the bus had left.

10. I arrived _____ this city _____ September third.

11. Your grades are wonderful. Your mother and I are very proud _____ you.

12. I'm looking forward _____ my holiday in Spain.

13. Canada belongs _____ the United Nations.

14. The army protected the president _____ his enemies. The rebels attacked the presidential palace. They tried to get rid _____ the president by force.

15. A: What are you doing under the sink?

    B: I'm looking _____ my ring. It went down the drain, and I've taken the pipe out.

16. A: Did you hear _____ my promotion?

    B: Yes. They told me to report to you _____ noon tomorrow.

17. I'm a little afraid _____ flying, so when I was buying an airplane ticket, I asked _____ a seat near the front because I thought it was safer near the main door. The person behind me insisted _____ having a seat near the back, because he thought it was safer there. The next person paid _____ his ticket only after they assured him that he could have a seat over the wing, which he felt was the safest location on the airplane. It's very confusing. _____ the future, I think I'll just sit wherever they put me.

18. The people of the Hawaiian islands are famous _____ their warm hospitality. When we visited the islands, everyone we met was extremely nice _____ us.

19. A: Barbara is telling Ben something _____ you. I think she's complaining _____ you. Is she angry _____ you?

    B: I borrowed some money _____ her a long time ago, and I never paid her back. I'd better try to see her _____ the morning and give her the money I owe her. I'd also better apologize _____ her _____ waiting so long.

20. My chemistry examination consisted _____ all of the things I didn't understand during the semester. I couldn't concentrate _____ it at all. I'm sure that I didn't pass.

CHAPTER 9
Connecting Ideas

◇ **PRACTICE 1—SELFSTUDY: Connecting ideas with *and*. (Chart 9-1)**

Directions: <u>Underline</u> the words that are connected with **AND**. Label these words as NOUNS, VERBS, or ADJECTIVES.

                  noun + noun +   noun
1. The farmer has a <u>cow</u>, a <u>goat</u>, and a black <u>horse</u>.
          adjective + adjective
2. Danny is a <u>bright</u> and <u>happy</u> child.
  verb   + verb
3. I <u>picked</u> up the telephone and <u>dialed</u> Steve's number.

4. The cook washed the vegetables and put them in boiling water.

5. My feet were cold and wet.

6. Sara is responsible, considerate, and trustworthy.

7. The three largest land animals are the elephant, the rhinoceros, and the hippopotamus.

8. A hippopotamus rests in water during the day and feeds on land at night.

◇ PRACTICE 2—SELFSTUDY: Punctuating a series with *and.* (Chart 9-1)

Directions: Add COMMAS where necessary.

1. Rivers streams lakes and oceans are all bodies of water.
   → *Rivers, streams, lakes, and oceans are all bodies of water.* OR
     Rivers, streams, lakes and oceans are all bodies of water.

2. My oldest brother my neighbor and I went shopping yesterday.

3. Ms. Parker is intelligent friendly and kind.

4. Did you bring copies of the annual report for Sue Dan Joe and Mary?

5. In the early 1600s, the Chinese made wallpaper by painting birds flowers and landscapes on large sheets of rice paper.

6. Can you watch television listen to the radio and read the newspaper at the same time?

7. Lawyers doctors teachers and accountants all have some form of continuing education throughout their careers.

8. Gold is beautiful workable indestructible and rare.

9. My mother father grandfather and sisters welcomed my brother and me home.

10. My husband imitates animal sounds for our children. He moos like a cow roars like a lion and barks like a dog.

◇ PRACTICE 3—GUIDED STUDY: Punctuating a series with *and.* (Chart 9-1)

Directions: Make a list for each of the topics below. Then write sentences using this list. Use AND in your sentence.

Example: three things you are afraid of
List: *heights*
poisonous snakes
guns

Possible sentences:
   → *I'm afraid of heights, poisonous snakes, and guns.*
   → *Three of the things I'm afraid of are heights, poisonous snakes, and guns.*
   → *Heights, poisonous snakes, and guns make me feel afraid.*

1. your three favorite sports
2. three adjectives that describe a person whom you admire
3. four cities that you would like to visit
4. three characteristics that describe (*name of this city*)
5. three or more separate things you did this morning
6. the five most important people in your life
7. three or more things that make you happy
8. three or more adjectives that describe the people in your country

◇ PRACTICE 4—SELFSTUDY: Connecting ideas with *and*. (Chart 9-1)

Directions: Each of the following sentences contains two independent clauses. Find the SUBJECT (**S**) and VERB (**V**) of each clause. Add a COMMA or a PERIOD. CAPITALIZE as necessary.

      S   **V**   **S**   **V**
1. Birds fly, and fish swim.

      S   **V**   **S**   **V**
2. Birds fly. F/fish swim.

3. Dogs bark lions roar.

4. Dogs bark and lions roar.

5. A week has seven days a year has 365 days.

6. A week has seven days and a year has 365 days.

7. Bill raised his hand and the teacher pointed at him.

8. Bill raised his hand the teacher pointed at him.

◇ PRACTICE 5—SELFSTUDY: Using *and*, *but*, and *or*. (Chart 9-2)

Directions: Add COMMAS where appropriate.

1. I talked to Amy for a long time but she didn't listen.

    → *I talked to Amy for a long time, but she didn't listen.*

2. I talked to Tom for a long time and asked him many questions.

    → *(no change)*

3. I talked to Bob for a long time and he listened carefully to every word.

    → *I talked to Bob for a long time, and he listened carefully to every word.*

4. Please call Jane or Ted.

5. Please call Jane and Ted.

6. Please call Jane Ted or Anna.

7. Please call Jane Ted and Anna.

8. I waved at my friend but she didn't see me.

9. I waved at my friend and she waved back.

10. I waved at my friend and smiled at her.

11. Was the test hard or easy?

12. My test was short and easy but Ali's test was hard.

◇ PRACTICE 6—SELFSTUDY: Using *and, but, or,* and *so.* (Charts 9-1 → 9-3)

Directions: Write in the correct completion.

1. I was tired, ____*so*____ I went to bed.
   A. but   B. or   C. so

2. I sat down on the sofa _____ opened the newspaper.
   A. but   B. and   C. so

3. The students were on time, _____ the teacher was late.
   A. but   B. or   C. so

4. I would like one pet. I'd like to have a dog _____ a cat.
   A. but   B. and   C. or

5. Our children are happy _____ healthy.
   A. but   B. and   C. or

6. I wanted a cup of tea, _____ I heated some water.
   A. but   B. and   C. so

7. The phone rang, _____ I didn't answer it.
   A. but   B. and   C. so

8. You can have an apple _____ an orange. Choose one.
   A. but   B. and   C. or

◇ PRACTICE 7—SELFSTUDY: Using *and, but, or,* and *so.* (Charts 9-1 → 9-3)

Directions: Add COMMAS where appropriate. Some sentences need no commas.

1. I washed and dried the dishes. → (*no change*)

2. I washed the dishes and my son dried them.

   → *I washed the dishes, and my son dried them.*

3. I called their house but no one answered the phone.

4. He offered me an apple or a peach.

5. I bought some apples peaches and bananas.

6. I was hungry so I ate an apple.

7. Bill was hungry and ate two apples.

8. My sister is generous and kind-hearted.

9. My daughter is affectionate shy independent and smart.

10. It started to rain so we went inside and watched television.

◇ PRACTICE 8—SELFSTUDY: Using *and, but, or,* and *so.* (Charts 9-1 → 9-3)

Directions: Add COMMAS where appropriate. Some sentences need no commas.

1. Gina wants a job as an air traffic controller. Every air traffic controller worldwide uses English so it is important for Gina to be fluent in the language.

2. Why do people with different cultural backgrounds sometimes fear and distrust each other?

3. Mozart was a great composer but he had a short and difficult life. During the last part of his life, he was penniless sick and unable to find work but he wrote music of lasting beauty and joy.

4. Nothing in nature stays the same forever. Today's land sea climate plants and animals are all part of a relentless process of change continuing through millions of years.

5. People and animals must share the earth and its resources.

6. According to one researcher, the twenty-five most common words in English are: *the and a to of I in was that it he you for had is with she has on at have but me my* and *not.*

◇ PRACTICE 9—SELFSTUDY: Separating sentences: periods and capital letters. (Charts 9-1 → 9-3)

Directions: Add PERIODS and CAPITAL LETTERS as necessary.

1. There are over 100,000 kinds of flies they live thoughout the world.

   → *There are over 100,000 kinds of flies.* **T***hey live throughout the world.*

2. I like to get mail from my friends and family it is important to me.

3. We are all connected by our humanity we need to help each other we can all live in peace.

4. There was a bad flood in Hong Kong the streets became raging streams luckily no one died in the flood.

5. People have used needles since prehistoric times the first buttons appeared more than two thousand years ago zippers are a relatively recent invention the zipper was invented in 1890.

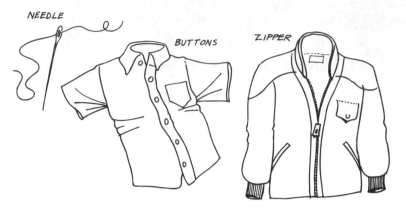

◇ PRACTICE 10—GUIDED STUDY: Punctuating with commas and periods. (Charts 9-1 → 9-3)

Directions: Add COMMAS, PERIODS, and CAPITAL LETTERS as necessary.

1. African elephants are larger than Asiatic elephants. Elephants native to Asia are easier to train and have gentler natures than African elephants.

2. Asiatic elephants live in jungles and forests in India Indonesia Malaysia Thailand India China and other countries in southeastern and southern Asia.

3. Elephants eat roots leaves bushes grass branches and fruit they especially like berries dates corn and sugar cane.

4. Elephants spend a lot of time in water and are good swimmers they take baths in rivers and lakes and like to roll around in muddy water they like to give themselves a shower by shooting water from their trunks.

5. After a bath, they often cover themselves with dirt the dirt protects their skin from the sun and insects.

6. Most elephants live in herds an older female (called a *matriarch*) leads a herd.

7. A female elephant is pregnant for approximately twenty months and almost always has only one baby a young elephant stays close to its mother for the first ten years of its life.

8. Elephants live peacefully together in herds but some elephants (called *rogues*) leave the herd and become mean these elephants usually are in pain from decayed teeth a disease or a wound.

9. Elephants are intelligent animals a well-trained elephant can kneel stand up or turn around on command.

10. Elephants are in danger of extinction so it is important to stop the illegal killing of elephants they are killed most often for their ivory.

◇ PRACTICE 11—GUIDED STUDY: Punctuating with commas and periods.
(Charts 9-1 → 9-3)

Directions: Add COMMAS, PERIODS, and CAPITAL LETTERS as necessary.

(1)   **A** a few days ago, a friend and I were driving from Benton Harbor to Chicago. **W** We were

(2)   in a lot of traffic, but it was moving smoothly.   **W** We didn't experience any delays for the

(3)   first hour but near Chicago we ran into some highway construction the traffic wasn't moving at

(4)   all my friend and I sat in the car and waited we talked about our jobs our families and the

(5)   terrible traffic slowly the traffic started to move

(6)   we noticed a black sports car at the side of the road the right blinker was blinking the driver

(7)   obviously wanted to get back into the line of traffic car after car passed without letting the

(8)   black sports car get in line I decided to do a good deed so I motioned for the black car to get

(9)   in line ahead of me the driver of the black car waved thanks to me and I waved back at him all

(10)   cars had to stop at a toll booth a short way down the road I held out my money to pay my toll

(11)   but the tolltaker just smiled and waved me on she told me that the man in the black sports car

(12)   had already paid my toll wasn't that a nice way of saying thank you?

◇ PRACTICE 12—SELFSTUDY: Using auxiliary verbs after *but* and *and*. (Chart 9-4)

Directions: Complete the sentences with AUXILIARY VERBS.

PART I: Auxiliaries after *but*.

1. Debra **reads** a lot of books, but her brothers _____*don't*_____.

2. Sam **isn't** in the school play this year, but Adam _____*is*_____.

3. I **will be** at home this evening, but my roommate _____.

4. Ducks **like** to swim, but chickens _____.

5. That phone **doesn't work,** but this one _____.

6. Joe **is** at home, but his parents _____.

7. I **can't swim,** but my dog _____.

8. Jack **has visited** my home, but Linda _____.

9. I'**m not going** to graduate this year, but my best friend _____.

10. My dog **crawls** under the bed when it thunders, but my cat _____.

PART II: Auxiliaries after *and*.

11. Debra **reads** a lot of books, and her sisters _____*do*_____ too.

12. Horses **are** domesticated animals, and camels _____ too.

13. Red **isn't** a dull color, and orange _____ either.

14. Jack **didn't go** to the picnic, and Paul _____ either.

15. I **work** at an airplane factory, and my brother _____ too.

16. Dick **won't work** late every evening, and Jean _____ either.

17. Fatima **is** in class today, and Pedro _____ too.

18. I **can't** sing, and my wife _____ either.

◇ PRACTICE 13—SELFSTUDY: Using auxiliary verbs after *but* and *and*. (Chart 9-4)

Directions: Complete the sentences with AUXILIARY VERBS.

1. I **like** rock music, and my roommate _____*does*_____ too.

2. My son **enjoys** monster movies, but I _____.

3. Paul **can't speak** Spanish, and Larry _____ either.

4. My neighbor **walks** to work every morning, but I _____.

5. Carl **can touch** his nose with his tongue, but most people _____.

6. I **am** exhausted from the long trip, and my mother _____ too.

7. I **don't have** a dimple in my chin, but my brother _____.

8. I **visited** the museum yesterday, and my friend _____ too.

9. Water **isn't** solid, but ice _____.

10. Clouds **aren't** solid, and steam _____ either.

◇ PRACTICE 14—SELFSTUDY: Using *too, so, either,* or *neither* after *and*. (Chart 9-5)

Directions: Complete the sentences.

PART I: Complete the sentences with an AUXILIARY + **too** or **either**.

1. Snow **is** white, and clouds _____*are too*_____.

2. I **can't cook,** and my roommate _____*can't either*_____.

3. Squirrels **have** long tails, and cats _____*do too*_____.

4. I **like** movies, and my wife _____.

5. I **don't like** salty food, and my wife _____.

6. Sugar **isn't** expensive, and salt _____.

7. Sugar **is** sweet, and honey _____.

8. Rosa Gomez **wasn't** in class yesterday, and Mr. Nazari _____.

9. Andy **didn't know** the answer to the question, and Tina _____.

10. I **couldn't understand** the substitute teacher, and Yoko _____.

11. Everyone in the room **laughed** at my foolish mistake, and I _____.

12. Fish **can't walk,** and snakes _____.

13. I **like** to fix things around the house, and Ted _____.

14. **I'd rather stay** home this evening, and my husband _____.

Connecting Ideas ◇ **183**

PART II: Complete the sentences with **SO** or **NEITHER** + an AUXILIARY.

15. Pasta **is** a famous Italian dish, and _____*so is*_____ pizza.

16. Anteaters **don't have** teeth, and _____*neither do*_____ most birds.

17. I **didn't go** to the bank, and _____ my husband.

18. Turtles **are** reptiles, and _____ snakes.

19. My sister **has** dark hair, and _____ I.

20. Gorillas **don't have** tails, and _____ human beings.

21. **I'm studying** English, and _____ Mr. Chu.

22. **I'm not** a native speaker of English, and _____ Mr. Chu.

23. Wood **burns**, and _____ paper.

24. Mountain climbing **is** dangerous, and _____ auto racing.

25. **I've never seen** a monkey in the wild, and _____ my children.

26. When we heard the hurricane warning, I **nailed** boards over my windows and _____ all of my neighbors.

27. My brother and I studied chemistry together. I **didn't pass** the course, and _____ he.

28. Ostriches **can't fly**, and _____ penguins.

> I WONDER HOW THEY DO THAT?
>
> SO DO I !

◇ PRACTICE 15—GUIDED STUDY: Using *so* or *neither* to respond. (Chart 9-5)

Directions: Pair up with another student (or friend, roommate, etc.).

STUDENT A: With your book open, say the given sentence. Complete the sentence with your own words if necessary.

STUDENT B: Respond to A's statement by using **SO** or **NEITHER**. Your book is closed.

Example: I'm confused.
STUDENT A: *I'm confused.*
STUDENT B: *So am I.* *

---

*This exercise is designed to practice the use of *so* and *neither* in conversational responses. If, however, STUDENT B doesn't want to agree with, echo, or support STUDENT A's statement, there are alternative responses. For example:

STUDENT A: I'm confused.
STUDENT B: **You are? What's the matter?**
STUDENT A: Frogs don't have tails.
STUDENT B: **Really? Is that so? Hmmmm. I didn't know know that. Are you sure?**
STUDENT A: Ivar's Seafood Restaurant is a good place to eat in Seattle.
STUDENT B: **Oh? I've never eaten there.**

Example: Frogs don't have tails.

STUDENT A: *Frogs don't have tails.*

STUDENT B: *Neither do human beings.*

Example: *(Name of a restaurant)* is a good place to eat in *(this city).*

STUDENT A: *Ivar's Seafood Restaurant is a good place to eat in Seattle.*

STUDENT B: *So is Hong Kong Gardens.*

1. I'm thirsty.
2. I'd like *(a kind of drink).*
3. I studied last night.
4. I study grammar every day.
5. I've never been in *(name of a country).*
6. I don't like *(a kind of food).*
7. . . . is a *(big/small)* country.
8. *(Name of a student)* is from *(name of a country).*
9. Soccer is . . . .
10. *(Name of a student)* has *(dark/red/black/etc.)* hair.
11. I like *(a kind of)* weather.
12. Monkeys climb trees.
13. Ice is cold.
14. (. . .) has a part in her/his hair.
15. *(name of a country)* is a large country.

Directions: Switch roles.

16. I *(write/don't write)* a lot of letters.
17. I *(get/don't get)* a lot of mail.
18. San Francisco is a seaport.
19. Fish live in water.
20. I've never seen an iceberg.
21. Swimming is an Olympic sport.
22. I *(like/don't like)* the weather today.
23. I'd rather go to *(name of a place)* than *(name of a place).*
24. *(name of a city)* is in South America.
25. Oxygen is colorless.
26. Elephants are big animals.
27. *(name of a country)* is in Africa.
28. I've never had caviar* (OR *name of another exotic food)* for breakfast.
29. Denmark has no volcanoes.
30. I don't have *(red/gray/white)* hair.

Caviar = fish eggs (an expensive delicacy in some cultures).

◇ PRACTICE 16—GUIDED STUDY: Using *too, so, either,* or *neither.* (Chart 9-5)

Directions: Create dialogues (either with a partner or in writing) between A and B. STUDENT A uses the given verb to make a statement (not a question). STUDENT B reacts to A's idea by using **TOO, SO, EITHER,** or **NEITHER** in a response.

Example: would like
STUDENT A: *I'd like to sail around the world someday.*
STUDENT B: *So would I.* OR *I would too.* *

Example: didn't want
STUDENT A: *Toshi didn't want to give a speech in front of the class.*
STUDENT B: *Neither did Ingrid.* OR *Ingrid didn't either.* *

1. don't have
2. can't speak
3. enjoy
4. isn't going to be
5. haven't ever seen
6. will be
7. can fly
8. would like
9. didn't go
10. are
11. is sitting
12. wasn't

◇ PRACTICE 17—SELFSTUDY: Adverb clauses with *because.* (Chart 9-6)

Directions: Underline the ADVERB CLAUSES. Find the SUBJECT (**S**) and VERB (**V**) of the adverb clause.

$$\qquad\qquad\qquad\qquad\qquad \textbf{S} \quad \textbf{V}$$
1. Johnny was late for work because [he] [missed] the bus.

2. I closed the door because the room was cold.

3. Because I lost my umbrella, I got wet on the way home.

4. Joe didn't bring his book to class because he couldn't find it.

◇ PRACTICE 18—SELFSTUDY: Adverb clauses with *because.* (Chart 9-6)

Directions: Add PERIODS, COMMAS, and CAPITAL LETTERS as necessary.

1. I opened the window because the room was hot we felt more comfortable then.

    → *I opened the window because the room was hot.* **W**e felt more comfortable then.

2. I can't use my bicycle because it has a flat tire. → *(no change)*

3. Because his coffee was cold Jack didn't finish it he left it on the table and walked away.

    → *Because his coffee was cold,* Jack didn't finish it. **H**e left it on the table and walked away.

---

*This practice asks you to use **too, so, either** or **neither** in conversational responses. Other responses are, of course, possible. For example:
A: I'd like to sail around the world someday.
B: **Really? Why?**
A: Toshi didn't want to give a speech in front of the class.
B: **Oh? Why not?**

4. Annie is very young because she is afraid of the dark she likes to have a light on in her bedroom at night.

5. My sister went to a doctor because she hurt her right knee.

6. Marilyn has a cold because she's not feeling well today she's not going to go to her office.

◇ PRACTICE 19—GUIDED STUDY: Adverb clauses with *because*. (Chart 9-6)

Directions: Add PERIODS, COMMAS, and CAPITAL LETTERS as necessary.

1. Because the weather was bad we canceled our trip into the city we stayed home and watched TV.

2. Mark is an intelligent and ambitious young man because he hopes to get a good job later in life he is working hard to get a good education now.

3. Many species of birds fly to warm climates in the winter because they can't tolerate cold weather.

4. Frank put his head in his hands he was angry and upset because he had lost a lot of work on his computer.

◇ PRACTICE 20—SELFSTUDY: *Because* vs. *so.* (Charts 9-3 and 9-6)

Directions: Give sentences with the same meaning. Use COMMAS as appropriate.

PART I: Restate the sentence, using **so**.

1. Jack lost his job because he never showed up for work on time.
   → *Jack never showed up for work on time, so he lost his job.*

2. Because I was sleepy, I took a nap.

3. I opened the window because the room was hot.

4. Because it was raining, I stayed indoors.

PART II: Restate the sentence, using **BECAUSE.**

5. Jason was hungry, so he ate.
   → *Because Jason was hungry, he ate.* OR *Jason ate because he was hungry.*

6. I was tired, so I went to bed.

7 The water in the river is polluted, so we can't go swimming.

8. My watch is broken, so I was late for my job interview.

◇ PRACTICE 21—GUIDED STUDY: Using *because*. (Chart 9-6)

Directions: Complete the sentences with your own words.

Example: My friend and I didn't . . . because . . . .
→ ***My friend and I didn't*** go to the party ***because*** *we didn't know anyone who was going to be there.*

1. Because I . . . , I . . . .
2. Sometimes people . . . because they . . . .
3. Parents . . . because . . . .
4. Because my parents . . . , ...
5. . . . had a problem. He couldn't . . . because . . . .
6. Because cats . . . , ...
7. My friend . . . yesterday. He didn't . . . because . . . .
8. Because . . . and . . . , they . . . .

◇ PRACTICE 22—SELFSTUDY: Using *because* and *even though*. (Charts 9-6 and 9-7)

Directions: Choose the correct completion.

1. Even though I was hungry, I __**B**__ a lot at dinner.
   A. ate   B. didn't eat

2. Because I was hungry, I _____ a lot at dinner.
   A. ate   B. didn't eat

3. Because I was cold, I _____ my coat.
   A. put on   B. didn't put on

4. Even though I was cold, I _____ my coat.
   A. put on   B. didn't put on

5. Even though Mike _____ sleepy, he stayed up to watch the end of the game on TV.
   A. was   B. wasn't

6. Because Linda _____ sleepy, she went to bed.
   A. was   B. wasn't

7. Because Kate ran too slowly, she _____ the race.
   A. won   B. didn't win

8. Even though Jessica ran fast, she _____ the race.
   A. won   B. didn't win

9. I _____ the test for my driver's license because I wasn't prepared.
   A. failed   B. didn't fail

10. I went to my daughter's school play because she _____ me to be there.
    A. wanted   B. didn't want

11. I bought a new suit for the business trip even though I _____ it.
    A. could afford B. couldn't afford

12. Even though I had a broken leg, I _____ to the conference in New York.
    A. went   B. didn't go

◇ PRACTICE 23—SELFSTUDY: Using *even though* and *although*. (Chart 9-7)

Directions: Choose the best completion.

1. Even though ostriches have wings, __**C**__.
   A. their feathers are large
   B. they are big birds
   C. they can't fly

2. Although _____, the hungry man ate every bit of it.
   A. an apple is both nutritious and delicious
   B. the cheese tasted good to him
   C. the bread was old and stale

3. The nurse didn't bring Mr. Hill a glass of water even though _____.
   A. she was very busy
   B. she forgot
   C. he asked her three times

4. Although _____, Eric got on the plane.
   A. he is married
   B. he is afraid of flying
   C. the flight attendant welcomed him aboard

5. Even though I looked in every pocket and every drawer, _____.
   A. my keys were under the bed
   B. my roommate helped me look for my keys
   C. I never found my keys

◇ PRACTICE 24—SELFSTUDY: Using *even though/although* and *because*.
                (Charts 9-6 and 9-7)

Directions: Choose the best completion.

1. It was a hot summer night. We went inside and shut the windows because _____.
   A. the rain stopped
   B. we were enjoying the cool breeze
   C. a storm was coming

2. Cats can't see red even though _____.
    A. it's a bright color
    B. many people like to wear that color
    C. many flowers are bright red

3. Although _____, my daughter and her friends went swimming in the lake.
    A. it was cold outside
    B. they love to play in the water
    C. the water was warm

4. Because _____, I joined my daughter and her friends in the lake.
    A. I don't know how to swim
    B. I like to swim
    C. it was cold outside

5. My partner and I worked late into the evening. Even though _____, we stopped at our favorite restaurant before we went home.
    A. we were very hungry
    B. we were very polite
    C. we were very tired

◇ PRACTICE 25—GUIDED STUDY: Using *even though/although* and *because*.
                              (Charts 9-6 and 9-7)

Directions: Choose the best completion.

Example: I gave him the money because ___C___.
                A. I didn't have any
                B. he had a lot of money
                C. I owed it to him

1. My brother came to my graduation ceremony although _____.
    A. he was sick
    B. he was eager to see everyone
    C. he was happy for me

2. Jack hadn't heard or read about the murder even though _____.
    A. he was the murderer
    B. it was on the front page of every newspaper
    C. he was out of town when it occurred

3. We can see the light from an airplane high in the sky at night before we can hear the plane because _____.
    A. light travels faster than sound
    B. airplanes travel at high speeds
    C. our eyes work better than our ears at night

4. Although _____, he finished the race in first place.
    A. John was full of energy and strength
    B. John was leading all the way
    C. John was far behind in the beginning

5. Snakes don't have ears, but they are very sensitive to vibrations that result from noise. Snakes can sense the presence of a moving object even though _____.
    A. they have ears
    B. they feel vibrations
    C. they can't hear

6. In mountainous areas, melting snow in the spring runs downhill into streams and rivers. The water carries with it sediment, that is, small particles of soil and rock. In the spring, mountain rivers become cloudy rather than clear because _____.
   A. mountain tops are covered with snow
   B. the water from melting snow brings sediment to the river
   C. ice is frozen water

7. Foxes can use their noses to find their dinners because _____.
   A. they have a keen sense of smell
   B. mice and other small rodents move very quickly
   C. they have keen vision

8. When she heard the loud crash, Marge ran outside in the snow although _____.
   A. her mother ran out with her
   B. she wasn't wearing any shoes
   C. she ran as fast as she could

9. Even though his shoes were wet and muddy, Brian _____.
   A. took them off at the front door
   B. walked right into the house and across the carpet
   C. wore wool socks

10. Robert ate dinner with us at our home last night. Although _____, he left right after dinner.
    A. he washed the dishes
    B. there was a good movie at the local theater
    C. I expected him to stay and help with the dishes

11. Alex boarded the bus in front of his hotel. He was on his way to the art museum. Because he _____, he asked the bus driver to tell him where to get off.
    A. was late for work and didn't want his boss to get mad
    B. was carrying a heavy suitcase
    C. was a tourist and didn't know the city streets very well

12. When I attended my first business conference out of town, I felt very uncomfortable during the social events because _____.
  A. we were all having a good time
  B. I didn't know anyone there
  C. I am very knowledgeable in my field

◇ PRACTICE 26—GUIDED STUDY: Punctuating with commas and periods.
     (Charts 9-1→ 9-7)

Directions: Add COMMAS, PERIODS, and CAPITAL LETTERS as necessary. (There are four adverb clauses in the following passage. Can you find and <u>underline</u> them?)

(1) What is the most common substance on earth? I*i*t isn't wood**,** iron**,** or sand**.** T*t*he most common substance on earth is water it occupies more than seventy percent of the earth's surface it is in lakes rivers and oceans it is in the ground and in the air it is practically everywhere.

(2) Water is vital because life on earth could not exist without it people animals and plants all need water in order to exist every living thing is mostly water a person's body is about sixty-seven percent water a bird is about seventy-five percent water most fruit is about ninety percent water.

(3) Most of the water in the world is saltwater ninety-seven percent of the water on earth is in the oceans because seawater is salty people cannot drink it or use it to grow plants for food only three percent of the earth's water is fresh only one percent of the water in the world is easily available for human use.

(4) Even though water is essential to life human beings often poison it with chemicals from industry and agriculture when people foul water with pollution the quality of all life— plant life animal life and human life—diminishes life cannot exist without fresh water so it is essential for people to take care of this important resource.

◇ PRACTICE 27—SELFSTUDY: Separable vs. nonseparable. (Charts 9-8 and 9-9)

Directions: If the given phrasal verb is separable, mark SEPARABLE. If it is inseparable, mark INSEPARABLE.

1. CORRECT: I *turned* the light *on.* *turn on =* ☒ SEPARABLE
    CORRECT: I *turned on* the light.   ☐ NONSEPARABLE

2. CORRECT: I *ran into* Mary.   *run into =* ☐ SEPARABLE
    (INCORRECT: I *ran* Mary *into.*)   ☒ NONSEPARABLE

3.	CORRECT: Joe *looked up* the definition. CORRECT: Joe *looked* the definition *up*.	*look up* =	☑ SEPARABLE ☐ NONSEPARABLE
4.	CORRECT: I *got off* the bus. (INCORRECT: I *got* the bus *off*.)	*get off* =	☐ SEPARABLE ☑ NONSEPARABLE
5.	CORRECT: I *took off* my coat. CORRECT: I *took* my coat *off*	*take off* =	☐ SEPARABLE ☐ NONSEPARABLE
6.	CORRECT: I *got in* the car and left. (INCORRECT: I *got* the car *in* and left.)	*got in* =	☐ SEPARABLE ☑ NONSEPARABLE
7.	CORRECT: I *figured out* the answer. CORRECT: I *figured* the answer *out*.	*figure out* =	☐ SEPARABLE ☐ NONSEPARABLE
8.	CORRECT: I *turned* the radio *off.* CORRECT: I *turned off* the radio.	*turn off* =	☐ SEPARABLE ☐ NONSEPARABLE

◇ PRACTICE 28—SELFSTUDY: Identifying phrasal verbs. (Charts 9-8 and 9-9)

Directions: <u>Underline</u> the second part of the phrasal verb in each sentence.

1. I *figured* the answer <u>out</u>.

2. The teacher *called* <u>on</u> me in class.

3. I *made* up a story about my childhood.

4. I feel okay now. I *got* over my cold last week.

5. The students *handed* their papers in at the end of the test.

6. I *woke* my roommate up when I got home.

7. I *picked* up a book and started to read.

8. I *turned* the radio on to listen to some music.

9. When I don't know how to spell a word, I *look* it up in the dictionary.

10. I opened the telephone directory and *looked* up the number of a plumber.

11. I *put* my book down and *turned* off the light.

◇ PRACTICE 29—SELFSTUDY: Using phrasal verbs (separable). (Chart 9-8)

Directions: Complete the sentences with the words in the following list.

away	*off*	*out*
down	*on*	*up*
in		

1. I'd like to listen to some music. Would you please *turn* the radio ____**on**____?

2. My husband *makes* _____ bedtime stories for our children.

3. My arms hurt, so I *put* the baby _____ for a minute, but he started crying right away, so I *picked* him _____ again.

4. A: We need a plumber to fix the kitchen sink. Call one today.

   B: I will.

   A: Don't *put* it ____off____.

   B: I won't. I'll call today. I promise.

5. A: Why are you wearing your new suit?

   B: I just *put* it _____ to see what it looked like.

   A: It looks fine. *Take* it ____off____ and hang it up before it gets wrinkled.

6. A: I found this notebook in the wastebasket. It's yours, isn't it?

   B: Yes. I *threw* it ____up____. I don't need it anymore.

   A: Okay. I thought maybe it had fallen in the wastebasket accidentally.

7. A: I need Jan's address again.

   B: I gave you her address just yesterday.

   A: I'm afraid I've lost it. Tell me again, and I'll *write* it _____.

   B: Just a minute. I have to *look* it ____up____ in my address book.

8. A: You'll never believe what happened in physics class today.

   B: What happened?

   A: We had a big test today. When I first looked it over, I realized that I couldn't *figure*

   _____ any of the answers. What happened is that he'd *handed* ____out, in____

   the wrong test. We hadn't covered that material in class yet.

9. A: *Wake* ____up____! It's six o'clock! Rise and shine!

   B: What are you doing!? *Turn* the light ____on____ and close the window curtain!

   A: My goodness but we're grumpy this morning. Come on. It's time to get up, dear. You
   don't want to be late.

◇ PRACTICE 30—SELFSTUDY: Phrasal verbs. (Charts 9-8 and 9-9)

Directions: Complete the sentences with PRONOUNS and PARTICLES. If the phrasal verb is SEPARABLE, circle SEP. If it is NONSEPARABLE, circle NONSEP.

1. I *got over* my cold . → I got _____ *over it* _____ .   SEP   (NONSEP)

2. I *made up* the story. → I made _____ *it up* _____ .   (SEP)   NONSEP

3. I *put off* my homework. → I put *off* _____ .   SEP   NONSEP

4. I *wrote down* the numbers. → I wrote *it down* _____ .   SEP   NONSEP

5. I *ran into* Robert. → I ran *into* _____ .   SEP   NONSEP

6. I *figured* the answer *out*. → I figured *it out* _____ .   SEP   NONSEP

7. I *took off* my shoes. → I took *it off* _____ .   SEP   NONSEP

8. I *called on* Susan. → I called *on* _____ .   SEP   NONSEP

9. I *turned off* the lights. → I turned *it off* _____ .   SEP   NONSEP

10. I *threw away* the newspaper. → I threw *it away* _____ .   SEP   NONSEP

◇ PRACTICE 31—SELFSTUDY: Phrasal verbs. (Charts 9-8 and 9-9)

Directions: Complete the sentences with PARTICLES. Include PRONOUNS in the completions if necessary.

1. I had the flu, but I got _____ *over it* _____ a couple of days ago.

2. I was wearing gloves. I took _____ before I shook hands with Mr. Zabidi.

3. Stacy needed to find the date that India became independent. She looked _____ in the encyclopedia and wrote _____ in her notebook.

4. The job was finished. I didn't need my tools anymore, so I put _____ .

5. It looked like rain, so I got my raincoat from the closet and put _____ before I left the apartment.

6. A: Have you seen Dan this morning?

   B: Not this morning. But I ran _____ at the movie last night.

7. A: Janet's car was stolen this morning!

   B: That's incredible! How did it happen?

   A: She had stopped at the store to pick _____ some groceries. When she returned to her car in the parking lot, she was carrying three bags. She put _____ to get her keys out of her purse. At that moment, a man grabbed the keys out of her hand, got _____ her car, started the engine, and drove away.

8. A: Why do you look so worried?

   B: I don't have my homework. My mother threw _____ with the trash this

   morning. If Ms. Anthony calls _____ in class to answer homework

   questions, I'll have to tell her what happened.

   A: She'll never believe your story. She'll think you made _____.

9. A: You're all wet!

   B: I know. A passing truck went through a big puddle and splashed me.

   A: You'd better take those clothes _____ and put _____

   something clean and dry before you go to work.

CHAPTER *10*
Gerunds and Infinitives

◇ PRACTICE 1—SELFSTUDY: Identifying gerunds and infinitives. (Charts 10-1 → 10-2)

Directions: Find and <u>underline</u> the gerunds and infinitives in the following sentences. Circle GER for GERUNDS. Circle INF for INFINITIVES.

1. GER (INF)   Ann promised <u>to wait</u> for me.

2. (GER) INF   I kept <u>walking</u> even though I was tired.

3. GER INF   Alex offered to help me.

4. GER INF   Karen finished writing a letter and went to bed.

5. GER INF   Don't forget to call me tomorrow.

6. GER INF   David was afraid of falling and hurting himself.

7. GER INF   Working in a coal mine is a dangerous job.

8. GER INF   It is easy to grow vegetables.

◇ PRACTICE 2—GUIDED STUDY: Verb + gerund. (Chart 10-2)

Directions: Complete the sentences in COLUMN A by using a verb from COLUMN B and your own words. Don't use a verb from COLUMN B more than one time.

Example: I often postpone + write
    → *I often postpone writing thank you notes, and then I have to apologize for sending them late.*

COLUMN A	COLUMN B		
1. I often postpone	A. buy	H. go	O. play
2. I enjoy	B. close	I. help	P. take
3. I'm considering	C. do	J. learn	Q. teach
4. Would you mind	D. eat	K. listen	R. try
5. I finished	E. exercise	L. love	S. watch
6. I'll never stop	F. finish	M. make	T. write
7. Do you ever think about	G. give	N. open	
8. You should keep			
9. Sometimes I put off			

◇ PRACTICE 3—SELFSTUDY: *Go + gerund.* (Chart 10-3)

Directions: Use the given ideas to complete the sentences with a form of **GO** + the appropriate GERUND to describe the activity.

1. I love to dance. Last night, my husband and I danced for hours.

   → Last night, my husband and I ___*went dancing*_____.

2. Later this afternoon, Ted is going to take a long walk in the woods.

   → Ted ____*is going to go hiking*_____ later today.

3. Yesterday Alice visited many stores and bought some clothes and makeup.

   → Yesterday, Alice _____.

4. Let's go to the beach and jump in the water.

   → Let's _____.

5. My grandfather takes his fishing pole to a farm pond every Sunday.

   → My grandfather _____ every Sunday.

6. When I visit a new city, I like to look around at the sights.

   → When I visit a new city, I like to _____.

7. I love to put up a small tent by a stream, make a fire, and listen to the sounds of the forest

   through the night.

   → I love to _____.

8. I want to take the sailboat out on the water this afternoon.

   → I want to _____ this afternoon.

9. Once a year, we take our skis to our favorite mountain resort and enjoy an exciting weekend.

   → Once a year, we _____

   at our favorite mountain resort.

10. Last year on my birthday, my friends

    and I went up in an airplane, put on

    parachutes, and jumped out of the

    plane at a very high altitude.

    → Last year, on my birthday,

    my friends and I

    _____.

◇ PRACTICE 4—SELFSTUDY: Verb + gerund vs. infinitive. (Charts 10-2 → 10-4)

Directions: Choose the correct completion.

1. I would like __**B**__ you and some of my other friends for dinner sometime.
   A. inviting   B. to invite

2. I enjoyed _____ with my family at the lake last summer.
   A. being   B. to be

3. Don agreed _____ me move out of my apartment this weekend.
   A. helping   B. to help

4. My parents can't afford _____ all of my college expenses.
   A. paying   B. to pay

5. Liang-Siok, would you mind _____ this letter on your way home?
   A. mailing   B. to mail

6. Do you expect _____ this course? If so, you'd better work harder.
   A. passing   B. to pass

7. Adam offered _____ for me tonight because I feel awful.
   A. working   B. to work

8. I refuse _____ your proposal. I've made up my mind.
   A. considering   B. to consider

9. I wish you would consider _____ my proposal. I know I can do the job.
   A. accepting   B. to accept

10. I don't think I'll ever finish _____ this report. It just goes on and on.
    A. writing   B. to write

11. I would enjoy _____ you in Cairo while you're studying there.
    A. visiting   B. to visit

12. The children seem _____ why they have to stay home tonight.
    A. understanding   B. to understand

13. Don't forget _____ all of the doors before you go to bed.
    A. locking   B. to lock

14. I'm really sorry. I didn't mean _____ your feelings.
    A. hurting   B. to hurt

15. Why do you keep _____ me the same question over and over again?
    A. asking   B. to ask

16. I've decided _____ for another job. I'll never be happy here.
    A. looking   B. to look

17. You need _____ harder if you want to get the promotion.
    A. trying   B. to try

18. Why do you pretend _____ his company? I know you don't like him.
    A. enjoying   B. to enjoy

19. Let's get together tonight. I want to talk about _____ a new business.
    A. opening   B. to open

20. I have a secret. Do you promise _____ no one?
    A. telling   B. to tell

21. The president plans _____ everyone a bonus at the end of the year.
    A. giving   B. to give

22. I have a good job, and I hope _____ myself all through school.
    A. supporting   B. to support

23. I can't wait _____ work today. I'm taking off on vacation tonight.
    A. finishing   B. to finish

24. My neighbor and I get up at six every morning and go _____.
    A. jogging   B. to jog

◇ PRACTICE 5—SELFSTUDY: Verb + gerund or infinitive. (Charts 10-2 → 10-5)

Directions: Choose the correct answer or answers. **Both answers may be correct.**

1. I want _____**B**_____ the comedy special on TV tonight.
   A. watching   B. to watch

2. I'm a people-watcher. I like _____**A, B**_____ people in public places.
   A. watching   B. to watch

3. I've already begun _____ ideas for my new novel.
   A. collecting   B. to collect

4. A group of Chinese scientists plan _____ their discovery at the world conference next spring.
   A. presenting   B. to present

5. Every time I wash my car, it starts _____.
   A. raining   B. to rain

6. Angela and I continued _____ for several hours.
   A. talking   B. to talk

7. I love _____ on the beach during a storm.
   A. walking   B. to walk

8. I would love _____ a walk today.
   A. taking   B. to take

9. Are you sure you don't mind _____ Johnny for me while I go to the store?
   A. watching   B. to watch

10. Annie hates _____ in the rain.
    A. driving   B. to drive

11. My roommate can't stand _____ to really loud rock music.
    A. listening   B. to listen

12. I don't like _____ in front of other people.
    A. singing   B. to sing

13. Would you like _____ to the concert with us?
    A. going   B. to go

14. Most children can't wait _____ their presents on their birthday.
    A. opening   B. to open

◇ PRACTICE 6—GUIDED STUDY: Verb + gerund or infinitive. (Chart 10-5)

Directions: In writing, or orally in small groups, discuss what you like and don't like to do. Use the given ideas to make sentences that begin with:

I like	*I don't like*	*I don't mind*
I love	*I hate*	
I enjoy	*I can't stand*	

1. cook
   → *I like to cook / I like cooking / I hate to cook / I hate cooking / I don't mind cooking.*
2. live in this city
3. wash dishes
4. fly
5. wait in airports
6. read novels in my spare time
7. eat a delicious meal slowly
8. drive on city streets during rush hour
9. speak in front of a large group
10. play cards for money
11. go to parties where I don't know a single person
12. listen to the sounds of the city while I'm trying to get to sleep
13. visit with friends I haven't seen in a long time
14. get in between two friends who are having an argument
15. travel to strange and exotic places

◇ PRACTICE 7—GUIDED STUDY: Gerunds vs. infinitives. (Charts 10-1 → 10-5)

Directions: Complete the sentences with the correct form, GERUND or INFINITIVE, of the words in parentheses.

A: Have you made any vacation plans?

B: I was hoping (1. go) _____**to go**_____ to an island off the Atlantic coast, but my wife

wanted (2. drive) _____ down the Pacific coast. We've decided

(3. compromise) _____ by going to neither coast. We've agreed (4. find)

_____ a place where both of us want (5. go) _____.

A: So where are you going?

B: Well, we've been considering (6. go) _____ (7. fish) _____

in Canada. We've also discussed (8. take) _____ a train across central and

western Canada. We also have been talking about (9. rent) _____

a sailboat and (10. go) _____ (11. sail) _____

in the Gulf of Mexico.

A: Have you ever thought about (12. stay) _____ home and (13. relax)

_____?

B: That's not a vacation to me. If I stay home during my vacation, I always end up doing all the

chores around home that I've put off (14. do) _____ for the past year. When

I go on a holiday, I like (15. visit) _____ new places and (16. do)

_____ new things. I enjoy (17. see) _____ parts of the

world I've never seen before.

A: What place would you like (18. visit) _____ the most?

B: I'd love (19. go) _____ (20. camp) _____ in New Zealand.

My wife loves (21. camp) _____ in new places too, but I'm afraid she might

refuse (22. go) _____ to New Zealand. She doesn't like long plane flights.

A: Why don't you just pick a spot on a map? Then call and make a hotel reservation.

B: Neither of us can stand (23. spend) _____ two whole weeks at a luxury hotel

somewhere. I don't mean (24. say) _____ anything bad about big hotels, but

both of us seem (25. like) _____ more adventurous vacations.

A: Well, keep (26. think) _____ about it. I'm sure you'll figure out a really great

place for your vacation.

B: We'll have to stop (27. think) _____ about it sometime soon and make a

decision.

B: I can't wait *(28. find)* _____ out where you decide *(29. go)*

_____. I'll expect *(30. hear)* _____ from you when you

make a decision. Don't forget *(31. call)* _____ me.

A: Hmmm. Maybe we should go *(32. ski)* _____ in Switzerland. Or perhaps

we could go *(33. water-ski)* _____ on the Nile. Then there's the possibility

of going *(34. hike)* _____ in the Andes. Of course, we'd probably enjoy

(35. swim) _____ off the Great Barrier Reef of Australia. And we shouldn't

postpone *(36. explore)* _____ the Brazilian rain forest much longer.

Someday I'd really like *(37. climb)* _____ to the top of an active volcano and

(38. look) _____ inside the crater. Or maybe we could . . . .

◇ PRACTICE 8—SELFSTUDY: Uncompleted infinitives. (Chart 10-6)

Directions: Cross out the unnecessary words in Speaker B's responses.

1. A: Did you pay the electric bill?
   B: Not yet. But I'm going to ~~pay the electric bill~~.
2. A: Why didn't you go to class this morning?
   B: I didn't want to go to class this morning.
3. A: Did you call your mother?
   B: No, but I ought to call my mother.
4. A: Have you taken your vacation yet this year?
   B: No, I haven't, but I intend to take my vacation.

◇ PRACTICE 9—GUIDED STUDY: Uncompleted infinitives. (Chart 10-6)

Directions: Complete the dialogues with your own words. Then explain the full meaning of the uncompleted infinitives.

1. A: Would you like ___*to go to a movie with us tonight*_____?

   B: I'd love to!   (→ *I'd love to go to a movie with you tonight.*)

2. A: Does _____*Yoko*_____enjoy _____*meeting new people*_____?

   B: She seems to.   (→ *She seems to enjoy meeting new people.*)

3. A: Did you _____?

   B: No.

   A: Well, you ought to.

4. A: Why didn't _____?

   B: I didn't want to.

5. A: Would you like to _____?

   B: Yes, but I can't afford to.

6. A: Do you _____?

   B: No, but I used to.

7. A: You should _____.

   B: I intend to.

8. A: I'm not going _____.

   B: But you have to!

9. A: Have you _____?

   B: Not yet, but I'm planning to.

10. A: _____?

    B: I'd really like to, but I can't.

◇ PRACTICE 10—SELFSTUDY: Preposition + gerund. (Chart 10-7 and Appendix 1)

Directions: Using the verbs in parentheses, complete the sentences with PREPOSITIONS and GERUNDS. Refer to the list of expressions with prepositions at the bottom of the page if necessary.*

1. I believe _____*in telling*_____ the truth no matter what. *(tell)*

2. I wish the weather would get better. I'm tired _____*of having to be*_____ inside all the time.

   (have to be)

---

*EXPRESSIONS WITH PREPOSITIONS:

be afraid of	*be* good at	plan on
apologize for	have the (bad) habit of	*be* responsible for
believe in	*be* in danger of	stop someone from
concentrate on	*be* in the habit of	succeed in
dream about	insist on	talk into doing
be excited about	*be* interested in	thank someone for
feel like	look forward to	*be* tired of
forgive someone for	*be* nervous about	worry about

3. I don't go swimming because I'm afraid _____. (drown)

4. Greg is nervous _____ his girlfriend's parents for the first time. (meet)

5. I don't know how to thank you _____ me. (help)

6. Are you interested _____ to a bullfight? (go)

7. I worked on it all night, but I didn't succeed _____ the problem. (solve)

8. I just can't get excited _____ Disneyland for the third time in two years. (visit)

9. Carlos has the irritating habit _____ gum very loudly. (chew)

10. Why do you constantly worry _____ your parents? (please)

11. Jonathan! Please concentrate _____ your assignment. (read)

12. Every summer, I look forward _____ a vacation with my family. (take)

13. Do you feel _____ me why you're so sad? (tell)

14. I apologize _____, but I was trying to protect you from the truth. Sometimes the truth hurts. (lie)

15. Why do you always insist _____ for everything when we go out for dinner? (pay)

16. I'm in the habit _____ every morning, but I'm too tired today. (jog)

17. I want you to know that I'm sorry. I don't know if you can ever forgive me _____ you so much trouble. (cause)

18. I'm not very good _____ names. (remember)

19. I'm not happy in my work. I often dream _____ my job. (quit)

20. How do you stop someone _____ something you know is wrong? (do)

21. You can't convince me to change my mind. After what she did, you'll never talk me _____ her. (forgive)

22. I'm too tired to cook, but I hadn't planned _____ out tonight. (eat)

23. Who's responsible _____ these coffee beans all over the floor? (spill)

24. You'd better be careful. You're in danger _____ this class. (fail)

25. Anna made a lot of big mistakes at work. That's why she was afraid _____ her job. (lose)*

---

*Note that *lose* is spelled with one "o." The word *loose*, with two "o's," is an adjective meaning "not tight." (e.g., My shirt is big and loose.) Pronunciation difference: *lose* = /luwz/; *loose* = /luws/.

◇ PRACTICE 11—GUIDED STUDY: Preposition + gerund. (Chart 10-7 and Appendix 1)

Directions: In writing or in groups, make up sentences that contain GERUNDS. Include the appropriate PREPOSITION in each.

Example: apologize to (. . .) + interrupt / be / call
→ *You should apologize to Tarik for interrupting him.*
I apologized to my friend for being late.
Rosa apologized to me for calling after midnight.

1. be nervous + *speak / go / get*
2. thank (. . .) + *open / help / invite*
3. feel like (. . .) + *go / have / take*
4. look forward + *do / stop / skydive*
5. apologize to (. . .) + *sell / give / leave*
6. worry + *lose / not have / be*
7. forgive (. . .) + *lie / take / forget*
8. be excited + *go / meet / move*
9. insist + *answer / drive / fly*
10. believe + *help / tell / trust*

◇ PRACTICE 12—SELFSTUDY: Using *by* + gerund. (Chart 10-8)

Directions: Describe what the people did by using **BY** + a GERUND.

1. *Mary:* How did you comfort the child?
    Sue: I held him in my arms.

    → Sue comforted the child _____*by holding*_____ him in her arms.

2. *Pat:* How did you improve your vocabulary?
    Nadia: I read a lot of books.

    → Nadia improved her vocabulary _____ a lot of books.

3. *Kirk:* How did Grandma amuse the children?
    Sally: She told them a story.

    → Grandma amused the children _____ them a story.

4. *Masako:* How did you improve your English?
    Pedro: I watched TV a lot.

    → Pedro improved his English _____ TV a lot.

5. *Jeffrey:* How did you catch up with the bus?
    Jim: I ran as fast as I could.

    → Jim caught up with the bus _____ as fast as he could.

6. *Sam:* How did you recover from your cold?
    Abdul: I stayed in bed and took care of myself.

    → Abdul recovered _____ in bed and _____ care of himself.

7. *Mr. Lee:* How did you earn your children's respect?
    Mr. Fox: I treated them with respect at all times.

    → Mr. Smith earned his children's respect _____
    them with respect at all times.

◇ PRACTICE 13—GUIDED STUDY: Using *by* + gerund. (Chart 10-8)

Directions: Complete the sentences in Column A with **BY** + an appropriate idea from Column B.

Example: I arrived on time by taking a taxi instead of the bus.

COLUMN A

1. I arrived on time
2. I put out the fire
3. Giraffes can reach the leaves at the top
4. I fixed the chair
5. Sara was able to buy an expensive stereo system
6. A hippopotamus can cross a river
7. I figured out how to cook the noodles
8. Pam finished her project on time
9. You can figure out how old a tree is

COLUMN B

A. tighten the loose screws
B. count the rings
C. read the directions on the package
D. walk on the bottom of the riverbed
E. pour water on it
F. work all through the night
G. stretch their long necks
H. save her money for two years
✔ I. take a taxi instead of a bus

CROSS-SECTION

20 RINGS
20 YEARS OLD

◇ PRACTICE 14—SELFSTUDY: Using *with*. (Chart 10-8)

Directions: Complete the sentences using **WITH** and appropriate words from the following list.

✔*a broom*	*a needle and thread*	*a shovel*
a hammer	*a pair of scissors*	*a spoon*
a key	*a saw*	*a thermometer*
a knife		

1. I swept the floor _____ **with a broom** _____.

2. I sewed the button on my shirt _____.

3. I cut the wood _____.

4. I took my temperature _____.

5. I stirred my coffee _____.

6. I opened the locked door _____.

7. I dug a hole in the ground _____.

8. I nailed two pieces of wood together _____.

9. I cut the meat _____.

10. I cut the paper _____.

◇ PRACTICE 15—SELFSTUDY: *By* vs. *with*. (Chart 10-8)

Directions: Complete the sentences with **BY** or **WITH**.

1. Alice greeted me _____ **with** _____ a smile.

2. Ms. Williams goes to work every day _____ **by** _____ bus.

3. I pounded the nail into the wood _____ a hammer.

4. Tom went to the next city _____ train.

5. I got in touch with Bill _____ phone.

6. Akihiko eats _____ chopsticks.

7. I didn't notice that the envelope wasn't addressed to me. I opened it _____ mistake.

8. I sent a message to Ann _____ fax.

9. Jack protected his eyes from the sun _____ his hand.

10. Janice put out the fire _____ a bucket of water.

11. I pay my bills _____ mail.

12. I solved the math problem _____ a calculator.

13. We traveled to Boston _____ car.

14. The rider kicked the sides of the horse _____ her heels.

15. Jim was extremely angry. He hit the wall _____ his fist.

16. At the beach, Julie wrote her name in the sand _____ her finger.

◇ PRACTICE 16—SELFSTUDY: Gerund as subject; *it* + infinitive. (Charts 10-9 → 10-10)

Directions: Complete the sentences by using a GERUND as the subject or IT + INFINITIVE. Add the word **IS** where appropriate. Use the verbs in the following list.

complete	eat	live
drive	✔ learn	swim

1. a. __**It is**__ easy for anyone __**to learn**__ how to cook an egg.

   b. __**Learning**__ how to cook an egg __**is**__ easy for anyone.

2. a. _____ nutritious food _____ important for your health.

   b. _____ important for your health _____ nutritious food.

3. a. _____ on the wrong side of the road _____ against the law.

   b. _____ against the law _____ on the wrong side of the road.

4. a. _____ fun for both children and adults _____ in the ocean.

   b. _____ in the ocean _____ fun for both children and adults.

5. a. _____ expensive _____ in a dormitory?

   b. _____ in a dormitory expensive?

6. a. _____ difficult _____ these sentences correctly?

   b. _____ these sentences correctly difficult?

◇ PRACTICE 17—GUIDED STUDY: Gerund as subject; *it* + infinitive. (Chart 10-9)

Directions: Make sentences by combining ideas from Column A and Column B. Use GERUND SUBJECTS or IT + INFINITIVE.

Example: Riding a bicycle is easy / dangerous / fun / relaxing.   OR
It is easy / dangerous / fun / relaxing to ride a bicycle.

COLUMN A	COLUMN B
1. ride a bicycle	A. against the law
2. read newspapers	B. boring
3. study grammar	C. dangerous
4. play tennis	D. easy
5. steal cars	E. educational
6. listen to a two-hour speech	F. embarrassing
7. predict the exact time of an earthquake	G. exciting
8. forget someone's name	H. frightening
9. walk alone through a dark forest at night	I. fun
10. go fishing with your friends	J. hard
11. know the meaning of every word in a dictionary	K. important
	L. impossible
12. be honest with yourself at all times	M. relaxing
13. change a flat tire	N. a waste of time
14. visit museums	

◇ PRACTICE 18—GUIDED STUDY: *It* + *for* (*someone*) + infinitive. (Chart 10-10)

Directions: Make sentences using IT + FOR (*someone*) + INFINITIVE by combining ideas from Columns A, B, and C. Add your own words if you wish.

Example: difficult
→ *It is difficult for me to be on time for class.*
It is difficult for some people to learn how to swim.
It's difficult for children to understand adults' behavior.

COLUMN A	COLUMN B	COLUMN C
1. difficult	anyone	spend time with friends
2. easy	children	predict the exact time of an earthquake
3. fun	me	change a flat tire
4. important	most people	be on time for class
5. impossible	some people	understand adults' behavior
6. enjoyable	students	obey their parents
7. interesting		observe animals in their wild habitat
8. possible		visit new places
		learn how to swim
		live on the planet Mars

◇ PRACTICE 19—GUIDED STUDY: *It + take.* (Charts 6-11 and 10-9 → 10-10)

Directions: Use your own words to complete the following sentences.

Example: It takes . . . hours to . . . .
→ ***It takes** five **hours to** fly from Los Angeles to Honolulu.*

Example: It takes a lot of work for . . . to . . . .
→ ***It takes a lot of work for** most small businesses **to** succeed.*

1. It takes time for . . . to . . . .
2. It takes a lot of money to . . . .
3. It takes . . . minutes to . . . .
4. How long does it take to . . . ?

5. It will take . . . years for . . . to . . . .
6. It takes patience / courage / skill to . . . .
7. It takes hard work for . . . to . . . .
8. It takes stamina and determination to . . . .

◇ PRACTICE 20—GUIDED STUDY: *It + for (someone) + infinitive.* (Chart 10-10)

Directions: Complete the sentences with your own words.

1. It is easy for . . . to . . . .
2. It's traditional for . . . to . . . .
3. It's impossible for . . . to . . . .
4. It takes *(a length of time)* for . . . to . . . .

5. It's sensible for . . . to . . . .
6. Is it necessary for . . . to . . . ?
7. It's important for . . . to . . . .
8. It's difficult for . . . to . . . .

◇ PRACTICE 21—SELFSTUDY: *(In order) to.* (Chart 10-11)

Directions: Complete the sentences in Column A by using the ideas in Column B. Connect the ideas with (**IN ORDER**) **TO**.

Example: I called the hotel desk (in order) to ask for an extra pillow.

COLUMN A	COLUMN B
1. I called the hotel desk	A. keep their feet warm and dry
2. I turned on the radio	B. reach the top shelf
3. I looked in the encyclopedia	C. listen to a ball game
4. People wear boots	D. find the population of Malaysia
5. Andy went to Egypt	✔ E. ask for an extra pillow
6. Ms. Lane stood on tiptoe	F. chase a stray dog away
7. The dentist moved the light closer to my face	G. help him pay the rent
8. I clapped my hands and yelled	H. get some fresh air and exercise
9. Maria took a walk in the park	I. see the ancient pyramids
10. I offered my cousin some money	J. look into my mouth

◇ PRACTICE 22—SELFSTUDY: Purpose: *to* vs. *for.* (Chart 10-11)

Directions: Complete the sentences with **TO** or **FOR**.

1. Sam went to the hospital _____***for***_____ an operation.

2. I hired a cab _____***to***_____ take me to the boat dock.

3. Frank stayed after school _____ get some extra help from the teacher.

4. I play tennis twice a week _____ exercise and relaxation.

5. I sent a card to Carol _____ wish her a happy birthday.

6. Two police officers came to my apartment _____ ask me about my cousin.

7. Mr. Wong works in his garden _____ the pure pleasure of it.

8. I looked in the encyclopedia _____ information about Ecuador.

9. Jennifer used some medicine _____ cure an infection on her arm.

10. I lent Yvette money _____ her school expenses.

11. My three brothers, two sisters, and parents all came to town _____ attend my graduation.

12. I went to my boss _____ permission to take the rest of the day off.

◇ PRACTICE 23—SELFSTUDY: *Too* and *enough* + infinitive. (Chart 10-12)

Directions: Complete the sentences by choosing from the given words. Use **TOO** or **ENOUGH** and an **INFINITIVE**.

1. *strong/lift*   I'm not _____**strong enough to lift**_____ a refrigerator.

2. *weak/lift*   Most people are _____**too weak to lift**_____ a refrigerator without help.

3. *full/hold*   My suitcase is _____ any more clothes.

4. *large/hold*   My suitcase isn't _____ all the clothes I want to take on my trip.

5. *busy/answer*   I was _____ _____ the phone. I let it keep ringing until the caller gave up.

6. *early/get*   We got to the concert _____ good seats.

7. *big/get*   Rex is _____ into Bobo's doghouse.

8. *big/hold*   Julie's purse is _____

_____ her dog Pepper.

◇ PRACTICE 24—SELFSTUDY: *Too* and *enough* + infinitive. (Chart 10-12)

Directions: Complete the sentences with **TOO** or **ENOUGH**. Write a slash (/) if nothing is needed in a blank.

1. Alan is _____ *too* _____ smart _____ */* _____ to make that kind of mistake.

2. Alan is _____ smart _____ to understand how to solve that

problem.

3. My pocket is _____ */* _____ big _____ *enough* _____ to hold my wallet. I always carry

my wallet there.

4. A horse is _____ big _____ for a person to lift.

5. I'm uncomfortable. This room is _____ hot _____. Why don't

you open the window?

6. That watch is _____ expensive _____. I can't afford it.

7. Are you _____ tall _____ to reach that book for me? The green

one on the top shelf. Thanks.

8. Ask John to help you move that box. He's _____ strong _____ to lift it.

9. I am _____ busy _____ to help you right now.

10. I think this problem is _____ important _____ to require our immediate attention.

11. Nora is not _____ tired _____ to finish the project before she goes home.

12. Our company is _____ successful _____ to start several new branches overseas.

◇ PRACTICE 25—SELFSTUDY: Gerunds vs. infinitives. (Charts 10-1 → 10-10)

Directions: Complete the sentences with the words in parentheses: GERUND or INFINITIVE.

1. It's difficult for me *(remember)* _____*to remember*_____ phone numbers.

2. My cat is good at *(catch)* _____*catching*_____ mice.

3. I bought a newspaper *(look)* _____ at the ads for apartments for rent.

4. Tourists like *(go)* _____ *(swim)* _____ in the warm ocean in Hawaii.

5. I called my friend *(invite)* _____ her for dinner.

6. Hillary talked about *(go)* _____ to graduate school.

7. Sarosh found out what was happening by *(listen)* _____ carefully to everything that was said.

8. Children, stop *(draw)* _____ pictures on the tablecloth!

9. Professor Amani has a strong accent. It is difficult for his students *(understand)* _____ him. He needs *(improve)* _____ his pronunciation if he wants *(be)* _____ a good lecturer. *(lecture)* _____ requires good communication skills.

10. A: Hi! I'm home!

   B: Welcome back. Did you have a good trip?

   A: Yes, thanks. How's everything? How are my goldfish? I hope you didn't forget *(feed)* _____ them.

   B: Oh, my gosh!

11. Dan's goldfish died when he was away on a trip because his roommate forgot *(feed)* _____ them. Dan is considering *(get)* _____ a new roommate.

12. My friend Akihiko has goldfish in a pond in his garden. He enjoys *(feed)* _____ them one by one with chopsticks.

13. Michelle Yin Yin Ko works sixteen hours a day *(earn)* _____ enough money *(take)* _____ care of her elderly parents as well as her three children.

14. It takes care, patience, and a little luck *(take)* _____ a really good photograph of wildlife.

15. No matter how wonderful a trip is, it's always good *(get)* _____ back home and *(sleep)* _____ in one's own bed.

16. A: Quit *(stare)* _____ at the phone. Greg isn't going to call.

    B: I keep *(think)* _____ the phone will ring any second.

    A: I don't mean *(be)* _____ unsympathetic, but I think you'd better forget about Greg. It's over.

17. It's important to your health for you *(work)* _____ at a job you like. If you hate *(go)* _____ to your job, you should seriously think about *(look)* _____ for a different kind of job. The stress of *(do)* _____ work you hate day in and day out can damage your health.

◇ PRACTICE 26—SELFSTUDY: Gerunds vs. infinitives. (Chart 10-1 → 10-10)

Directions: Find and underline the GERUNDS and INFINITIVES in the following.

1. Jim offered <u>to help</u> me with my work.

2. My son isn't old enough to stay home alone.

3. Do you enjoy being alone sometimes, or do you prefer to be with other people all the time?

4. I called my friend to thank her for the lovely gift.

5. Mary talked about going downtown tomorrow, but I'd like to stay home.

6. It is interesting to learn about earthquakes.

7. Approximately one million earthquakes occur around the world in a year's time. Six thousand can be felt by humans. Of those, one hundred and twenty are strong enough to cause serious damage to buildings, and twenty are violent enough to destroy a city.

8. It's important to respect the power of nature. A recent earthquake destroyed a bridge in California. It took five years for humans to build the bridge. It took nature fifteen seconds to knock it down.

9. Predicting earthquakes is difficult. I read about one scientist who tries to predict earthquakes by reading the daily newspaper's lost-and-found ads for lost pets. He believes that animals can sense an earthquake before it comes. He thinks they then begin to act strangely. Dogs and cats respond to the threat by running away to a safer place. By counting the number of ads for lost pets, he expects to be able to predict when an earthquake will occur.

◇ PRACTICE 27—GUIDED STUDY: Gerunds vs. infinitives. (Charts 10-1 → 10-10)

Directions: Complete the sentences with the words in parentheses: GERUND or INFINITIVE.

1. (study) _____**Studying**_____ English is fun.

2. My boss makes a habit of (jot)* _____ quick notes to her employees when they've done a good job.

3. From the earth, the sun and the moon appear (be) _____ almost the same size.

4. A: I don't like airplanes.

   B: Why? Are you afraid of (fly) _____ ?

   A: No, I'm afraid of (crash) _____ .

5. I keep (forget) _____ (call) _____ my friend Louise. I'd better write myself a note.

6. People in the modern world are wasteful of natural resources. For example, every three months, people in North America throw away enough aluminum (build) _____ an entire airplane.

7. I am so busy! I have just enough time (do) _____ what I need (do) _____, but not enough time (do) _____ what I'd like (do) _____.

8. (ask) _____ others about themselves and their lives is one of the secrets of (get) _____ along with other people. If you want (make) _____ and (keep) _____ friends, it is important (be) _____ sincerely interested in other people's lives.

9. A: Have you called Amanda yet?

   B: No. I keep (put) _____ it off.

   A: Why?

---

*Jot = write quickly and briefly.

B: She's mad at me for *(forget)* _____ *(send)* _____ a

card on her birthday.

A: It's silly for her *(get)* _____ mad about something like that. Just call her

and say you are sorry about *(remember, not)* _____ to wish

her a happy birthday. She can't stay mad at you forever.

10. In days of old, it was customary for a servant *(taste)* _____ the king's food

before the king ate *(make)* _____ sure it was not poisoned.

11. One of my good friends, Larry, has the bad habit of *(interrupt)* _____

others while they're talking.

12. I like *(travel)* _____ to out-of-the-way places. I don't like *(go)*

_____ to usual tourist places when I'm on holiday.

13. Large bee colonies have 80,000 workers. These worker bees must visit fifty million flowers

(make) _____ one kilogram (2.2 pounds) of honey. It's no wonder that

"busy as a bee" is a common expression.

14. Exercise is good for you. Why don't you walk up the stairs instead of *(take)*

_____ the elevator?

15. Stop *(crack)* _____ those nuts with your teeth! Here. Use a nutcracker.

Do you want *(be)* _____ toothless by the time you're thirty?

◇ PRACTICE 28—GUIDED STUDY: Gerunds vs. infinitives. (Charts 10-1 → 10-10)

Directions: Complete the sentences with the words in parentheses: GERUND or INFINITIVE.

1. A: Let's quit (argue) _____*arguing*_____. We're getting nowhere. Let's just agree

   (disagree) _____ and still (be) _____ friends.

   B: Sounds good to me. And I apologize for (raise) _____ my voice. I

   didn't mean (yell) _____ at you.

   A: That's okay. I didn't intend (get) _____ angry at you either.

2. A: David, why did you want (sneak) _____ into the movie theater without

   (pay) _____?

   B: I don't know, Mom. My friends talked me into (do) _____ it, I guess.

   A: That's not a very good reason. You are responsible for your actions, not your friends.

   B: I know. I'm sorry.

   A: How does this make you feel? Do you like yourself for (try) _____

   (sneak) _____ into the theater?

   B: No. It doesn't make me feel good about myself.

   A: You're young. We all have lessons like this to learn as we grow up. Just remember: It's

   essential for you (have) _____ a good opinion of yourself. It's very

   important for all of us (like) _____ ourselves. When we do something

   wrong, we stop (like) _____ ourselves, and that doesn't feel good. Do

   you promise never (do) _____ anything like that again?

   B: Yes. I promise! I'm really sorry, Mom.

3. Different cultures have different gestures. When North Americans meet someone, they usually

   offer a strong handshake and look the other person straight in the eye. In some countries,

   however, it is impolite (shake) _____ hands firmly, and (look)

   _____ the person in the eye is equally rude.

4. How close do you stand to another person when you are speaking? North Americans prefer

   (stand) _____ just a little less than an arm's length from someone. Many

   people in the Middle East and Latin America prefer (move) _____ in

   closer than that during a conversation.

5. (Smile) _____ at another person is a universal, cross-cultural gesture.

   Everyone throughout the world understands the meaning of a smile.

6. A: What do you feel like *(do)* _____ex 6_____ this afternoon?

   B: I feel like *(go)* _____ *(shop)* _____ at the mall.

   A: I feel like *(go)* _____ to a used car lot and *(pretend)*

   _____ *(be)* _____ interested in *(buy)*

   _____ a car.

   B: You're kidding. Why would you want *(do)* _____ that?

   A: I like cars. Maybe we could even take one out for a test drive. You know I'm planning *(get)*

   _____ a car as soon as I can afford *(buy)* _____

   one. I can't wait *(have)* _____ my own car. Maybe we'll find the car

   of my dreams at a used car lot. Come on. It sounds like fun.

   B: Nah. Not me. You go ahead. *(pretend)* _____ *(be)*

   _____ interested in *(buy)* _____ a used car

   doesn't sound like my idea of fun.

◇ PRACTICE 29—SELFSTUDY: Phrasal verbs (separable). (Chart 10-13)

Directions: Complete the sentences with the correct PARTICLE from the list below.

away	back	down	off	on	out	up

1. When are you going to *pay* me ____**back**____ the money you owe me?

2. *Turn* _____ the radio! It's too loud! I can't hear myself think.

3. Debra *put* _____ the fire in the wastebasket with a fire extinguisher.

4. After I wash and dry the dishes, I *put* them _____. In other words, I put them in the
   cupboard where they belong.

5. Before you buy shoes, you should *try* them _____ to see if they fit.

6. I can't hear the TV. Could you please *turn* it _____? Thanks. No, don't *shut* it
   _____! I want to hear the news. I wanted you to make it louder, not turn it off.

7. A: That's mine! *Give* it _____!

   B: No, it's not. It's mine!

   C: Now children. Don't fight.

8. A: I don't hear anyone on the other end of the phone.

   B: Just *hang* _____. It's probably a wrong number.

9. A: I hear that Tom *asked* you _____ for next Saturday night.

   B: Yes, he did. He called a couple of hours ago. We're going to the symphony concert.

   A: The concert's been *called* _____. Didn't you hear about it? The musicians are on strike.

   B: No, I didn't. I'd better *call* Tom _____ and ask him what he wants to do.

◇ PRACTICE 30—SELFSTUDY: Phrasal verbs (separable). (Chart 10-13)

Directions: Complete the sentences with appropriate PRONOUNS and these PARTICLES:

| *away* | *back* | *down* | *off* | *on* | *out* | *up* |

1. When the children finished playing with *their toys*, they put _____***them away***_____.

2. If you don't want *your shirt* to get wrinkled, you'd better hang_____.

3. I wanted to see if *the shoes* were the right size, so I tried _____.

4. *The radio* was too loud, so I turned _____ a little.

5. I feel like talking to *Jim*. I think I'll call _____.

6. Rick poured some water on *the campfire* to put _____.

7. Whenever I borrow *money*, I make sure to pay _____ as soon as I can.

8. I can't hear *the TV*. Could you please turn _____? Thanks.

9. There's a phone message here from *Mary*. She sounds worried. You'd better call _____ as soon as possible.

10. If you leave *your computer* for a short while, you don't need to shut _____.

11. Because of crowd violence, *the championship match* was canceled. The authorities called _____.

12. No, Tommy, we're not going to buy *that candy bar*. Put _____ where you got it.

13. Tom invited *Linda* to go to a concert with him. In other words, he asked _____.

14. I'll lend you *my grammar book,* but be sure to give _____ to me before class tomorrow.

CHAPTER 11
The Passive

◇ PRACTICE 1—SELFSTUDY: Active vs. passive. (Chart 11-1)

Directions: Circle ACTIVE if the given sentence is active; circle PASSIVE if it is passive. Underline the VERB.

1. (ACTIVE)   PASSIVE   Farmers <u>grow</u> corn.
2. ACTIVE   (PASSIVE)   Corn <u>is grown</u> by farmers.
3. ACTIVE   PASSIVE   Sara wrote the letter.
4. ACTIVE   PASSIVE   The letter was written by Sara.
5. ACTIVE   PASSIVE   The teacher explained the lesson.
6. ACTIVE   PASSIVE   The lesson was explained by the teacher.
7. ACTIVE   PASSIVE   Bridges are designed by engineers.
8. ACTIVE   PASSIVE   Engineers design bridges.
9. ACTIVE   PASSIVE   The mouse ate the cheese.
10. ACTIVE   PASSIVE   The cheese was eaten by the mouse.

◇ PRACTICE 2—SELFSTUDY: Review of past participles. (Chart 2-3)

Directions: Write the PAST PARTICIPLES of the verbs. The list contains both regular and irregular verbs.

	SIMPLE FORM	SIMPLE PAST	PAST PARTICIPLE			SIMPLE FORM	SIMPLE PAST	PAST PARTICIPLE
1.	bring	brought	___*brought*___	14.	play	played	_____
2.	build	built	_____	15.	read	read*	_____
3.	buy	bought	_____	16.	save	saved	_____
4.	eat	ate	_____	17.	send	sent	_____
5.	plan	planned	_____	18.	speak	spoke	_____
6.	give	gave	_____	19.	spend	spent	_____
7.	grow	grew	_____	20.	take	took	_____
8.	hit	hit	_____	21.	teach	taught	_____
9.	hurt	hurt	_____	22.	go	went	_____
10.	leave	left	_____	23.	visit	visited	_____
11.	lose	lost	_____	24.	wear	wore	_____
12.	make	made	_____	25.	write	wrote	_____
13.	find	found	_____	26.	do	did	_____

◇ PRACTICE 3—SELFSTUDY: Passive form. (Charts 11-1, 11-2, and 11-6)

Directions: Use the given form of BE (WAS, IS, GOING TO BE, etc.) and complete the sentences with the PAST PARTICIPLES of any verbs in the list in Practice 2.

1. *was*   There's no more candy. All the candy _____*was eaten*_____ by the children.

2. *is*   Arabic _____ by the people of Syria and Iraq.

3. *are*   Books _____ by authors.

4. *was*   My friend _____ in an accident. He broke his nose.

5. *is going to be*   Bombay, India, _____ by thousands of tourists this year.

6. *has been*   *War and Peace* is a famous book. It _____ by millions of people.

_____
*The simple past and past participle of *read* are pronounced "red," as the color red.

7. *will be* The championship game _____ in Milan next week.

8. *can be* Everyone _____ to read. I'll teach you if you'd like.

9. *are going to be* Our pictures _____ by a professional photographer at the wedding.

10. *have been* Oranges _____ by farmers in Jordan since ancient times.

11. *is* Special fire-resistant clothing _____ by firefighters.

12. *will be* A new bridge across the White River _____ by the city government next year.

◇ PRACTICE 4—SELFSTUDY: Tense forms of the passive. (Chart 11-1 and 11-2)

Directions: Complete the sentences with the passive form of the given verbs.

PART I: Use the **SIMPLE PRESENT** with:

    ✔ collect   grow   understand
       eat   pay   write

1. Taxes _____**are collected**_____ by the government.

2. Small fish _____ by big fish.

3. Rice _____ by farmers in Korea.

4. I _____ for my work by my boss.

5. Books _____ by authors.

6. The meaning of a smile _____ by everyone.

PART II: Use the **SIMPLE PAST** with:

    build   collect   destroy   write

7. Yesterday the students' papers _____**were**_____ by the teacher at the end of the test.

8. The Great Wall of China _____ by Chinese emperors over 2500 years ago.

9. The book *War and Peace* _____ by Leo Tolstoy, a famous Russian novelist.

10. Several small buildings _____ by the recent earthquake in Los Angeles.

PART III: Use the *PRESENT PERFECT* with:

> read   speak   visit   wear

11. The pyramids in Egypt _____ *have* _____ by millions of tourists through the years.

12. Spanish _____ by people in Latin America for nearly 600 years.

13. Mark Twain's books _____ by millions of people through the years.

14. Perfume _____ by both men and women since ancient times.

PART IV: Use *WILL* with:

> discover   visit

15. New information about the universe _____ *will* _____ by scientists in the twenty-first century.

16. Hawaii _____ by thousands of tourists this year.

PART V: Use *BE GOING TO* with:

> elect   hurt   offer   save

17. Your friend _____ *is going* _____ by your unkind remark when she hears about it.

18. New computer courses _____ by the university next year.

19. Tigers _____ from extinction by people who care.

20. A new leader _____ by the people in my country next month.

◇ PRACTICE 5—SELFSTUDY: Passive to active. (Charts 6-2, 11-1 and 11-2)

Directions: Change the passive sentences to ACTIVE. Keep the same verb tense.

1. Taxes are collected by the government. → *The government collects taxes.*

2. Small fish are eaten by big fish.

3. The meaning of a smile is understood by everyone.

4. *War and Peace* was written by Leo Tolstoy.

5. The pyramids in Egypt have been visited by millions of tourists.

6. New information about the universe will be discovered by scientists in the twenty-first century.

◇ PRACTICE 6—SELFSTUDY: Passive to active. (Charts 6-2, 11-1 and 11-2)

Directions: Change the passive sentences to ACTIVE. Keep the same tense. Some of the sentences are questions.

1. The letter was signed by Mr. Rice. → *Mr. Rice signed the letter.*
2. Was the letter signed by Mr. Foster? → *Did Mr. Foster sign the letter?*
3. The fax was sent by Ms. Owens.
4. Was the other fax sent by Mr. Chu?
5. Will Adam be met at the airport by Mr. Berg?
6. Adam will be met at the airport by Mrs. Berg.
7. Have you been invited to the reception by Mrs. Jordan?
8. I have been invited to the reception by Mr. Lee.
9. Is the homework going to be collected by the teacher?
10. The homework is going to be collected by the teacher.

◇ PRACTICE 7—GUIDED STUDY: Passive to active. (Charts 6-2, 11-1 and 11-2)

Directions: Change the passive sentences to active. Keep the same tense. Some of the sentences are questions.

1. Were you taught to read by your parents?

   → *Did your parents teach you to read?*

2. I was taught to read by my parents.

   → *My parents taught me to read.*

3. Was the riot stopped by the police?
4. Love and understanding are needed by all children.
5. The ball was kicked by the captain of the soccer team.
6. Was the chalkboard washed by a student?
7. My suitcase was inspected by a customs officer.
8. Are we going to be met at the train station by your cousin?
9. The plans for the new hospital have already been drawn by the architect.
10. The bear was chased up a tree by a dog.

◇ PRACTICE 8—SELFSTUDY: Transitive vs. Intransitive. (Chart 11-3)

Directions: Circle TRANSITIVE if the verb takes an object; circle INTRANSITIVE if it does not. **Underline** the OBJECT OF THE VERB.

1. (TRANSITIVE)   INTRANSITIVE   Alex wrote <u>a letter</u>.
2. TRANSITIVE   (INTRANSITIVE)   Alex waited for Amy. *(There is no object of the verb.)*
3. TRANSITIVE   INTRANSITIVE   Rita lives in Mexico.

4.	TRANSITIVE	INTRANSITIVE	Sam walked to his office.
5.	TRANSITIVE	INTRANSITIVE	Kate caught the ball.
6.	TRANSITIVE	INTRANSITIVE	My plane arrived at six-thirty.
7.	TRANSITIVE	INTRANSITIVE	Emily is crying.
8.	TRANSITIVE	INTRANSITIVE	A falling tree hit my car.
9.	TRANSITIVE	INTRANSITIVE	I returned the book to the library yesterday.
10.	TRANSITIVE	INTRANSITIVE	A bolt of lightning appeared in the sky last night.

◇ PRACTICE 9—SELFSTUDY: Active and passive. (Charts 11-1 → 11-3)

Directions: <u>Underline</u> the OBJECT OF THE VERB if the given sentence has one. Then change the sentence to the passive. Some sentences cannot be changed to the passive.

ACTIVE   PASSIVE

1. A noise awakened <u>me</u>.   **I *was awakened by a noise.***
                                       (*no change*)

2. It rained hard yesterday.

3. Alice discovered the mistake.

4. We stayed at a hotel last night.

5. Dinosaurs existed millions of years ago.

6. I usually agree with my sister.

7. Many people die during a war.

8. In the fairy tale, a princess kissed a frog.

9. I slept only four hours last night.

10. Anita fixed the chair.

11. Did Susan agree with Prof. Hill?

12. Did the Koreans invent gunpowder?

13. The /*th*/ sound doesn't occur in my native language.

14. Research scientists will discover a cure for AIDS* someday.

15. A cloud of migrating butterflies appeared out of nowhere.

_____
*AIDS = a disease (**A**uto **I**mmune **D**eficiency **S**yndrome).

Directions: If the sentence contains a BY-phrase, underline it. Then answer the question. If you don't know the exact person or people who performed the action, write UNKNOWN. (NOTE: Most of the sentences are passive, but some are active.)

1. The mail is usually delivered to Bob's apartment around eleven o'clock.
   Who delivers the mail?   **unknown**

2. The wastebasket was emptied <u>by Fred</u>.
   Who emptied the wastebasket?   **Fred**

3. Paul carried the suitcases into the airport for his elderly father.
   Who carried the suitcases?

4. The Eiffel Tower was designed by Alexandre Eiffel.
   Who designed the Eiffel Tower?

5. The Eiffel Tower was erected in 1889.
   Who erected the Eiffel Tower?

6. Nicole visited the Eiffel Tower when she was in France last year.
   Who visited the Eiffel Tower?

7. Our classroom building was built in the 1950s.
   Who built the classroom building?

8. Our exam papers will be corrected by Ms. Brown.
   Who will correct the exam papers?

9. Coffee is grown in Brazil.
   Who grows coffee in Brazil?

10. Sara accepted Mike's invitation to the international street fair next Saturday.
    Who accepted the invitation?

11. Eric Wong's new book will be translated into many languages.
    Who will translate Eric Wong's new book?

12. Rebecca's bicycle was stolen yesterday from in front of the library.
    Who stole Rebecca's bicycle?

◇ PRACTICE 11—GUIDED STUDY: The *by*-phrase. (Chart 11-4)

Directions: <u>Underline</u> the passive verbs. Answer the questions. If you don't know the exact person or people who performed the action, write UNKNOWN.

1. Soft duck feathers <u>are used</u> to make pillows.
   Who uses duck feathers to make pillows?   **unknown**

2. The mail <u>was opened</u> by Shelley.
   Who opened the mail?   **Shelley**

3. All the tickets for the school play tonight have been sold.
   Who sold the tickets to the school play?

4. My flight was canceled because of the heavy fog.
   Who canceled the flight?

5. Aunt Mary's favorite glass bowl was accidentally broken by her nephew David.
   Who broke the glass bowl?

6. Malawi is a country in southeastern Africa. A new highway is going to be built in Malawi next year.
   Who is going to build the new highway?

7. The invention of the printing press changed the world because it allowed many people instead of few to have copies of books. It was invented by Johannes Gutenberg around 1440. Before that, people wrote books by hand. Writing books by hand was a slow process.
Who invented the printing press?

8. One of the most significant inventions in the history of civilization is the wheel. It was invented around five thousand years ago. It allowed people to pull things in carts instead of carrying everything on their backs or in their arms.
Who invented the wheel?

9. Yesterday there was almost a tragedy at the swimming pool. A young boy who didn't know how to swim jumped in the deep end. He panicked★ when he couldn't swim to the side of the pool. He was saved from drowning by a lifeguard at the pool. It's lucky that she was alert.
Who saved the boy?

10. The name *Thailand* means "land of the free." The Thai people have never been ruled by a foreign power. Thailand is a constitutional monarchy. The prime minister is nominated by the National Assembly and then is appointed by the monarch. Senators are chosen by the prime minister and representatives are elected by the people.
Who nominates the prime minister?
Who appoints the prime minister?
Who chooses the senators?
Who elects the representatives?
What countries have ruled Thailand?

★*To panic* is a verb that means "to become suddenly and greatly frightened." Notice that a "k" is added before the *-ed* ending.

◇ PRACTICE 12—SELFSTUDY: Active vs. passive. (Charts 11-1 → 11-4)

    Directions: Complete the sentences with the correct forms of the verbs in parentheses.

1. Almost everyone (enjoy) _____*enjoys*_____ visiting a zoo. Today zoos are common.

2. The first zoo (establish) _____ around 3500 years ago by an Egyptian

   queen for her personal enjoyment. Five hundred years later, a Chinese emperor (establish)

   _____ a huge zoo to show his power and wealth. Later zoos (establish)

   _____ for the purpose of studying animals.

3. Some of the early European zoos were dark holes or dirty cages. People (disgust)

   _____ by the bad conditions and the mistreatment of the animals. In

   the nineteenth century, these early zoos (replace) _____ by scientific

   institutions where animals (study) _____ and (keep)

   _____ in good condition. These research centers (become)

   _____ the first modern zoos.

4. As early as the 1940s, scientists (understand) _____ that many kinds of

   wild animals faced extinction. Since that time, zoos (become) _____ a

   place to save many endangered species such as the rhinoceros. In the 1980s, the number of

   rhinos in the world (reduce) _____ from 10,000 to 400. Some wildlife

   biologists fear that the species (become) _____ extinct in the wild in the

   near future. Some scientists (believe) _____ that half of the animal

   species in zoos will be in danger of extinction by the middle of the twenty-first century.

5. Because zoos want to treat animals humanely and encourage breeding, animals (put, now)

   _____ in large, natural settings instead of small cages. They (watch)

   _____ carefully for any signs of disease and (feed) _____

   a balanced diet. Most zoos (have) _____ a hospital for animals and

   specially trained veterinarians.

6. Today food (prepare) _____ in the zoo kitchen. The food program

   (design) _____ to satisfy the animals' particular needs. For example,

   some snakes (feed) _____ only once a week, and some birds (feed)

   _____ several times a day.

7. Today zoo animals (treat) _____ well, and zoo breeding programs are

   important in the attempt to save many species of wildlife.

◇ PRACTICE 13—SELFSTUDY: Progressive tenses in passive. (Chart 11-5)

Directions: <u>Underline</u> the PROGRESSIVE VERB. Then complete the sentence with the correct PASSIVE form.

1. Some people <u>are considering</u> a new plan.

   → A new plan _____***is being considered***_____.

2. The grandparents are watching the children.

   → The children _____ by their grandparents.

3. Some painters are painting Mr. Rivera's apartment this week.

   → Mr. Rivera's apartment _____ this week.

4. Many of the older people in the neighborhood were growing vegetables.

   → Vegetables _____ by many of the older people in the

   neighborhood.

5. Eric's cousins are meeting him at the airport this afternoon.

   → Eric _____ by his cousins at the airport this afternoon.

6. I watched while the movers were moving the furniture from my apartment to a truck.

   → I watched while the furniture _____ from my apartment

   to a truck.

◇ PRACTICE 14—GUIDED STUDY: Progressive tenses in passive. (Chart 11-5)

Directions: Complete the sentences with the correct PASSIVE form.

1. Mr. Rice is teaching our class today.

   → Our class _____***is being taught***_____ by Mr. Rice today.

2. Scientists are still discovering new species of plants and animals.

   → New species of plants and animals _____.

3. Everyone looked at the flag while they were singing the national anthem.

   → Everyone looked at the flag while the national anthem _____.

4. Dogs usually wag their tails while people are petting them.

   → Dogs usually wag their tails while they _____.

5. According to one scientific estimate, we are losing 20,000 species of plants and animals each

   year due to the destruction of rain forests.

   → According to one scientific estimate, 20,000 species of plants and animals

   _____ each year due to the destruction of rain forests.

◇ PRACTICE 15—GUIDED STUDY: Active vs. passive. (Charts 11-1 → 11-7)

Directions: Circle ACTIVE if the sentence is active; circle PASSIVE if it is passive. Underline the verb.

1. (ACTIVE) PASSIVE   People have used sundials since ancient times.

2. ACTIVE (PASSIVE)   Sundials have been used for almost three thousand years.

3. ACTIVE PASSIVE   Sundials, clocks, and watches are used to tell time.

4. ACTIVE PASSIVE   Some watches show the date as well as the time.

5. ACTIVE PASSIVE   On digital watches, the time is shown by lighted numbers.

6. ACTIVE PASSIVE   The first watches were made in Europe six hundred years ago.

7. ACTIVE PASSIVE   The earliest watches were worn around a person's neck.

8. ACTIVE PASSIVE   Pocket watches became popular in the 1600s.

9. ACTIVE PASSIVE   Today most people wear wristwatches.

10. ACTIVE PASSIVE   Close to seventy million watches are sold in the United States each year.

11. ACTIVE PASSIVE   How many watches are made and sold throughout the world in one year?

12. ACTIVE PASSIVE   Somewhere in the world, a watch is being sold at this very moment.

13. ACTIVE PASSIVE   Many different styles of watches can be bought today.

14. ACTIVE PASSIVE   Do you own a watch?

15. ACTIVE PASSIVE   Where was it made?

16. ACTIVE PASSIVE   Some watches can be worn underwater.

DO YOU HAVE THE TIME?

◇ PRACTICE 16—SELFSTUDY: Passive modals. (Chart 11-6)

Directions: Complete the sentences by changing the active modals to PASSIVE MODALS.

1. Someone must send this letter immediately.

→ This letter _____ **must be sent** _____ immediately.

2. You can find flowers in almost every part of the world.

→ Flowers _____ in almost every part of the world.

3. Someone ought to wash these dirty dishes soon.

→ These dirty dishes _____ soon.

4. People may cook carrots or eat them raw.

→ Carrots _____ or _____ raw.

5. Our air conditioner doesn't work. Someone has to fix it before the hot weather comes.

→ Our air conditioner _____ before the hot weather comes.

6. If the river floods, water might destroy the village.

→ The village _____ if the river floods.

7. Someone may call off the picnic if it rains.

→ The picnic _____ if it rains.

8. You must keep medicine out of the reach of children.

→ Medicine _____ out of the reach of children.

9. You shouldn't pronounce the "b" in "lamb."

→ The "b" in "lamb" _____.

10. People should remove coffee stains on cotton immediately with cold water.

→ Coffee stains on cotton _____ immediately with cold water.

◇ PRACTICE 17—GUIDED STUDY: Passive modals. (Chart 11-6)

Directions: Complete the sentences by using the words in the list with the MODALS in parentheses. All of the completions are PASSIVE.

build	know	teach
divide	✔ put off	tear down
kill	sell	write

1. Don't postpone things you need to do. Important work _____ **shouldn't be put off** _____ until the last minute. *(should not)*

2. Your application letter _____ in ink, not pencil. *(must)*

3. Dogs _____ to do tricks. *(can)*

4. Mrs. Papadopolous didn't want her son to go to war because he _____

   _____. (could)

5. My son's class is too big. It _____ into two classes. (ought to)

6. A: Hey, Tony. These bananas are getting too ripe. They _____

   today. Reduce the price. (must)

   B: Right away, Mr. Rice.

7. It takes time to correct an examination that is taken by ten thousand students nationwide. The

   test results _____ for at least four weeks. (will not)

8. The big bank building on Main Street was severely damaged in the earthquake. The structure

   is no longer strong or safe. The building _____. Then

   a new bank _____ in the same place. (has to, can)

◇ PRACTICE 18—SELFSTUDY: Active vs. passive. (Charts 11-1 → 11-7)

   Directions: Complete the sentences with the verbs in parentheses; use ACTIVE or PASSIVE.

   1. Flowers (love) _____ *are loved* _____ throughout the world. Their beauty

   (bring) _____ *brings* _____ joy to people's lives. Flowers (use, often)

   _____ to decorate homes or tables in restaurants. Public

   gardens (can find) _____ in almost every country in the world.

   2. Around 250,000 different kinds of flowers (exist) _____ in the

   world. The majority of these species (can find) _____ only in

   the tropics. Nontropical areas (have) _____ many fewer kinds

   of flowering plants than tropical regions.

   3. Flowers may spread from their native region to other similar regions. Sometimes seeds (carry)

   _____ by birds or animals. The wind also (carry)

   _____ some seeds. In many cases throughout history,

   flowering plants (introduce) _____ into new areas by humans.

   4. Flowers (appreciate) _____ mostly for their beauty, but they

   can also be a source of food. For example, honey (make) _____

   from the nectar which (gather) _____ from flowers by bees.

   And some flower buds (eat) _____ as food; for example,

   broccoli and cauliflower are actually flower buds.

5. Some very expensive perfumes *(make)* _____ from the petals

   of flowers. Most perfumes today, however, *(come, not)* _____

   from natural fragrances. Instead, they are synthethic; they *(make)* _____

   from chemicals in a laboratory.

6. Some kinds of flowers *(may plant)* _____ in pots and *(grow)*

   _____ indoors. Most flowers, however, *(survive)*

   _____ best outdoors in their usual environment.

◇ PRACTICE 19—GUIDED STUDY: Active vs. passive. (Charts 11-1 → 11-7)

Directions: All of the sentences in the following passage are active. Some of the sentences should be passive because it is unknown or unimportant to know exactly who performs certain actions. Change sentences to the PASSIVE AS APPROPRIATE. Discuss your reasons for making changes and for not making changes.

(1) Cheese has been a principal food throughout much of the world for thousands of years.

The first cheese was probably made

(2) ~~Someone probably made the first cheese~~ in Asia around four thousand years ago.

(3) Today people eat it in almost all the countries of the world.   (4) People can eat it alone, or

they may eat it with bread.   (5) People can melt it and add it to noodles or vegetables.

(6) People can use it as part of a main course or as a snack.   (7) Throughout most of the

world, cheese adds enjoyment and nutrition to many people's daily diets.

(8) Cheese is a milk product.   (9) Cheesemakers make most cheese from cow's milk, but

they can make it from the milk of goats, camels, yaks and other animals, including zebras.

(10) Some kinds of cheese, such as cheddar, are common in many parts in the world, but you

can find other kinds only in small geographical areas.

(11) Cheesemakers produce cheese in factories.   (12) They have to treat the milk in

special ways.   (13) They must heat it several times during the process.   (14) At the end, they

add salt and they pack it into molds.   (15) They age most cheese for weeks or months before

they package and sell it.   (16) They usually sell cheese to stores in large round pieces that

they seal in wax.

(17) You can see these big rounds of cheese in food stores like delicatessens. (18) I like cheese and buy it often. (19) I don't know all the names of different kinds of cheese. (20) Often I can't pronounce the foreign name of the cheese I want. (21) When I go to the delicatessen near my apartment, I simply point to a kind of cheese that looks good to me. (22) I hold my thumb and forefinger wide apart if I want a lot of cheese or close together if I want just a little. (23) Frank and Anita, who work behind the cheese counter at the deli, always seem to give me just the right amount. (24) I'm glad cheese is nutritious because it's one of my favorite kinds of food.

◇ PRACTICE 20—SELFSTUDY: Stative passive. (Chart 11-8)

Directions: Complete the sentences with the appropriate form, ACTIVE or PASSIVE, of the verbs in parentheses. Include PREPOSITIONS as necessary. Use the SIMPLE PRESENT.

1. Loud noises _____ **_scare_** _____ small children. *(scare)*

2. Most children _____ **_are scared of_** _____ loud noises. *(scare)*

3. New ideas _____ me. *(interest)*

4. Jane _____ ecology. *(interest)*

5. My bad grades _____ my parents. *(disappoint)*

6. My parents _____ me because of my low grades. *(disappoint)*

7. My boss _____ my work. *(please)*

8. My work _____ my boss. *(please)*

9. My progress in English _____ me. *(satisfy)*

10. I _____ my progress in English. *(satisfy)*

◇ PRACTICE 21—SELFSTUDY: Participial adjectives. (Chart 11-9)

Directions: Complete the sentences with the appropriate **-ED** or **-ING** form of the words in parentheses.

Ben is reading a book. He really likes it. He can't put it down. He has to keep reading.

1. The book is really _____**interesting**_____. *(interest)*

2. Ben is really _____. *(interest)*

3. The story is _____. *(excite)*

4. Ben is _____ about the story. *(excite)*

5. Ben is _____ by the characters in the book. *(fascinate)*

6. The people in the story are _____. *(fascinate)*

7. Ben doesn't like to read books when he is _____ and
   _____. *(bore, confuse)*

8. Ben didn't finish that last book he started because it was _____ and
   _____. *(bore, confuse)*

9. What is the most _____ book you've read lately? *(interest)*

10. I just finished a _____ mystery story that had a very
    _____ ending. *(fascinate, surprise)*

◇ PRACTICE 22—GUIDED STUDY: Participial adjectives. (Chart 11-9)

Directions: Complete the sentences with the appropriate **-ED** or **-ING** form of the words in parentheses.

Julie was walking along the edge of the fountain outside her office building. She was with her co-worker and friend Paul. Suddenly she lost her balance and accidentally fell in.

1. Julie was really _____. *(embarrass)*

2. Falling into the fountain was really _____. *(embarrass)*

3. Her friend Paul was _____. *(shock)*

4. It was a _____ sight. *(shock)*

5. The people around the office building were very _____ when they saw Julie in the fountain. *(surprise)*

6. It was a _____ sight. *(surprise)*

7. The next day Julie was _____ because she thought she had made a fool of herself. *(depress)*

8. When she fell into the fountain, some people laughed at her. It was a _____ experience. *(depress)*

9. Her friend Paul told her not to lose her sense of humor. He told her it was just another _____ experience in life. *(interest)*

10. He said that people would be _____ in hearing about how she fell into a fountain. *(interest)*

◇ PRACTICE 23—GUIDED STUDY: Participial adjectives. (Chart 11-9)

Directions: Complete the sentences with your own words.

Example: I'm bored . . . .
→ *I am bored by people who talk about themselves all the time.*

Example: . . . is/are boring.
→ *Self-centered people are boring.*

1. I am interested in . . . .
2. . . . is/are interesting to me.
3. I am fascinated by . . . .
4. . . . is/are fascinating to me.
5. . . . is/are exciting.
6. . . . is/are confusing.
7. I was excited when . . . .
8. I was confused when . . . .
9. I was surprised when . . . .
10. I'll be surprised if . . . .

◇ PRACTICE 24—SELFSTUDY: *Get* + adjective and past participle. (Chart 11-10)

Directions: Complete the sentences with appropriate forms of **GET** and the words in the given list.

busy	dress	invite	tired
dark	dry	marry	well
dizzy	hungry	✔sunburn	wet

1. When I stayed out in the sun too long yesterday, I _____**got sunburned**_____.

2. If you're sick, stay home and take care of yourself. You won't _____ if you don't take care of yourself.

3. Jane and Greg are engaged. They are going to _____ a year from now.

4. Sarah doesn't eat breakfast, so she always _____ by ten or ten-thirty.

5. In the winter, the sun sets early. It _____ outside by six or even earlier.

6. Yes, I have an invitation to Joan and Paul's wedding. Don't worry. You'll _____ _____ to the wedding, too.

7. Put these socks back in the dryer. They didn't _____ the first time.

8. Let's stop working for a while. I'm _____. I need to rest.

9. Sam is wearing one brown sock and one blue sock today. He _____ in a hurry this morning and didn't pay attention to the color of his socks.

10. This work has to be done before we leave. We'd better _____ and stop wasting time.

11. Some people are afraid of heights. They _____ and have trouble keeping their balance.

12. Sally _____ when she stood near the pool of dolphins. They splashed her more than once.

◇ PRACTICE 25—GUIDED STUDY: *Get* + adjective and past participle. (Chart 11-10)

Directions: Complete the sentences with appropriate forms of GET and the words in the given list.

cold	excite	lose	steal
crowd	involve	rich	thirsty
dirty	kill	sleepy	✔worry

1. Sue has to vacate her apartment next week, and she hasn't found a new place to live. She's

_____ ***getting worried*** _____.

2. Sitara always _____ after she eats salty food.

3. Toshiro was in a terrible car wreck and almost _____. He's lucky to be alive.

4. The temperature is dropping. Brrr! I'm _____. Can I borrow your sweater?

5. We were in a strange city without a map. It was easy for us to _____. We had to ask a shopkeeper how to get back to our hotel.

6. Did you _____ when your team won the game? Did you clap and yell when they won?

7. Good restaurants _____ around dinner time. It's hard to find a seat because there are so many people.

8. When little Annie _____, her father gave her a bottle and put her to bed.

9. It's hard to work in a garage and stay clean. Paul's clothes always _____ from all the grease and oil.

10. Don't waste your money gambling. You won't ever _____ that way.

11. Tarik was afraid his important papers or his jewelry might _____, so he had a wall safe installed in his home.

12. I left when Ellen and Joe began to argue. I never _____ in other people's quarrels.

◇ PRACTICE 26—SELFSTUDY: *Used to* vs. *be accustomed to.* (Charts 2-9 and 11-11)

Directions: Choose the correct completions. **More than one** completion may be correct.

1. Frank has lived alone for twenty years. He __**B, C**__ alone.
   A. used to live   B. is used to living   C. is accustomed to living

2. I ___**A**___ with my family, but now I live alone.
   A. used to live   B. am used to living   C. am accustomed to living

3. Rita rides her bike to work every day. She _____ her bike to work.
   A. used to ride   B. is used to riding   C. is accustomed to riding

4. Tom rode his bike to work for many years, but now he takes the bus. Tom _____ his bike to work.
   A. used to ride   B. is used to riding   C. is accustomed to riding

5. Carl showers every day. He _____ a shower every day.
   A. used to take   B. is used to taking   C. is accustomed to taking

6. Carl _____ a bath only once a week, but now he showers every day.
   A. used to take   B. is used to taking   C. is accustomed to taking

◇ PRACTICE 27—SELFSTUDY: *Used to* vs. *be used to.* (Charts 2-9 and 11-11)

Directions: Complete the sentences with USED TO or BE USED TO/BE ACCUSTOMED TO and the correct form of the verb in parentheses.

1. Nick stays up later now than he did when he was in high school. He *(go)*

   _____**used to go**_____ to bed at ten, but now he rarely gets to bed before midnight.

2. I got used to going to bed late when I was in college, but now I have a job and I need my sleep.

   These days I *(go)* _____**am used to going/am accustomed to going**_____ to bed

   around ten-thirty.

3. I am a vegetarian. I *(eat)* _____ meat, but now I eat only meatless

   meals.

4. Mrs. Wu has had a vegetable garden all her life. She *(grow)* _____

   her own vegetables.

5. Oscar has lived in Brazil for ten years. He *(eat)* _____ Brazilian food.

   He doesn't like any other kind.

6. Georgio moved to Germany to open his own restaurant. He *(have)* _____

   a small bakery in Italy.

7. I have taken the bus to work every day for the past five years. I *(take)* _____

   the bus.

8. Juanita travels by plane on company business. She *(go)* _____ by train,

   but now the distances she needs to travel are too great.

◇ PRACTICE 28—GUIDED STUDY: *Be used/accustomed to* and *get used/accustomed to.* (Chart 11-11)

Directions: Discuss or write about the following topics.

1. James graduated from high school last month. Three days after graduation, he got married. The next week he got a job at a paint store. Within two weeks, his life changed a lot. What did he have to get used to?

2. Jane is going to leave her parents' house next week. She is going to move in with two of her cousins who work in the city. Jane will be away from her home for the first time in her life. What is she going to have to get used to?

3. Think of a time you traveled in or lived in a foreign country. What weren't you used to? What did you get used to? What didn't you ever get used to?

4. Think of the first day of a job you have had. What weren't you used to? What did you get used to?

◇ PRACTICE 29—SELFSTUDY: *Be supposed to.* (Chart 11-12)

Directions: Find the mistakes and correct them.

1. INCORRECT: I'm supposed $\overset{to}{\wedge}$ call my parents tonight.

2. INCORRECT: We're not suppose to tell anyone about the surprise.

3. INCORRECT: You don't supposed to talk to Alan about the surprise.

4. INCORRECT: My friend was supposing to call me last night, but he didn't.

5. INCORRECT: Children supposed to respect their parents.

6. INCORRECT: Didn't you supposed be at the meeting last night?

◇ PRACTICE 30—SELFSTUDY: *Be supposed to.* (Chart 11-12)

Directions: Make sentences with **BE SUPPOSED TO** by combining the subjects in Column A with the ideas in Column B. Use the SIMPLE PRESENT.

Example: Doctors are supposed to care about their patients.

COLUMN A	COLUMN B
1. Doctors	A. listen to their parents
2. Visitors at a zoo	B. buckle their seatbelts before takeoff
3. Employees	C. not . . . feed the animals
4. Air passengers	D. not . . . talk during a performance
5. Theatergoers	E. be on time for work
6. Soldiers on sentry duty	F. obey its trainer
7. Children	G. pay their rent on time
8. Heads of state	✔H. care about their patients
9. A dog	I. not . . . fall asleep
10. People who live in apartments	J. be diplomatic

◇ PRACTICE 31—GUIDED STUDY: *Be supposed to.* (Chart 11-12)

Directions: Think of things the following people are or were supposed to do. Use BE SUPPOSED TO.

Example: a good friend of yours

→ *My friend Ji Ming is supposed to help me paint my apartment this weekend. Benito was supposed to go to dinner with me last Wednesday, but he forgot. Nadia is supposed to call me tonight.*

1. a good friend of yours
2. your roommate or spouse*
3. children
4. a student in your English class
5. your English teacher
6. the leader of your country
7. one or both of your parents
8. one of your siblings or cousins
9. yourself
10. (. . .)

◇ PRACTICE 32—GUIDED STUDY: Verb form review. (Chapters 1 → 11)

Directions: Complete the sentences by writing the correct form of the verb in parentheses.

What is your most *(1. embarrass)* _____ experience? Let me tell you what happened to my uncle when he *(2. go)* _____ to Norway for a business meeting last year.

First, I must tell you about my Uncle Ernesto. He *(3. be)* _____ a businessman from Buenos Aires, Argentina. He *(4. manufacture)* _____ a new kind of computer compass for ships. Computer compasses *(5. manufacture)* _____ by many companies in the world, so my uncle *(6. have)* _____ a lot of competition for his product. In order to sell his product, he *(7. need)* _____ *(8. meet)* _____ with companies that might want to buy it. He *(9. travel)* _____ frequently to other countries.

Last year, he *(10. go)* _____ to Norway *(11. meet)* _____ with a shipping company. It was his first trip to Europe. My Uncle Ernesto *(12. speak)* _____ Spanish, of course, and also *(13. know)* _____

---
*If you have neither a roommate nor a spouse, invent one or simply skip to the next item.

a little English, but he *(14. know, not)* _____ any Norwegian. While he *(15. stay)* _____ in Norway, he *(16. have)* _____ a problem.

Uncle Ernesto *(17. stay)* _____ at a large, modern hotel in Oslo. One morning, while he *(18. get)* _____ ready to take a shower, he *(19. hear)* _____ a knock at the door. He *(20. walk)* _____ to the door, *(21. open)* _____ it, and *(22. find)* _____ no one. He *(23. take)* _____ a step out of his room and *(24. look)* _____ down the hall. He *(25. see)* _____ no one. So he *(26. turn)* _____ *(27. go)* _____ back into his room, but the door *(28. close)* _____! It *(29. lock)* _____, and he *(30. have, not)* _____ his key. This was a very big problem for my uncle because he *(31. dress, not)* _____ properly. In fact, he *(32. wear)* _____ nothing but a towel. Poor Uncle Ernesto! "What *(33. do, I)* _____?" he asked himself.

Instead of *(34. stand)* _____ in the hallway with only a towel, he *(35. decide)* _____ *(36. get)* _____ help. So he *(37. start)* _____ *(38. walk)* _____ down the hall toward the elevator. He was too *(39. embarrass)* _____ *(40. knock)* _____ on someone else's door *(41. ask)* _____ for help.

When he *(42. reach)* _____ the elevator, he *(43. push)* _____ the down button and *(44. wait)* _____. When it *(45. come)* _____, Uncle Ernesto *(46. take)* _____ a deep breath and *(47. get)* _____ into the elevator. The other people in the elevator *(48. surprise)* _____ when they *(49. see)* _____ a man who *(50. wrap)* _____ in a towel.

Uncle Ernesto *(51. think)* _____ about *(52. try)* _____ *(53. explain)* _____ his problem, but he *(54. know, not)* _____ any Norwegian. He said, in English, "Door. Locked. No key." A businessman in the elevator *(55. nod)* _____, but he *(56. smile, not)* _____. Another man *(57. look)* _____ at Uncle Ernesto and *(58. smile)* _____ broadly.

After an eternity, the elevator *(59. reach)* _____ the ground floor. Uncle

Ernesto *(60. walk)* _____ straight to the front desk and *(61. look)*

_____ at the hotel manager helplessly. The hotel manager *(62. have to*

understand, not) _____ any language *(63. figure)*

_____ out the problem. My uncle *(64. have to say, not)* _____

_____ a word. The manager *(65. grab)* _____ a key,

(66. take) _____ my uncle by the elbow, and *(67. lead)* _____

_____ him to the nearest elevator.

My uncle *(68. embarrass, still)* _____ about this incident.

But he always *(69. laugh)* _____ a lot when he *(70. tell)* _____

the story.

CHAPTER *12*
Adjective Clauses

◇ PRACTICE 1—SELFSTUDY: Using *who* in adjective clauses. (Charts 12-1 → 12-2)

Directions: Find and <u>underline</u> the ADJECTIVE CLAUSE in the long sentence. Then complete the change of the long sentence into two short sentences.*

1. *Long sentence:*   I thanked the man <u>who helped me move the refrigerator</u>.

   Short sentence 1:   _____**I thanked**_____ the man.

   Short sentence 2:   _____**He helped**_____ me move the refrigerator.

2. *Long sentence:*   A woman who was wearing a gray suit asked me for directions.

   Short sentence 1:   _____ me for directions.

   Short sentence 2:   _____ a gray suit.

3. *Long sentence:*   I saw a man who was wearing a blue coat.

   Short sentence 1:   _____ a man.

   Short sentence 2:   _____ a blue coat.

4. *Long sentence:*   The woman who aided the rebels put her life in danger.

   Short sentence 1:   _____ her life in danger.

   Short sentence 2:   _____ the rebels.

---

*In grammar terminology, the "long sentence" is called **a complex sentence** and the "short sentence" is called **a simple sentence**:

- A complex sentence has an independent clause and a dependent clause. For example:
  I thanked the man who helped me. = a complex sentence consisting of one independent clause (*I thanked the man*) and one dependent clause (*who helped me*).
- A simple sentence has only an independent clause. For example:
  I thanked the man. = a simple sentence consisting of one independent clause.
  He helped me. = a simple sentence consisting of one independent clause.

5. *Long sentence:*   I know some people who live on a boat.

   Short sentence 1:   _____ some people.

   Short sentence 2:   _____ on a boat.

◇   PRACTICE 2—SELFSTUDY: Using *who* in adjective clauses. (Chart 12-2)

   Directions: Combine the two short sentences into one long sentence using "sentence 2" as an
   ADJECTIVE CLAUSE. Use **WHO**. <u>Underline</u> the adjective clause.

1. *Short sentence 1:*   The woman was polite.
   Short sentence 2:   She answered the phone.

   Long sentence: **The woman <u>who answered the phone</u> was polite.**

2. *Short sentence 1:*   The man has a good voice.
   Short sentence 2:   He sang at the concert.

   Long sentence:

3. *Short sentence 1:*   We enjoyed the actors.
   Short sentence 2:   They played the leading roles.

   Long sentence:

4. *Short sentence 1:*   The girl is hurt.
   Short sentence 2:   She fell down the stairs.

   Long sentence:

◇ PRACTICE 3—SELFSTUDY: Using *who* in adjective clauses. (Chart 12-2)

Directions: Insert **WHO** where it is necessary.

1. The man who answered the phone was polite.

2. I liked the people sat next to us at the soccer game.

3. People paint houses for a living are called house painters.

4. I'm uncomfortable around married couples argue all the time.

5. While I was waiting at the bus stop, I stood next to an elderly gentleman started a conversation

   with me about my educational plans.

◇ PRACTICE 4—SELFSTUDY: Using *who* and *whom* in adjective clauses. (Chart 12-2)

Directions: Find and underline the ADJECTIVE CLAUSE. Identify the SUBJECT and VERB of the adjective clause. Then complete the change from one long sentence to two short sentences, and identify the SUBJECT and VERB of the second short sentence.

1. *Long sentence:*   The people who live next to me are nice.
   Short sentence 1: The people are nice.

   Short sentence 2: **They live next to me.**

2. *Long sentence:*   The people whom Kate visited yesterday were French.
   Short sentence 1: The people were French.

   Short sentence 2: **Kate visited them yesterday.**

3. *Long sentence:*   The people whom I saw at the park were having a picnic.
   Short sentence 1: The people were having a picnic.

   Short sentence 2:

4. *Long sentence:*   The students who go to this school are friendly.
   Short sentence 1: The students are friendly.

   Short sentence 2:

5. *Long sentence:*   The woman whom you met last week lives in Mexico.
   Short sentence 1: The woman lives in Mexico.

   Short sentence 2:

Directions: Change the two short sentences into one long sentence with an ADJECTIVE CLAUSE.
Use **WHO** or **WHOM**. <u>Underline</u> the adjective clause.

1. *Short sentence 1:*   The woman was polite.
   Short sentence 2:   Jack met her.

   Long sentence: **The woman <u>whom Jack met</u> was polite.**

2. *Short sentence 1:*   I like the woman.
   Short sentence 2:   She manages my uncle's store.

   Long sentence: **I like the woman <u>who manages my uncle's store</u>.**

3. *Short sentence 1:*   The singer was wonderful.
   Short sentence 2:   We heard him at the concert.

   Long sentence:

4. *Short sentence 1:*   The people brought a small gift.
   Short sentence 2:   They came to dinner.

   Long sentence:

5. *Short sentence 1:*   What is the name of the woman?
   Short sentence 2:   Tom invited her to the dance.

   Long sentence:

Directions: Complete the sentences with **WHO** or **WHO(M)**.*

1. I know a man _____*who*_____ works at the post office.

2. One of the people _____*who(m)*_____ I watched at the race track lost a huge amount of money.

3. My neighbor is a kind person _____ is always willing to help people in trouble.

4. The people _____ we visited gave us tea and a light snack.

5. The doctor _____ lives on my street is a surgeon.

6. My mother is a woman _____ I admire tremendously.

7. I thanked the man _____ helped me.

8. The woman _____ I helped thanked me.

_____

*There are parentheses around the "m" in *who(m)* to show that, in everyday informal English, *who* may be used as an object pronoun instead of *whom*.

◇ PRACTICE 7—GUIDED STUDY: Using *who* and *who(m)* in adjective clauses. (Chart 12-2)

Directions: Complete the sentences with WHO or WHO(M).

1. The children _____*who*_____ live down the street in the yellow house are always polite.

2. The children _____*who(m)*_____ I watched at the park were feeding ducks in a pond.

3. People _____ listen to very loud music may suffer gradual hearing loss.

4. There are many good people in the world _____ you can trust to be honest and honorable at all times.

5. Marie and Luis Escobar still keep in touch with many of the students _____ they met in their English class five years ago.

6. My husband is a person _____ enjoys good food and good friends.

7. At the supermarket yesterday, one of the store employees caught a man _____ had put a beefsteak in his coat pocket and attempted to walk out without paying.

8. The couple _____ I invited to dinner at my home were an hour late. I thought that was very rude. They didn't call. They didn't have an excuse. I'll never invite them again.

◇ PRACTICE 8—SELFSTUDY: Using *that* or Ø in adjective clauses. (Chart 12-3)

Directions: Cross out the word THAT if possible.

1. That man ~~that~~ I saw was wearing a black hat.

2. The people that visited us stayed too long. *(no change)*

3. The fruit that I bought today at the market is fresh.

4. My high school English teacher is a person that I will never forget.

5. The puppy that barked the loudest got the most attention in the pet store.

6. The girl that is sitting in front of Richard has long black hair that she wears in a ponytail.

◇ PRACTICE 9—SELFSTUDY: Using *who, who(m), that* and Ø in adjective clauses. (Chart 12-3)

Directions: In the box write every possible PRONOUN that can be used to connect the adjective clause to the main clause: **WHO, WHO(M),** or **THAT**. Also, write Ø if the pronoun can be omitted.

1. The woman | *who* *that* | sat next to me on the plane talked a lot.

2. The woman | *who(m)* *that* *Ø* | I met on the plane talked a lot.

3. Three men | | I didn't know walked into my office.

4. The three men | | walked into my office were strangers.

5. My cousin's wife is the woman | | is talking to Mr. Horn.

6. I like the woman | | my brother and I visited.

◇ PRACTICE 10—SELFSTUDY: *Who* and *who(m)* vs. *which.* (Charts 12-2 → 12-4)

Directions: Choose the correct answer.

1. The magazine ___**C**___ I read on the plane was interesting.
   A. who   B. who(m)   C. which

2. The artist _____ drew my picture is very good.
   A. who   B. who(m)   C. which

3. I really enjoyed the experiences _____ I had on my trip to Nigeria.
   A. who   B. who(m)   C. which

4. Most of the games _____ we played as children no longer amuse us.
   A. who   B. who(m)   C. which

5. All of the people _____ I called yesterday can come to the meeting on Monday.
   A. who   B. who(m)   C. which

6. The teacher _____ was ill canceled her math class.
   A. who   B. who(m)   C. which

◇ PRACTICE 11—SELFSTUDY: Using *which, that,* and Ø in adjective clauses. (Chart 12-4)

Directions: Write the PRONOUNS that can be used to connect the adjective clause to the main clause: WHICH or THAT. Also write Ø if the pronoun can be omitted.

1. I really enjoyed the show | **which** **that** **Ø** | we saw last night.

2. Tim liked the show | | was playing at the Fox Theater.

3. The plane | | I took to Korea arrived on time.

4. The plane | | flew to the Gold Coast left on time.

5. The books | | Jane ordered came in the mail today.

6. Jane was glad to get the books | | came in the mail today.

◇ PRACTICE 12—SELFSTUDY: Object pronouns in adjective clauses: error analysis. (Charts 12-3 → 12-4)

Directions: Find and cross out the incorrect PRONOUNS in the ADJECTIVE CLAUSES.

1. The books I bought ~~them~~ at the bookstore were expensive.
2. I like the shirt you wore it to class yesterday.
3. Amanda Jones is a person I would like you to meet her.
4. The apartment we wanted to rent it had two bedrooms.
5. My wife and I are really enjoying the TV set that we bought it for ourselves last week.
6. The woman you met her at Aunt Martha's house is a pharmacist.

◇ PRACTICE 13—GUIDED STUDY: Object pronouns in adjective clauses: error analysis.
(Charts 12-3 and 12-4)

Directions: Find and cross out the incorrect PRONOUNS in the ADJECTIVE CLAUSES.

1. I enjoy the relatives I visited ~~them~~ in Mexico City last year.
2. The coffee that I drank it was cold and tasteless.
3. The tennis shoes I was wearing them in the garden got wet and muddy.
4. My cousin Ahmed is a person I've known and loved him since he was born.
5. I have a great deal of respect for the wonderful woman I married her eleven years ago.
6. Anna has a cat that it likes to catch birds.
7. The birds that Anna's cat catches them are very frightened.
8. Yesterday, Anna rescued a bird that the cat had brought it into the house. She set it free. It flew away quickly.

◇ PRACTICE 14—GUIDED STUDY: Using *who, who(m), which, that,* and Ø in adjective
clauses. (Charts 12-3 and 12-4)

Directions: Write the PRONOUNS that can be used to connect the adjective clause to the main
clause: WHICH, WHO, WHO(M) or THAT. Also write Ø if the pronoun can be omitted.

Example: The manager . . . fired Tom is a difficult person to work for.

→ *The manager* $\begin{Bmatrix} who \\ that \end{Bmatrix}$ *fired Tom is a difficult person to work for.*

1. The box . . . I mailed to my sister was heavy.
2. The people . . . sat in the stadium cheered for the home team.
3. The calendar . . . hangs in Paul's office has pictures of wildlife.
4. The teenagers counted the money . . . they earned at the car wash.
5. The people . . . my brother called didn't answer their phone.
6. The tree branch . . . was lying in the street was a hazard to motorists.

◇ PRACTICE 15—SELFSTUDY: Pronoun usage in adjective clauses. (Charts 12-2 → 12-4)

Directions: Choose the correct answers. NOTE: There is **more than one correct answer** for each sentence.

1. I liked the teacher ____**A, C, D**____ I had for chemistry in high school.
   A. whom   B. which   C. that   D. Ø

2. The university scientist _____ did research in the Amazon River basin found many previously unknown species of plants
   A. who   B. whom   C. which   D. that   E. Ø

3. The children enjoyed the sandwiches _____ Mr. Rice made for them.
   A. who   B. whom   C. which   D. that   E. Ø

4. Have you ever read any books by the author _____ the teacher mentioned in class this morning?
   A. whom   B. which   C. that   D. Ø

5. The fans _____ crowded the ballpark roared their approval.
   A. who   B. whom   C. which   D. that   E. Ø

6. Have you been to the York Art Gallery? It has a new exhibit _____ includes the work of several local artists.
   A. who   B. whom   C. which   D. that   E. Ø

7. The operation _____ the surgeon performed on my uncle was very dangerous.
   A. who   B. whom   C. which   D. that   E. Ø

8. Bricks are made of soil _____ has been placed in molds, pounded down, and dried.
   A. who   B. whom   C. which   D. that   E. Ø

◇ PRACTICE 16—GUIDED STUDY: Pronoun usage in adjective clauses. (Charts 12-2 → 12-4)

Directions: Choose the correct answers. NOTE: There is **more than one correct answer** for each sentence.

1. The actors ____**A, C, D**____ we saw at Stratford performed out-of-doors.
   A. whom   B. which   C. that   D. Ø

2. Many of the games _____ children play teach them about the adult world.
   A. who   B. whom   C. which   D. that   E. Ø

3. When Jason arrived at the reunion, the first person _____ he encountered was Sally Sellers, one of his best friends when he was in high school.
   A. whom   B. which   C. that   D. Ø

4. The earth receives less than one-billionth of the enormous amount of heat _____ the sun produces. The rest of the sun's energy disappears into outer space.
   A. who   B. whom   C. which   D. that   E. Ø

5. Two hundred years ago, people on ships and in coastal towns greatly feared the pirates _____ sailed the South China Sea and the Gulf of Thailand.
   A. who   B. whom   C. which   D. that   E. Ø

6. Piranhas are dangerous fish _____ can tear the flesh off an animal as large as a horse in a few minutes.
   A. who   B. whom   C. which   D. that   E. Ø

7. Fire swept through an old apartment building in the center of town. I know some of the people _____ the firefighters rescued. They lost all their possessions. They were grateful simply to be alive.

      A. whom   B. which   C. that   D. Ø

8. Most of the islands in the Pacific are the tops of volcanic mountains _____ rise from the floor of the ocean.

      A. who   B. whom   C. which   D. that   E. Ø

◇ PRACTICE 17—GUIDED STUDY: Adjective clauses. (Charts 12-1 → 12-4)

Directions: Answer the questions in complete sentences. Use any appropriate pattern of ADJECTIVE CLAUSE. Use **THE** with the noun that is modified by the adjective clause.

1. We ate some food from our garden.
   We ate some food at a restaurant.
   Which food was very expensive?
   → **The** *food we ate at a restaurant was very expensive.* **The** *food we ate from our garden was not expensive at all.*

2. One phone wasn't ringing.
   The other phone was ringing.
   Which phone did Sam answer?
   → *Sam answered* **the** *phone that was ringing. He didn't answer* **the** *phone that wasn't ringing.*

3. One girl won the foot race.
   The other girl lost the foot race.
   Which girl is happy?

4. One man was sleeping.
   Another man was listening to the radio.
   One of them heard the news bulletin about the earthquake in China. Which one?

5. One person raised her hand in class.
   Another person sat quietly in his seat.
   One of them asked the teacher a question. Which one?

6. One person bought a *(brand name of a car)*.
   Another person bought a *(brand name of a car)*.
   Which person spent more money than the other?

7. Pretend I'm at the market. Some of the bananas are completely brown.
   Some of the bananas are green.
   Which bananas should I buy?

8. Amanda bought some canned vegetables at a small food store.
   Tom picked some vegetables from his grandfather's garden.
   Which vegetables tasted fresh?

9. One young musician practiced hours and hours every day.
   The other young musician had a regular job and practiced only in the evenings and on the weekends.
   Which musician showed a great deal of improvement during the course of a year?

10. One city provides clean water and a modern sewer system for its citizens.
    Another city uses its rivers and streams as both a source of water and a sewer.
    Which city has a high death rate from infectious diseases such as typhoid and cholera?

◇ PRACTICE 18—GUIDED STUDY: Adjective clauses. (Charts 12-1 → 12-4)

Directions: Complete the definitions that begin in COLUMN A with the information given in COLUMN B. Use ADJECTIVE CLAUSES in the definitions.

Example: An architect is someone who designs buildings.

COLUMN A

1. An architect is someone . . . .
2. A vegetarian is a person . . . .
3. Steam is gas . . . .
4. A turtle is an animal . . . .
5. A ring is a circle of metal . . . .
6. An expressway is a road . . . .
7. A hermit is a person . . . .
8. A banana tree is a plant . . . .
9. Plastic is a synthetic material . . . .
10. A mystery is something . . . .

COLUMN B

A. It is built for fast driving.
B. It is worn on a finger for decoration.
C. It cannot be understood or explained.
D. S/he leaves society and lives completely alone.
E. It can be shaped and hardened to form many useful things.
F. It grows in hot climates and produces large bunches of yellow fruit.
✔ G. S/he designs buildings.
H. It has a hard shell and can live in water or on land.
I. It forms when water boils.
J. S/he doesn't eat meat.

◇ PRACTICE 19—GUIDED STUDY: Adjective clauses. (Charts 12-1 → 12-4)

Directions: In groups or pairs, provide definitions for the words listed below. Consult your dictionaries if necessary.

Example: A telephone directory is a book . . . .
→ *A telephone directory is a book that lists telephone numbers.*

1. A dictionary is a book . . . .
2. An author is someone . . . .
3. A giraffe is an animal . . . .
4. Parents are people . . . .
5. A key is a piece of metal . . . .
6. A prisoner is a person . . . .
7. Water is a substance . . . .
8. Photographers are people . . . .
9. A hero is a person . . . .
10. An adjective is a word . . . .
11. A triangle is a geometric form . . . .
12. Friends are people . . . .

◇ PRACTICE 20—SELFSTUDY: Subject-verb agreement in adjective clauses. (Chart 12-5)

Directions: Complete the sentence with the correct form of the verb in parentheses. Use the SIMPLE PRESENT. Underline the noun that determines whether the verb in the ADJECTIVE CLAUSE is singular or plural.

1. A saw is a <u>tool</u> that _____ *is* _____ used to cut wood. *(be)*

2. Hammers are <u>tools</u> that _____ *are* _____ used to pound nails. *(be)*

3. I recently met a woman who _____ in Montreal. *(live)*

4. Most of the people who _____ in Montreal speak French as their first language. *(live)*

5. I have a cousin who _____ as a coal miner. *(work)*

6. Some coal miners who _____ underground suffer from lung disease. *(work)*

7. A professional athlete who _____ tennis for a living is called a tennis pro. *(play)*

8. Professional athletes who _____ tennis for a living can make a lot of money. *(play)*

9. A carpenter is a person who _____ things out of wood. *(make)*

10. Sculptors are artists who _____ things from clay or other materials. *(make)*

◇ PRACTICE 21—SELFSTUDY: Prepositions in adjective clauses. (Chart 12-6)

Directions: The adjective clauses in the following sentences need PREPOSITIONS. Add the prepositions and give all the possible patterns for the ADJECTIVE CLAUSE. Write "Ø" if nothing is needed.

1. The bus _____ *that* _____ we were waiting ____ *for* ____ was an hour late.

   The bus _____ *which* _____ we were waiting ____ *for* ____ was an hour late.

   The bus _____ *Ø* _____ we were waiting ____ *for* ____ was an hour late.

   The bus ____ *for which* ____ we were waiting ____ *Ø* ____ was an hour late.

2. The music _____ I listened _____ was pleasant.

   The music _____ I listened _____ was pleasant.

   The music _____ I listened _____ was pleasant.

   The music _____ I listened _____ was pleasant.

3. Ecology is one of the subjects _____ I am very interested _____.

   Ecology is one of the subjects _____ I am very interested _____.

   Ecology is one of the subjects _____ I am very interested _____.

   Ecology is one of the subjects _____ I am very interested _____.

4. Tom argued with a man about politics.

   The man _____ Tom was arguing _____ was very angry.

   The man _____ Tom was arguing _____ was very angry.

   The man _____ Tom was arguing _____ was very angry.

   The man _____ Tom was arguing _____ was very angry.

◇ PRACTICE 22—GUIDED STUDY: Prepositions in adjective clauses. (Chart 12-6)

Directions: Complete the given sentences with PRONOUNS and PREPOSITIONS, as necessary. Give all the possible patterns for the ADJECTIVE CLAUSES.

Example: The movie . . . we went . . . was good.
→ *The movie that we went to was good.*
  The movie which we went to was good.
  The movie Ø we went to was good.
  The movie to which we went was good.

1. I enjoyed meeting the people . . . you introduced me . . . yesterday.

2. English grammar is a subject . . . I am quite familiar . . . .

3. The woman . . . Mr. Low told us . . . works for the government.

◇ PRACTICE 23—SELFSTUDY: Prepositions in adjective clauses. (Chart 12-6)

Directions: Supply appropriate PREPOSITIONS in the blanks. Write "Ø" if no preposition is necessary. In sentence b., put brackets around the ADJECTIVE CLAUSE.

1. a. I enjoyed the CD. We listened _____*to*_____ it at Sara's apartment.

   b. I enjoyed the CD [we listened _____*to*_____ at Sara's apartment.]

2. a. I paid the shopkeeper for the glass cup. I accidentally broke _____*Ø*_____ it.

   b. I paid the shopkeeper for the glass cup [I accidentally broke _____*Ø*_____.]

3. a. The bus was only three minutes late. We were waiting _____ it.

   b. The bus we were waiting _____ was only three minutes late.

4. a. Mrs. Chan is someone. I always enjoy talking _____ her about politics.

   b. Mrs. Chan is someone I always enjoy talking _____ about politics.

5. a. I showed my roommate the letter. I had just written _____ it.

   b. I showed my roommate the letter I had just written _____.

6. a. One of the subjects is global economics. I've been interested _____ it for a long time.

   b. One of the subjects I've been interested _____ for a long time is global economics.

◇ PRACTICE 24—SELFSTUDY: Prepositions in adjective clauses. (Chart 12-6)

Directions: Put brackets around the ADJECTIVE CLAUSE in each sentence. Add an appropriate PREPOSITION, if necessary. If no preposition is needed, write "Ø."

1. The book catalogue [I was looking _____*at*_____] had hundreds of interesting titles.

2. The book [I wanted _____*Ø*_____] wasn't available at the library.

3. I really enjoyed the music we were listening _____ at Jim's yesterday.

4. The man I was staring _____ started to stare back at me.

5. My father is someone I've always been able to depend _____ when I need advice or help.

6. The suitcases I was carrying _____ got so heavy that my arms started to ache.

7. Organic chemistry is a subject that I'm not familiar _____.

8. The news article we talked _____ in class concerned a peace conference.

9. Chris looks angry. The man she is arguing _____ is her cousin.

10. Jennifer and David stopped at a sidewalk cafe. The food they ate _____ at the cafe was delicious.

11. The sailor you waved _____ is walking toward us. What are you going to say?

12. The bank I borrowed money _____ charges high interest on its loans.

◇ PRACTICE 25—GUIDED STUDY: Prepositions in adjective clauses. (Chart 12-6)

Directions: Put brackets around the ADJECTIVE CLAUSE in each sentence. Add an appropriate PREPOSITION, if necessary. If no preposition is needed, write "Ø."

1. The people [I talked ____*to/with*____ at the reception] were interesting.

2. One of the places [I want to visit ____*Ø*____ next year] is Mexico City.

3. My sister and I have the same ideas about almost everything. She is the one person [____*with*____ whom I almost always agree.]

4. The man _____ whom I spoke at the airline counter asked to see my passport and ticket.

5. The furniture I bought _____ was expensive.

6. What's the name of the person you introduced me _____ at the restaurant last night? I've already forgotten.

7. Botany is a subject I'm not familiar _____.

8. The bags I was carrying _____ were really heavy.

9. The guy I borrowed these tools _____ wants them back today.

10. English grammar is one of the subjects _____ which I enjoy studying the most.

11. The friend I waved _____ didn't wave back. Maybe he just didn't see me.

12. The people _____ whom Alex was waiting were over an hour late.

13. What was that tape you were just listening _____ ? I really liked it.

14. The newspaper I was reading _____ had the latest news about the election.

15. Your building supervisor is the person _____ whom you should complain if you have any problems with your apartment.

16. My parents are people I can always rely _____ for support and help.

17. Taking out the garbage is one of the chores our fourteen-year-old is responsible _____.

18. The interviewer wanted to know the name of the college I had graduated _____.

◇ PRACTICE 26—SELFSTUDY: Adjective clauses with *whose*. (Chart 12-7)

Directions: Find and <u>underline</u> the ADJECTIVE CLAUSE in the long sentence. Then change the long sentence into two short sentences.

1. *Long sentence:*   I know a man <u>whose daughter is a pilot</u>.

   Short sentence 1:   ____*I know* **a man.**____

   Short sentence 2:   **His daughter is a pilot.**

2. *Long sentence:* The woman <u>whose husband is out of work</u> found a job at Mel's Diner.

   Short sentence 1:   *The woman* **found a job at Mel's Diner.**

   Short sentence 2:   **Her**

3. *Long sentence:* The man whose wallet I found gave me a reward.

   Short sentence 1:   *The man*

   Short sentence 2:

4. *Long sentence:* I know a girl whose family never eats dinner together.

   Short sentence 1:

   Short sentence 2:

5. *Long sentence:* The people whose window I broke got really angry.

   Short sentence 1:

   Short sentence 2:

Directions: Use the given information to complete the sentences with ADJECTIVE CLAUSES. Omit the PRONOUN from the adjective clause if possible.

> *I share their views.*
>
> *Their children were doing poorly in her class.*
>
> *They disrupted the global climate and caused mass extinctions of animal life.*
>
> ✔ *The man's son was in an accident.*
>
> *Ted bought them for his wife on their anniversary.*
>
> *I slept on it at the hotel last night.*
>
> *They had backbones.*
>
> ✔ *James chose the color of paint for his bedroom walls.*
>
> *It is used to carry boats with goods and/or passengers.*

1. The man _____*whose son was in an accident*_____ called an ambulance.

2. The color of paint_____*James chose for his bedroom walls*_____ was an unusual blue.

3. My back hurts today. The mattress _____

   was too soft.

4. A waterway is a river or stream _____.

5. The second grade teacher talked to all the parents _____

   _____.

6. The flowers _____

   wilted in the heat before he got home.

7. The candidates _____will get my votes.

8. According to scientists, the first animals _____

   were fish. They appeared on the earth about 500 million years ago.

9. Approximately 370 million years ago, seventy percent of the earth's marine species

   mysteriously vanished. Approximately 65 million years ago, the dinosaurs and two-thirds of all

   marine animal species became extinct. According to some scientific researchers, the earth was

   struck by speeding objects from space _____.

◇ PRACTICE 28—GUIDED STUDY: Adjective clauses. (Charts 12-1 → 12-7)

Directions: Use the given information in the list to complete the sentences with ADJECTIVE CLAUSES. Omit the OBJECT PRONOUN from the adjective clause if possible.

Their specialty is heart surgery.

Its mouth was big enough to swallow a whole cow in one gulp.

You drink it.

It erupted in Indonesia recently.

They lived in the jungles of Southeast Asia.

These molecules have been used countless times before in countless ways.

They continued week after week.

1. A volcano _____ killed six people

   and damaged large areas of rice, coconut, and clove crops.

2. Doctors and nurses _____ are some

   of the best-trained medical personnel in the world.

3. Early human beings hunted animals for food, including chickens. Originally, chickens were

   wild birds _____.

   At some point in time, humans learned how to domesticate them and raise them for food.

4. In prehistoric times, there was a dinosaur _____.

   _____

5. Several years ago, tons of fish in the Seine River died from lack of oxygen when the river

   became polluted. Heavy rains _____ caused the

   sewer system to overflow into the river, bypassing the sewage treatment plant.

6. Every glass of water _____ has molecules

   _____.

◇ PRACTICE 29—SELFSTUDY: Adjective clauses. (Charts 12-1 → 12-7)

Directions: Which of the following can be used in the blanks: WHO, WHO(M), WHICH, THAT, WHOSE, or Ø?

1. The people _____*who/that*_____ moved into town are Italian.

2. The lamp _____ I bought downtown is beautiful and quite expensive.

3. Everyone _____ came to the audition got a part in the play.

4. Ms. Laura Rice is the teacher _____ class I enjoy most.

5. Flowers _____ grow in tropical climates usually have vibrant colors.

6. The man _____ I found in the doorway had collapsed from exhaustion.

7. Flying squirrels _____ live in tropical rain forests stay in the trees their entire lives without ever touching the ground.

8. The girl _____ skirt was caught in the classroom door seemed very embarrassed.

◇ PRACTICE 30—GUIDED STUDY: Adjective clauses. (Charts 12-1 → 12-7)

Directions: Which of the following can be used in the blanks: WHO, WHO(M), WHICH, THAT, WHOSE, or Ø?

1. What do you say to people _____ *who/that* _____ ask you personal questions that you don't want to answer?

2. In my country, any person _____ is twenty-one years old or older can vote. I turned twenty-one last year. The person _____ I voted for in the national election lost. I hope the next candidate for _____ I vote has better luck. I'd like to vote for a winning candidate.

3. Vegetarians are people _____ do not eat meat. True vegetarians do not eat flesh _____ comes from any living creature, including fish. Some vegetarians even exclude any food _____ is made from animal products such as milk and eggs.

4. A: A magazine _____ I read at the doctor's office had an article _____ you ought to read. It's about the importance of exercise in dealing with stress.

   B: Why do you think I should read an article _____ deals with exercise and stress?

   A: If you stop and think for a minute, you can answer that question yourself. You're under a lot of stress, and you don't get any exercise.

   B: The stress _____ I have at work doesn't bother me. It's just a normal part of my job. And I don't have time to exercise.

   A: Well, you should make time. Anyone _____ job is as stressful as yours should make physical exercise part of a daily routine.

◇ PRACTICE 31—SELFSTUDY: Adjective clauses. (Charts 12-1 → 12-7)

Directions: Find and underline the ADJECTIVE CLAUSES in the following passages. Circle the NOUN that each adjective clause modifies.

1. (Flowers) that bloom year after year are called perennials. (Flowers) that bloom only one season are called annuals.

2. A: Who's that boy?

   B: Which boy? Are you talking about the boy who's wearing the striped shirt or the boy who has on the T-shirt?

   A: I'm not talking about either one of them. I'm talking about the boy who just waved at us. Look. Over there. Do you see the kid that has the red baseball cap?

   B: Sure. I know him. That's Al Jordan's kid. His name is Josh or Jake or Jason. Nice kid. Did you wave back?

3. Hiroki is from Japan. When he was sixteen, he spent four months in South America. He stayed with a family who lived near Quito, Ecuador. Their way of life was very different from his. At first, all of the things they did and said seemed strange to Hiroki: their eating customs, political views, ways of expressing emotion, work habits, sense of humor, and more. He felt homesick for people who were like him in their customs and habits. But as time went on, he began to appreciate the way of life that his host family followed. Many of the things Hiroki did with his host family began to feel natural to him. He developed a strong bond of friendship with them. At the beginning of his stay in Ecuador, he had noticed only the things that were different between his host family and himself. At the end, he understood how many things they had in common as human beings despite their differences in cultural backgrounds.

4. Many of the problems that exist today have existed since the beginning of recorded history. One of these problems is violent conflict between people who come from different geographical areas or cultural backgrounds. One group may distrust and fear another group of people who are different from themselves in language, customs, politics, religion, and/or appearance. These irrational fears are the source of much of the violence that has occurred throughout the history of the world.

◇ PRACTICE 32—GUIDED STUDY: Adjective clauses. (Charts 12-1 → 12-7)

Directions: Find and <u>underline</u> the ADJECTIVE CLAUSES in the following passage. Circle the NOUN that each adjective clause modifies.

Parents are (people) <u>who provide love, care, and education for children</u>. Parents may be defined as the principal people who raise a child. These people may or may not have physically produced the child. Many children are brought up by relatives or other caring adults when their biological parents, through death, disability or uncontrollable circumstances, are not present to care for them. The role of any parents, biological or not, is to take care of their children's emotional, physical, and social needs.

Children need love and affection to grow strong emotionally. It is important for all children to have at least one adult with whom they can form a loving, trusting relationship. A strong bond with adults is essential from birth through adolescence. For example, babies who are not picked up frequently and held lovingly may have slow physical and mental growth even though they receive adequate food and exercise. Youngsters who are raised in an institution without bonding with an older person who functions as a parent may often have difficulty forming trusting relationships when they are adults.

In addition to love, children need physical care. Babies are completely dependent upon adults for food, shelter, and safety. Children who are denied such basics in their early lives may suffer chronic health problems and feelings of insecurity throughout their lifetimes. One of the greatest responsibilities that parents have is to provide for the physical well-being of their children.

Children's education is also the responsibility of the parents. Girls and boys must learn to speak, dress themselves, eat properly, and get along with others. They must learn not to touch fire, to look carefully before they cross the street, and not to use violence to solve problems. The lessons that parents teach their children are numerous. As children get older and enter school, teachers join parents in providing the education that young people need in order to become independent, productive members of society.

◇ PRACTICE 33—GUIDED STUDY: Adjective clauses. (Chapter 12)

Directions: Discuss or write about the following topics. Incorporate ADJECTIVE CLAUSES into sentences whenever possible.

1. What are the qualities of a friend?
2. What kind of neighbors do you like to have?
3. What kind of people make good leaders?
4. What kind of people make good parents?
5. What is your idea of the ideal roommate?
6. What qualities do you expect in a boss?
7. What is one of the things you enjoy most about living here?
8. What is one of the things you dislike about living here?
9. Describe your dream house.
10. Describe your ideal vacation.

◇ PRACTICE 34—SELFSTUDY: Phrasal verbs. (Chart 12-8)

Directions: Complete the sentences with the given PARTICLES.

down	in	off	out	over	up

1. If I quit a bad habit like smoking, that means I give it _____**up**_____.

2. If I don't want to include something when I write a letter, I leave it _____.

3. When I write words in this practice, I am filling _____ the blanks.

4. When I discover new information, that means I find something _____.

5. Sometimes when I recite a poem, I forget a line. So I go back to the beginning and start

   _____.

6. When buildings are old and dangerous, we tear them _____.

7. If I write a letter and I don't like what I've written, I will write it again. That means I'll do it

   _____.

8. When I remove a piece of paper from a spiral notebook, I tear the paper _____ of

   my notebook.

9. When I write something that I don't want anybody else to see, I tear the paper into tiny pieces.

   I tear _____ the note.

10. When I write information on an application form, I fill the form _____.

11. When I make a mistake in something I write, I erase the mistake if I'm using a pencil. If I'm

    using a pen, I cross the mistake _____ by drawing a line through it.

12. When my tea cup is empty, I fill it _____ again if I'm still thirsty.

Directions: Complete each sentence with **two** PARTICLES.

1. When I cross a busy street, I'm careful. I look _____*out*_____ _____*for*_____ cars and trucks.

2. Some friends visited me last night. I hadn't expected them. They just dropped _____ _____ me.

3. Maria was born and raised in Brazil. in other words, she grew _____ _____ Brazil.

4. If I like people and enjoy their company, that means I get _____ _____ them.

5. My cousin never does anything useful. He just fools _____ _____ his friends all day wasting time.

6. When somebody uses the last spoonful of sugar in the kitchen, we don't have any more sugar. That means we have run _____ _____ sugar and need to go to the market.

7. I'm glad when I finish my homework. When I get _____ _____ my homework, I can go out and play tennis or do whatever else I feel like doing.

8. In some places, it's important to be careful about pickpockets. There are places where tourists have to watch _____ _____ pickpockets.

9. If you return from a trip, that means you get _____ _____ a trip.

10. Sometimes students have to quit school because they need to get a job, fail their courses, or lose interest in their education. There are various reasons why students drop _____ _____ school.

CHAPTER **13**
Comparisons

◇ PRACTICE 1—SELFSTUDY: *As . . . as.* (Chart 13-1)

Directions: Using the given information and the words in parentheses, complete the comparisons using **AS . . . AS.** Use **NOT** with the verb as necessary.

1. Dogs make more noise than cats do. *(be noisy)*

   → Cats _____**aren't as noisy as**_____ dogs.

2. Both Anne and her sister Amanda are lazy. *(be lazy)*

   → Anne _____**is as lazy as**_____ her sister Amanda.

3. Adults have more strength than children. *(be strong)*

   → Children _____ adults.

4. Tom and Jerry are the same height. *(be tall)*

   → Tom _____ Jerry.

5. It's more comfortable to live at home than in a dormitory. *(be comfortable)*

   → Living in a dormitory _____ living at home.

6. Both the bride and the groom were nervous before the wedding. *(be nervous)*

   → The bride _____ the groom.

7. A basketball is bigger than a soccer ball. *(be big)*

   → A soccer ball _____ a basketball.

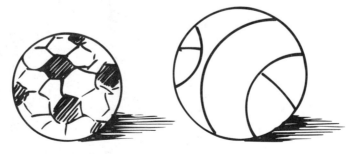

SOCCER
BALL

BASKETBALL

8. The air in a big city is more polluted than the air in the countryside. *(be fresh and clean)*

    → The air in a big city _____ the air in the countryside.

9. My sister wants to be a famous and successful businesswoman. I don't have any plans for my future. *(be ambitious)*

    → I _____ my sister.

10. Some school subjects interest me, and others don't. *(be interesting)*

    → Some school subjects _____ others.

◇ PRACTICE 2—SELFSTUDY: *As . . . as.* (Chart 13-1)

Directions: Complete the sentences with one of the following:

> *just as*
> *almost as/not quite as*
> *not nearly as*

PART I: Compare the boxes.

1. Box B is _____ **almost as / not quite as** _____ big as Box A.

2. Box E is _____ big as Box A.

3. Box C is _____ big as Box B.

4. Box E is _____ big as Box D.

PART II: Meeting time: 9:00 A.M. Compare the arrival times.

> Arrival times:
> David   9:01 A.M.
> Julia   9:14 A.M.
> Laura   9:15 A.M.
> Paul   9:15 A.M.
> James   9:25 A.M.

5. Paul was _____ late as Laura.

6. David was _____ late as James.

7. Julia was _____ late as Laura.

8. Julia was _____ late as Paul.

PART III: Compare world temperatures today.

Bangkok	92°F/33°C
Cairo	85°F/30°C
Madrid	90°F/32°C
Moscow	68°F/20°C
Tokyo	85°F/30°C

9. Tokyo is _____ hot as Cairo.

10. Moscow is _____ hot as Bangkok.

11. Madrid is _____ hot as Bangkok.

PART IV: Compare world temperatures yesterday and today.

	Yesterday	Today
Bangkok	95°F/35°C	92°F/33°C
Cairo	95°F/35°C	85°F/30°C
Madrid	90°F/32°C	90°F/32°C
Moscow	70°F/21°C	68°F/20°C
Tokyo	81°F/27°C	85°F/30°C

12. Cairo was _____ hot as Bangkok yesterday.

13. It's _____ warm in Moscow today as yesterday.

14. Madrid is _____ hot today as yesterday.

15. It was _____ hot in Tokyo yesterday as in Bangkok.

16. It's _____ hot in Bangkok today as yesterday.

◇ PRACTICE 3—GUIDED STUDY: *As . . . as.* (Chart 13-1)

Directions: Complete the sentences with your own words.

Example: . . . not as sharp as . . . .
> → *A pencil point isn't as sharp as a needle.*
> → *A kitchen knife isn't as sharp as a razor blade.*
> → *My mind isn't as sharp in the afternoon as it is in the morning.*

1. . . . just as important as . . . .

2. . . . not as comfortable as . . . .

3. . . . not nearly as interesting as . . . .

4. . . . just as good as . . . .

5. . . . not quite as difficult as . . . .

6. . . . not as quiet as . . . .

7. . . . almost as good as . . . .

8. . . . not as friendly as . . . .

9. . . . not as heavy as . . . .

10. . . . just as soft as . . . .

◇ PRACTICE 4—SELFSTUDY: *As . . . as.* (Chart 13-1)

Directions: Choose the best sentence completion from the given list.

A. *as bad as she said it was*   ✔E. *as much as possible*
B. *as easy as it looks*   F. *as often as I can*
C. *as fast as I could*   G. *as often as I used to*
D. *as good as they looked*   H. *as soon as possible*

1. I have a lot of homework. I will finish _____**E**_____ before I go to bed.

2. I'm sorry I'm late. I drove _____.

3. I saw some chocolates at the candy store. They looked delicious, so I bought some. They tasted just _____.

4. When I was in college, I went to at least two movies every week. Now I'm very busy with my job and family, so I don't go to movies _____.

5. It took Julie years of lessons to be able to play the piano well. She makes it look easy, but we all know that playing a musical instrument isn't _____.

6. I need to finish working on this report, so go ahead and start the meeting without me. I'll be there _____.

7. Even though I'm very busy, I'm usually just sitting at my desk all day. I need more exercise, so I try to walk to and from work _____.

8. My friend told me the movie was terrible, but I went anyway. My friend was right. The movie was just _____.

◇ PRACTICE 5—SELFSTUDY: Comparative and superlative forms. (Chart 13-3)

Directions: Give the COMPARATIVE and SUPERLATIVE forms of the words below.

	COMPARATIVE			SUPERLATIVE	
1. strong	*stronger*	than	the	*strongest*	of all
2. important	*more important*	than	the	*most important*	of all
3. soft	_____	than	the	_____	of all
4. lazy	_____	than	the	_____	of all
5. wonderful	_____	than	the	_____	of all
6. calm	_____	than	the	_____	of all
7. tame	_____	than	the	_____	of all
8. dim	_____	than	the	_____	of all
9. convenient	_____	than	the	_____	of all
10. clever	_____	than	the	_____	of all
11. good	_____	than	the	_____	of all

12. bad	_____ than	the _____ of all
13. far	_____ than	the _____ of all
14. slow	_____ than	the _____ of all
15. slowly	_____ than	the _____ of all

◇ PRACTICE 6—GUIDED STUDY: Comparative and superlative forms. (Charts 13-2 and 13-3)

Directions: As a class or in smaller groups, divide into two teams. Each team will try to score points by (1) giving the meaning of an adjective and (2) giving its comparative and superlative forms. (3) Bonus points will be awarded for every correct sentence the team creates using the comparative or superlative of the given adjective.

Each team has thirty seconds or a minute (or any other agreed upon length of time) for each word. (Someone in the class needs to be the timekeeper.) The teams should prepare for the contest by discussing the words in the list, looking them up in the dictionary if necessary, and making up possible sentences.

SCORING:
(1) one point for the correct *meaning* of the given adjective
(2) one point for the correct *comparative and superlative forms* of that adjective
(3) one point for each clear *sentence* with the correct comparative or superlative form

Example: dependable

LEADER: What does "dependable" mean?

TEAM: "Dependable" means "responsible, reliable, trustworthy." For example, it describes people who do their jobs well every day.

LEADER: Yes. That's one point. Now, comparative and superlative forms?

TEAM: More dependable than, the most dependable of all.

LEADER: Correct. That's one point. Sentences?

TEAM: Adults are more dependable than children.

LEADER: Good. One point.

TEAM: Vegetables are more dependable than fruit.

LEADER: What? That doesn't make any sense. No point.

TEAM: My parents always support me. They are the most dependable people I know.

LEADER: Great sentence! One point.—Time is up. Your total points as a team: Four.

List of adjectives:

1. wonderful	8. heavy	15. bright
2. high	9. dangerous	16. pleasant
3. easy	10. humid	17. polite
4. intelligent	11. confusing	18. soft
5. calm	12. clever	19. sour
6. dim	13. fresh	20. common
7. wild	14. friendly	

◇ PRACTICE 7—SELFSTUDY: Comparatives. (Charts 13-2 and 13-3)

Directions: Complete the sentences with the correct COMPARATIVE form (**MORE/-ER**) of the given adjectives.

bad	cold	funny	pretty
careful	confusing	generous	✔ soft
clean	expensive	lazy	thin

1. I like to sit on pillows. They are a lot _____*softer*_____ than a hardwood seat.

2. The average temperature in Moscow is _____ than the average temperature in Hong Kong.

3. This gold ring costs much more than that silver one. Can you tell me why gold is _____ than silver?

4. Bobby! How did you get all covered with mud? Hurry and take a bath. Even the floor is _____ than you are.

5. Fresh flowers not only smell good, but they're a lot _____ than artificial flowers.

6. Sandy, when you drive to the airport today, you have to be _____ than you were the last time you went. You almost had an accident because you weren't paying attention to your driving.

7. I heard a little polite laughter when I told my jokes, but everyone laughed loudly when Janet was telling hers. Her jokes are always much _____ than mine.

8. I have trouble understanding Professor Larson. Her lectures are much _____ than Professor Sato's.

9. Your father seems to give you plenty of money for living expenses. He is _____ than mine.

10. My handwriting isn't very good, but my wife's handwriting is practically illegible. Her handwriting is much _____ than mine.

11. Cardboard has thickness, but paper doesn't. Paper is _____ than cardboard.

12. I don't like to work hard, but my sister does. I'm a lot _____ than my sister.

◇ PRACTICE 8—GUIDED STUDY: Comparatives. (Charts 13-2 and 13-3)

Directions: Complete the sentences with the correct COMPARATIVE form (MORE/-ER) of the given adjectives and adverbs.

comfortable	*expensive*	*softly*
dangerous	*friendly*	✔ *sweet*
dark	*slowly*	*wet*

1. Lemons aren't _____*sweeter*_____ than oranges. Lemons are sour.

2. Refrigerators cost a lot. They are much _____ than microwave ovens.

3. Children seem to be able to appear out of nowhere. When I'm near a school, I always drive _____ than I have to.

4. In my experience, old shoes are usually a lot _____ than new shoes.

5. People in villages seem to be _____ than people in large cities. They seem to enjoy talking to strangers.

6. Babies don't like loud noises. Most people speak _____ than usual when they're talking to a baby.

7. Many more people die in car accidents than in plane accidents. Statistics show that driving your own car is _____ than flying in an airplane.

8. A: Why does wet sand look _____ than dry sand?

   B: Because wet sand reflects less light.

9. If a cat and a duck are out in the rain, the cat will get much _____ than the duck. The water will simply roll off of the duck's feathers but will soak into the cat's fur.

◇ PRACTICE 9—SELFSTUDY: *Farther* and *further.* (Chart 13-3)

Directions: Choose the correct answer or answers. **Both** answers may be correct.

1. Ron and his friend went jogging. Ron ran two miles, but his friend got tired after one mile. Ron ran __**A, B**__ than his friend did.
   A. farther   B. further

2. If you have any ___**B**___ questions, don't hesitate to ask.
   A. farther   B. further

3. The planet Earth is _____ from the sun than the planet Mercury is.
   A. farther   B. further

4. I like my new apartment, but it is _____ away from school than my old apartment is.
   A. farther   B. further

5. Thank you for your help, but I'll be fine now. I don't want to cause you any _____ trouble.
   A. farther   B. further

6. I have no _____ need of this equipment. I'm going to sell it.
   A. farther   B. further

7. Paris is _____ north than Tokyo.
   A. farther   B. further

8. A: Mr. President, will you describe your new plans for the economy?
   B: I have no _____ comment. This press conference is over.
   A. farther   B. further

9. I'm tired. I walked _____ than I should have.
   A. farther   B. further

10. I gave my old typewriter to my younger sister because I had no _____ use for it.
    A. farther   B. further

◇ PRACTICE 10—GUIDED STUDY: Comparatives. (Charts 13-2 and 13-3)

Directions: Choose any appropriate adjective from the list (or any adjective of your own choosing) to make comparisons of the given items. Use the COMPARATIVE form (**MORE/-ER**).

bright	*fast*	*relaxing*	*thick*
easy	*flexible*	*shallow*	*thin*
enjoyable	*heavy*	*short*	*wide and deep*

1. traveling by air/traveling by bus
   → *Traveling by air is faster than traveling by bus.*
   Traveling by air is easier than traveling by bus. (Etc.)

2. a pool/a lake

3. an elephant's neck/a giraffe's neck

4. sunlight/moonlight

5. iron/wood

6. walking/running

7. river/stream

8. rubber/wood

9. nothing/sitting in a garden on a quiet summer day

10. a butterfly's wing/a blade of grass

◇ PRACTICE 11—SELFSTUDY: Completing comparisons with pronouns. (Chart 13-4)

Directions: Complete the comparisons with a PRONOUN and an appropriate AUXILIARY VERB.

1. Bob arrived at ten. I arrived at eleven.

→ Bob arrived earlier than _____*I did*_____.

2. Linda is a good painter. Steven is better.

→ He is a better painter than _____*she is*_____.

3. Alex knows a lot of people. I don't know many people at all.

→ He knows a lot more people than _____.

4. I won the race. Patty came in second.

→ I ran faster than _____.

5. My parents were nervous about my motorcycle ride. I was just a little nervous.

→ They were a lot more nervous than _____.

6. My aunt will stay with us for two weeks. My uncle has to return home to his job after a couple of days.

→ She will be here with us a lot longer than _____.

7. Ms. Ross speaks clearly. Mr. Mudd mumbles.

→ She speaks a lot more clearly than _____.

8. I've been here for two years. Sam has been here for two months.

→ I've been here a lot longer than _____.

9. I had a good time at the picnic yesterday. Mary didn't enjoy it.

→ I had a lot more fun at the picnic than _____.

10. I can reach the top shelf of the bookcase. Tim can only reach the shelf next to the top.

→ I can reach higher than _____.

◇ PRACTICE 12—GUIDED STUDY: Unclear comparisons. (Chart 13-3)

Directions: The following are unclear comparisons. Discuss the possible meanings.

1. UNCLEAR: Ann likes her dog better than her husband.
   POSSIBLE MEANINGS:
   → *Ann likes her dog better than her husband does.*
      (Meaning: *Ann likes her dog better than her husband likes her dog.*)
   → *Ann likes her dog better than she does her husband.*
      (Meaning: *Ann likes her dog better than she likes her husband.*)

2. UNCLEAR: I know John better than Mary.

3. UNCLEAR: Sam likes football better than his wife.

4. UNCLEAR: Frank helps me more than Debra.

5. UNCLEAR: I pay my plumber more than my dentist.

◇ PRACTICE 13—SELFSTUDY: *Very* vs. *a lot/much/far.* (Chart 13-4)

Directions: Circle the correct answer or answers. **More than one** answer may be correct.

1. This watch is not _____ expensive.
   A. very B. a lot C. much D. far

2. That watch is _____ more expensive than this one.
   A. very B. a lot C. much D. far

3. My nephew is _____ polite.
   A. very B. a lot C. much D. far

4. My nephew is _____ more polite than my niece.
   A. very B. a lot C. much D. far

5. Simon is _____ taller than George.
   A. very B. a lot C. much D. far

6. Simon is _____ tall.
   A. very B. a lot C. much D. far

7. I think astronomy is _____ more interesting than geology.
   A. very B. a lot C. much D. far

8. I think astronomy is _____ interesting.
   A. very B. a lot C. much D. far

◇ PRACTICE 14—SELFSTUDY: *Less . . . than* and *not as . . . as.* (Chart 13-4)

Directions: Circle the correct answer or answers.

1. My nephew is _____ ambitious _____ my niece.
   A. less . . . than B. not as . . . as

2. My nephew is _____ old_____ my niece.
   A. less . . . than B. not as . . . as

3. A bee is _____ big _____ a bird.
   A. less . . . than B. not as . . . as

4. Money is _____ important _____ good health.
   A. less . . . than B. not as . . . as

5. The last exercise was _____ difficult _____ this one.
   A. less . . . than B. not as . . . as

6. My brother is _____ interested in planning for the future _____ I am.
   A. less . . . than B. not as . . . as

7. I am _____ good at repairing things _____ Diane is.
   A. less . . . than B. not as . . . as

8. Some students are _____ serious about their schoolwork _____ others.
   A. less . . . than B. not as . . . as

◇ PRACTICE 15—GUIDED STUDY: Completing a comparative. (Chart 13-4)

Directions: Answer the questions. Begin your answer with **"Yes, I've never . . . ."** Use COMPARATIVES (**MORE/-ER**) in your answer.

Example: Your friend told a story at the party last night. Was it funny?
→ *Yes, I've never heard a funnier story.* *

1. You took a test yesterday. Was it difficult?
2. You read a book that you liked very much. Was it a good book?
3. Someone said something bad to you. Were you angry?
4. I hope you liked staying in our guest room. Were you comfortable?
5. You've been carrying things and moving furniture all day. Are you tired?
6. Congratulations on the birth of your daughter. Are you happy?
7. You have known many people in your lifetime, but one person is special. Is this person kind? Is this person considerate? Is this person generous? wise? compassionate?
8. You have had many good experiences in your lifetime, but you remember one in particular. Was it an interesting experience? Was it a good experience? exciting? memorable?

◇ PRACTICE 16—SELFSTUDY: Adjectives vs. adverbs in the comparative. (Chart 13-4)

Directions: Complete each sentence using the COMPARATIVE + the correct ADJECTIVE or ADVERB. If it is an adjective, circle ADJ. If it is an adverb, circle ADV.

1. *slow*
   slowly
   I like to drive fast, but my brother William doesn't. As a rule, he drives
   _____ **more slowly** _____ than I do. ADJ **(ADV)**

2. *slow*
   slowly
   Alex is a _____ **slower** _____ driver than I am. **(ADJ)** ADV

3. *serious*
   seriously
   Some workers are _____ about their jobs than
   others. ADJ ADV

4. *serious*
   seriously
   Some workers approach their jobs _____ than
   others. ADJ ADV

5. *polite*
   politely
   Why is it that my children behave _____
   at other people's houses than at home? ADJ ADV

6. *polite*
   politely
   Why are they _____ at Mrs. Miranda's
   house than at home? ADJ ADV

7. *careful*
   carefully
   I'm a cautious person when I express my opinions, but my sister will say anything to
   anyone. I'm much _____ when I speak to others than
   my sister is. ADJ ADV

_____

*The understood completion of the comparison is: *I've never heard a funnier story* **in my lifetime than the story my friend told at the party last night.**

8. *careful* I always speak _____ in public than my sister

   carefully does. **ADJ** **ADV**

9. *clear* I can't understand Mark's father very well when he talks, but I

   clearly can understand Mark. He speaks much _____ than

   his father. **ADJ** **ADV**

10. *clear* Mark is a much _____ speaker than his

    clearly father. **ADJ** **ADV**

◇ PRACTICE 17—SELFSTUDY: Nouns in the comparative. (Chart 13-5)

Directions: Choose from the given words to complete the sentences with the COMPARATIVE
(**MORE/-ER**). If the word you use in the comparative is an adjective, circle ADJ. If it is an adverb,
circle ADV. If it is a noun, circle NOUN.

books	friends	✔ newspapers
carefully	homework	pleasant
easily	loud	snow

1. My husband always wants to know everything that is going on in the world. He reads many

   ___*more newspapers*___ than I do. ADJ ADV (NOUN)

2. University students study hard. They have a lot _____ than high

   school students. **ADJ** **ADV** **NOUN**

3. There is far _____ in winter in Alaska than there is in Texas.

   ADJ **ADV** **NOUN**

4. I'm lonely. I wish I had _____ to go places with and spend time

   with. **ADJ** **ADV** **NOUN**

5. A warm, sunny day is _____ than a cold, windy day.

   ADJ **ADV** **NOUN**

6. Don picks up languages with little difficulty. For me, learning a second language is slow and

   difficult. I guess some people just learn languages a lot _____ than

   others. **ADJ** **ADV** **NOUN**

7. The New York City Public Library has many _____ than the

   public library in Portland, Oregon. **ADJ** **ADV** **NOUN**

8. I have been driving _____ since my accident. **ADJ** **ADV** **NOUN**

9. Karen doesn't need a microphone when she speaks to the audience. She's the only person I

   know whose voice is _____ than mine. **ADJ** **ADV** **NOUN**

◇ PRACTICE 18—GUIDED STUDY: Making comparisons: *as . . . as* and *more/-er.*
(Charts 13-1 → 13-4)

Directions: Compare the following. Use **AS . . . AS, LESS,** and **MORE/-ER.** How many points of comparison can you think of?

Example: the sun and the moon

→ *The sun is larger than the moon.*
The sun is hotter than the moon.
The sun is more important to life on earth than the moon is.
The sun is much brighter than the moon.
The moon is closer to the earth than the sun is.
The moon is less important than the sun.
The moon isn't as far away as the sun.

1. two stores in this city
2. two seasons
3. two kinds of music
4. fingers and toes
5. two classes
6. two restaurants in this city
7. iron and aluminum (American English)/aluminium (British English)
8. a cloudy day and a sunny day

◇ PRACTICE 19—SELFSTUDY: Repeating a comparative. (Chart 13-6)

Directions: Complete the sentences by **REPEATING A COMPARATIVE.** Use the words in the list.

angry	✔ fast	hard
big	good	weak
cold		wet

1. When I get excited, my heart beats _____**faster**_____ and _____**faster**_____.

2. I was really mad! I got _____ and _____ until my sister

   touched my arm and told me to calm down.

3. When you blow up a balloon, it gets _____ and _____.

4. As we continued traveling north, the weather got _____ and

   _____. Eventually, everything we saw was frozen.

5. My English is improving. It is getting _____ and _____

   every day.

6. As I continued walking in miserable weather, it rained _____ and

_____. I got _____ and _____. By the time

I got home, I was completely soaked.

7. As I continued to row the boat, my arms got _____ and

_____ until I had almost no strength left in them at all.

◇ PRACTICE 20—SELFSTUDY: Double comparatives. (Chart 13-7)

Directions: Complete the sentences with DOUBLE COMPARATIVES (THE MORE/-ER . . .
THE MORE/-ER).

1. If the fruit is *fresh,* it tastes *good.*

→ _____*The fresher*_____ the fruit is, _____*the better*_____ it tastes.

2. We got *close* to the fire. We felt *warm.*

→ _____ we got to the fire, _____ we felt.

3. If a knife is *sharp,* it is *easy* to cut something with.

→ _____ a knife (is), _____ it is to cut

something.

4. The party got *noisy* next door. I got *angry.*

→ I had a terrible time getting to sleep last night. My neighbors were having a loud party.

_____ it got, _____ I got. Finally, I banged

on the wall and told them to be quiet.

5. Bill talked very *fast.* I became *confused.*

→ Bill was trying to explain some complicated physics problems to me to help me prepare for

an exam. He kept talking faster and faster. _____ he talked,

_____ I became.

◇ PRACTICE 21—SELFSTUDY: Superlatives (Chart 13-8)

Directions: Complete the sentences in COLUMN A with the ideas in COLUMN B. Use the SUPERLATIVE of the adjective in parentheses. If you don't know the right answer, guess.

Example: Kangaroos are the most familiar Australian grassland animals.

COLUMN A
1. Kangaroos . . .
2. Giraffes . . .
3. Apes and monkeys . . .
4. Bottle-nosed dolphins . . .
5. African elephants . . .
6. Horses . . .

COLUMN B
A. (large) eyes of all four-legged land animals
B. (large) ears of all animals
C. (long) necks of all animals
✔ D. (familiar) Australian grassland animals
E. (intelligent) animals that live in water
F. (intelligent) animals that live on land (besides human beings)

◇ PRACTICE 22—SELFSTUDY: Superlatives. (Chart 13-8)

Directions: Use the given phrases to complete the sentences with SUPERLATIVES.

big bird
clean air
✔ deep ocean
high mountains on earth
large living animal

long river in South America
popular forms of entertainment
three common street names
two great natural dangers

1. The Pacific is _____ **the deepest ocean** _____ in the world.

2. There is almost no air pollution at the South Pole. The South Pole has _____

_____ in the world.

3. _____ are in the Himalayan Range in Asia.

4. Most birds are small, but not the flightless North African ostrich. It is _____

_____ in the world.

5. _____ to ships are fog and icebergs.

6. One of _____ throughout the

world is the motion picture.

7. _____ in the United States are

Park, Washington, and Maple.

8. _____ in South America is the

Amazon.

9. The blue whale is huge. It is _____ in the world.

Directions: Complete the sentences with SUPERLATIVES and the appropriate PREPOSITION, IN or OF.

1. Jack is *lazy*. He is _____*the laziest*_____ student ___*in*___ the class.

2. Mike and Julie were *nervous*, but Amanda was _____*the most nervous of*_____ all.

3. Costa Rico is *beautiful*. It is one of _____ countries _____ the world.

4. Scott got a *bad* score on the test. It was one of _____ scores _____ the whole school.

5. Pluto is *far* from the sun. In fact, it is _____ planet from the sun _____ our solar system.

6. There are a lot of *good* cooks in my family, but my mom is _____ cook _____ all.

7. Alaska is *big*. It is _____ state _____ the United States.

8. My grandfather is very *old*. He is _____ person _____ the town where he lives.

9. That chair in the corner is *comfortable*. It is _____ chair _____ the room.

10. Everyone who ran in the race was *exhausted*, but I was _____ _____ all.

Directions: Complete the sentences with an appropriate SUPERLATIVE and the PRESENT PERFECT of the words in parentheses.

1. I have had many *good* experiences. Of those, my trip to Honduras was one of ___*the best*___ experiences I (*have, ever*) _____*have ever had*_____.

2. I know many *responsible* people. Maria is one of _____*the most responsible*_____ people I (*know, ever*) _____*have ever known*_____.

3. I've had many *nice* times, but my birthday party was one of _____ times I (*have, ever*) _____.

4. I've taken many *difficult* courses, but statistics is _____ course I (*take, ever*) _____.

5. I've tasted a lot of *good* coffee, but this is _____ coffee I (*have, ever*) _____.

6. I've made a lot of *bad* mistakes in my life, but I'm afraid lending my cousin a lot of money was

_____ mistake I *(make, ever)* _____.

7. There are many *beautiful* buildings in the world, but the Taj Mahal is one of _____

_____ buildings I *(see, ever)* _____.

8. A: How do you think you did on the exam this morning?

B: I think I did pretty well. It was an *easy* test. In fact, it was one of _____

exams I *(take, ever)* _____.

◇ PRACTICE 25—GUIDED STUDY: Completing superlatives with adjective clauses. (Chart 13-8)

Directions: Create sentences with **ONE OF** plus a SUPERLATIVE and your own words. Use the following patterns:

PATTERN A: *ONE OF* + SUPERLATIVE + PLURAL NOUN + *IS*
PATTERN B: *IS* + *ONE OF* + SUPERLATIVE + PLURAL NOUN

Example: There are many good students in this class. Who is one of the best?

→ PATTERN A: *One of* **the best students** in this class *is* (Nazir).   OR
→ PATTERN B: (Nazir) *is one of* **the best students** in this class.

Example: You have known many interesting people. Who is one of the most interesting you've known?

→ PATTERN A: *One of* **the most interesting people** I've ever known *is* (Ms. Lee).   OR
→ PATTERN B: (Ms. Lee) *is one of* **the most interesting people** I've ever known.

1. There are many beautiful countries in the world. What is one of them?
2. There are many famous people in the world. Who is one of them?
3. There are many long rivers in the world. What is one of them?
4. You've seen some good movies. What is one of the best movies you've seen recently?
5. Have you seen any bad movies? What is one of them?
6. You've visited some interesting cities. What is one of them?
7. You know some wonderful people. Who is one of them?
8. Have you ever taken any difficult classes? What is one of them?
9. You have had many good experiences. What is one of the best experiences you've ever had?
10. There are a lot of interesting animals in the world. What is one of them?
11. What is one of the strangest things you've ever seen?
12. There are many important people in your life among your family, friends, teachers, co-workers, and others. Who is one of these people?
13. Who is one of the most important people in world politics or the history of your country?
14. Think of some happy days in your life. What was one of them?
15. Talk about one of the best trips you've taken, the funniest things you've seen, the most exciting things you've done, the easiest jobs you've had, the coldest places you've been, the best times you've had, the most decent people you've known.

◇ PRACTICE 26—SELFSTUDY: Comparatives and superlatives. (Charts 13-2 → 13-4 and 13-8)

Directions: Complete with BETTER, THE BEST, WORSE, or THE WORST.

1. I just finished a terrible book. It's _____ *the worst* _____ book I've ever read.

2. The weather was bad yesterday, but it's terrible today. The weather is
   _____ *worse* _____ today than it was yesterday.

3. This cake is really good. It's _____ cake I've ever eaten.

4. My grades this term are great. They're much _____ than last term.

5. Being separated from my family in time of war is one of _____
   experiences I can imagine.

6. I broke my nose in a football game yesterday. Today it's very painful. For some reason, the
   pain is _____ today than it was yesterday.

7. The fire spread and burned down an entire city block. It was _____ fire
   we've ever had in our town.

8. I think my cold is almost over. I feel a lot _____ than I did yesterday. I
   can finally breathe again.

◇ PRACTICE 27—GUIDED STUDY: Comparatives and superlatives. (Charts 13-1 → 13-8)

Directions: Ask and answer questions with COMPARATIVES and SUPERLATIVES.
STUDENT A: Ask a question that uses either a comparative or a superlative.
STUDENT B: Answer the question. Use complete sentences.

Example: what . . . sweet
STUDENT A: *What is sweeter than sugar?*
STUDENT B: *Nothing is sweeter than sugar.*

Example: what . . . dangerous
STUDENT A: *What is more dangerous than riding a motorcycle without a helmet?*
STUDENT B: *Climbing a mountain without a safety rope is more dangerous than riding a motorcycle without a helmet.*

Example: who is . . . wonderful
STUDENT A: *Who is the most wonderful person you've ever known?*
STUDENT B: *That's a hard question. Probably my mother is the most wonderful person I've ever known.*

1. what is . . . important
2. who is . . . famous
3. what is . . . good
4. what is . . . bad
5. whose hair is . . . long
6. what is . . . interesting
7. which car is . . . expensive
8. what country is . . . near
9. what is . . . dangerous
10. who is . . . old
11. what is . . . beautiful
12. who is . . . kind

◇ **PRACTICE 28—GUIDED STUDY:** *As . . . as, more/-er, most/-est.* (Charts 13-1 → 13-8)

Directions: Complete comparisons for the following three parts.

PART I: Compare the cost of the listed items. Use the given expressions.

ITEMS TO COMPARE:

a telephone
a pencil
a pair of socks
a motorcycle

1. is less expensive than

   A telephone is less expensive than a motorcycle.

   A pencil is less expensive than a pair of socks.

   Etc.

2. is much more expensive than
3. is not as expensive as
4. are more expensive than
5. are both less expensive than
6. is not nearly as expensive as
7. are all more expensive than

PART II: Compare the waterfalls by using the given expressions.

8. much higher
9. almost as high
10. highest
11. not nearly as high
12. not quite as high

Waterfalls of the World

   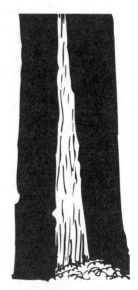

Niagara Falls	Giessbach Falls	Cuquenán Falls	Angel Falls
United States and Canada	Switzerland	Venezuela	Venezuela
53 meters	604 meters	610 meters	807 meters

PART III: Compare the weight of the listed items. Use the given expressions.

ITEMS TO COMPARE:

> *water*
> *iron*
> *wood*
> *air*

13. heavier
14. lighter
15. heaviest
16. not as heavy
17. lightest
18. not nearly as light
19. both heavier

◇ PRACTICE 29—SELFSTUDY: Review of comparatives and superlatives. (Charts 13-2 → 13-8)

Directions: Complete the sentences. Use any appropriate form of the words in parentheses and add any other necessary words. There may be more than one possible completion.

1. Lead is a very heavy metal. It is *(heavy)* _____**heavier than**_____ gold or silver. It is one of *(heavy)* _____**the heaviest**_____ metals ____**of**____ all

2. Dogs are usually *(friendly)* _____ cats.

3. One of *(famous)* _____ volcanoes _____ the world is Mount Etna in Sicily.

4. A car has two *(wheels)* _____ a bicycle.

5. Mrs. Cook didn't ask the children to clean up the kitchen. It was *(easy)* _____ for her to do it herself _____ to nag them to do it.

6. Duck eggs and chicken eggs are different. Duck eggs are *(large)* _____ chicken eggs. Also, the yolk of a duck egg is *(dark)* _____ yellow _____ the yolk of a chicken egg.

7. One of *(safe)* _____ places to be during a lightning storm is inside a car.

8. Small birds have a much *(fast)* _____ heartbeat _____ large birds.

9. Are your feet exactly the same size? Almost everyone's left foot is *(big)* _____ their right foot.★

10. The volcanic explosion of Krakatoa near Java in 1883 may have been *(loud)* _____ noise _____ recorded history. It was heard 2,760 miles (4,441 kilometers) away.

★ Grammar note: In formal English, a singular pronoun is used to refer to *everyone:*
   Almost **everyone's** left foot is bigger than **his or her** right foot.
   In everyday informal usage, a plural pronoun is frequently used:
   Almost **everyone's** left foot is bigger than **their** right foot.

11. In terms of area, *(large)* _____ state _____ the United States is Alaska, but it has one of *(small)* _____ populations _____ all the states.

12. Nothing is *(important)* _____ good health. Certainly gaining wealth is much *(important)* _____ enjoying good health.

13. I need more facts. I can't make my decision until I get *(information)* _____.

14. Rebecca is a wonderful person. I don't think I've ever met a *(kind)*
_____ and *(generous)* _____ person.

15. You can trust her. You will never meet a *(honest)* _____ person _____
she is.

16. I'm leaving! This is *(bad)* _____ movie I've ever seen! I won't sit through another second of it.

17. *(important)* _____ piece of equipment for birdwatching
is a pair of binoculars.

18. Although both jobs are important, being a teacher requires *(education)* _____
_____ being a bus driver.

19. The Great Wall of China is the *(long)* _____ structure that has ever been
built.

20. Howard Anderson is one of *(delightful)* _____ people I've ever met.

21. *(hard)* _____ I tried, *(impossible)* _____ it seemed to
solve the math problem.

22. Perhaps *(common)* _____ topic of everyday conversation _____
the world is the weather.

23. No animals can travel *(fast)* _____ birds. Birds are *(fast)* _____ _____ animals _____ all.

24. Most birds have small eyes, but not ostriches. Indeed, the eye of an ostrich is *(large)* _____ its brain.

25. *(great)* _____ variety of birds _____ a single area can be found in the rain forests of Southeast Asia and India.

26. I feel *(safe)* _____ in a plane _____ I do in a car.

27. Jakarta is *(large)* _____ city _____ Indonesia.

◇ PRACTICE 30—GUIDED STUDY: Review of comparatives and superlatives.
(Charts 13-1 → 13-8)

Directions: Complete the sentences. Use any appropriate form of the words in parentheses and add any other necessary words.

1. Sometimes I feel like all of my friends are *(intelligent)* __***more intelligent than***__ I am, and yet sometimes they tell me that they think I am *(smart)* __***the smartest***__ person __***in***__ the class.

2. One of *(popular)* _____ holidays _____ Japan is New Year's.

3. A mouse is *(small)* _____ a rat.

4. Europe is first in agricultural production of potatoes. *(potatoes)* _____ are grown in Europe _____ on any other continent.

5. Mercury is *(close)* _____ planet to the sun. It moves around the sun *(fast)* _____ any other plant in the solar system.

6. Human beings must compete with other species for the food of the land. The *(great)* _____ competitors we have for food are insects.

7. When the temperature stays below freezing for a long period of time, the Eiffel Tower becomes six inches (fifteen centimeters) *(short)* _____ .

8. Have you every been bothered by a fly buzzing around you? *(easy)* _____ way _____ all to get a fly out of a room is to darken the room and turn on a light somewhere else.

9. Mountain climbing takes *(strength)* _____ walking on a level path.

10. Cheese usually tastes *(good)* _____ at room temperature _____ it does just after you take it out of the refrigerator.

11. World Cup Soccer is *(big)* _____ sporting event _____ the world. It is viewed on TV by *(people)* _____ any other event in sports.

12. The wall of a soap bubble is very, very thin. A human hair is approximately ten thousand times *(thick)* _____ the wall of a soap bubble.

13. English has approximately 600,000 words. Because of the explosion of scientific discoveries and new technologies, there are *(words)* _____ in English _____ in any other language.

14. You'd better buy the tickets for the show soon. *(long)* _____ you wait, *(difficult)* _____ it will be to get good seats.

15. I've seen a lot of funny movies over the years, but the one I saw last night is *(funny)* _____ all.

16. Riding a bicycle can be dangerous. *(people)* _____ were killed in bicycle accidents last year _____ have been killed in airplane accidents in the last four years.

17. Young people have *(high)* _____ rate of automobile accidents _____ all drivers.

18. Some people build their own boats from parts that they order from a manufacturer. They save money that way. It is *(expensive)* _____ to build your own boat _____ to buy a boat.

19. It's easy to drown a houseplant. *(houseplants)* _____ die from too much water _____ not enough water.

20. Mr. Hochingnauong feels (comfortable) _____ speaking his native

     language _____ he does speaking English.

21. My friend has studied many languages. He thinks Japanese is (difficult) _____

     _____ all the languages he has studied.

22. One of (bad) _____ nuclear accidents _____ the world occurred at

     Chernobyl in 1986.

23. I think learning a second language is (hard) _____ studying

     chemistry or mathematics.

24. (low) _____ temperature ever recorded in Alaska was minus 80°F (-27° C) in

     1971.

25. Computers are complicated machines, but one of (complex) _____

     things _____ the universe is the human brain.

◇   PRACTICE 31—SELFSTUDY: *The same, similar, different, like,* and *alike.* (Chart 13-9)

    Directions: Complete the sentences with AS, TO, FROM, or Ø if no word is necessary.

1. Geese are similar _____*to*_____ ducks. They are both large water birds.

2. But geese are not the same _____*as*_____ ducks. Geese are usually larger and have longer

    necks.

3. Geese are different _____*from*_____ ducks.

4. Geese are like _____*Ø*_____ ducks in some ways, but geese and ducks are not exactly alike

    _____*Ø*_____.

5. An orange is similar _____ a grapefruit. They are both citrus fruits.

6. But an orange is not the same _____ a grapefruit. A grapefruit is usually larger and

    sourer.

7. An orange is different _____ a grapefruit.

8. An orange is like _____ a grapefruit in some ways, but they are not exactly alike

    _____.

9. Gold is similar _____ silver. They are both valuable metals that people use for jewelry.

    But they aren't the same _____. Gold is not the same color _____ silver. Gold

    is also different _____ silver in cost. Gold is more expensive than silver.

10. Look at the two zebras. Their names are Zee and Bee. Zee looks like _____ Bee. Is

Zee exactly the same _____ Bee? The pattern of the stripes on each zebra in the world

is unique. No two zebras are exactly alike _____. Even though Zee and Bee are similar

_____ each other, they are different _____ each other in the exact pattern of

their stripes.

◇ PRACTICE 32—SELFSTUDY: *The same, similar, different, like,* and *alike.* (Chart 13-9)

Directions: Circle the correct completions.

1. My coat is   (different,) the same   from yours.

2. Our apartment is   *like, similar*   to my cousin's.

3. The news report on channel four was   *similar, the same*   as the report we heard on

channel six last night.

4. My sister and I look   *like, alike*   and talk   *like, alike,*   but our personalities

are quite   *different, similar to.*

5. Does James act   *like, alike*   his brother?

6. My dictionary is   *different, similar*   from yours.

7. A: I'm sorry, but I believe you have my umbrella.

B: Oh? Yes, I see. It looks almost exactly   *like, alike*   mine, doesn't it?

8. A: How do you like the spaghetti I made for you? Is it   *similar, the same*   to yours?

B: It's a little   *similar, like*   mine, but not exactly   *like, alike.*

9. A: Your jacket is exactly the same   *as, like*   mine.

B: Isn't that amazing? I bought mine in New York, and you bought yours in Tokyo, and yet

they're exactly   *the same, like.*

10. A: Some people think that we look   *like, alike.*   What do you think?

B: Well, the color of your hair is   *similar, the same*   to mine, and your eyes are almost

a similar, the same   color as mine. I guess there's a resemblance.

◇ PRACTICE 33—GUIDED STUDY: *The same, similar, different, like,* and *alike.* (Chart 13-9)

Directions: Compare the figures. Complete the sentences using THE SAME, SIMILAR, DIFFERENT, LIKE, and ALIKE.

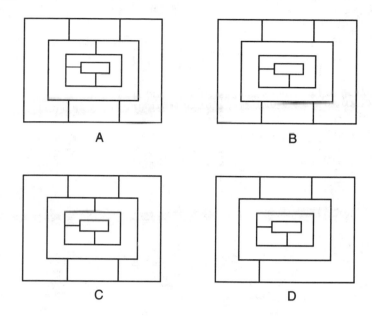

1. All of the figures are _____*similar to*_____ each other.

2. Figure A is _____ Figure B.

3. Figure A and Figure B are _____.

4. A and C are _____.

5. A and C are _____ D.

6. C is _____ A.

7. B isn't _____ D.

◇ PRACTICE 34—GUIDED STUDY: *The same, similar, different, like,* and *alike.* (Chart 13-9)

Directions: Compare the figures.

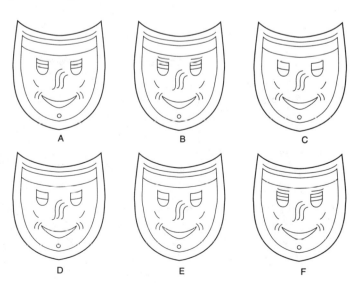

◇ PRACTICE 35—GUIDED STUDY: Making comparisons. (Chapter 13)

Directions: Compare the pictures. How many differences can you find?

Example: *The boy in Picture B isn't the same height as the boy in Picture A .*

◇ PRACTICE 36—GUIDED STUDY: Making comparisons. (Chapter 13)

Directions: Ask three (or more) classmates four (or more) questions.
First decide what you want to ask your classmates. Below are some suggestions.
Next fill out the chart with the topics of the questions.
Then write in the names of the classmates you talk to and ask them the questions.
After you have all of your information, compare the answers using SAME, DIFFERENT, SIMILAR, LIKE, ALIKE, AS . . . AS, MORE/-ER and MOST/-EST.

Example:

	eye-color	favorite sport	length of time at this school	educational goals	size of family
Hamid	brown	soccer	3 mo.	engineering degree	5
Hiroki	brown	baseball	3 mo.	business degree	4
Maria	brown	baseball	4 mo.	journalism degree	7

Possible comparisons:

I'm comparing three people: Hamid, Hiroki, and Maria.

• All three have **the same** eye color.

• Hiroki and Maria like **the same** sport, baseball. Hamid's favorite sport is **different from** theirs. He likes soccer.

• Maria has been at this school **longer than** Hamid and Hiroki.

• Their educational goals are **similar.** All of them want to get university degrees.

• Maria has **the largest** family. Hiroki's immediate family is **the smallest**.

Suggestions for questions to ask your classmates:

1. How long have you been at this school?
2. What color are your eyes?
3. What is your favorite kind of music?
4. What is your favorite sport?
5. What do you usually wear to class?
6. What are your educational goals?
7. How many people are there in your immediate family?*
8. How big is your hometown?
9. What kind of books do you like to read?
10. What kind of movies do you prefer?
11. What country would you most like to visit?
12. What is your favorite food?
13. When did you last visit home?
14. What kind of vacation do you prefer?
15. How tall are you?

Use this chart to record your information. Write in the topics of your questions, the names of the people you interview, and then their answers.

Immediate family = mother, father, and children (not including cousins, aunts, uncles, grandparents, etc.).

CHAPTER 14
Noun Clauses

◇ PRACTICE 1—SELFSTUDY: Noun clauses and information questions.
(Charts 6-2 and 14-2)

Directions: If the sentence contains a NOUN CLAUSE, <u>underline</u> it and circle NOUN CLAUSE. If the question word introduces a question, circle QUESTION. Add appropriate final punctuation: a PERIOD (.)* or a QUESTION MARK (?).

1. I don't know <u>where Jack bought his new boots</u>.	(NOUN CLAUSE)	QUESTION
2. Where did Jack buy his new boots?	NOUN CLAUSE	(QUESTION)
3. I don't understand why Ann left	NOUN CLAUSE	QUESTION
4. Why did Ann leave	NOUN CLAUSE	QUESTION
5. I don't know where your book is	NOUN CLAUSE	QUESTION
6. Where is your book	NOUN CLAUSE	QUESTION
7. When did Bob come	NOUN CLAUSE	QUESTION
8. I don't know when Bob came	NOUN CLAUSE	QUESTION
9. What does "calm" mean	NOUN CLAUSE	QUESTION
10. Tarik knows what "calm" means	NOUN CLAUSE	QUESTION
11. I don't know how long the earth has existed	NOUN CLAUSE	QUESTION
12. How long has the earth existed	NOUN CLAUSE	QUESTION

◇ PRACTICE 2—SELFSTUDY: Noun clauses and information questions.
(Charts 6-2 and 14-2)

Directions: PART I: <u>Underline</u> the NOUN CLAUSE in each sentence. Find the SUBJECT (**S**) and VERB (**V**) of the noun clause.

                             S   **V**
1. I don't know <u>where [Patty] [went] last night</u>.

---

*A *period* is called a *full stop* in British English.

2. Do you know where [Joe's parents] [live]?*

$$\begin{array}{cc} \textbf{S} & \textbf{V} \end{array}$$

3. I know where Joe lives.

4. Do you know what time   the movie   begins?

5. She explained where   Brazil   is.

6. I don't believe what   Estefan   said.

7. I don't know when the packages will arrive.

8. Please tell me how far it is to the post office.

9. I don't know who knocked on the door.

10. I wonder what happened at the party last night.

PART II: Change the underlined NOUN CLAUSE to a QUESTION.

1. QUESTION: **_Where did Patty go last night_**   ?

   NOUN CLAUSE: I don't know where Patty went last night.

2. QUESTION: **_Where do Joe's parents live_**   ?

   NOUN CLAUSE: I don't know where Joe's parents live.

3. QUESTION: _____   ?

   NOUN CLAUSE: I don't know where Joe lives.

4. QUESTION: _____   ?

   NOUN CLAUSE: I don't know what time the movie begins.

5. QUESTION: _____   ?

   NOUN CLAUSE: I don't know where Pine Street is.

6. QUESTION: _____   ?

   NOUN CLAUSE: I don't know what Estefan said.

7. QUESTION: _____   ?

   NOUN CLAUSE: I don't know when the packages will arrive.

8. QUESTION: _____   ?

   NOUN CLAUSE: I don't know how far it is to the post office.

---

*A question mark is used at the end of this noun clause because the main subject and verb of the sentence (*Do you know*) are in question word order.

     Example: *Do you know where Joe lives?*

Do you know asks a question; *where Joe lives* is a noun clause.

9. QUESTION: _____ ?

   NOUN CLAUSE: I don't know <u>who knocked on the door</u>.

10. QUESTION: _____ ?

   NOUN CLAUSE: I don't know <u>what happened at the party last night</u>.

◇ PRACTICE 3—SELFSTUDY: Noun clauses that begin with a question word. (Chart 14-2)

Directions: Complete the dialogues by changing the questions to NOUN CLAUSES.

1. A: Where does Jim go to school?

   B: I don't know _____ ***where Jim goes*** _____ to school.

2. A: Where did Alex go yesterday?

   B: I don't know. Do you know _____ ***where Alex went*** _____ yesterday?

3. A: Why is Maria laughing?

   B: I don't know. Does anybody know _____ ?

4. A: Why is fire hot?

   B: I don't know _____ hot.

5. A: How much does a new Honda cost?

   B: Peter can tell you _____ .

6. A: Why is Mike always late?

   B: Don't ask me. I don't understand _____ late.

7. A: How long do birds live?

   B: I don't know _____ .

8. A: When was the first wheel invented?

   B: I don't know. Do you know _____ ?

9. A: How many hours does a light bulb burn?

    B: I don't know exactly _____.

10. A: Where did Emily buy her computer?

    B: I don't know _____ her computer.

11. A: Who lives next door to Kate?

    B: I don't know _____ next door to Kate.

12. A: Who(m) did Julie talk to?

    B: I don't know _____ to.

◇ PRACTICE 4—SELFSTUDY: Noun clauses and information questions.
                        (Charts 6-2 and 14-2)

   Directions: Complete the sentences with the words in parentheses.

   1. A: Do you know where *(Jason, work)* _____**Jason works**_____?

       B: Who?

       A: Jason. Where *(he, work)* _____**does he work**_____?

       B: I don't know.

   2. A: Where *(Susan, eat)* _____ lunch yesterday?

       B: I don't know where *(she, eat)* _____ lunch yesterday.

   3. A: Excuse me.

       B: Yes. How can I help you?

       A: How much *(that camera, cost)* _____?

       B: You want to know how much *(this camera, cost)* _____,
           is that right?

       A: No, not that one. The one next to it.

   4. A: How far *(you, can run)* _____ without stopping?

       B: I have no idea. I don't know how far *(I, can run)* _____
           without stopping. I've never tried.

   5. A: Where *(you, see)* _____ the ad for the computer sale last
           week?

       B: I don't remember where *(I, see)* _____ it. One of the local
           papers, I think.

   6. A: Could you please tell me where *(Mr. Gow's office, is)* _____?

       B: I'm sorry. I didn't understand.

       A: Where *(Mr. Gow's office, is)* _____ ?

       B: Ah. Down the hall on the right.

7. A: Ann was out late last night, wasn't she? What time *(she, get)* _____ in?

B: Why do you want to know what time *(she, get)* _____ home?

A: Just curious.

8. A: What time *(it, is)* _____?

B: I don't know. I'll ask Sara. Sara, do you know what time *(it, is)* _____?

C: Almost four-thirty.

9. A: What was your score on the test?

B: I don't know yet.

A: How soon *(you, know)* _____ ?

B: I don't know how soon *(I, know)* _____. I won't know until the professor hands the exams back.

10. A: How often *(you, go)* _____ shopping every week?

B: *(you, mean)* _____ grocery shopping?

A: Yes.

B: Why? I don't understand why *(you, want)* _____ to know how often *(I, go)* _____ shopping every week.

A: My mother goes to the market every day. She thinks I'm lazy because I go shopping only once a week. I just wonder how often *(other people, go)* _____ shopping.

B: I see. Well, once a week is enough for me.

11. A: *(who, invent)* _____ the first refrigerator?

B: I don't know *(who, invent)* _____ it. Do you?

12. A: Whose car *(Toshi, borrow)* _____ yesterday?

B: I don't know whose car *(Toshi, borrow)* _____.

13. A: When *(Rachel, plan)* _____ to return to class?

B: No one knows when *(she, return)* _____ to class. She left the hospital two weeks ago.

A: Why *(she, be)* _____ in the hospital?

B: I haven't heard why *(she, be)* _____ in the hospital. I just know that she's living at home with her parents.

14. A: Where *(Tom, go)* _____ last night?

B: I'm sorry. I didn't hear what *(you, say)* _____.

A: I wanted to know where *(Tom, go)* _____ last night.

◇ PRACTICE 5—SELFSTUDY: Noun clauses with *who, what, whose + be.* (Chart 14-3)

Directions: Find the SUBJECT (**S**) and VERB (**V**) of the NOUN CLAUSE.

                          S   **V**
1. I don't know who [that man] [is].

                       S   **V**
2. I don't know [who] [called].

3. I don't know who those people are.

4. I don't know who that person is.

5. I don't know who lives next door to me.

6. I don't know who my teacher will be next semester.

7. I don't know who will teach us next semester.

8. I don't know what a lizard is.

9. I don't know what happened in class yesterday.

10. I don't know whose hat this is.

11. I don't know whose hat is on the table.

◇ PRACTICE 6—SELFSTUDY: Noun clauses with *who, what, whose + be.* (Chart 14-3)

Directions: Add the word **IS** to each sentence in the correct place.

1. I don't know who _____ that woman _____**is**_____.

2. I don't know who _____**is**_____ on the phone _____.

3. I don't know what _____ a crow _____.

4. I don't know what _____ in that bag _____.

5. I don't know whose car _____ in the driveway _____.

6. I don't know whose car _____ that _____.

7. I don't know who _____ Bob's doctor _____.

8. I don't know who _____ in the doctor's office _____.

◇ PRACTICE 7—SELFSTUDY: Noun clauses with *who, what, whose + be.* (Chart 14-3)

Directions: Complete the dialogues by changing the QUESTIONS to NOUN CLAUSES.

1. A: Whose car is that?

   B: I don't know _____*whose car that is*_____.

2. A: Whose car is in front of Sam's house?

   B: I don't know _____*whose car is in front of Sam's house*_____.

3. A: Who has the scissors?

   B: Not me. I don't know _____.

4. A: Who are the best students?

   B: Ask the teacher _____.

5. A: What is a violin?

   B: I don't know _____.

   C: It's a musical instrument that has strings.

6. A: What causes earthquakes?

   B: You should ask your geology professor _____.

7. A: What kind of fruit is that?

   B: I can't tell you _____. I've never seen it before.

8. A: Whose hammer is this?

   B: I don't know. Hey, Hank, do you know _____?

   A: It's Ralph's.

9. A: The phone's for you.

   B: Who is it?

   A: I don't know _____. Want me to find out?

   B: Yeah.

   A: Okay. Could I please ask who's calling? Oh, hi, Jennifer! It's Jennifer.

   B: Where is she?

   A: Betsy wants to know _____. Okay. She's at home.

   B: What time does she want me to meet her at the theater?

   A: Here. You talk to her yourself.

◇ PRACTICE 8—GUIDED STUDY: Noun clauses and information questions.
              (Charts 6-2, 14-2 and 14-3)

   Directions: Complete the sentences with the words in parentheses.

   1. A: How long (the oldest whales, live) ___*do the oldest whales live*___?

      B: Nobody knows for sure how long (the oldest whales, live) ___*the oldest whales live*___.

   2. A: Do you know how old (Amanda, be) _____?

      B: Why do you want to know how old (Amanda, be) _____?

      A: Just answer my question. How old (Amanda, be) _____?

      B: I won't tell you until you tell me why (you, want) _____ to

      know.

3. A: The boss wants to know why *(David, leave)* _____ the office

   early yesterday. Do you know?

   B: No. I'll ask Sara. Hey, Sara, why *(David, leave)* _____

   early yesterday?

   C: He had to go to a meeting at his son's school.

4. A: How *(airplanes, stay)* _____ up in the air?

   B: What? What are you talking about?

   A: I'm talking about airplanes. I wonder how *(they, stay)* _____

   up in the air. Do you know?

   B: Sure. It has something to do with the movement of air.

5. A: Where *(you, go)* _____ last night?

   B: I don't have to tell you where *(I, go)* _____ last night.

   A: Why don't you want to tell me where *(you, go)* _____ last night?

   B: It's none of your business.

   A: Well!

6. A: What *(an apricot, be)* _____ ?

   B: Why do you want to know what *(an apricot, be)* _____ ?

   A: I'm studying my vocabulary list. I'm trying to learn twenty new words every day.

   B: I see. An apricot is a small, sweet, orange fruit.

7. A: Do you know why *(Jane, bring)* _____

   her suitcase to work with her this morning?

   B: No. I'll ask Mike. Mike, why *(Jane, bring)* _____

   her suitcase to work with her this morning? Did she tell you?

   C: Yes. Right after work today she's leaving for Springfield to visit her fiancé.

8. A: Whose red sports car *(that, be)* _____ ?

   B: I'll ask Don. I think he knows whose red sports car *(that, be)* _____ .

   A: Wish it were mine.

9. A: What *("chief," mean)* _____ ?

   B: What's the word?

   A: "Chief." I want to know what *("chief," mean)* _____ ?

   B: I don't know. Pablo, do you know what *("chief," mean)* _____ ?

   C: No. I'll ask the teacher. Ms. Sills, what *("chief," mean)* _____ ,

   as in "the chief reason"?

   D: It means "Principal, main, most important."

10. A: Mom, why *(some people, be)* _____ cruel to other people?

    B: Honey, I don't really understand why *(some people, be)* _____

    cruel to others. It's difficult to explain.

11. A: Mr. Wortman! Why *(you, tell, not)* _____ me about

    this problem sooner?

    B: I'm sorry, sir. I don't know why *(I, tell, not)* _____

    you about it sooner. I guess I forgot.

12. A: What kind of camera *(Barbara, have)* _____ ?

    B: I don't know, but you should find out what kind of camera *(she, have)*

    _____ before you decide what to get for yourself. She knows a lot

    about cameras.

13. A: How many French francs *(there, be)* _____ in one U.S. dollar?

    B: I don't know. Call your friend Pierre if you want to know how many French francs *(there,*

    be) _____ in one U.S. dollar.

14. A: Susan looks sad. Why *(she, be)* _____ so unhappy today?

    B: I can't say why *(she, be)* _____ unhappy. She swore me to secrecy.

15. A: I don't care about the future. All I care about is today.

    B: Oh? Well, answer this question for me. Where *(you, spend)* _____

    _____ the rest of your life?

    A: What do you mean?

    B: I mean it's important to pay attention to the future. That's where *(you, spend)*

    _____ the rest of your life.

◇ PRACTICE 9—GUIDED STUDY: Information questions and noun clauses.
(Charts 6-2, 14-2, and 14-3)

Directions: Ask information questions and respond using NOUN CLAUSES.

STUDENT A: Using the given question word, ask a question that you are sure Student B cannot
answer. (You don't have to know the answer to the question.)
STUDENT B: Respond to the question by saying "I don't know . . ." followed by a NOUN CLAUSE.
Then you can guess at an answer if you wish.

Example: when
STUDENT A. *When was the first book printed?*
STUDENT B: *I don't know when the first book was printed. Probably three or four hundred years ago.*

1. where   6. whose
2. who   7. when
3. how far   8. why
4. what kind   9. what
5. what time   10. how much

◇ PRACTICE 10—SELFSTUDY: *Yes/no* questions and noun clauses. (Charts 6-2 and 14-4)

Directions: Change the **YES/NO** QUESTION to a NOUN CLAUSE.

1. YES/NO QUESTION: Is Tom coming?

   NOUN CLAUSE: I wonder _____ **if (whether) Tom is coming** _____.

2. YES/NO QUESTION: Can Jennifer play the piano?

   NOUN CLAUSE: I don't know _____.

3. YES/NO QUESTION: Did Paul go to work yesterday?

   NOUN CLAUSE: I don't know _____.

4. YES/NO QUESTION: Is Susan coming to work today?

   NOUN CLAUSE: Can you tell me _____?

5. YES/NO QUESTION: Will Mr. Pips be at the meeting?

   NOUN CLAUSE: Do you know _____?

6. YES/NO QUESTION: Is Barcelona a coastal town?

   NOUN CLAUSE: I can't remember _____.

7. YES/NO QUESTION: Would Carl like to come with us?

   NOUN CLAUSE: I wonder _____.

8. YES/NO QUESTION: Do you still have Yung Soo's address?

   NOUN CLAUSE: I don't know _____.

Directions: Complete the dialogues by completing the NOUN CLAUSES. Use IF to introduce the noun clause.

1. A: Are you tired?

   B: Why do you want to know _____ ***if I am*** _____ tired?

   A: You look tired. I'm worried about you.

2. A: Are you going to be in your office later today?

   B: What? Sorry. I didn't hear you.

   A: I need to know _____ in your office later today.

3. A: Do all birds have feathers?

   B: Well, I don't really know for sure _____ feathers,

   but I suppose they do.

4. A: Did Bill take my dictionary off my desk?

   B: Who?

   A: Bill. I want to know _____ my dictionary off my desk.

5. A: Can Uncle Pete babysit tonight?

   B: Sorry. I wasn't listening. I was thinking about something else.

   A: Have you talked to Uncle Pete? We need to know _____ tonight.

6. A: Does Al have a flashlight in his car?

   B: I'll ask him. Hey, Al! Al! Fred wants to know _____

   a flashlight in your car.

7. A: Are you going to need help moving the furniture to your new apartment?

   B: I don't know _____ help. Thanks for asking. I'll

   let you know.

8. A: Should I take my umbrella?

   B: How am I supposed to know _____ your umbrella? I'm

   not a weather forecaster.

   A: You're kind of grumpy today, aren't you?

9. A: Is white a color?

   B: What?

   A: I wonder _____ a color, you know, like blue or red.

   B: Of course it is.

10. A: Can fish smell?

B: Why do you want to know _____ ?

A: Just wondering. Do fish breathe?

B: You want to know _____ , is that right?

A: Yes. Do they?

B: Sort of. They get oxygen from water through their gills.

◇ PRACTICE 12—GUIDED STUDY: Noun clauses. (Charts 14-1 → 14-4)

Directions: What are some of the things you wonder about? Consider the given topics. Create sentences with "**I wonder . . . (why, when, how, if, whether, etc.).**"

1. birds → *I wonder how many birds there are in the world.*
   I wonder how many different kinds of birds there are in the world.
   I wonder how long birds have lived on earth.
   I wonder whether birds can communicate with each other.
   I wonder if birds in cages are unhappy.

2. fish

3. the earth

4. (*name of a person you know*)

5. events in the future

6. electricity

7. dinosaurs

8. (*topic of your own choosing*)

◇ PRACTICE 13—GUIDED STUDY: Questions and noun clauses.
(Charts 6-2 and 14-1 → 14-4)

Directions: Make up questions and report them using NOUN CLAUSES.

STUDENT A: Write five questions you want to ask Student B about his/her life or opinions. Sign your name. Hand the questions to Student B.

STUDENT B: Report to the class or a smaller group what Student A wants to know and then provide the information if you can or want to. Use " . . . wants to know . . ." each time you report a question.

Example:

STUDENT A's list of questions:

1. Where were you born?

2. What is your favorite color?

3. What do you think about the recent election in your country?

4. Who do you admire most in the world?

5. Do you have a red car?

STUDENT B's report:

1. (Student A) wants to know where I was born. I was born in (Caracas).

2. S/he wants to know what my favorite color is. Well, blue, I guess.

3. S/he wants to know what I think about the recent election in my country. I'm very pleased. The new leader will be good for my country.

4. (S/he) wants to know who I admire most in the world. I'll have to think about that for a minute.

5. Finally, (s/he) wants to know if I have a red car. I wonder why s/he wants to know that. The answer is no. I don't have a red car, or a black car, or a blue car.

◇ PRACTICE 14—GUIDED STUDY: Questions and noun clauses. (Charts 6-2, 14-1 → 14-4)

Directions: Make up questions and answer them using NOUN CLAUSES.

STUDENT A: Ask a question. Use the suggestions below.
STUDENT B: Answer the question if you can. If you can't, respond by saying "I don't know . . ." followed by a NOUN CLAUSE. Then you can guess at the answer if you wish.

Example: location of X★
STUDENT A: *Where is Mr. Chin's briefcase right now?*
STUDENT B: *Under his desk.* OR
I don't know where his briefcase is right now. I suppose he left it at home today.

1. location of X
2. cost of X
3. year that X happened
4. reason for X
5. person who did X
6. owner of X
7. the meaning of X
8. time of X
9. amount of X
10. country X is from
11. type of X
12. distance from X to Y

◇ PRACTICE 15—SELFSTUDY: *That*-clauses. (Chart 14-5)

Directions: Add the word THAT to the following sentences at the appropriate places to mark the beginning of a noun clause.

1. I believe $\stackrel{\textbf{\textit{that}}}{\wedge}$ we need to protect endangered species of animals.

2. Last night I dreamed I was at my aunt's house.

3. I think most people have kind hearts.

4. I know Matt walks a long distance to school every day. I assume he doesn't have a bicycle.

5. I heard Sara dropped out of school.

6. Did you notice Ji Ming wasn't in class yesterday? I hope he's okay.

---

*"X" simply indicates that the questioner should supply her/his own ideas.

7. I trust Linda. I believe what she said. I believe she told the truth.

8. A: Can Julia prove her watch was stolen?

   B: I suppose she can't, but she suspects her roommate's friend took it.

9. A: Did you know leopards sometimes keep their dead prey in trees?

   B: Really?

   A: Yes. I understand they save their food for later if they're not hungry.

10. A: Do you believe a monster really exists in Loch Ness in Scotland?

    B: I don't know. Look at this story in the newspaper. It says some scientists have proved the Loch Ness Monster exists.

    A: You shouldn't always believe what you read in the newspapers. I think the monster is purely fictional.

◇ PRACTICE 16—SELFSTUDY: *That*-clauses. (Charts 14-5 and 14-7)

Directions: Add the word **THAT** to the following sentences at the appropriate places to mark the beginning of a noun clause.

1. I'm sorry ∧ *that* you won't be here for Joe's party.

2. I'm glad it's warm today.

3. I'm surprised you bought a car.

4. Are you certain Mr. McVay won't be here tomorrow?

5. John is pleased Claudio will be here for the meeting.

6. Carmella was convinced I was angry with her, but I wasn't.

7. Jason was angry his father wouldn't let him use the family car.

8. Andy was fortunate you could help him with his algebra. He was delighted he got a good grade on the exam.

9. It's a fact the Nile River flows north.

10. It's true some dinosaurs could fly.

11. Are you aware dinosaurs lived on earth for one hundred and twenty-five million (125,000,000) years?

12. Is it true human beings have lived on earth for only four million (4,000,000) years?

◇ PRACTICE 17—GUIDED STUDY: *That*-clauses. (Charts 14-5 and 14-7)

Directions: Add the word **THAT** to the following sentences at the appropriate places to mark the beginning of a noun clause.

1. A: Are you sure ∧ *that* you'll be in class tomorrow?

   B: Yes. I'm certain ∧ *that* I'll be in class tomorrow. It's a test day.

2. A: Guido is delighted you can speak Italian.

   B: I'm surprised he can understand my Italian. It's not very good.

3. A: How do you know it's going to be nice tomorrow?

   B: I heard the weather report.

   A: So? The weather report is often wrong, you know. I'm still worried it'll rain on our picnic.

4. A: Are you afraid another diasaster like the one at Chernobyl might occur?

   B: Yes. I'm convinced it can happen again.

5. A: Are you aware you have to pass the English test to get into the university?

   B: Yes, but I'm not worried about it. I'm positive I'll do well on it.

6. A: Mrs. Lane hopes we can come with her to the museum tomorrow.

   B: I don't think I can go with you. I'm supposed to babysit my little brother tomorrow.

   A: Oh, too bad. I wish you could come.

7. A: Is it a fact blue whales are the largest creatures on earth?

   B: Yes. In fact, I believe they are the largest creatures that have ever lived on earth.

8. A: Do you think technology benefits humankind?

   B: Of course. Everyone knows modern inventions make our lives better.

   A: I'm not sure that's true. For example, cars and buses provide faster transportation, but they

   pollute our air. Air pollution can cause lung disease and other illnesses.

◇ PRACTICE 18—GUIDED STUDY: *That*-clauses. (Charts 14-5 and 14-7)

Directions: Read each dialogue. Then use the expressions in parentheses to explain what the people are talking about.

DIALOGUE 1. ALICIA: I really like my English teacher.
            BONNIE: Great! That's wonderful. It's important to have a good English teacher.
                     (think that, be delighted that)
     → *Alicia thinks that her English teacher is very good.*
        Bonnie is delighted that Alicia likes her English teacher.
        Alicia is delighted that she has a good English teacher.
        Bonnie thinks that it's important to have a good English teacher.

DIALOGUE 2. MR. GREEN: Why didn't you return my call?
            MS. WHITE: I truly apologize. I just got too busy and it slipped my mind.
                        (be upset that, be sorry that,)
     → *Mr. Green is upset that Ms. White didn't return his call.*
        Ms. White is upset that she forgot to call Mr. Green.
        Ms. White is sorry that she didn't call Mr. Green.

DIALOGUE 3. MRS. DAY: How do you feel, honey? You might have the flu.
            BOBBY: I'm okay, Mom. Honest. I don't have the flu.
                       (be worried that, be sure that)

DIALOGUE 4. KIM: Did you really fail your chemistry course? How is that possible?
            TINA: I didn't study hard enough. I was too busy having fun with my
                   friends. I feel terrible about it.
                   (be surprised that, be disappointed that)

DIALOGUE 5. KAY: Oh no! My dog is lost! My poor little dog!
             SARA: Call your neighbor. Your dog is probably visiting your neighbor's dog.
                    (be afraid that, think that)

DIALOGUE 6. DAVID: Mike! Hello! It's nice to see you.
             MIKE: It's nice to be here. Thank you for inviting me.
                    (be glad/happy/pleased that)

DIALOGUE 7. FRED: Susan has left. Look. Her closet is empty. Her suitcases are gone. She
                    won't be back. I just know it!
             ERICA: She'll be back.
                    (be afraid that, be upset that, be sure that)

DIALOGUE 8. JOHN: I heard you were in jail. I couldn't believe it!
             ED: Neither could I! I was arrested for robbing a house on my block. Can you
                    believe that? It was a case of mistaken identity. I didn't have to stay in jail
                    long.
                    (be shocked that, be relieved that)

◇ PRACTICE 19—GUIDED STUDY: *That*-clauses. (Charts 14-5 and 14-7)

Directions: What are your views on the following topics? Introduce your opinion with an
expression in the given list, then state your opinion in a **THAT**-CLAUSE.

am certain that	*believe that*	*hope that*
am convinced that	*can prove that*	*predict that*
am sure that	*have concluded that*	*think that*

Example: guns
→ *I believe that ordinary people shouldn't have guns in their homes.*
   I think anyone should be able to have any kind of gun.
   I have concluded that countries in which it is easy to get a gun have a higher
   *   rate of murder than other countries do.*

1. smoking (cigarettes, cigars, pipes)
2. a controversy at your school (perhaps something that has been on the front pages of a student
    newspaper)
3. a recent political event in the world (something that has been on the front pages of the
    newspapers)
4. the exploration of outer space
5. the older generation vs. the younger generation
6. strong laws to protect the environment and endangered species
7. freedom of the press vs. government controlled news
8. solutions to world hunger

◇ PRACTICE 20—SELFSTUDY: Substituting *so* for a *that*-clause. (Chart 14-6)

Directions: Give the meaning of **SO** by writing a **THAT**-clause.

1. A: Does Alice have a car?
    B: I don't think so. (= *I don't think* _____**that Alice has a car**_____ .)

2. A: Did Alex pass his French course?

   B: I think so. (= *I think* _____.)

3. A: Is Mr. Kozari going to be at the meeting?

   B: I hope so. (= *I hope* _____.)

4. A: Can cats swim?

   B: I think so. (= *I think* _____.)

5. A: Do gorillas have tails?

   B: I don't think so. (= *I don't think* _____.)

6. A: Will Janet be at Omar's wedding?

   B: I suppose so. (= *I suppose* _____.)

◇ PRACTICE 21—GUIDED STUDY: Substituting *so* for a *that*-clause. (Chart 14-6)

   Directions: Working with another student, complete the dialogues with your own words.

   STUDENT A: Complete the question.
   STUDENT B: Complete the response using **THINK, BELIEVE, HOPE,** or **SUPPOSE.**

1. A: Does Maria have ____**any brothers or sisters**_____?

   B: I ____**don't think**____ so.

2. A: Do you know if ____**Mr. Miranda will be in class**_____ tomorrow?

   B: I _____**hope**_____ so .

3. A: Is Singapore farther north than _____?

   B: I _____ so.

4. A: Will peace be a reality soon in _____?

   B: I _____ so.

5. A: Can most adults _____?

   B: I _____ so.

6. A: Do you have _____ in your _____?

   B: I _____ so.

7. A: Is _____ soon?

   B: I _____ so.

8. A: Will our teacher _____?

   B: I _____ so.

9. A: Is _____ a holiday in India?

   B: I _____ so.

10. A: Was _____?

    B: I _____ so.

CHAPTER 15
Quoted Speech and Reported Speech

◇ PRACTICE 1—SELFSTUDY: Quoted speech. (Chart 15-1)

> Directions: All of the following present quoted speech. Punctuate as necessary by adding QUOTATION MARKS ("..."),* COMMAS (,), PERIODS (.),** and QUESTION MARKS (?). Also use capital letters as necessary.

Example: My roommate   said   the door is open   could you close it

   →   My roommate   said, **"T**he door is open. **C**ould you close it**?"**

1. Alex   said   do   you   smell   smoke

2. He   said   something   is   burning

3. He   said   do   you   smell   smoke   something   is   burning

4. Rachel   said   the   game   starts   at   seven

5. She   said   the   game   starts   at   seven   we   should   leave   here   at   six

6. She   said   the   game   starts   at   seven   we   should   leave   here   at   six   can   you

   be   ready   to   leave   then

---

* Quotation marks are called *inverted commas* in British English.
** A *period* is called a *full stop* in British English.

◇ PRACTICE 2—SELFSTUDY: Quoted speech. (Chart 15-1)

(a) "Cats are fun to watch," Jane said.	In (a): Notice that a comma (not a period) is used at the end of the quoted **sentence** when *Jane said* comes after the quote.
(b) "Do you own a cat?" Mike said.	In (b): Notice that a question mark (not a comma) is used at the end of the quoted **question**

Directions: Notice the punctuation in examples (a) and (b) above. All of the following present quoted speech. Punctuate as necessary by adding QUOTATION MARKS ("..."), COMMAS (,), PERIODS (.), and QUESTION MARKS (?). Also use CAPITAL LETTERS as necessary.

Example: The door is open my roommate said.

→ *"The door is open," my roommate said.*

Example: The door is open could you close it my roommate said

→ *"The door is open. Could you close it?" my roommate said.*

1. Do you smell smoke   Alex said

2. Something is burning   he said

3. Do you smell smoke   something is burning   he said

4. The game starts at seven   Rachel said

5. The game starts at seven   we should leave here at six   she said

6. Can you be ready to leave at six   she asked

7. The game starts at seven   we should leave here at six   can you be ready to leave then she said

8. The game starts at seven   she said   we should leave here at six   can you be ready to leave then

◇ PRACTICE 3—SELFSTUDY: Quoted speech. (Chart 15-1)

Directions: All of the following present quoted speech. Punctuate by adding QUOTATION MARKS ("..."), COMMAS (,), PERIODS (.), and QUESTION MARKS (?) wherever needed. Also use CAPITAL LETTERS as necessary.

Example: Jack said please wait for me

→ Jack said, *"Please wait for me."*

1. Mrs. Hill said my children used to take the bus to school

2. She said we moved closer to the school

3. Now my children can walk to school Mrs. Hill said

4. Do you live near the school she asked

5. Yes, we live two blocks away I replied

6. How long have you lived here Mrs. Hill wanted to know.

7. I said we've lived here for five years how long have you lived here

8. We've lived here for two years Mrs. Hill said how do you like living here

9. It's a nice community I said it's a good place to raise children

◇ PRACTICE 4—SELFSTUDY: Quoted speech. (Chart 15-1)

Directions: Following are two passages which use quoted speech. Punctuate as necessary by adding QUOTATION MARKS (" . . . "), COMMAS (,), PERIODS (.), QUESTION MARKS (?), and EXCLAMATION MARKS (!). Notice that a new paragraph begins each time the speaker changes.

CONVERSATION 1:

"Why weren't you in class yesterday?" Mr. Garcia asked me.

I had to stay home and take care of my pet bird I said. He wasn't feeling well.

What? Did you miss class because of your pet bird Mr. Garcia demanded to know.

I replied yes, sir. That's correct. I couldn't leave him alone. He looked so miserable.

Now I've heard every excuse in the world Mr. Garcia said. Then he threw his arms in the air and walked away.

CONVERSATION 2:

Both of your parents are deaf, aren't they I asked Robert.

Yes, they are he replied.

I'm looking for someone who knows sign language I said. Do you know sign language I asked.

Of course I do. I've been using sign language with my parents since I was a baby he said. It's a beautiful and expressive language. I often prefer it to spoken language.

Well, a deaf student is going to visit our class next Monday. Could you interpret for her I asked.

That's great he answered immediately and enthusiastically. I'd be delighted to. I'm looking forward to meeting her. Can you tell me why she is coming?

She's interested in seeing what we do in our English classes I said.

◇ PRACTICE 5—GUIDED STUDY: Quoted speech. (Chart 15-1)

Directions: Following are two passages that use quoted speech. Punctuate by adding QUOTATION MARKS ("..."") and COMMAS (,) as necessary. Notice that a new paragraph begins each time the speaker changes.

One day my friend Laura and I were sitting in her apartment. We were having a cup of tea together and talking about the terrible earthquake that had just occurred in Iran. Laura asked me, "Have you ever been in an earthquake?"

Yes, I have I replied.

Was it a big earthquake she asked.

I've been in several earthquakes, and they've all been small ones I answered. Have you ever been in an earthquake?

There was an earthquake in my village five years ago Laura said. I was in my house. Suddenly the ground started shaking. I grabbed my little brother and ran outside. Everything was moving. was scared to death. And then suddenly it was over.

I'm glad you and your brother weren't hurt I said.

Yes, we were very lucky. Has everyone in the world felt an earthquake sometime in their lives Laura wondered. Do earthquakes occur everywhere on the earth?

Those are interesting questions I said but I don't know the answers.

◇ PRACTICE 6—GUIDED STUDY: Quoted speech. (Chart 15-1)

Directions: Rewrite the following. Punctuate as necessary by adding QUOTATION MARKS ("...") and COMMAS (,). Begin a new paragraph each time the speaker changes.

How did you do on the test my friend asked me. I replied I don't know yet. I won't know until tomorrow. He said I know that it's an important test. Are you worried about your score? No, not really I answered. I feel good about it. I think I did well on the test. That's great! he said. I like people who have self-confidence.

◇ PRACTICE 7—SELFSTUDY: Reported speech: pronoun usage. (Charts 15-2 and 15-3)

Directions: Change the pronouns from quoted speech to REPORTED SPEECH.

1. QUOTED: Mr. Smith said, "I need help with my luggage."

   REPORTED: Mr. Smith said (that) _____*he*_____ needed help with _____*his*_____ luggage.

2. My roommate said to me, "You should call your brother."

   → My roommate said (that) _____*I*_____ should call _____*my*_____ brother.

3. Sarah said, "I like sugar in my coffee."

   → Sarah said (that) _____ liked sugar in _____ coffee.

4. Joe said to me, "I will call you."

   → Joe said (that) _____ would call _____.

5. My aunt said to me, "I want your new telephone number."

   → My aunt said (that) _____ wanted _____ new telephone number.

6. Sue and Tom said, "We don't like our new apartment."

   → Sue and Tom said (that) _____ didn't like _____ new apartment .

7. Sam said to me, "I've lost my book."

   → Sam said (that) _____ had lost _____ book.

8. Paul said to me, "I want you to help me with my homework."

   → Paul said (that) _____ wanted _____ to help _____ with _____ homework.

◇ PRACTICE 8—SELFSTUDY: Reported speech: sequence of tenses.
                        (Charts 15-2 and 15-3)

Directions: Complete the reported speech sentences. Use the formal sequence of tenses.

1. QUOTED: Sara said, "I need some help."

   REPORTED: Sara said (that) she _____*needed*_____ some help.

2. Tom said, "I'm meeting David for dinner."

→ Tom said (that) he _____*was meeting*_____ David for dinner.

3. Ms. Davis said, "I have studied in Cairo."

→ Ms. Davis said (that) she _____ in Cairo.

4. Bill said, "I forgot to pay my electric bill."

→ Bill said (that) he _____ to pay his electric bill.

5. Barbara said, "I am exhausted."

→ Barbara said (that) she _____ exhausted.

6. I said, "I'll carry the box up the stairs."

→ I said (that) I _____ the box up the stairs.

7. Jerry said to me, "I can teach you to drive."

→ Jerry said (that) he _____ me to drive.

8. My sister said, "I have to attend a conference in London."

→ My sister said (that) she _____ a conference in London.

9. George said, "I should leave on Friday."

→ George said (that) he _____ on Friday.

10. Ed said, "I want a CD player."

→ Ed said (that) he _____ a CD player.

◇ PRACTICE 9—GUIDED STUDY: Reported speech: pronoun usage and sequence of tenses. (Charts 15-2 and 15-3)

Directions: Complete the reported speech sentences. Use the formal sequence of tenses.

1. QUOTED: David said to me, "I'm going to call you on Friday."

REPORTED: David said (that) _____*he was going*_____

_____*to call me*_____ on Friday.

2. John said to Ann, "I have to talk to you."

→ John told Ann _____

_____ to _____.

3. Diane said to me, "I can meet you after work."

→ Diane said _____

_____ after work.

4. Maria said to Bob, "I wrote you a note."

→ Maria told Bob _____

_____ a note.

5. I said to David, "I need your help to prepare for the exam."

→ I told David _____

_____ help to prepare

for the exam.

6. David said, "You should study with me."

→ David said _____

_____ with _____.

7. Julie asked Mike, "When will I see you again?"

→ Julie asked Mike when _____

_____ again.

8. Hillary said to Bill, "What are you doing?"

→ Hillary asked Bill _____

_____.

9. Mr. Fox said to me, "I'm going to meet Jack and you at the restaurant."

→ Mr. Fox said_____

_____ Jack and _____ at the restaurant.

10. A strange man looked at me and said, "I'm sure I've met you before."

→ A strange man looked at me and said _____ before.

I was sure I'd never seen this person before in my whole life.

◇ PRACTICE 10—SELFSTUDY: *Say* vs. *tell.* (Chart 15-4)

Directions: Complete the sentences with **SAID** or **TOLD**.

1. Ann _____*told*_____ me that she was hungry.

2. Ann _____*said*_____ that she was hungry.

3. Jack _____ that I had a message.

4. Jack _____ me that I had a message.

5. My neighbor and I had a disagreement. I _____ my neighbor that he was wrong.

6. My neighbor _____ me that I was wrong.

7. Fumiko _____ the teacher that Fatima wasn't going to be in class.

8. Ellen _____ she enjoyed the movie last night.

9. When the storm began, I _____ the children to come into the house.

10. When I talked to Mr. Grant, he _____ he would be at the meeting.

◇ PRACTICE 11—SELFSTUDY: Reporting questions. (Chart 15-5)

Directions: Change the quoted questions to REPORTED QUESTIONS. Use formal sequence of tenses.

1. QUOTED: Eric said to me, "How old are you?"

   REPORTED: Eric asked me ___*how old* I was_____.

2. Ms. Rush said to Mr. Long, "Are you going to be at the meeting?"

   → Ms. Rush asked Mr. Long ___*if he was going to be*_____ at the meeting.

3. My mother said to me, "Can you hear the radio?"

   → My mother asked me _____ the radio.

4. I said to Abdullah, "Have you ever seen a panda?"

   → I asked Abdullah _____ a panda.

5. Mr. Lee said to his daughter, "Are you passing your biology class?"

   → Mr. Lee asked his daughter _____ biology class.

6. Larry said to Ms. Ho, "Do you have time to help me?"

   → Larry asked Ms. Ho _____ time to help him.

7. Janet said to Bill, "When will you get back from your holiday?"

   → Janet asked Bill _____ holiday.

8. Don said to Robert, "Did you change your mind about going to Reed College?"

   → Don asked Robert _____ mind about going to Reed College.

◇ PRACTICE 12—GUIDED STUDY: Reporting questions. (Chart 15-5)

Directions: Change the quoted questions to REPORTED QUESTIONS. Use **ASKED (SOMEONE)** to report the question. Use the formal sequence of tenses.

1. Igor said to me, "How long have you been a teacher?"

   → *Igor asked me how long I had been a teacher.*

2. Kathy said to Mr. May, "Will you be in your office around three?"
→ *Kathy asked Mr. May if he would be in his office around three.*

3. My brother said to me, "When do you plan to go to Bangkok?"

4. The teacher said to Maria, "Why are you laughing?"

5. My uncle said to me, "Have you ever considered a career in business?"

6. My boss said to me, "Did you bring the report with you?

7. I said to Tina, "Can you speak Swahili?"

8. Bill said to Ann, "Are you tired?"

◇ PRACTICE 13—GUIDED STUDY: Reported vs. quoted speech. (Charts 15-2 → 15-5)

Directions: Change the reported speech to QUOTED SPEECH. Begin a new paragraph each time the speaker changes. Pay special attention to PRONOUNS, VERB FORMS, and WORD ORDER.

Example: This morning my mother asked me if I had gotten enough sleep last night. I told her that I was fine. I explained that I didn't need a lot of sleep. She told me that I needed to take better care of myself.

Written: *This morning my mother said, "Did you get enough sleep last night?"*
"I'm fine," I replied. "I don't need a lot of sleep."
She said, "You need to take better care of yourself."

1. In the middle of class yesterday, my friend tapped me on the shoulder and asked me what time it was. I told her it was two-thirty.

2. I met Mr. Redford at the reception for international students. He asked me where I was from. I told him I was from Argentina.

3. When I was putting on my hat and coat, Robert asked me where I was going. I told him that I had a date with Anna. He wanted to know what we were going to do. I told him that we were going to a movie.

◇ PRACTICE 14—GUIDED STUDY: Reported speech. (Charts 15-1 → 15-5)

Directions: Change the quoted speech to REPORTED SPEECH. Use formal sequence of tenses. In addition to using SAID, use verbs such as TOLD, ASKED, WONDERED, WANTED TO KNOW, ANSWERED, REPLIED.

Example:
QUOTED: "Where's Bill?" Susan asked me.
"He's in the lunch room," I replied.
"When will he be back in his office?" she wanted to know.
I said, "He'll be back around two."

REPORTED: *Susan asked me where Bill was. I replied (that) he was in the lunch room. She wanted to know when he would be back in his office. I said (that) he would be back around two.*

1. "What are you doing?" Mr. Singh asked me.
"I'm doing a grammar exercise," I told him.

2. "Where's my cane?" Grandfather asked me.
   "I don't know," I told him. "Do you need it?" I asked.
   "I want to walk to the mailbox," he said.
   I told him, "I'll find it for you."

3. "Can you help me clean the hall closet?" my wife asked me.
   "I'm really busy," I told her.
   "What are you doing?" she wanted to know.
   "I'm fixing the zipper on my winter jacket," I said.
   Then she asked me, "Will you have some time to help me after you fix the zipper?"
   I said, "I can't because I have to change a light bulb in the kitchen."
   With a note of exasperation in her voice, she finally said, "I'll clean the closet myself."

◇ PRACTICE 15—SELFSTUDY: Verb + infinitive to report speech. (Chart 15-6)

Directions: Change the quoted speech to reported speech by using a REPORTING VERB from the given list and an INFINITIVE. Use each verb from the list only one time.

advise	*invite*	*remind*
✔*ask*	*order*	*warn*
encourage	*permit*	

1. My son said, "Could you help me with my homework after dinner?"

   → My son _____**asked**_____ me _____**to help**_____ him with his

   homework after dinner.

2. Jennifer said to Kate, "Would you like to have dinner with me?"

   → Jennifer _____ Kate _____ dinner with her.

3. Mr. Crane said to his daughter, "You should take music lessons. You already sing very well. You would enjoy studying music. Wouldn't like you to learn how to play the piano?"

   → Mr Crane _____ his daughter _____ music

   lessons.

4. Nicole said to Heidi, "You should call Julie and apologize. At least, that's what I think."

   → Nicole _____ Heidi _____ Julie and

   _____.

5. Professor Wilson said to Bill, "Yes, you may use my name as a reference on your job application."

   → Professor Wilson _____ Bill _____ her name as

   a reference.

6. Robert said to his dog, "Sit."

   → Robert _____ his dog _____.

7. Kate said, "Don't forget to order some more large envelopes."

   → Kate _____ her secretary _____ some more

   large envelopes.

8. Mrs. Silverman said to her son, "Don't go near the water! I'm warning you! It's dangerous!"

   → Mrs. Silverman _____ her son _____ near the

   water.

◇ PRACTICE 16—GUIDED STUDY: Verb + infinitive to report speech. (Chart 15-6)

Directions: Change the quoted speech to reported speech by using a REPORTING VERB from the given list and completing the sentence.

    ✔ advise   order   remind
      encourage   permit   warn

1. I said to my daughter, "You should quit your job if you are unhappy."

   → I _____*advised my daughter to quit her job if she was unhappy*_____ .

2. The rebel commander said to his army, "Retreat!"

   → The rebel commander _____ .

3. My aunt and uncle said to my husband and me, "Why don't you spend a week with us in August?"

   → My aunt and uncle _____ .

4. Mr. Gordon said to his teenaged son, "Don't forget to make your bed."

   → Mr. Gordon _____ .

5. The tour guide said to us, "Watch out for pickpockets in the marketplace."

   → The tour guide _____ .

6. The teacher said to the students, "You may not leave the room in the middle of the examination."

   → The teacher didn't _____ .

◇ PRACTICE 17—GUIDED STUDY: Verb + infinitive to report speech. (Chart 15-6)

Directions: Change the reported speech to QUOTED SPEECH. There is more than one possible completion. Use quotation marks and other punctuation as necessary.

1. Alex warned his friend not to drive faster than the speed limit.
   → Alex said to his friend . . . .
   Alex said to his friend, *"Don't drive faster than the speed limit."*
   Alex said to his friend, *"You'd better not drive faster than the speed limit."*

2. Paul had tickets to a soccer game. He invited Erica to go with him.
   → Paul said to Erica . . . .
   Paul said to Erica, *"Would you like to go to a soccer game with me?"*
   Paul said to Erica, *"Can you go to a soccer game with me?"*

3. Dr. Aqua advised his patient to drink eight glasses of water a day.

   → Dr. Aqua said to his patient . . . .

4. Mr. Nottingham allowed the children to go to the two o'clock movie at the mall.

   → Mr. Nottingham said to the children . . . .

5. Richard's school counselor encouraged him to enroll in a technical school.

   → Richard's school counselor said to him . . . .

6. The swimming instructor warned her beginning class not to go into the deep end of the pool.

→ The swimming instructor said to her beginning class . . . .

7. Debbie's mother reminded her not to forget her music lesson after school.

→ Debbie's mother said . . . .

8. Sue asked her neighbor Ann to look after the baby for a little while.

→ Sue said to her neighbor . . . .

9. Bill told us to wait for him at the corner of 6th and Pine.

→ Bill said to us . . . .

10. The CEO* ordered his staff to give him their financial reports by five o'clock.

→ The CEO said to his staff . . . .

◇ PRACTICE 18—GUIDED STUDY: Verb + infinitive to report speech. (Chart 15-6)

Directions: Use Student A's original ideas to report speech using a verb and infinitive.

STUDENT A: Speak to Student B, following the directions given in each item below.
STUDENT B: Report what Student A said to you using the *italicized* verb.

Example: advise Student B to do something
STUDENT A (Masako): *Maria, I think you should use an English–English dictionary instead of a Spanish–English dictionary.*
STUDENT B (Maria): *Masako advised me to use an English–English dictionary instead of a Spanish–English dictionary.*

1. *ask* Student B to do something
2. *remind* Student B to do something
3. *warn* Student B not to do something
4. *invite* Student B to do something
5. *advise* Student B to do (or not to do) something
6. *allow* Student B to do something
7. *encourage* Student B to do something
8. *tell* Student B to do (or not to do) something

◇ PRACTICE 19—GUIDED STUDY: Reporting speech. (Chapter 15)

Directions: Use your imagination. Who are these people and what are they saying?

STUDENT A: Give names to the people in the cartoons. Write what you imagine the people are saying in the empty cartoon balloons.
STUDENT B: Read what Student A wrote in the cartoon balloons. Write a story about the people in the cartoons. Write about who said what to whom.

Example: For Story 1, STUDENT A could name the people Mrs. Lee and Mr. Lee, and then write in the balloons:
Mrs. Lee: Dinner's ready.   Mr. Lee: Okay. I'll be there in a minute.
Mrs. Lee: It's getting cold.   Mr. Lee: I have to hear the end of this news report.

---

*CEO = an abbreviation for **C**hief **E**xecutive **O**fficer, meaning the head of a company or corporation.

Example of STUDENT B's written story, using **present tense reporting verbs**:

> Mr. and Mrs. Lee are at home. It's evening, around dinner time. Mr. Lee is watching TV. Mrs. Lee walks in and says, "Dinner's ready." Mr. Lee tells her that he'll be there in a minute. Mrs. Lee warns him that the dinner is getting cold, but Mr. wants to hear the end of a news report before he has his dinner.

Example of STUDENT B's written story, using **past tense reporting verbs**:

> Mr. and Mrs. Lee were at home yesterday evening around dinner time. Mr. Lee was watching TV when Mrs. came into the room and told him dinner was ready. He told her he would be there in a minute, but Mrs. Lee knew her husband meant more than a minute. She got a little impatient and warned him that their dinner was getting cold. Mr. Lee didn't get up from his chair. He told his wife that he had to hear the end of a news report he was watching.

STORY 1:

STORY 2:

STORY 3:

◇ PRACTICE 20—SELFSTUDY: Using *advise, suggest,* and *recommend.* (Chart 15-7)

Directions: Choose the correct completion.

1. I advised him __**A**__ more time at the library.
   A. to spend   B. spending   C. should spend

2. I advised _____ more time at the library.
   A. to spend   B. spending   C. should spend

3. I suggested _____ to the zoo.
   A. to go   B. going   C. should go

4. I suggested that we _____ to the zoo.
   A. to go   B. going   C. should go

5. Bill recommended _____ to Luigi's Restaurant.
   A. to go   B. going   C. should go

6. Bill recommended that we _____ to Luigi's Restaurant.
   A. to go   B. going   C. should go

7. My mother advised me _____ in school.
   A. to stay   B. staying   C. should stay

8. My brother advised _____ in school, too.
   A. to stay   B. staying   C. should stay

9. My father suggested that I _____ for a job.
   A. to look   B. looking   C. should look

10. My uncle suggested _____ for a job, too.
    A. to look   B. looking   C. should look

11. My sister recommended that I _____ around the world for a year.
    A. to travel   B. traveling   C. should travel

12. My aunt recommended _____ around the world for a year, too.
    A. to travel   B. traveling   C. should travel

◇ PRACTICE 21—GUIDED STUDY: Using *advise, suggest,* and *recommend.* (Chart 15-7)

Directions: Use the given information to complete the sentences.

1. The teacher said to Pierre, "You should spend more time on your studies."

   → The teacher advised Pierre _____ *to spend* _____ more time on his studies.

2. Ms. Wah said to Anna, "You should go to Mills College."

   → Ms. Wah suggested to Anna (that) _____ to Mills College.

3. My gardening book says, "Plant tomatoes in June."

   → My gardening book recommends _____ tomatoes in June.

4. When we were planning our vacation, my wife said, "How about Argentina? Let's go there."

   → My wife suggested _____ to Argentina on our vacation.

5. Nutrition experts say, "People should eat a lot of fresh fruit."

   → Nutrition experts recommend _____ a lot of fresh fruit.

6. My field of study is geology. My sister said, "You should change your major to biology."

   → My sister advised me _____ my major to biology.

7. My brother said, "I think you should change to chemistry."

   → My brother suggested _____ my major to chemistry.

8. My aunt said, "I think you ought to change your major to business."

   → My aunt recommended _____ my major to business.

◇ PRACTICE 22—GUIDED STUDY: Reporting speech. (Charts 15-1 → 15-7)

Directions: Report on the people in the pictures and what they say. Use the formal sequence of tenses.

Example:

At the Restaurant

Possible written report:

   One day Susan and Paul were at a restaurant. Susan picked up her menu and looked at it. Paul left his menu on the table. Susan asked Paul what he was going to have. He said he wasn't going to have anything (OR: was going to have nothing) because he wasn't hungry. He'd already eaten. Susan was surprised. She asked him why he had come to the restaurant with her. He told her (that) he needed to talk to her about a problem he was having at work.

Before School in the Morning

◇ PRACTICE 23—GUIDED STUDY: Questions and noun clauses. (Chapters 6, 14, and 15)

Directions: Ask questions and write reports as directed below.

STUDENT A: (1) Make up five to ten questions to ask a classmate, friend, roommate, etc.
(2) Ask the questions and write a report of the information you received. Then give your report to STUDENT B. Don't show STUDENT B your list of questions.

STUDENT B: (3) Read STUDENT A's report. Try to figure out and write down the questions that STUDENT A asked.
(4) Then write a report on the interview using REPORTED SPEECH. Use a separate sentence to report each question. Use the formal sequence of tenses.

Example:
(1) STUDENT A's list of questions:
   1. Where do you live?
   2. How long have you been here?
   3. What is your favorite color?
   4. Are you married?
   5. What are you studying?

(2) STUDENT A's written report:

My friend Po lives in Reed Hall. He's been here for eight months. His favorite color is sky blue. He's not married. He's studying chemical engineering.

(3) STUDENT B's list of probable questions:

1. Where do you live?
2. How long have you been at this school?
3. What's your favorite color?
4. Are you married?
5. What subject are you studying?

(4) STUDENT B's report of the interview, using reported speech:

(Student A) asked his friend Po where he lived. He asked him how long he had been here. He wanted to know what his favorite color was. He wanted to know if he was married. And finally, he asked him what he was studying.

CHAPTER 16
Using Wish; Using If

◇ **PRACTICE 1—SELFSTUDY:** Making wishes. (Charts 16-1 and 16-2)

Directions: Circle the correct answer, then answer the questions.

Sara, David, and Heidi are twelve years old. They're lost in the woods because they left the main path. Sara didn't listen to her mother, who told her not to come to the woods. None of them has a flashlight. It's dark.

1. Is Sara safe at home?

   YES (NO)

   What does she wish?

   → *She wishes she were safe at home.*

2. Did David come to the woods?

   YES   NO

   What does he wish?

3. Can Heidi remember how to get back to town?

   YES   NO

   What does she wish?

4. Did Sara listen to her mother?

   YES   NO

   What does she wish?

5. Docs David have a flashlight?

   YES   NO

   What does he wish?

6. Did the three leave the main path?

   YES   NO

   What does Heidi wish?

DAVID   SARA   HEIDI

◇ PRACTICE 2—SELFSTUDY: Making wishes. (Chart 16-1)

Directions: Using the given information, complete the sentences.

1. In truth, I _____**don't have**_____ a dog, but I really like dogs.

   I *wish* I _____**had**_____ a dog.

2. In truth, Linda _____**has**_____ a cat, but it ruins her furniture.

   She *wishes* she _____**didn't have**_____ a cat.

3. In truth, Mr. Mills _____**doesn't teach**_____ my math class. He's a good teacher.

   I *wish* Mr. Mills _____ my math class.

4. In truth, it _____**snows**_____ here in winter, and I don't like snow.

   I *wish* it _____ here in winter.

5. In truth, I _____**don't understand**_____ my friend Pierre.

   I *wish* I _____ him.

6. In truth, I _____**can't sing**_____ very well, but I like to sing.

   I *wish* I _____ well.

7. In truth, I _____**have**_____ four roommates.

   I *wish* I _____ four roommates.

   I *wish* I _____ only one roommate.

8. In truth, I _____**have to study**_____ tonight.

   I *wish* I _____ tonight.

9. In truth, I _____**am not**_____ at home with my family. I'd like to be with them.

   I *wish* I _____ at home.

10. In truth, Tom _____**isn't**_____ here. I'd like to see him.

    I *wish* he _____ here.

◇ PRACTICE 3—SELFSTUDY: Using auxiliaries after *wish*. (Charts 6-1 and 16-1)

Directions: Complete the dialogues with auxiliary verbs.

1. A: Do you have a TV set?

   B: No, I _____**don't**_____ , but I *wish* I _____**did**_____ .

2. A: Do you have a cold?

   B: Yes, I _____ , but I *wish* I _____ .

3. A: Is Bob here?

   B: No, he _____ , but I *wish* he _____ .

4. A: Does Rita speak Chinese?

   B: No, she _____ , but I *wish* she _____ .

5. A: Are you shy?

   B: Yes, I _____ , but I *wish* I _____ .

6. A: Can you stay home from work today?

   B: No, I _____ , but I *wish* I _____ .

◇ PRACTICE 4—SELFSTUDY: Making wishes about the past. (Chart 16-2)

Directions: Using the given information, complete the sentences.

1. In truth, I _____ **didn't have** _____ a dog when I was a child. I like dogs.

   I *wish* I _____ ***had had*** _____ a dog.

2. In truth, Linda _____ **had** _____ a cat, but it ruined her furniture.

   She *wishes* she _____ ***hadn't had*** _____ a cat.

3. In truth, I _____ **didn't understand** _____ Pierre's problem. I couldn't help him.

   I *wish* I _____ his problem.

4. In truth, I _____ **lost** _____ the keys to my apartment. I couldn't get in.

   I *wish* I _____ them.

5. In truth, I _____ **wasn't** _____ at the meeting yesterday.

   I *wish* I _____ at the meeting yesterday.

◇ PRACTICE 5—SELFSTUDY: Using auxiliaries after *wish*. (Charts 6–1, 16-1, and 16-2)

Directions: Complete the dialogues with auxiliary verbs.

1. A: Did you lose your keys?

   B: Yes, I _____ ***did*** _____ , but I wish I _____ ***hadn't*** _____ .

2. A: Did you go to the party?

   B: No, I _____ , but I wish I _____ .

3. A: Did you go to the concert?

   B: Yes, I _____ , but I wish I _____ . It was boring.

4. A: Do you know Jennifer Hayakawa?

   B: No, I _____ , but I wish I _____ .

5. A: Are you busy today?

   B: Yes, I _____ , but I wish I _____ .

◇ PRACTICE 6—GUIDED STUDY: Using *wish.* (Charts 16-1 and 16-2)

Directions: What do the following people probably wish?

1. *Rosa:* I don't have a bicycle. I can't ride a bike to school. I have to walk. I didn't buy a bicycle last year.

   → *Rosa wishes that she had a bicycle.*
   She wishes she could ride a bike to school.
   She wishes she . . . .

2. *Hiroki:* I can't speak Spanish. I can't understand Maria and Roberto when they speak Spanish. I didn't study Spanish in high school.

3. *Dennis:* I didn't go to the meeting last night. I didn't know about it. My boss was really angry. Bob forgot to tell me about the meeting.

4. *Linda:* I have to clean up the kitchen this morning. My roommate didn't wash the dishes last night. I can't go to the beach. I'm not at the beach in the sun right now.

◇ PRACTICE 7—SELFSTUDY: Using *if:* contrary-to-fact. (Charts 16-3 → 16-6)

Directions: Answer the questions and complete the sentences.

1. Does David have matches? YES (NO)

   Can they build a fire? YES (NO)

   But if David _____*had*_____

   matches, they _____*could build*_____

   a fire.

2. Is Sara at home? YES NO

   Is she afraid? YES NO

   But if Sara _____ at home,

   she _____ afraid.

3. Does Heidi have a flashlight? YES NO

   Can she lead them out of the woods? YES NO

   But if Heidi _____ a flashlight, she

   _____ them out of the woods.

HEIDI   DAVID   SARA

4. Did Sara listen to her mother?   YES   NO

   Did she come to the woods?   YES   NO

   But if Sara _____ to her mother, she _____ to the woods.

5. Did David, Heidi, and Sara leave the main path?   YES   NO

   Did they get lost?   YES   NO

   But if David, Heidi, and Sara _____ the main path, they _____

   lost.

◇ PRACTICE 8—SELFSTUDY: Using *if:* contrary-to-fact. (Chart 16-3)

Directions: Use the given information to complete the sentences.

1. In truth, I _____**am not**_____ from Italy. I _____**can't speak**_____ Italian.

   But *if* I _____**were**_____ from Italy, I _____**could speak**_____ Italian.

2. In truth, Al _____**has**_____ enough money. He_____**won't ask**_____ for a loan.

   But *if* Al _____**didn't have**_____ enough money, he _____**would ask**_____ for a loan.

3. In truth, Tom _____**doesn't need**_____ a new coat. He_____**won't buy**_____ one.

   But *if* Tom _____ a new coat, he _____ one.

4. In truth, Kate _____**is**_____ tired. She_____**won't finish**_____ her work.

   But *if* Kate _____ tired, she_____ her work.

5.   In truth, I _____**don't have**_____ a ticket. I _____**can't go**_____ to the concert.

   But *if* I _____ a ticket, I_____ to the concert.

6.   In truth, I _____**am not**_____ an artist. I _____**can't paint**_____ your picture.

   But *if* I _____ an artist, I _____ your picture.

7. In truth, John __**doesn't understand**__ the problem. He _____**can't solve**_____ it.

   But *if* John _____ the problem, he_____ it.

◇ PRACTICE 9—GUIDED STUDY: Using *if:* contrary-to-fact. (Chart 16-3)

Directions: Answer the questions.

PART I: If you were the following, what would (or could) you do?

1. hungry → *If I were hungry, I'd eat a Big Mac.*

2. tired

3. lost in a big city

4. *(the name of someone)*

5. fluent in five languages

6. the most powerful person in the world

PART II: If you had the following things, what would (or could) you do?

7. a horse → *If I had a horse, I would ride it to school.*
8. a boat
9. six apples
10. a gun
11. a car with a phone in it
12. my own private jet airplane

PART III: If you were in the following places, what would (or could) you do?

13. in India → *If I were in India, I would visit the Taj Mahal.*
14. on a beach
15. at home right now
16. *(choose one)* Paris, Damascus, Tokyo, Rio de Janeiro
17. on a spaceship in outer space
18. *(name of a local place)*

◇ PRACTICE 10—SELFSTUDY: *If:* true vs. contrary-to-fact. (Charts 16-4 and 16-5)

Directions: Using the given information, complete the sentences with the words in parentheses.

1. I may need a new bike this year.

   If I *(need)* _____**need**_____ a new bike, I *(buy)* _____**will/can buy**_____ one.

2. I don't need a new bike this year

   However, if I *(need)* _____**needed**_____ a new bike, I *(buy)* _____**would/could buy**_____ one.

3. I didn't need a new bike last year.

   However, if I *(need)* _____**had needed**_____ a new bike last year, I *(buy)*
   _____**would have/could have bought**_____ one.

4. I may go to Japan next month.

   If I *(go)* _____ to Japan, I *(see)* _____ Yoko.

5. I won't go to Japan next week.

   However, if I *(go)* _____ to Japan, I *(see)* _____ Yoko.

6. I didn't go to Japan last month.

   However, if I *(go)* _____ to Japan last month, I *(see)* _____ Yoko.

7. I may have a pen right now.

   If I *(have)* _____ a pen, I *(write)* _____ a letter.

8. I don't have a pen right now.

   However, if I *(have)* _____ a pen, I *(write)* _____ a letter.

9. I didn't have a pen while I was waiting for my plane at the airport yesterday.

   However, if I *(have)* _____ a pen, I *(write)* _____ a letter.

◇ PRACTICE 11—SELFSTUDY: *If:* contrary-to-fact in the past. (Chart 16-5)

Directions: Using the given information, complete the sentences with the words in parentheses.

1. I didn't go to work this morning, so I didn't finish my report.

   → If I *(go)* _____**had gone**_____ to work this morning, I *(finish)* _**would/could have**_ _____**finished**_____ my report.

2. I didn't hear the doorbell, so I didn't answer the door.

   → I *(answer)* _____ the door if I *(hear)* _____ _____ the doorbell.

3. You didn't tell me about your problem, so I didn't help you.

   → If you *(tell)* _____ me about your problem, I *(help)* _____ _____ you.

4. Joe didn't come with us to the Rocky Mountains, so he didn't see the beautiful scenery.

   → Joe *(see)* _____ some beautiful scenery if he *(come)* _____ with us to the Rocky Mountains.

5. Barbara didn't read the story before class, so she couldn't talk about it during the class discussion.

   → If Barbara *(read)* _____ the book before class, she *(talk)* _____ about it during the class discussion.

6. We didn't offer you a ride because we didn't see you standing near the road.

   → If we *(see)* _____ you standing near the road, we *(offer)* _____ you a ride.

7. My brother had to get a job, so he didn't complete his education.

   → If my brother *(have to get, not)* _____ a job, he *(complete)* _____ his education.

◇ PRACTICE 12—SELFSTUDY: Contracting *had* and *would.* (Charts 16-1 → 16-6)

Directions: Change the contraction with apostrophe + **d** to the full word, **HAD** or **WOULD**.

          had   *would*
1. If you'd asked me, I'd have told you the truth.

2. I'd be careful if I were you.

3. If I'd known that you were sick, I'd have brought you some flowers.

4. If Jack were here, he'd help us.

5. If I'd told them, they'd have laughed at me.

Directions: Choose the correct completion.

1. If I'd studied, I _____ the test yesterday.
   A. passed   B. had passed   C. would pass   D. would have passed

2. I'd go to the concert with you tomorrow if I _____ the time, but I'm going to be too busy.
   A. have   B. had   C. would have   D. would have had

3. If you let me know when your computer comes, I _____ you connect it .
   A. helped   B. help   C. will help   D. would help

4. If you'd listened to the radio last night, you _____ about the riot at the soccer game.
   A. heard   B. will hear   C. had heard   D. would have heard

5. I would have picked you up at the airport if you _____ me your arrival time.
   A. had told   B. would tell   C. tell   D. did tell

6. I don't mind driving, but I don't know the way. I _____ if you read the map and give me directions.
   A. drive   B. drove   C. will drive   D. would have driven

7. The weather is too cold today. If it _____ so cold, we could go swimming.
   A. isn't   B. weren't   C. hadn't been   D. wouldn't have been

8. If you _____ my baby while I go to the store, I'll get your groceries for you. Okay?
   A. watch   B. watched   C. had watched   D. would have watched

9. I would have embarrassed my parents if I _____ during the wedding ceremony.
   A. laugh   B. will laugh   C. would laugh   D. had laughed

10. You shouldn't spend all day at your desk. If you took long walks every day, you _____ better.
   A. feel   B. will feel   C. felt   D. would feel

◇ PRACTICE 14—GUIDED STUDY: Using *wish* and *if*. (Chapter 16)

Directions: Answer the questions in complete sentences.

Example: a. What do you wish were different about your room?
   → *I wish my room were larger.*

   b. What would/could you do if that were different?
   → *If my room were larger, I would put a sofa in it.*

1. a. What do you wish you had?
   b. What would/could you do if you had it/them?

2. a. Where do you wish you were?
   b. What would/could you do if you were there?

3. a. Who do you wish were here right now?
   b. What would/could you do if she/he/they were here?

4. a. What do you wish you had done yesterday/last week/last year?
   b. What would/could you have done if you had done that?

5. a. Where do you wish you had gone yesterday/last week/last year?
   b. What would/could you have done if you had gone there?

6. a. Who do you wish you had seen or talked to yesterday?
   b. What would/could you have done if you had seen or talked to her/him/them?

Directions: Read the story, and then complete the sentences with the correct form of the verbs in parentheses.

Sara, David, and Heidi decided to stop walking aimlessly in the woods. They huddled together under a tree and fell asleep. In the morning, they stayed in the same place. Over and over again, they yelled as loudly as they could, "Help! Help! We're lost! Help!"

A woman by the name of Mrs. Lark was in the woods. She was watching birds early in the morning while her husband was fishing in a nearby stream. She heard the children's cries and found them. The Larks knew the way out of the woods. The children were saved. They happily followed the Larks back to town. At last, they reached the open arms of their very worried parents.

If Mrs. Lark *(1. be, not)* _____**hadn't been**_____ in the woods, she *(2. find, not)*

_____ the children. If the children *(3. yell, not)*

_____ or if they *(4. walk)* _____ to a

different part of the woods, Mrs. Lark *(5. hear, not)* _____

them. If the children *(6. yell, not)* _____ , they *(7. found, not)*

_____ by Mrs. Lark. If the Larks *(8. know, not)*

_____ the way out of the woods, the children *(9. have to*

spend) _____ another night there. The childen are fortunate

that Mrs. Lark likes to go birdwatching. All of the children wish they *(10. go, not)* _____

_____ into the woods alone.

Directions: Complete the sentences with the correct form of the verbs in parentheses.

Yesterday Sam *(1. have)* _____**had**_____ an automobile accident. While he *(2. drive)*

_____ down the road, a squirrel *(3. run)* _____ in front of his car.

Sam *(4. drive)* _____ off the road

to miss the squirrel. His car *(5. hit)*

_____ a tree. The squirrel *(6. run)*

_____ up the tree, so it *(7. kill, not)*

_____ by Sam's car.

Sam *(8. have, not)* _____ an automobile accident

yesterday if a squirrel *(9. run, not)* _____ in front of his car. Sam

(10. drive, not) _____ off the road if there *(11. be, not)*

_____ a squirrel in the way. If he *(12. drive, not)* _____

_____ off the road, he *(13. hit, not)* _____

a tree. If the squirrel *(14. run, not)* _____

up the tree, it *(15. kill)* _____ by Sam's car. Both Sam and the

squirrel are lucky to be alive.

◇ PRACTICE 17—SELFSTUDY: Review of verb forms with *if.* (Chapter 16)

Directions: Choose the correct completion.

1. I don't have a word processor. But if I *(have)* _____**had**_____ my own word processor, it

(take) _____**would take**_____ me less time to write papers for school.

2. I'm not a carpenter, but if I *(be)* _____ , I *(build)* _____
my own house.

3. Pluto is the farthest planet from the sun. If you *(be)* _____ on Pluto right now,
the sun *(look)* _____ like a bright star.

4. Watching a fish tank can be relaxing. Most people begin to relax if they *(watch)*
_____ fish swimming in a tank.

5. If you light a candle on earth, the flame *(be)* _____ oval. If, however, you were
in outer space and lit a candle, the flame *(be)* _____ perfectly round.

6. Ten percent of the earth's surface is covered with ice. If the world's ice caps melted
completely, the sea level *(rise)* _____ enough to put half of the cities
in the world completely under water.

7. A: The colors of the rainbow are not all mixed together. But if the colors in a rainbow *(be)*
_____ all mixed together, what color *(the rainbow, be)* _____
_____?

   B: Purple?

   A: No. It *(be)* _____ gray.

8. A: If you rub onion juice on your skin, insects *(stay)* _____ away. It's true!
Didn't you know that?

   B: Listen, if I rubbed onion juice on myself, my wife *(stay)* _____
away from me forever! Are you trying to fool me?

9. Right now there is not a fire in this room, but think for a second. What *(you, do)*
_____ if there *(be)* _____ a fire in this room? *(you,
run)* _____ out of the room? *(you, call)* _____
the fire department? *(you, use)* _____ a fire extinguisher?

10. Mike bought a used car. While he was cleaning under the seats this morning, he found a bag
full of money. What should he do? What *(you, do)* _____ if you *(be)*
_____ Mike?

11. A: What would you be able to do if you *(have)* _____ three hands? Use your
imagination.

    B: That's a strange question. Let me see. If I *(have)* _____ three hands, I
(carry) _____ my tray at the cafeteria with two hands and *(pick)*
_____ up food with the other. Hmmm. That would be
convenient.

12. A: I wonder how long it would take me to get to one million by adding one, plus one, plus one and so on using my calculator.

B: If you entered a thousand ones an hour, it *(take)* _____ you a thousand hours to get to a million.

◇ PRACTICE 18—GUIDED STUDY: Conditional sentences. (Chapter 16)

Directions: Talk about wishes and "if's." Use the suggested topics or make up your own.

STUDENT A: Finish the sentence **"I wish . . . ."**
STUDENT B: Create a sentence with *if*. Imagine what would happen if STUDENT A's wish came true.

Example: dorm life
STUDENT A: *I wish I had a pet bird in my dorm room.*
STUDENT B: *If you had a pet bird in your dorm room, you'd get in trouble with the dorm manager. It's against the rules to have pets in dorm rooms.*

Example: peace
STUDENT A: *I wish there were peace throughout the world.*
STUDENT B: *If there were peace throughout the world, everybody would be very happy.*

Suggested topics to make wishes about:

1. this school
2. food
3. the world
4. a skill you'd like to have
5. language
6. sports
7. season of the year
8. money
9. friends
10. weather
11. the environment
12. etc.

◇ PRACTICE 19—GUIDED STUDY: Conditional sentences. (Chapter 16)

Directions: Discuss or write about the following topics.

1. If you could live in a different time period, which would you choose?
2. If you could ask *(name of a world leader)* one question, what would you say? Why? What do you think the answer would be?
3. If you had only two career choices—to be an artist or to be a scientist—which would you choose and why?
4. What would the earth be like today if there were no humans and never had been any?

Index

---

*The abbreviation "*fn.*" means "footnote." A footnote is found at the bottom of a chart or a page. Footnotes contain additional information.

Answer Key

Answers to the Selfstudy Practices

Chapter 1: PRESENT TIME

◇ **PRACTICE 1, p. 1.**

A: Hi. My name __is__ Kunio.

B: Hi. My __name__ is Maria. I __'m__ glad to meet you.

KUNIO: I__'m__ glad to __meet__ you, too. Where __are you from__ ?

MARIA: I __'m__ from Mexico. Where __are you from__ ?

KUNIO: I __'m__ from Japan.

MARIA: Where __are you__ living now?

KUNIO: On Fifth Avenue in __an__ apartment. And you?

MARIA: I__'m__ living in a dorm.

KUNIO: __What's__ (**What is**) your field of study?

MARIA: Business. After I study English, I__'m__ going to attend the School of Business Administration. How __about__ you? __What's__ your major?

KUNIO: Chemistry.

MARIA: What __do__ you like to do in your free time? __Do you__ have any hobbies?

KUNIO: I __like__ to swim. How __about__ you?

MARIA: I read a lot and I __collect__ stamps from all over the world.

KUNIO: Really? __Would__ you like some stamps from Japan?

MARIA: Sure! That would be great. Thanks.

KUNIO: I have __to__ write your full name on the board when I introduce __you__ to the class. __How__ do you spell your name?

MARIA: My first __name__ is Maria. M-A-R-I-A. My last __name__ is Lopez. L-O-P-E-Z.

KUNIO: My __first__ name is Kunio. K-U-N-I-O. My __last__ name is Akiwa. A-K-I-W-A.

MARIA: Kunio Akiwa. __Is__ that right?

KUNIO: Yes, it __is__ . It's been nice talking with you.

MARIA: I enjoyed it, too.

◇ PRACTICE 4, p. 3.

1. am sitting
2. am reading
3. am looking
4. am writing
5. am doing
6. sit . . . am sitting
7. read . . . am reading
8. look . . . am looking
9. write . . . am writing
10. do . . . am doing

◇ PRACTICE 5, p. 3.

Part I:
1. speak
2. speak
3. speaks
4. speak
5. speaks

Part II:
1. do not (don't) speak
2. do not (don't) speak
3. does not (doesn't) speak
4. do not (don't) speak
5. does not (doesn't) speak

Part III:
1. Do you speak
2. Do they speak
3. Does he speak
4. Do we speak
5. Does she speak

◇ PRACTICE 6, p. 4.

1. like __s__
2. watch __es__
3. do __es__ n't . . . like __I__
4. climb __I__
5. Do __I__ . . . like __I__
6. Do __es__ . . . like __I__
7. like __s__
8. wash __es__
9. go __es__
10. make __I__
11. visit __s__
12. get __s__
13. get __I__
14. Do __es__ . . . get __I__
15. do __es__ n't . . . get __I__
16. carr __ies__
17. play __s__
18. catch __es__
19. live __I__
20. liv __es__

◇ PRACTICE 8, p. 5.

Part I:
1. am speaking
2. are speaking
3. is speaking
4. are speaking

Part II:
1. am not speaking
2. are not (aren't) speaking
3. is not (isn't) speaking
4. are not (aren't) speaking

Part III:
1. Are you speaking
2. Are they speaking
3. Is she speaking
4. Are we speaking

◇ PRACTICE 9, p. 6.

1. does
2. Do
3. /
4. is
5. Are
6. are
7. Is
8. Do
9. /
10. is
11. is
12. are
13. /
14. /
15. Do
16. Does
17. Is
18. Are
19. are
20. /
21. are
22. is

◇ PRACTICE 11, p. 7.

1. often
2. rarely/seldom
3. always
4. usually/often
5. sometimes
6. usually
7. rarely/seldom
8. rarely/seldom
9. never
10. always
11. often
12. rarely/seldom
    (also possible: sometimes)

◇ PRACTICE 13, p. 9.

Expected answers:
1. He's swimming.
   He's doing the crawl.
2. He's cutting her hair.
   He's using scissors.
   She's getting a haircut.
3. She's sleeping.
   She's dreaming.
   She's having a pleasant dream.
4. He's crying.
   He's wiping his tears with his hand.
5. She's kicking a ball.
   She's playing soccer.
6. He's hitting a golf ball.
   He's playing golf.
   He's golfing.
   He's swinging a golf club.
7. She's riding a motorcycle.
   She's wearing a helmet.
8. They're dancing.
   They're smiling.
   They're having a good time.

PRACTICE 15, p. 11.

1. is snowing
2. takes
3. drive
4. am watching
5. prefer
6. need
7. are playing
8. is looking ... sees
9. sings
10. bite
11. writes
12. understand
13. belongs
14. is shining ... is raining

PRACTICE 16, p. 12.

1. A: Are   B: I am   OR   I'm not
2. A: Do   B: they do   OR   they don't
3. A: Do   B: I do   OR   I don't
4. A: Does   B: she does OR   she doesn't
5. A: Are   B: they are OR   they aren't
6. A: Do   B: they do   OR   they don't
7. A: Is   B: he is   OR   he isn't
8. A: Are   B: I am   OR   I'm not
9. A: Is   B: it is   OR   it isn't
10. A: Does   B: it does   OR   it doesn't

PRACTICE 19, p. 14.

1. is ... is blowing ... are falling
2. eats ... don't eat ... do you eat
3. A: Do you shop   B: don't ... usually shop
   A: are you shopping   B: am trying
4. am buying ... buy
5. A: Do you read
   B: do ... read ... subscribe ... look
6. B: am ... am trying   A: is resting
7. A: am I studying ... do I want ... need
8. lose ... rest ... grow ... keep ... stay ... don't
   grow ... don't have ... Do trees grow

PRACTICE 23, p. 18.

1. of
2. to
3. to
4. with
5. for
6. to
7. with/at
8. of
9. from
10. to
11. at
12. for

Chapter 2:   PAST TIME

PRACTICE 1, p. 19.

1. walked ... yesterday
2. talked ... last
3. opened ... yesterday
4. went ... last
5. met ... last
6. Yesterday ... made ... took
7. paid ... last
8. Yesterday ... fell
9. left ... last

PRACTICE 2, p. 20.

1. started
2. went
3. saw
4. stood
5. arrived
6. won
7. had
8. made
9. finished
10. felt
11. fell
12. heard
13. sang
14. explored
15. asked
16. brought
17. broke
18. ate
19. watched
20. built
21. took
22. paid
23. left
24. wore

PRACTICE 3, p. 20.

1. A: Did you answer
   B: I did ... I answered
   OR I didn't ... I didn't answer
2. A: Did he see
   B: he did ... He saw
   OR he didn't ... He didn't see
3. A: Did they watch
   B: they did ... They watched
   OR they didn't ... They didn't watch
4. A: Did you understand
   B: I did ... I understood
   OR I didn't ... I didn't understand
5. A: Were you
   B: I was... I was
   OR I wasn't ... I wasn't

PRACTICE 4, p. 21.

1. shook
2. stayed
3. swam
4. jumped
5. held
6. fought
7. taught
8. froze
9. thought
10. called
11. rode
12. sold

PRACTICE 6, p. 22.

Expected answers:

1. swept
2. flew
3. caught/held/took
4. taught
5. froze
6. felt
7. drew/got/made
8. heard
9. fell ... broke
10. won
11. drove/took
12. fought
13. hid/put
14. shut
15. ran
16. led
17. paid
18. drank/had
19. bought/chose
20. wore
21. gave/lent

END OF VERB	DOUBLE THE CONSONANT?	SIMPLE FORM	-ING	-ED
-e	**NO**	*excite*	**exciting**	**excited**
Two Consonants	**NO**	*exist*	**existing**	**existed**
Two Vowels + One Consonant	**NO**	*shout*	**shouting**	**shouted**
One Vowel + One Consonant	**YES**	ONE-SYLLABLE VERBS *pat*	**patting**	**patted**
	NO	TWO-SYLLABLE VERBS (STRESS ON **FIRST** SYLLABLE) *visit*	**visiting**	**visited**
	YES	TWO-SYLLABLE VERBS (STRESS ON **SECOND** SYLLABLE) *admit*	**admitting**	**admitted**
-y	**NO**	*pray* *pry*	**praying** **prying**	**prayed** **pried**
-ie	**NO**	*tie*	**tying**	**tie**

◇ PRACTICE 11, p. 26.

1. wai **t** ing . . . wait
2. pa **tt** ing . . . pat
3. bi **t** ing . . . bite
4. si **tt** ing . . . sit
5. wri **t** ing . . . write
6. figh **t** ing . . . fight
7. wai **t** ing . . . wait
8. ge **tt** ing . . . get
9. star **t** ing . . . start
10. permi **tt** ing . . . permit
11. lif **t** ing . . . lift
12. ea **t** ing . . . eat
13. tas **t** ing . . . taste
14. cu **tt** . . . cut
15. mee **t** ing . . . meet
16. visi **t** ing . . . visit

◇ PRACTICE 12, p. 27.

1. A: Did you hear
   B: didn't . . . didn't hear . . . was
2. A: Do you hear   B: don't . . . don't hear
3. A: Did you build   B: didn't . . . built
4. A: Is a fish   B: it is   A: Are they
   B: they are   B: don't know
5. A: want . . . look . . . Do you want
   B: have . . . bought . . . don't need
6. offer . . . is . . . offered . . . didn't accept
7. took . . . found . . . didn't know . . . isn't . . . didn't want . . . went . . . made . . . heated . . . seemed . . . am not
8. likes . . . worry . . . is . . . trust . . . graduated (also possible: was graduated) . . . went . . . didn't travel . . . rented . . . rode . . . was . . . worried (also possible: were worried) . . . were . . . saw . . . knew

◇ PRACTICE 13, p. 28.

1. was standing
2. was eating
3. was answering
4. was singing
5. was walking
6. were climbing
7. was beginning
8. was counting
9. was melting
10. was looking . . . was driving

◇ PRACTICE 15, p. 30.

1. While I was climbing the stairs, the doorbell rang.   OR   The doorbell rang while I was climbing the stairs.
2. I gave Alan his pay after he finished his chores.   OR   After Alan finished his chores, I gave him his pay.
3. The firefighters checked the ashes one last time before they went home.   OR   Before the firefighters went home, they checked the ashes one last time.
4. When Mr. Novak stopped by our table at the restaurant, I introduced him to my wife.   OR   I introduced Mr. Novak to my wife when he stopped by our table at the restaurant.
5. While the kitten was sitting on the roof, an eagle flew over the house.   OR   An eagle flew over the house while the kitten was sitting on the roof.
6. My father was listening to a baseball game on the radio while he was watching a basketball game on television.   OR   While my father was watching a basketball game on television, he was listening to a baseball game on the radio.

◇ PRACTICE 16, p. 30.

1. began (also possible: was beginning) . . . were walking
2. was washing . . . dropped . . . broke
3. hit . . . was using
4. was walking . . . fell . . . hit
5. knew . . . were attending . . . mentioned . . . were . . . were staying (also possible: stayed)
6. was looking . . . started/was starting . . . took . . . was taking . . . (was) enjoying . . . came . . . asked . . . told . . . thanked . . . went . . . came . . . covered . . . went

◇ PRACTICE 19, p. 33.

1. used to hate school
2. used to think
3. used to be a secretary
4. used to have a rat
5. used to go bowling
6. used to raise chickens
7. used to have fresh eggs
8. used to crawl under his bed . . . (used to) put his hands over his ears

◇ PRACTICE 25, p. 38.

1. on
2. at . . . in
3. in . . . on . . . At . . . In
4. In . . . at . . . in
5. in . . . at
6. at
7. In . . . In . . . on . . . on
8. in (also possible: during)

◇ PRACTICE 26, p. 39.

1. at . . . in
2. for . . . in
3. on . . . at . . . in . . . from . . . at/with . . . at
4. with . . . in (also possible: during)
5. on . . . of . . . on . . . in
6. of . . . in

Chapter 3:   FUTURE TIME

◇ PRACTICE 1, p. 40.

1. a. arrives
   b. arrived
   c. is going to arrive OR will arrive
2. a. Does . . . arrive
   b. Did . . . arrive
   c. Is . . . going to arrive OR Will . . . arrive
3. a. does not (doesn't) arrive
   b. did not (didn't) arrive
   c. is not (isn't) going to arrive OR will not (won't) arrive
4. a. eats
   b. ate
   c. is going to OR will eat
5. a. Do . . . eat
   b. Did . . . eat
   c. Are . . . going to eat OR Will . . . eat
6. a. do not (don't) eat
   b. did not (didn't) eat
   c. am not going to eat OR will not (won't) eat

◇ PRACTICE 2, p. 41.

1. B: Do . . . get
   A: do . . . get
   B: Did . . . get
   A: did . . . got
   B: Are . . . going to get
   A: am . . . am going to get
2. B: Do . . . study
   A: do . . . study
   B: Did . . . study
   A: did . . . studied
   B: are . . . going to study
   A: am . . . am going to study

◇ PRACTICE 4, p. 41.

1. A: are you going to do   B: am going to finish
2. A: is Ryan going to be   B: is going to be
3. A: Are you going to have   B: am not going to eat
4. A: Are you going to finish   B: am going to finish
5. A: Are you going to call   B: am not going to call her . . . am going to write
6. A: is Laura going to talk   B: is going to discuss

◇ PRACTICE 7, p. 43.

1. A: Will you help   B: I will   OR   I won't
2. A: Will Paul lend   B: he will   OR   he won't
3. A: Will Jane graduate   B: she will   OR   she won't
4. A: Will her parents be   B: they will   OR   they won't
5. A: Will I benefit   B: you will   OR   you won't

◇ PRACTICE 8, p. 43.

1. probably won't
2. will probably
3. will probably
4. probably won't
5. will probably
6. probably won't
7. will probably
8. will probably

◇ PRACTICE 11, p. 45.

1. I am going to
2. will
3. am going to
4. will
5. am going to
6. will
7. am going to . . . will

◇ PRACTICE 12, p. 46.

1. I am going to
2. will
3. will
4. am going to
5. will
6. am going to
7. A: are . . . going to
    B: am going to
8. will

◇ PRACTICE 13, p. 46.

1. <u>When I call Mike tomorrow</u>, I'll tell him the good news.   OR

   I'll tell Mike the good news <u>when I call him tomorrow.</u>

2. Ann will lock all the doors <u>before she goes to bed.</u>   OR

   <u>Before Ann goes to bed</u>, she'll lock all the doors.   OR

   (<u>Before she goes to bed</u>, Ann will lock all the doors.)

3. <u>When I am in London</u>, I'm going to visit the Tate Museum.   OR

   I'm going to visit the Tate Museum <u>when I am in London.</u>

4. The show will start <u>as soon as the curtain goes up.</u>   OR

   <u>As soon as the curtain goes up</u>, the show will start.

5. Nick is going to change the oil in his car <u>after he takes a bath.</u>   OR

   <u>After Nick takes a bath</u>, he's going to change the oil in his car.   OR

   (<u>After he takes a bath</u>, Nick is going to change the oil in his car.)

6. We'll call you <u>before we drive over to pick you up.</u>   OR

   <u>Before we drive over to pick you up</u>, we'll call you.

7. I'll call you <u>when I get an answer from the bank about the loan.</u>   OR

   <u>When I get an answer from the bank about the loan</u>, I'll call you.

8. I'll pay my rent <u>as soon as I get my paycheck.</u>   OR

   <u>As soon as I get my paycheck</u>, I'll pay my rent.

◇ **PRACTICE 14, p. 47.**
1. will read . . . take
2. will call . . . returns
3. won't be . . . come
4. go . . . will prepare
5. visits . . . will take
6. will move . . . graduates . . . finds

◇ **PRACTICE 15, p. 47.**
1. is . . . won't go
2. get . . . will pay
3. will be . . . don't go
4. will stop . . . tells
5. gets . . . will eat . . . is . . . will be

◇ **PRACTICE 17, p. 48.**
1. was listening . . . (and) (was) doing
2. are going to meet . . . (and) (are going to) study
3. will rise . . . (and) (will) set
4. was carrying . . . (and) (was) climbing
   flew . . . (and) sat
   dropped . . . (and) spilled
5. is going to meet . . . (and) (is going to) go
6. moves . . . (and) starts
7. slipped . . . (and) fell
8. am getting . . . (and) (am) walking
9. arrived . . . (and) started
   was . . . (and) felt
   was watching . . . (and) (was) feeling
   knocked . . . (and) asked
   see . . . (and) usually spend
   are borrowing . . . (and) (are) going
   are going to take . . . (and) (are going to) go

◇ **PRACTICE 18, p. 49.**
1. will retire . . . (will) travel   OR
   are going to retire . . . (are going to) travel
2. close . . . think
3. is watching . . . (is) studying
4. takes . . . buys
5. go . . . tell
6. will take . . . (will) forget   OR
   am going to take . . . (am going to) forget
7. will discover . . . (will) apologize   OR
   is going to discover . . . (is going to) apologize
8. saw . . . ran . . . caught . . . knocked . . . went . . .
   sat . . . was waiting . . . got . . . understood . . . put
   . . . took

◇ **PRACTICE 20, p. 51.**
1. is traveling (travelling)
2. are arriving
3. am meeting
4. am getting

5. is . . . taking
6. am studying
7. am leaving
8. is attending . . . am seeing
9. is speaking
10. am spending . . . am visiting

◇ **PRACTICE 21, p. 52.**
Possible answers:
1. Fred is eating/having dinner with Emily on Sunday.
2. He is seeing Dr. Wood at 1:00 p.m. on Monday.
3. He is going to Jean's birthday party at 7:00 p.m. on Tuesday.
4. He is probably eating lunch with Jack on Wednesday.
5. He is meeting Tom's plane on Thursday at 2:00 p.m.
6. He is attending a financial seminar on Friday.
7. He is taking his children to the zoo on Saturday.

◇ **PRACTICE 24, p. 53.**
1. A: does . . . begin/start
   B: begins/starts
2. opens
3. arrives/gets in/lands
4. B: begins/starts
   A: does . . . end/finish
   B: ends/finishes
5. A: does . . . close
   B: closes
6. begins/starts

◇ **PRACTICE 25, p. 54.**
1. The chimpanzee is about to eat a banana.
2. Sam is about to leave.
3. The plane is about to land.
4. The woman is about to answer the phone.

◇ **PRACTICE 26, p. 54.**
1. don't need
2. is planning/plans . . . Are you coming/Are you going to come
3. A: do you usually get
   B: take
4. was watching . . . became . . . stopped . . . found
5. A: am going/am going to go
   B: are going/are going to go
6. will probably call/is probably going to call . . . go
7. A: is . . . are flashing
   B: know . . . know . . . see
   A: is going . . . Are you speeding
   B: am going   A: is passing
8. is going to land/will land . . . think
9. ride . . . was raining . . . drove . . . arrived . . . discovered
10. will give
11. are you wearing/are you going to wear . . . am planning/plan . . . bought . . . is . . . will show . . . will get . . . (will) bring
12. B: is wearing
    A: didn't lend
    B: will be/is going to be

◇ **PRACTICE 27, p. 56.**
(1) made . . . did not have . . . were not . . . wore
(2) make . . . comes . . . buy
(3) is . . . wear . . . wear
(4) exist . . . wear . . . are
(5) will probably be/are probably going to be . . . will wear/are going to wear . . . Will we all dress/Are we all going to dress . . . show . . . do you think

◇ **PRACTICE 31, p. 60.**
1. at
2. at
3. in
4. with
5. for
6. to . . . with
7. for
8. from
9. about
10. for

◇ **PRACTICE 32, p. 60.**
1. to
2. from . . . for
3. to . . . at
4. to
5. of
6. from . . . for
7. in . . . with
8. for . . . with . . . to

Chapter 4: NOUNS AND PRONOUNS

◇ **PRACTICE 1, p. 61.**
1. <u>Chicago</u> has busy <u>streets</u> and <u>highways</u>.
2. <u>Boxes</u> have six <u>sides</u>.
3. Big <u>cities</u> have many <u>problems</u>.
4. <u>Bananas</u> grow in hot, humid <u>areas</u>.
5. <u>Insects</u> don't have <u>noses</u>.
6. <u>Lambs</u> are the <u>offspring</u> of <u>sheep</u>.
7. <u>Libraries</u> keep <u>books</u> on <u>shelves</u>.
8. <u>Parents</u> support their <u>children</u>.
9. <u>Indonesia</u> has several active <u>volcanoes</u>.
10. <u>Baboons</u> are big <u>monkeys</u>. They have large <u>heads</u> and sharp ***teeth***. They eat <u>leaves</u>, <u>roots</u>, <u>insects</u>, and <u>eggs</u>.

◇ **PRACTICE 2, p. 61.**
1. mouse
2. pockets
3. tooth
4. tomato
5. fish
6. woman
7. branches
8. friends
9. duties
10. highways
11. thief
12. beliefs
13. potatoes
14. radios
15. offspring
16. child
17. seasons
18. customs
19. businesses
20. century
21. occurrences
22. phenomenon
23. sheep
24. loaf

◇ **PRACTICE 5, p. 63.**
1. [Bridges *S*] [cross *V*] [rivers *O*].
2. [A terrible earthquake *S*] [occurred *V*] [in Turkey *PP*].
3. [Airplanes *S*] [fly *V*] [above the clouds *PP*].
4. [Trucks *S*] [carry *V*] [large loads *O*].
5. [Rivers *S*] [flow *V*] [toward the sea *PP*].
6. [Salespeople *S*] [treat *V*] [customers *O*] [with courtesy *PP*].
7. [Bacteria *S*] [can cause *V*] [diseases *O*].
8. [Clouds *S*] [are floating *V*] [across the sky *PP*].
9. [The audience *S*] [in the theater *PP*] [applauded *V*]
   [the performers *O*] [at the end *PP*] [of the show *PP*].
10. [Helmets *S*] [protect *V*] [bicyclists *O*] [from serious injuries *PP*].

◇ PRACTICE 6, p. 63.

1. v.	9. n.	16. n.
2. n.	10. v.	17. n.
3. n.	11. v.	18. v.
4. v.	12. n.	19. v.
5. v.	13. v.	20. n.
6. n.	14. n.	21. n.
7. n.	15. v.	22. v.
8. v.		

◇ PRACTICE 8, p. 64.

Expected answers:

1. old	9. hard/difficult	17. expensive
2. old	10. narrow	18. light
3. hot	11. dirty	19. light
4. slow	12. full	20. private
5. happy	13. safe	21. right
6. bad	14. quiet	22. right
7. dry	15. deep	23. strong
8. hard	16. sour	24. short

◇ PRACTICE 9, p. 65.

1. Paul has a (loud) voice.

2. Sugar is (sweet.)

3. The students took an (easy) test.

4. Air is (free.)

5. We ate some (delicious) food at a (Mexican) restaurant.

6. An encyclopedia contains (important) facts about a (wide) variety of subjects.

7. The child was (sick.)

8. The (sick) child crawled into his (warm) bed and sipped (hot) tea.

◇ PRACTICE 11, p. 66.

1. newspaper articles	6. city governments
2. page numbers	7. duck ponds
3. paper money	8. shoulder pads
4. apartment buildings	9. pocket knives
5. key chains	10. traffic lights

◇ PRACTICE 12, p. 66.

1. bottles . . . caps
2. seats
3. students . . . experiments . . . classes
4. Houseflies . . . pests . . . germs
5. Computers . . . operators
6. kinds . . . flowers
7. reporters . . . jobs
8. manners
9. tickets
10. lives . . . ways . . . years . . . lamps . . . candles . . . houses . . . chickens . . . fires

◇ PRACTICE 14, p. 68.

1. me (*O of vb*)
2. I (*S*) . . . me (*O of prep*)
3. He (*S*) . . . it (*O of vb*) . . . It (*S*) . . . him (*O of vb*)
4. me (*O of prep*) . . . We (*S*) . . . her (*O of vb*) . . . she (*S*) . . . us (*O of vb*) . . . We (*S*) . . . her (*O of prep*)
5. He (*S*) . . . them (*O of vb*) . . . them (*O of vb*) . . . They (*S*)
6. I (*S*) . . . him and me (*O of prep*) . . . He and I (*S*)

◇ PRACTICE 15, p. 68.

1. She = *Janet* . . . it = *a green apple*
2. her = *Betsy*
3. They = *Nick and Rob*
4. they = *phone messages*
5. him = *Louie* . . . He = *Louie* . . . her = *Alice* . . . She = *Alice*
6. She = *Jane* . . . it = *letter* . . . them = *Mr. and Mrs. Moore* . . . They = *Mr. and Mrs. Moore* . . . her = *Jane*

◇ PRACTICE 16, p. 68.

1. It
2. He . . . them
3. They . . . her
4. it
5. it . . . it . . . him . . . he
6. they . . . them . . . they
7. them
8. it
9. it . . . It
10. them . . . They . . . They . . . them

◇ PRACTICE 17, p. 69.

1. me
2. He
3. him
4. he
5. her
6. She
7. me . . . He . . . us
8. her . . . They
9. I . . . They . . . us . . . it . . . We . . . them
10. them
11. me . . . him
12. she
13. I . . . him and me

◇ PRACTICE 18, p. 70.

1. friend's	9. person's
2. friends'	10. people's
3. son's	11. teacher's
4. sons'	12. teachers'
5. baby's	13. man's
6. babies'	14. men's
7. child's	15. earth's
8. children's	

◇ PRACTICE 19, p. 70.
1. A king's chair
2. Kings' chairs
3. Babies' toys
4. a baby's toys
5. the caller's words
6. A receptionist's job . . . callers' names
7. yesterday's news . . . today's events
8. The pilots' seats
9. the earth's surface
10. Mosquitoes' wings
11. A mosquito's wings
12. A cat's heart . . . an elephant's heart
13. the elephants' tricks
14. the animals' bodies
15. an animal's footprints

◇ PRACTICE 22, p. 73.
1. your . . . yours
2. her . . . hers
3. his . . . his
4. your . . . yours
5. their . . . our . . . theirs . . . ours

◇ PRACTICE 24, p. 74.
1. myself
2. himself
3. ourselves
4. yourself
5. yourselves
6. herself
7. themselves

◇ PRACTICE 25, p. 74.
1. blamed myself
2. are going to/will cut yourself
3. introduced myself
4. was talking to himself
5. work for ourselves
6. taught themselves
7. killed himself
8. wished myself
9. is taking care of herself
10. believe in ourselves
11. felt sorry for myself
12. help themselves

◇ PRACTICE 26, p. 75.
1. me . . . him
2. yourselves
3. itself
4. its . . . its
5. hers
6. him
7. yourself . . . your
8. our . . . our
9. ours
10. themselves
11. itself
12. himself

◇ PRACTICE 28, p. 77.
1. The other
2. a. Another
3. b. The other
3. a. Another
   b. Another
   c. Another
   d. another
4. The other
5. Another
6. The other
7. a. Another
   b. the other
8. a. another
   b. another
   c. another
   d. another
   e. another

◇ PRACTICE 29, p.78.
1. The other
2. The others
3. a. Other
   b. Others
   c. Others
   d. Other
4. a. the other
   b. The others
5. a. other
   b. others
6. others
7. other
8. Others
9. Other
10. a. The other
    b. The others

◇ PRACTICE 30, p.79.
1. A
2. C
3. D
4. B
5. E
6. C
7. A
8. D
9. B
10. E

◇ PRACTICE 32, p. 80.
1. Robert Jones
2. (no change)
3. Uncle Joe . . . Aunt Sara
4. (no change)
5. Susan W. Miller
6. Prof. Miller's
7. January
8. (no change)
9. Monday
10. Los Angeles
11. California
12. (no change)
13. United States of America
14. (no change)
15. Atlantic Ocean
16. (no change)
17. Market Street . . . Washington High School
18. (no change)
19. Hilton Hotel . . . Bangkok
20. Japanese . . . German

◇ PRACTICE 33, p. 81.
1. for
2. A: to . . . about
   B: at . . . for
3. to
4. from
5. for
6. A: on
   B: about
7. in
8. of
9. with . . . about/on
10. to

◇ PRACTICE 34, p. 82.

1. about
2. from
3. of
4. to . . . with
5. to
6. for
7. from
8. with
9. with
10. to
11. in
12. at
13. for . . . at
14. at
15. A: with . . . about
    C: to
    A: to . . . about . . . with

Chapter 5: MODAL AUXILIARIES

◇ PRACTICE 1, p. 83.

1. must ___Ø___
2. has ___to___
3. should ___Ø___
4. ought ___to___
5. May I ___Ø___
6. can ___Ø___
7. must ___Ø___
8. can't ___Ø___
9. have got ___to___
10. A: Should I ___Ø___
    B: have ___to___ . . . could ___Ø___
    A: ought ___to___ . . . might ___Ø___ . . .
       Would ___Ø___
    B: should ___Ø___ . . . can ___Ø___ . . .
       will ___Ø___
    A: must ___Ø___ . . . can't ___Ø___

◇ PRACTICE 3, p. 84.

1. zebra
2. cat
3. Elephants
4. Monkeys
5. camels
6. cow
7. horse
8. donkey
9. squirrel
10. ants

◇ PRACTICE 6, p. 86.

1. can . . . can't
2. may
3. can
4. may . . . may not
5. may
6. may
7. can't
8. may
9. might . . . might not
10. can . . . can't
11. might
12. can . . . might . . . might not
13. can't . . . Can . . . might

◇ PRACTICE 7, p. 87.

1. A
2. B
3. B
4. B
5. B
6. A
7. B
8. A

◇ PRACTICE 10, p. 88.

1. Can
2. may
3. Would
4. could
5. Can
6. A: Could
   B: May
7. A: Can
   B: Will
8. Could

◇ PRACTICE 12, p. 89.

1. A
2. C
3. B
4. A
5. B
6. C
7. A
8. C
9. B
10. C

◇ PRACTICE 14, p. 90.

1. C
2. A
3. D
4. C
5. B
6. A
7. D
8. C

◇ PRACTICE 16, p. 91.

1. must not
2. don't have to
3. must not
4. don't have to
5. don't have to
6. must not
7. don't have to
8. must not
9. must not
10. don't have to

◇ PRACTICE 17, p. 92.

1. have to/must
2. doesn't have to
3. don't have to
4. must not
5. has to/must
6. doesn't have to
7. has to/must
8. must not

◇ PRACTICE 20, p. 94.

1. must
2. must not
3. must
4. must
5. must not
6. must not
7. must

◇ PRACTICE 22, p. 95.

1. Wait
2. Don't wait
3. Read
4. Don't put
5. Come in . . . have
6. Don't cross
7. Don't just stand . . . Do
8. Call
9. Take . . . Go . . . Walk . . . give
10. Capitalize . . . Put . . . use

◇ PRACTICE 24, p. 96.

1. A: go . . . fly
   B: see
2. B: get
   A: take
3. A: go
   B: play
4. A: take
   B: take . . . save
5. A: stop . . . fill up
   B: pick up/get
6. A: go
   A: call . . . see

◇ PRACTICE 26, p. 98.

1. prefer
2. like
3. would rather
4. prefer
5. would rather
6. A: prefer
   B: likes
   B: would rather
7. would rather
8. would rather
9. B: prefer
   A: like
10. prefer

◇ PRACTICE 28, p. 99.

1. A
2. C
3. A
4. A
5. B
6. C
7. B
8. C
9. B
10. A
11. C
12. A
13. B
14. C
15. B

◇ PRACTICE 32, p. 104.

1. A: with/to
   B: about
2. for
3. to
4. of
5. A: in
   B: for
6. to
7. of
8. for
9. of (also possible: about)
10. for
11. of
12. for
13. from

Chapter 6: QUESTIONS

◇ PRACTICE 1, p. 106.

Possible completions:

1. (*Supply your own name.*)
2. What is (What's) your name?
3. Is that your first name? / Is Anna your first name?
4. What's your last name?
5. How do you spell that? / How do you spell your last name?
6. Where are you from? / What country are you from? / What country do you come from?
7. What city? (What city are you from?) / Where in Poland? (Where do you come from in Poland?) / What's your hometown?
8. When did you come to (*name of this city/country/school*)? / When did you arrive here?
9. Why did you come here?
10. What is your major? / What are you going to study? / What are you studying? / What field are you in? / What's your field?
11. How long are you going to stay here? / How long do you plan to stay?
12. Where are you living?
13. Do you live far from / a long way from school? / Is their house far from school?
14. How far is it? / How far is their house from school? / How far away are you?
15. How do you get to school every day?
16. How do you like going to school here? / Do you like it here too?

◇ PRACTICE 2, p. 107.

1. A: Do
   B: I don't
2. A: Is
   B: it is
3. A: Do
   B: they don't
4. A: Are
   B: I am

5. A: Does
   B: it does
6. A: Are
   B: they aren't
7. A: Do
   B: they do
8. A: Are
   B: I am

9. A: Is
   B: it isn't
10. A: Do
    B: they do
11. A: Does
    B: it does

◇ PRACTICE 3, p. 108.

helping verb	subject	main verb	rest of sentence
1. Do	you	like	coffee?
2. Does	Tom	like	coffee?
3. Is	Ann	watching	TV?
4. Are	you	having	lunch with Rob?
5. Did	Sara	walk	to school?
6. Was	Ann	taking	a nap?
7. Will	Ted	come	to the meeting?
8. Can	Rita	ride	a bicycle?

form of *be*	subject		rest of sentence
9. Is	Ann		a good artist?
10. Were	you		at the wedding?

◇ PRACTICE 5, p. 109.

(question word)	helping verb	subject	main verb	rest of sentence
1. Ø	Did	you	hear	the news yesterday?
2. When	did	you	hear	the news?
3. Ø	Is	Eric	reading	today's paper?
4. What	is	Eric	reading	Ø?
5. Ø	Did	you	find	your wallet?
6. Where	did	you	find	your wallet?
7. Why	does	Mr. Li	walk	to work?
8. Ø	Does	Mr. Li	walk	to work?
9. Ø	Will	Ms. Cook	return	to her office at one o'clock?
10. When	will	Ms. Cook	return	to her office?

(question word)	form of *be*	subject		rest of sentence
11. Ø	Is	the orange juice		in the refrigerator?
12. Where	is	the orange juice		Ø?

◇ PRACTICE 6, p. 110.

1. What time/When do the fireworks start
2. Why are you waiting
3. When does Rachel start
4. What time/When do you usually leave
5. Why didn't you get
6. Where can I buy*
7. What time/When are you leaving
8. Where did you study . . . Why did you study . . . Why didn't you go
9. When do you expect
10. Where will the spaceship go

---

* Also possible: *Where can **you** buy?* In this case, *you* is used as an impersonal pronoun meaning *someone, anyone,* or *all people.*

◇ **PRACTICE 10, p. 113.**

    S
1. Who knows?
    O
2. Who(m) did you ask?
    S
3. Who knocked on the door?
    O
4. Who(m) did Sara meet?
    S
5. Who will help us?
    O
6. Who(m) will you ask?
    O
7. Who(m) is Eric talking to on the phone? OR
    O
    To whom is Eric talking on the phone?
    S
8. Who is knocking on the door?
    S
9. What surprised them?
    O
10. What did Mike learn?
    S
11. What will change Ann's mind?
    O
12. What can Tina talk about? OR
    O
    About what can Tina talk?

◇ **PRACTICE 11, p. 113.**
1. Who taught you to play chess?
2. What did Robert see?
3. Who got a good look at the bank robber?
4. Who(m) are you making the toy for? OR
    For whom are you making the toy?
5. Who(m) does the calculator belong to? OR
    To whom does the calculator belong?
6. What do you have in your pocket?
    [also possible: What have you (got) in your
    pocket?]
7. What did the cat kill?
8. What killed the cat?
9. Who(m) did you get a letter from? OR
    From whom did you get a letter?
10. Who wrote a note on the envelope?
11. What makes an apple fall to the ground from a
    tree?

◇ **PRACTICE 12, p. 114.**
1. What is Alex doing?
2. What should I do if someone calls while you're
    out?
3. What do astronauts do?
4. What should I do?
5. What are you going to do Saturday morning?
6. What do you do when you get sick?
7. What can I do to help you?
8. What did Sara do when she heard the good
    news?

◇ **PRACTICE 16, p. 116.**
1. Which
2. What
3. Which
4. What
5. What . . . Which
6. What
7. Which
8. which

◇ **PRACTICE 17, p. 117.**
1. Who
2. Whose
3. Whose
4. Who
5. Who
6. Whose
7. Whose
8. Who

◇ **PRACTICE 19, p. 118.**
1. hot . . . hot
2. soon
3. expensive
    (also common: how much)
4. busy . . . busy
5. serious . . . serious
6. well . . . well
7. fresh . . . fresh . . . fresh
8. safe

◇ **PRACTICE 20, p. 119.**
1. far
2. long
3. far
4. far
5. long
6. far
7. long
8. long
9. far
10. long

◇ **PRACTICE 21, p. 119.**
1. often
2. long
3. many
4. far
5. many
6. many
7. long
8. many
9. often
10. many
11. long
12. often
13. far
14. many
15. often
16. far
17. long

◇ PRACTICE 23, p. 121.

1. When are you going to buy a new bicycle?
2. How are you going to pay for it?
3. How long (How many years) did you have your old bike?
4. How often (How many times a week) do you ride your bike?
5. How do you (usually) get to work?
6. Are you going to ride your bike to work tomorrow?
7. Why didn't you ride your bike to work today?
8. When did Jason get his new bike?
9. Who broke Jason's new bike?
10. What (Whose bike) did Billy break?
11. What (Whose bike) is broken?
12. How did Billy break Jason's bike?
13. Does your bike have a comfortable seat?
    [also possible: Has your bike (got) a comfortable seat?]
14. What kind of bicycle do you have?
    [also possible: What kind of bike have you (got)?]
15. Which bicycle is yours, the red one or the blue one?
16. Where do you keep your bicycle at night?
17. Who(m) does that bike belong to?   OR
    To whom does that bike belong?
18. Whose bike did you borrow?
19. Where is Rita?
20. What is she doing?
21. How far did Rita ride her bike yesterday?
22. How do you spell "bicycle?"

◇ PRACTICE 28, p. 125.

1. a. don't
   b. doesn't
   c. don't
   d. doesn't
   e. isn't
   f. aren't
   g. does
   h. is
2. a. didn't
   b. did
   c. were
   d. wasn't
3. a. aren't
   b. is
   c. is
   d. weren't
   e. was
4. a. can't
   b. will
   c. shouldn't
   d. wouldn't
   e. do
   f. didn't

◇ PRACTICE 29, p. 126.

1. wasn't he
2. can't they
3. don't they
4. is he
5. wouldn't you
6. aren't they
7. isn't it
8. can it
9. shouldn't you
10. won't she
11. doesn't he
12. did you
13. is it
14. do I
15. is it
16. weren't they
17. will she
18. doesn't it

◇ PRACTICE 32, p. 127.

1. about
2. with
3. to
4. at
5. to
6. A: to
   B: for
7. about/of
8. for
9. about . . . about
10. from

Chapter 7:   THE PRESENT PERFECT AND THE PAST PERFECT

◇ PRACTICE 1, p. 128.

1. A: Have you ever eaten
   B: have . . . have eaten   OR
      haven't . . . have never eaten
2. A: Have you ever talked
   B: have . . . have talked   OR
      haven't . . . have never talked
3. A: Has Erica ever rented
   B: has . . . has rented   OR
      hasn't . . . has never rented
4. A: Have you ever seen
   B: have . . . have seen   OR
      haven't . . . have never seen
5. A: Has Joe ever caught
   B: has . . . has caught   OR
      hasn't . . . has never caught
6. A: Have you ever had
   B: have . . . have had   OR
      haven't . . . have never had

◇ PRACTICE 2, p. 129.

1. have used
2. has risen
3. have never played
4. have won
5. hasn't spoken
6. hasn't eaten
7. has given
8. haven't saved
9. Have you ever slept
10. have never worn
11. has improved
12. have looked

◇ PRACTICE 3, p. 129.

1. have already called . . . called
2. have already begun . . . began
3. have already eaten . . . ate
4. have already bought . . . bought
5. has already left . . . left
6. have already locked . . . locked

◇ PRACTICE 4, p. 130.

1. began . . . have begun
2. bent . . . have bent
3. broadcast . . . has broadcast
4. caught . . . have caught
5. came . . . have come
6. cut . . . have cut
7. dug . . . have dug
8. drew . . . has drawn
9. fed . . . have fed
10. fought . . . have fought
11. forgot . . . have forgotten
12. hid . . . have hidden
13. hit . . . has hit
14. held . . . has held
15. kept . . . have kept
16. led . . . has led
17. lost . . . has lost
18. met . . . have met
19. rode . . . have ridden
20. rang . . . has rung
21. saw . . . have seen
22. stole . . . has stolen
23. stuck . . . have stuck
24. swept . . . have swept
25. took . . . have taken
26. upset . . . have upset
27. withdrew . . . have withdrawn
28. wrote . . . have written

◇ PRACTICE 6, p. 134.

1. since	8. for
2. for	9. since
3. since	10. for
4. for	11. since
5. for	12. for
6. since	13. since
7. since	14. for

◇ PRACTICE 7, p. 135.

1. have known . . . were
2. has changed . . . started
3. was . . . have been
4. haven't slept . . . left
5. met . . . hasn't been
6. has had . . . bought
7. A: have you eaten . . . got up
   B: have eaten
8. had . . . was . . . left . . . have taken . . . have had
   . . . have learned

◇ PRACTICE 10, p. 136.

1. A: has Eric been studying
   B: has been studying . . . two hours
2. A: has Kathy been working at the computer
   B: has been working . . . two o'clock
3. A: has it been raining
   B: has been raining . . . two days
4. A: has Liz been reading
   B: has been reading . . . half an hour/thirty
   minutes
5. A: has Boris been studying English
   B: has been studying English . . . 1990
6. A: has Nicole been working at the Silk Road
   Clothing Store
   B: has been working at the Silk Road Clothing
   Store . . . three months.
7. A: has Ms. Rice been teaching at this school
   B: has been teaching at this school . . . September
   1992
8. A: has Mr. Fisher been driving a Chevy
   B: has been driving a Chevy . . . twelve years
9. A: has Mrs. Taylor been waiting to see her doctor
   B: has been waiting to see her doctor . . . an hour
   and a half
10. A: have Ted and Erica been playing tennis
    B: have been playing tennis . . . two o'clock

◇ PRACTICE 11, p. 137.

1. B
2. B
3. A
4. B
5. A
6. A
7. B
8. A

◇ PRACTICE 15, p. 140.

PART I:

1.	Ø	*is*	always
2.	always	*finishes*	Ø
3.	always	*finished*	Ø
4.	Ø	*will*	always
5.	Ø	*has*	always
6.	always	*helped*	Ø
7.	Ø	*are*	always
8.	always	*help*	Ø
9.	Ø	*have*	always
10.	Ø	*can*	always
11.	Ø	*are*	usually
12.	usually	*help*	Ø
13.	Ø	*have*	usually
14.	Ø	*can*	usually

PART II:

15.	*Do*	Ø	you	usually
16.	*Is*	Ø	Mike	usually
17.	*Did*	Ø	your mom	usually
18.	*Were*	Ø	you	usually
19.	*Can*	Ø	students	usually
20.	*Do*	Ø	you	ever
21.	*Is*	Ø	Mike	ever
22.	*Did*	Ø	your mom	ever
23.	*Were*	Ø	you	ever
24.	*Can*	Ø	students	ever

PART III:

25. probably	*won't*	Ø
26. probably	*isn't*	Ø
27. probably	*doesn't*	Ø
28. probably	*hasn't*	Ø
29. Ø	*won't*	ever
30. Ø	*isn't*	ever
31. Ø	*doesn't*	always
32. Ø	*hasn't*	always

◇ **PRACTICE 17, p. 142.**
1. B
2. D
3. A
4. D
5. C

◇ **PRACTICE 19, p. 143.**
1. a. *1st*
   b. *2nd*
2. a. *2nd*
   b. *1st*
3. a. *1st*
   b. *2nd*
4. a. *2nd*
   b. *1st*
5. a. *1st*
   b. *2nd*
6. a. *2nd*
   b. *1st*
7. a. *1st*
   b. *2nd*
8. a. *2nd*
   b. *1st*

◇ **PRACTICE 20, p. 145.**
1. has already left
2. had already left
3. have already slept
4. had already slept
5. have already met
6. had already met
7. have already seen
8. had already seen
9. have made
10. had made

◇ **PRACTICE 21, p. 145.**
1. B
2. A
3. A
4. B
5. B
6. A
7. B
8. B

◇ **PRACTICE 22, p. 146.**
1. was sleeping
2. have never been
3. had already heard
4. was still snowing
5. had passed
6. were making
7. Hasn't he come
8. had never been
9. was wearing ... had never worn ...
   hasn't worn

◇ **PRACTICE 23, p. 147.**
1. A
2. C
3. B
4. D
5. A
6. B
7. D
8. C
9. D
10. B

◇ **PRACTICE 25, p. 148.**
1. (up)on
2. from
3. of
4. (up)on
5. to
6. to ... for ... for ... (up)on
7. for
8. to/with
9. of
10. for

Chapter 8: COUNT/NONCOUNT NOUNS AND ARTICLES

◇ **PRACTICE 1, p. 149.**
1. ____/____ furniture → noncount
2. __one__ table → count
3. __one__ ring → count
4. ____/____ jewelry → noncount
5. ____/____ homework → noncount
6. __one__ assignment → count
7. __one__ job → count
8. ____/____ work → noncount
9. __one__ question → count
10. ____/____ information → noncount
11. __one__ new word → count
12. ____/____ new vocabulary → noncount

◇ **PRACTICE 2, p. 149.**
1. __some__ furniture
2. __a__ table
3. __a__ ring
4. __some__ jewelry
5. __some__ homework
6. __an__ assignment
7. __a__ job
8. __some__ work
9. __a__ question
10. __some__ information
11. __a__ new word
12. __some__ new vocabulary

◇ PRACTICE 3, p. 150.

1. furniture /
2. table __s__
3. ring __s__
4. jewelry /
5. homework /
6. assignment __s__
7. job __s__
8. work /
9. question __s__
10. information /
11. word __s__
12. vocabulary /

◇ PRACTICE 4, p. 150.

1. (*no change*)
2. **two** tables
3. **two** rings
4. (*no change*)
5. (*no change*)
6. **two** assignments
7. **two** jobs
8. (*no change*)
9. **two** questions
10. (*no change*)
11. **two** new words
12. (*no change*)

◇ PRACTICE 5, p. 151.

1. **a lot of** furniture
2. **a lot of** tables
3. **a lot of** rings
4. **a lot of** jewelry
5. **a lot of** homework
6. **a lot of** assignments
7. **a lot of** jobs
8. **a lot of** work
9. **a lot of** questions
10. **a lot of** information
11. **a lot of** new words
12. **a lot of** new vocabulary

◇ PRACTICE 6, p. 151.

1. __much__ furniture
2. __many__ tables
3. __many__ rings
4. __much__ jewelry
5. __much__ homework
6. __many__ assignments
7. __many__ jobs
8. __much__ work
9. __many__ questions
10. __much__ information
11. __many__ words
12. __much__ new vocabulary

◇ PRACTICE 7, p. 152.

1. __a little__ furniture
2. __a few__ tables
3. __a few__ rings
4. __a little__ jewelry
5. __a little__ homework
6. __a few__ assignments
7. __a few__ jobs
8. __a little__ work
9. __a few__ questions
10. __a little__ information
11. __a few__ new words
12. __a little__ new vocabulary

◇ PRACTICE 8, p. 152.

1. __a__ game
2. __a__ rock
3. __a__ store
4. __an__ army
5. __an__ egg
6. __an__ island
7. __an__ ocean
8. __an__ umbrella
9. __a__ university
10. __a__ horse
11. __an__ hour
12. __a__ star
13. __an__ eye
14. __a__ new car
15. __an__ old car
16. __a__ used car
17. __an__ uncle
18. __a__ house
19. __an__ honest mistake
20. __a__ hospital
21. __a__ hand
22. __an__ aunt
23. __an__ ant
24. __a__ neighbor

◇ PRACTICE 9, p. 153.

1. __a__ letter
2. __some__ mail
3. __some__ equipment
4. __a__ tool
5. __some__ food
6. __an__ apple

7. __some__ clothing

8. __an__ old shirt

9. __some__ advice

10. __a__ suggestion

11. __an__ interesting story

12. __some__ interesting news

13. __a__ poem

14. __some__ poetry

15. __a__ song

16. __some__ Indian music

17. __a__ new idiom

18. __some__ new slang

◇ **PRACTICE 10, p. 153.**

1. grammar /

2. noun **s**

3. language **s**

4. English /

5. makeup /

6. scenery /

7. mountain **s**

8. traffic /

9. automobile **s**

10. sand /

11. dust /

12. beach **es**

13. slang /

14. mistake **s**

15. information /

16. fact **s**

17. game **s**

18. weather /

19. thunder /

20. water /

21. parent **s** . . . health /

22. circle / . . . degree **s**

23. Professor **s** . . . knowledge /

24. family / . . . luck /

25. neighbor **s** . . . help /

26. factor **ies** . . . pollution /

27. pride / . . . children /

28. people / . . . intelligence /

◇ **PRACTICE 13, p. 155.**

1. many letter **s** *are*

2. much mail /

3. many **men** *have*

4. many famil **ies** *are*

5. many word **s** *are*

6. many sentence **s** *are*

7. much chalk / *is*

8. much English /

9. much English literature /

10. many English word **s**

11. much gasoline / (much petrol /)

12. much homework /

13. many grandchild **ren**

14. many page **s** *are*

15. many librar **ies** * *are*

16. many bone **s** *are*

17. many **teeth** /

18. much water /

19. many cup **s**

20. much tea /

21. many glass **es**

22. much fun /

23. much education /

24. much soap /

25. many island **s** *are*

26. many people / *were*

27. many human being **s** *are*

28. many people /

29. many zero **es** OR zero **s** *are*

30. many butterfl **ies** *

◇ **PRACTICE 14, p. 156.**

1. a little music /

2. a few song **s**

3. a little help /

4. a little English /

5. a few more apple **s**

6. a little honey /

7. a little advice /

8. a few suggestion **s**

9. a few question **s**

10. a few people /

11. a few more minute **s**

12. a little light /

13. a little homework /

*The -y is changed to -i and then -es is added. Example: *baby → babies*. (See Chart 4-1.)

◇ PRACTICE 15, p. 157.

1. How many children do the Millers have?
2. How much money does Jake make?
3. How many players are there on a soccer team?
4. How much homework do you have tonight?
5. How many feet are there in a mile?
6. How many meters/metres are there in a kilometer/kilometre?
7. How many suitcases did you take on the plane to Florida?
8. How much suntan oil did you take with you?
9. How many pairs of sandals did you take?
10. How much toothpaste / How many tubes of toothpaste did you take?
11. How long did the flight take?
12. How many times have you been in Florida?
13. How many apples are there in the two baskets?
14. How much fruit is there in the two baskets?

◇ PRACTICE 16, p. 158.

Expected answers. Others may be possible.
PART I:
1. can/jar
2. box
3. bottle
4. jar
5. can
6. box
7. can
8. bag/box
9. bottle
10. can/bag
11. can/bag
12. bag
13. bottle/can
14. can

PART II:
15. cup/glass
16. bowl
17. slice/piece
18. slice/piece
19. slice/piece
20. glass
21. bowl/cup
22. piece
23. glass
24. bowl/cup
25. glass/cup
26. bowl
27. slice/piece
28. bowl/cup
29. bowl

◇ PRACTICE 20, p. 160.

1. D
2. G
3. F
4. B
5. E
6. C
7. A

◇ PRACTICE 22, p. 161.

1. **A** bird . . . Birds have feathers.
2. Ø Corn . . . (*none possible*)
3. Ø Milk . . . (*none possible*)
4. **A** flower . . . Flowers are beautiful.
5. Ø Water . . . (*none possible*)
6. **A** horse . . . Horses are strong.
7. Ø Jewelry . . . (*none possible*)
8. Ø Honey . . . (*none possible*)
9. **A** shirt . . . Shirts have sleeves.
10. Ø Soap . . . (*none possible*)

◇ PRACTICE 23, p. 161.

1. **a** bird . . . I saw some birds.
2. **some** corn . . . (*none possible*)
3. **some** milk . . . (*none possible*)
4. **a** flower . . . I picked some flowers.
5. **some** water . . . (*none possible*)
6. **a** horse . . . I fed grass to some horses.
7. **some** jewelry . . . (*none possible*)
8. **some** honey . . . (*none possible*)
9. **a** new shirt . . . Tom bought some new shirts.
10. **some** soap . . . (*none possible*)

◇ PRACTICE 24, p. 161.

1. **a** dog
2. **the** dog
3. **the** radio
4. **a** radio . . . **a** tape player
5. **a** desk, **a** bed, **a** chest of drawers
6. **the** desk . . . **the** top drawer
7. **the** basement
8. **a** basement
9. **a** subject and **a** verb
10. **the** subject . . . **the** verb
11. **a** meeting
12. **the** meeting
13. **a** long distance . . . **a** telephone
14. **The** distance . . . **the** sun . . . **the** earth
15. **the** telephone
16. **a** question
17. **the** problem
18. **a** poem
19. **the** lecture . . . **The** speaker . . . **an** interesting talk
20. **a** cup . . . **the** cafe . . . **the** corner

◇ **PRACTICE 25, p. 163.**

1. Ø Dogs
2. **the** dogs
3. Ø Fruit
4. **The** fruit
5. Ø Children
6. **the** children
7. Ø Paper . . . Ø trees
8. **The** paper
9. **the** potatoes
10. Ø Potatoes . . . Ø vegetables
11. Ø Nurses
12. **the** nurses
13. Ø Frogs . . . Ø small animals . . . Ø tails . . . Ø turtles . . . Ø tails . . . Ø hard shells
14. **The** frogs . . . **The** turtles
15. Ø books . . . Ø textbooks . . . Ø workbooks . . . Ø dictionaries . . . Ø encyclopedias . . . Ø entertainment . . . Ø novels . . . Ø poetry
16. **The** books
17. Ø plants . . . Ø fruit . . . Ø vegetables . . . Ø plants . . . Ø meat . . . Ø plants
18. **The** plants
19. **An** engineer . . . Ø engineers . . . Ø bridges . . . Ø rivers . . . Ø valleys . . . Ø highways . . . Ø railroad tracks . . . Ø other places
20. **the** bridges

◇ **PRACTICE 26, p. 164.**

1. **a** banana . . . **an** apple . . . **the** banana . . . **the** apple
2. **some** bananas . . . **some** apples . . . **the** bananas . . . **the** apples
3. **some** coffee . . . **some** milk . . . **The** coffee . . . **The** milk
4. **a** desk . . . **a** bed . . . **The** desk . . . **The** bed
5. **a** pen . . . **some** paper . . . **the** pen . . . **the** paper
6. **a** bag . . . **some** sugar . . . **some** cookies . . . **The** sugar . . . **the** flour . . . **the** flour . . . **some** little bugs . . . **the** little bugs . . . **a** new bag . . . **The** new bag
7. **some** birds . . . **a** tree . . . **a** cat . . . **the** tree . . . **The** birds . . . **the** cat . . . **the** cat . . . **the** birds
8. Once upon a time, **a** princess fell in love with **a** prince. **The** princess wanted to marry **the** prince, who lived in a distant land. She summoned **a** messenger to take **some** things to **the** prince to show him her love. **The** messenger took **the** jewels and **a** robe made of yellow and red silk to **the** prince. **The** princess anxiously awaited **the** messenger's return. She hoped that **the** prince would send her **some** tokens of his love. But when **the** messenger returned, he brought back **the** jewels and

the beautiful silk robe that **the** princess had sent. Why? Why? she wondered. Then **the** messenger told her: **The** prince already had **a** wife.

◇ **PRACTICE 28, p. 166.**

1. **An** egg . . . **the** egg
2. Ø Eggs
3. **a** scientific fact . . . Ø steam . . . Ø water
4. **the** tape player . . . **the** shelves . . . **the** batteries
5. Ø Chalk . . . **a** necessity
6. **the** plumber . . . **The** sink . . . **the** water supply . . . **the** house . . . **the** leak
7. Ø Water . . . **the** water . . . **The** pollution
8. **a** taxi
9. **the** car . . . **a** minute . . . **the** kids . . . **the** car . . . **a** minute
10. Ø Newspapers . . . **an** important source . . . Ø information
11. **The** sun . . . **a** star . . . **the** sun . . . Ø heat . . . Ø light . . . Ø energy
12. Ø Ducks
13. **the** letter . . . **A** strong wind . . . **the** floor . . . **the** dog . . . **the** scraps . . . **the** wastebasket
14. **An** efficient transportation system . . . **an** essential part
15. **the** alarm . . . **the** door . . . **the** stove . . . **the** windows . . . **the** lights
16. **an** exceptionally talented person
17. Ø Money . . . Ø trees
18. Ø sick people . . . **A** farmer . . . Ø crops . . . **An** architect . . . Ø buildings . . . **An** artist . . . Ø new ways . . . **the** world . . . Ø life
19. Ø Earthquakes . . . Ø relatively rare events
20. **an** earthquake . . . **the** earthquake . . . **The** ground

◇ **PRACTICE 30, p. 170.**

1. one
2. it
3. one
4. it . . . it
5. it
6. one
7. one
8. it
9. one
10. it

◇ **PRACTICE 32, p. 171.**

1. it
2. some
3. some
4. it
5. them
6. some
7. any
8. it

◇ PRACTICE 34, p. 173.

1. from
2. about . . . for
3. to . . . about
4. to . . . from . . . into . . . by
5. for
6. on
7. about/of . . . with
8. from . . . to
9. about . . . from

◇ PRACTICE 35, p. 174.

1. for
2. in
3. In . . . to
4. for
5. with
6. at
7. of
8. to
9. at
10. in . . . on
11. of
12. to
13. to
14. from . . . of
15. for
16. about/of . . . at
17. of . . . for . . . (up)on . . . for . . . In
18. for . . . to
19. A: about . . . about . . . with/at
    B: from . . . in . . . to . . . for
20. of . . . on

Chapter 9: CONNECTING IDEAS

◇ PRACTICE 1, p. 175.

1. The farmer has a <u>cow</u>, a <u>goat</u>, and a black <u>horse</u>.
   NOUN + NOUN + NOUN

2. Danny is a <u>bright</u> and <u>happy</u> child.
   ADJ + ADJ

3. I <u>picked</u> up the telephone and <u>dialed</u> Steve's number.
   VERB + VERB

4. The cook <u>washed</u> the vegetables and <u>put</u> them in boiling water.
   VERB + VERB

5. My feet were <u>cold</u> and <u>wet</u>.
   ADJ + ADJ

6. Sara is <u>responsible</u>, <u>considerate</u>, and <u>trustworthy</u>.
   ADJ + ADJ + ADJ

7. The three largest land animals are the <u>elephant</u>, the <u>rhinoceros</u>, and the <u>hippopotamus</u>.
   NOUN + NOUN + NOUN

8. A hippopotamus <u>rests</u> in water during the day and <u>feeds</u> on land at night.
   VERB + VERB

◇ PRACTICE 2, p. 176.

1. Rivers, streams, lakes, and oceans are all bodies of water.
2. My oldest brother, my neighbor, and I went shopping yesterday.
3. Ms. Parker is intelligent, friendly, and kind.
4. Did you bring copies of the annual report for Sue, Dan, Joe, and Mary?
5. In the early 1600s, the Chinese made wallpaper by painting birds, flowers, and landscapes on large sheets of rice paper.
6. Can you watch television, listen to the radio, and read the newspaper at the same time?
7. Lawyers, doctors, teachers, and accountants all have some form of continuing education throughout their careers.
8. Gold is beautiful, workable, indestructible, and rare.
9. My mother, father, grandfather, and sisters welcomed my brother and me home.
10. My husband imitates sounds for our children. He moos like a cow, roars like a lion, and barks like a dog.

◇ PRACTICE 4, p. 177.

1. Birds fly, and fish swim.
   S V   S V
2. Birds fly. Fish swim.
   S V   S V
3. Dogs bark. Lions roar.
   S V   S V
4. Dogs bark, and lions roar.
   S V   S V
5. A week has seven days. A year has 365 days.
   S V   S V
6. A week has seven days, and a year has 365 days.
   S V   S V
7. Bill raised his hand, and the teacher pointed at him.
   S V   S V
8. Bill raised his hand. The teacher pointed at him.
   S V   S V

◇ PRACTICE 5, p. 177.

1. I talked to Amy for a long time, but she didn't listen.
2. *(no change)*
3. I talked to Bob for a long time, and he listened carefully to every word.
4. *(no change)*
5. *(no change)*
6. Please call Jane, Ted, or Anna.
7. Please call Jane, Ted, and Anna.
8. I waved at my friend, but she didn't see me.
9. I waved at my friend, and she waved back.
10. *(no change)*
11. *(no change)*
12. My test was short and easy, but Ali's test was hard.

◇ PRACTICE 6, p. 178.

1. so
2. and
3. but
4. or
5. and
6. so
7. but
8. or

◇ PRACTICE 7, p. 178.

1. *(no change)*
2. I washed the dishes, and my son dried them.
3. I called their house, but no one answered the phone.
4. *(no change)*
5. I bought some apples, peaches, and bananas.
6. I was hungry, so I ate an apple.
7. *(no change)*
8. *(no change)*
9. My daughter is affectionate, shy, independent, and smart.
10. It started to rain, so we went inside and watched television.

◇ PRACTICE 8, p. 179.

1. Gina wants a job as an air traffic controller. Every air traffic controller worldwide uses English, so it is important for her to be fluent in the language.
2. *(no change)*
3. Mozart was a great composer, but he had a short and difficult life. During the last part of his life, he was penniless, sick, and unable to find work, but he wrote music of lasting beauty and joy.
4. Nothing in nature stays the same forever. Today's land, sea, climate, plants, and animals are all part of a relentless process of change continuing through millions of years.
5. *(no change)*
6. According to one researcher, the twenty-five most common words in English are: *the, and, a, to, of, I, in, was, that, it, he, you, for, had, is, with, she, has, on, at, have, but, me, my,* and *not.*

◇ PRACTICE 9, p. 179.

1. There are over 100,000 kinds of flies. They live throughout the world.
2. I like to get mail from my friends and family. It is important to me.
3. We are all connected by our humanity. We need to help each other. We can all live in peace.
4. There was a bad flood in Hong Kong. The streets became raging streams. Luckily no one died in the flood.
5. People have used needles since prehistoric times. The first buttons appeared more than two thousand years ago. Zippers are a relatively recent invention. The zipper was invented in 1890.

◇ PRACTICE 12, p. 182.

Part I:	Part II:
1. don't	11. do
2. is	12. are
3. won't	13. isn't
4. don't	14. didn't
5. does	15. does
6. aren't	16. won't
7. can	17. is
8. hasn't	18. can't
9. is	
10. doesn't	

◇ PRACTICE 13, p. 183.

1. does
2. don't
3. can't
4. don't
5. can't
6. is
7. does
8. did
9. is
10. isn't

◇ PRACTICE 14, p. 183.

Part I:	Part II:
1. are too	15. so is
2. can't either	16. neither do
3. do too	17. neither did
4. does too	18. so are
5. doesn't either	19. so do
6. isn't either	20. neither do
7. is too	21. so is
8. wasn't either	22. neither is
9. didn't either	23. so does
10. couldn't either	24. so is
11. did too	25. neither have
12. can't either	26. so did
13. does too	27. neither did
14. would too	28. neither can

◇ PRACTICE 17, p. 186.

1. Johnny was late for work <u>because [he] [missed] the</u>
                          S   **V**
   <u>bus</u>.

2. I closed the door <u>because [the room] [was] cold</u>.
                          S   **V**

3. <u>Because [I] [lost] my umbrella</u>, I got wet on the way
           S   **V**
   home.

4. Joe didn't bring his book to class <u>because [he]</u>
                                     S

   <u>[couldn't find] it</u>.
     V

◇ PRACTICE 18, p. 186.

1. I opened the window because the room was hot. **W**e felt more comfortable then.
2. *(no change)*
3. Because his coffee was cold, Jack didn't finish it. **H**e left it on the table and walked away.
4. Annie is very young. **B**ecause she is afraid of the dark, she likes to have a light on in her bedroom at night.
5. *(no change)*
6. Marilyn has a cold. **B**ecause she's not feeling well today, she's not going to go to her office.

◇ PRACTICE 20, p. 187.

Part I:
1. Jack never showed up for work on time, so he lost his job.
2. I was sleepy, so I took a nap.
3. The room was hot, so I opened the window.
4. It was raining, so I stayed indoors.

Part II:
5. Because Jason was hungry, he ate. OR: Jason ate because he was hungry.
6. Because I was tired, I went to bed.
7. We can't go swimming because the water in the river is polluted.
8. I was late for my job interview because my watch is broken.

◇ PRACTICE 22, p. 188.

1. B   7. B
2. A   8. B
3. A   9. A
4. B   10. A
5. A   11. B
6. A   12. A

◇ PRACTICE 23, p. 189.

1. C
2. C
3. C
4. B
5. C

◇ PRACTICE 24, p. 189.

1. C
2. A
3. A
4. B
5. C

◇ PRACTICE 27, p. 192.

1. separable
2. nonseparable
3. separable
4. nonseparable
5. separable
6. nonseparable
7. separable
8. separable

◇ PRACTICE 28, p. 193.

1. out   7. up
2. on   8. on
3. up   9. up
4. over   10. up
5. in   11. down . . . off
6. up

◇ PRACTICE 29, p. 193.

1. on
2. up
3. down . . . up
4. off
5. B: on   A: off
6. away
7. A: down   B: up
8. out . . . out
9. A: up   B: off

◇ PRACTICE 30, p. 195.

1. over it — NONSEP
2. it up — SEP
3. it off — SEP
4. them down — SEP
5. into him → NONSEP
6. it out — SEP
7. them off — SEP
8. on her — NONSEP
9. them off — SEP
10. it away — SEP

◇ PRACTICE 31, p. 195.

1. over it
2. them off
3. it up . . . it down
4. them away
5. it on
6. into him
7. up . . . them down . . . into
8. B: it away . . . on me   A: it up
9. off . . . on

Chapter 10:   GERUNDS AND INFINITIVES

◇ PRACTICE 1, p. 197.

1. (INF) Ann promised <u>to wait</u> for me.
2. (GER) I kept <u>walking</u> even though I was tired.
3. (INF) Alex offered <u>to help</u> me.
4. (GER) Karen finished <u>writing</u> a letter and went to bed.
5. (INF) Don't forget <u>to call</u> me tomorrow.
6. (GER) David was afraid of <u>falling</u> and <u>hurting</u> himself.
7. (GER) <u>Working</u> in a coal mine is a dangerous job.
8. (INF) It is easy <u>to grow</u> vegetables.

◇ PRACTICE 3, p. 198.

1. went dancing
2. is going to go hiking
3. went shopping
4. go swimming
5. goes fishing
6. go sightseeing
7. go camping
8. go sailing/boating
9. go skiing
10. went skydiving

◇ PRACTICE 4, p. 199.

1. B
2. A
3. B
4. B
5. A
6. B
7. B
8. B
9. A
10. A
11. A
12. B
13. B
14. B
15. A
16. B
17. B
18. B
19. A
20. B
21. B
22. B
23. B
24. A

◇ PRACTICE 5, p. 200.

1. B
2. A, B
3. A, B
4. B
5. A, B
6. A, B
7. A, B
8. B
9. A
10. A, B
11. A, B
12. A, B
13. B
14. B

◇ PRACTICE 8, p. 203.

1. Not yet. But I'm going to ~~pay the electric bill~~.
2. I didn't want to ~~go to class this morning~~.
3. No, but I ought to ~~call my mother~~.
4. No, I haven't, but I intend to ~~take my vacation~~.

◇ PRACTICE 10, p. 204.

1. in telling
2. of having to be
3. of drowning
4. about meeting
5. for helping
6. in going
7. in solving
8. about visiting
9. of chewing
10. about pleasing
11. on reading
12. to taking
13. like telling
14. for lying
15. on paying
16. of jogging
17. for causing
18. at remembering
19. about quitting
20. from doing
21. into forgiving
22. on eating
23. for spilling
24. of failing
25. of losing

◇ PRACTICE 12, p. 206.

1. by holding
2. by reading
3. by telling
4. by watching
5. by running
6. by staying . . . taking
7. by treating

◇ PRACTICE 14, p. 208.

1. with a broom
2. with a needle and thread
3. with a saw
4. with a thermometer
5. with a spoon
6. with a key
7. with a shovel
8. with a hammer
9. with a knife
10. with a pair of scissors

◇ PRACTICE 15, p. 208.

1. with
2. by
3. with
4. by
5. by
6. with
7. by
8. by
9. with
10. with
11. by
12. with
13. by
14. with
15. with
16. with

◇ PRACTICE 16, p. 209.

1. a. It is . . . to learn
   b. Learning . . . is
2. a. Eating . . . is
   b. It is . . . to eat
3. a. Driving . . . is
   b. It is . . . to drive
4. a. It is . . . to swim
   b. Swimming . . . is
5. a. Is it . . . to live
   b. Is living
6. a. Is it . . . to complete
   b. Is completing

◇ PRACTICE 21, p. 211.

1. (E) I called the hotel desk (in order) to ask for an extra pillow.
2. (C) I turned on the radio (in order) to listen to a ball game.
3. (D) I looked in the encyclopedia (in order) to find the population of Malaysia.
4. (A) People wear boots (in order) to keep their feet warm and dry.
5. (I) Andy went to Egypt (in order) to see the ancient pyramids.
6. (B) Ms. Lane stood on tiptoe (in order) to reach the top shelf.
7. (J) The dentist moved the light closer to my face (in order) to look into my mouth.
8. (F) I clapped my hands and yelled (in order) to chase a stray dog away.
9. (H) Maria took a walk in the park (in order) to get some fresh air and exercise.
10. (G) I offered my cousin some money (in order) to help him pay the rent.

◇ PRACTICE 22, p. 211.

1. for
2. to
3. to
4. for
5. to
6. to
7. for
8. for
9. to
10. for
11. to
12. for

◇ PRACTICE 23, p. 212.

1. strong enough to lift
2. too weak to lift
3. too full to hold
4. large enough to hold
5. too busy to answer
6. early enough to get
7. too big to get
8. big enough to hold

◇ PRACTICE 24, p. 213.

1. Alan is **too** smart *l* to make that kind of mistake.
2. Alan is *l* smart **enough** to understand how to solve that problem.
3. My pocket is *l* big **enough** to hold my wallet.
4. A horse is **too** big *l* for a person to lift.
5. This room is **too** hot *l* .
6. That watch is **too** expensive *l* .
7. Are you *l* tall **enough** to reach that book for me?
8. He's *l* strong **enough** to lift it.
9. I am **too** busy *l* to help you right now.
10. I think this problem is *l* important **enough** to require our immediate attention.
11. Nora is not **too** tired *l* to finish the project before she goes home.
12. Our company is *l* successful **enough** to start several new branches overseas.

◇ PRACTICE 25, p. 214.

1. to remember
2. catching
3. (in order) to look
4. to go swimming
5. (in order) to invite
6. going
7. listening
8. drawing
9. to understand . . . to improve . . . to be . . . Lecturing
10. to feed
11. to feed . . . getting
12. feeding
13. to earn . . . to take
14. to take
15. to get . . . (to) sleep
16. staring . . . thinking . . . to be
17. to work . . . to go/going . . . looking . . . doing

◇ PRACTICE 26, p. 215.

1. Jim offered to help me with my work.
2. My son isn't old enough to stay home alone.
3. Do you enjoy being alone sometimes, or do you prefer to be with other people all the time?
4. I called my friend to thank her for the lovely gift.
5. Mary talked about going downtown tomorrow, but I'd like to stay home.
6. It is interesting to learn about earthquakes.
7. Approximately one million earthquakes occur around the world in a year's time. Six thousand can be felt by humans. Of those, one hundred and twenty are strong enough to cause serious damage to buildings, and twenty are violent enough to destroy a city.
8. It's important to respect the power of nature. A recent earthquake destroyed a bridge in California. It took five years for humans to build the bridge. It took nature fifteen seconds to knock it down.
9. Predicting earthquakes is difficult. I read about one scientist who tries to predict earthquakes by reading the daily newspaper's lost-and-found ads for lost pets. He believes that animals can sense an earthquake before it comes. He thinks they then begin to act strangely. Dogs and cats respond to the threat by running away to a safer place. By counting thenumber of ads for lost pets, he expects to be able to predict when an earthquake will occur.

◇ PRACTICE 29, p. 219.

1. back
2. down/off
3. out
4. away
5. on
6. up . . . off
7. back
8. up
9. out . . . off . . . back/up

◇ PRACTICE 30, p. 220.

1. them away
2. it up
3. them on
4. it down
5. him up
6. it out
7. it back
8. it up
9. her back
10. it off
11. it off
12. it back
13. her out
14. it back

Chapter 11: THE PASSIVE

◇ PRACTICE 1, p. 221.

1. ACTIVE: Farmers <u>grow</u> corn.
2. PASSIVE: Corn <u>is grown</u> by farmers.
3. ACTIVE: Sara <u>wrote</u> the letter.
4. PASSIVE: The letter <u>was written</u> by Sara.
5. ACTIVE: The teacher <u>explained</u> the lesson.
6. PASSIVE: The lesson <u>was explained</u> by the teacher.
7. PASSIVE: Bridges <u>are designed</u> by engineers.
8. ACTIVE: Engineers <u>design</u> bridges.
9. ACTIVE: The mouse <u>ate</u> the cheese.
10. PASSIVE: The cheese <u>was eaten</u> by the mouse.

◇ PRACTICE 2, p. 222.

1. brought	14. played
2. built	15. read
3. bought	16. saved
4. eaten	17. sent
5. planned	18. spoken
6. given	19. spent
7. grown	20. taken
8. hit	21. taught
9. hurt	22. gone
10. left	23. visited
11. lost	24. worn
12. made	25. written
13. found	26. done

◇ PRACTICE 3, p. 222.

1. was eaten	7. will be played
2. is spoken	8. can be taught
3. are written	9. are going to be taken
4. was hurt	10. have been grown
5. is going to be visited	11. is worn
6. has been read	12. will be built

◇ PRACTICE 4, p. 223.

Part I:
1. are collected
2. are eaten
3. is grown
4. am paid
5. are written
6. is understood

Part II:
7. were collected
8. was built
9. was written
10. were destroyed

Part III:
11. have been visited
12. has been spoken
13. have been read
14. has been worn

Part IV:
15. will be discovered
16. will be visited

Part V:
17. is going to be hurt
18. are going to be offered
19. are going to be saved
20. is going to be elected

◇ PRACTICE 5, p. 224.

1. The government collects taxes.
2. Big fish eat small fish.
3. Everyone understands the meaning of a smile.
4. Leo Tolstoy wrote *War and Peace*.
5. Millions of tourists have visited the pyramids in Egypt.
6. Scientists in the twenty-first century will discover new information about the universe. OR
   Scientists will discover new information about the universe in the twenty-first century.

◇ PRACTICE 6, p. 225.

1. Mr. Rice signed the letter.
2. Did Mr. Foster sign the letter?
3. Ms. Owens sent the fax.
4. Did Mr. Chu send the other fax?
5. Will Mr. Berg meet Adam at the airport?
6. Mrs. Berg will meet Adam at the airport.
7. Has Mrs. Jordan invited you to the reception?
8. Mr. Lee has invited me to the reception.
9. Is the teacher going to collect the homework?
10. The teacher is going to collect the homework.

◇ PRACTICE 8, p. 225.

1. TRANSITIVE: Alex wrote <u>a letter</u>.
2. INTRANSITIVE
3. INTRANSITIVE
4. INTRANSITIVE
5. TRANSITIVE: Kate caught <u>the ball</u>.
6. INTRANSITIVE
7. INTRANSITIVE
8. TRANSITIVE: A falling tree hit <u>my car</u>.
9. TRANSITIVE: I returned <u>the book</u> to the library yesterday.
10. INTRANSITIVE

◇ PRACTICE 9, p. 226.

1. A noise awakened <u>me</u>.   I was awakened by a noise.
2. *(no change)*
3. Alice discovered <u>the mistake</u>. The mistake was discovered by Alice.
4. *(no change)*
5. *(no change)*
6. *(no change)*
7. *(no change)*
8. In the fairy tale, a princess kissed <u>a frog</u>. In the fairy tale, a frog was kissed by a princess.
9. *(no change)*
10. Anita fixed <u>the chair</u>. The chair was fixed by Anita.
11. *(no change)*
12. Did the Koreans invent <u>gunpowder</u>?   Was gunpowder invented by the Koreans?
13. *(no change)*
14. Research scientists will discover <u>a cure</u> for AIDS someday.
    A cure for AIDS will be discovered someday.   OR
    A cure for AIDS will someday be discovered.
15. *(no change)*

◇ PRACTICE 10, p. 227.

1. *unknown*
2. The wastebasket was emptied <u>by Fred</u>. Fred
3. Paul
4. The Eiffel Tower was designed <u>by Alexandre Eiffel</u>. Alexandre Eiffel
5. *unknown*
6. Nicole
7. *unknown*
8. Our exam papers will be corrected <u>by Ms. Brown</u>. Ms. Brown
9. *unknown*
10. Sara
11. *unknown*
12. *unknown*

◇ PRACTICE 12, p. 229.

1. enjoys
2. was established . . . established . . . were established
3. were disgusted . . . were replaced . . . were studied . . . (were) kept . . . became
4. understood . . . have become . . . was reduced . . . would become . . . believe
5. are now put . . . are watched . . . are fed . . . have
6. is prepared . . . is designed . . . are fed . . . are fed
7. are treated

◇ PRACTICE 13, p. 230.

1. Some people <u>are considering</u> a new plan.
   . . . is being considered
2. The grandparents <u>are watching</u> the children.
   . . . are being watched
3. Some painters <u>are painting</u> Mr. Rivera's apartment this week.
   . . . is being painted
4. Many of the older people in the neighborhood <u>were growing</u> vegetables.
   . . . were being grown
5. Eric's cousins <u>are meeting</u> him at the airport this afternoon.
   . . . is being met
6. I watched while the movers <u>were moving</u> the furniture from my apartment to a truck.
   . . . was being moved

◇ PRACTICE 16, p. 232.

1. must be sent
2. can be found
3. ought to be washed
4. may be cooked or (may be) eaten
5. has to be fixed
6. might be destroyed
7. may be called off
8. must be kept
9. shouldn't be pronounced
10. should be removed

◇ PRACTICE 18, p. 233.

1. are loved . . . brings . . . are often used . . . can be found
2. exist . . . can be found . . . have
3. are carried . . . carries . . . have been introduced
4. are appreciated . . . is made . . . is gathered . . . are eaten
5. are made . . . do not come . . . are made
6. may be planted . . . (may be) grown . . . survive

◇ PRACTICE 20, p. 235.

1. scare
2. are scared of
3. interest
4. is interested in
5. disappoint

6. are disappointed in
7. is pleased with
8. pleases
9. satisfies
10. am satisfied with

◇ PRACTICE 21, p. 236.

1. interesting
2. interested
3. exciting
4. excited
5. fascinated
6. fascinating
7. bored and confused
8. boring and confusing
9. interesting
10. fascinating . . . surprising

◇ PRACTICE 24, p. 238.

1. got sunburned
2. get well
3. get married
4. gets hungry
5. gets dark
6. get invited
7. get dry
8. getting tired
9. got dressed
10. get busy
11. get dizzy
12. got wet

◇ PRACTICE 26, p. 240.

1. B, C
2. A
3. B, C
4. A
5. B, C
6. A

◇ PRACTICE 27, p. 240.

1. used to go
2. am used to going/am accustomed to going
3. used to eat
4. is used to growing/is accustomed to growing
5. is used to eating/is accustomed to eating
6. used to have
7. am used to taking/am accustomed to taking
8. used to go

◇ PRACTICE 29, p. 241.

1. I'm supposed *to* call my parents tonight.
2. We're not suppose*d* to tell anyone about the surprise.
3. You *aren't* supposed to talk to Alan about the surprise.
4. My friend was suppose*d* to call me last night, but he didn't.
5. Children *are* supposed to respect their parents.
6. *Weren't* you supposed *to* be at the meeting last night?

◇ PRACTICE 30, p. 241.

1. (H) Doctors are supposed to care about their patients.
2. (C) Visitors at a zoo are not supposed to feed the animals.
3. (E) Employees are supposed to be on time for work.
4. (B) Air passengers are supposed to buckle their seatbelts before takeoff.
5. (D) Theatergoers are not supposed to talk during a performance.
6. (I) Soldiers on sentry duty are not supposed to fall asleep.
7. (A) Children are supposed to listen to their parents.
8. (J) Heads of state are supposed to be diplomatic.
9. (F) A dog is supposed to obey its trainer.
10. (G) People who live in apartments are supposed to pay their rent on time.

Chapter 12: ADJECTIVE CLAUSES

◇ PRACTICE 1, p. 245.

1. I thanked the man <u>who helped me move the refrigerator</u>.
   I thanked the man.
   He helped me move the refrigerator.
2. A woman <u>who was wearing a gray suit</u> asked me for directions.
   1: A woman asked me for directions.
   2: She was wearing a gray suit.
3. I saw a man <u>who was wearing a blue coat</u>.
   1: I saw a man.
   2: He was wearing a blue coat.
4. The woman <u>who aided the rebels</u> put her life in danger.
   1: The woman put her life in danger.
   2: She aided the rebels.
5. I know some people <u>who live on a boat</u>.
   1: I know some people.
   2: They live on a boat.

◇ PRACTICE 2, p. 246.

1. The woman <u>who answered the phone</u> was polite.
2. The man <u>who sang at the concert</u> has a good voice.
3. We enjoyed the actors <u>who played the leading roles</u>.
4. The girl <u>who fell down the stairs</u> is hurt.

◇ PRACTICE 3, p. 247.

1. The man **who** answered the phone was polite.
2. I liked the people **who** sat next to us at the soccer game.
3. People **who** paint houses for a living are called house painters.
4. I'm uncomfortable around married couples **who** argue all the time.
5. While I was waiting at the bus stop, I stood next to an elderly gentleman **who** started a conversation with me about my educational plans.

◇ PRACTICE 4, p. 247.

       S **V**
1. The people <u>who live next to me</u> are nice.

       S **V**
   2: They live next to me.

              S **V**
2. The people <u>whom Kate visited yesterday</u> were French.

       S **V**
   2: Kate visited them yesterday.

            S **V**
3. The people <u>whom I saw at the park</u> were having a

        S **V**
picnic.   2: I saw them at the park.

          S **V**
4. The students <u>who go to this school</u> are friendly.

      S **V**
   2: They go to this school.

            S **V**
5. The woman <u>whom you met last week</u> lives in

        S **V**
Mexico.   2: You met her last week.

◇ PRACTICE 5, p. 248.

1. The woman <u>whom Jack met</u> was polite.
2. I like the woman <u>who manages my uncle's store</u>.
3. The singer <u>whom we heard at the concert</u> was wonderful.

4. The people <u>who came to dinner</u> brought a small gift.
5. What is the name of the woman <u>whom Tom invited to the dance</u>?

◇ PRACTICE 6, p. 248.

1. who
2. who(m)
3. who
4. who(m)
5. who
6. who(m)
7. who
8. who(m)

◇ PRACTICE 8, p. 249.

1. ~~that~~
2. (no change)
3. ~~that~~
4. ~~that~~
5. (no change)
6. (no change) . . . ~~that~~

◇ PRACTICE 9, p. 250.

1. who
   that
2. who(m)
   that
   Ø
3. who(m)
   that
   Ø
4. who
   that
5. who
   that
6. who(m)
   that
   Ø

◇ PRACTICE 10, p. 250.

1. C
2. A
3. C
4. C
5. B
6. A

◇ PRACTICE 11, p. 251.

1. which
   that
   Ø
2. which
   that
3. which
   that
   Ø
4. which
   that
5. which
   that
   Ø
6. which
   that

◇ PRACTICE 12, p. 251.

1. ~~them~~
2. ~~it~~
3. ~~her~~
4. ~~it~~
5. ~~it~~
6. ~~her~~

◇ PRACTICE 15, p. 253.

1. A, C, D
2. A, D
3. C, D, E
4. A, C, D
5. A, D
6. C, D
7. C, D, E
8. C, D

◇ PRACTICE 20, p. 256.

1. tool . . . is
2. tools . . . are
3. woman . . . lives
4. people . . . live
5. cousin . . . works
6. coal miners . . . work
7. athlete . . . plays
8. athletes . . . play
9. person . . . makes
10. artists . . . make

◇ PRACTICE 21, p. 257.

1. that . . . for
   which . . . for
   Ø . . . for
   for which . . . Ø
2. that . . . to
   which . . . to
   Ø . . . to
   to which . . . Ø
3. that . . . in
   which . . . in
   Ø . . . in
   in which . . . Ø
4. that . . . with
   who(m) . . . with
   Ø . . . with
   with whom . . . Ø

◇ PRACTICE 23, p. 258.

1. a. to   b. [we listened **to** at Sara's apartment]
2. a. Ø   b. [I accidentally broke **Ø**]
3. a. for   b. [we were waiting **for**]
4. a. to   b. [I always enjoy talking **to** about politics]
5. a. Ø   b. [I had just written **Ø**]
6. a. in   b. [I've been interested **in** for a long time]

◇ PRACTICE 24, p. 258.

1. [I was looking **at**]
2. [I wanted **Ø**]
3. [we were listening **to** at Jim's yesterday]
4. [I was staring **at**]
5. [I've always been able to depend **on**]
6. [I was carrying **Ø**]
7. [that I'm not familiar **with**]
8. [we talked **about** in class]
9. [she is arguing **with**]
10. [they ate **Ø** at the cafe]
11. [you waved **at**]
12. [I borrowed money **from**]

◇ PRACTICE 26, p. 259.

1. I know a man whose daughter is a pilot.
   I know a man. His daughter is a pilot.
2. The woman whose husband is out of work found a
   job at Mel's Diner.
   The woman found a job at Mel's Diner. Her husband
   is out of work.

3. The man <u>whose wallet I found</u> gave me a reward.
   The man gave me a reward. I found his wallet.
4. I know a girl <u>whose family never eats
   dinner together</u>.
   I know a girl. Her family never eats
   dinner together.
5. The people <u>whose window I broke</u> got really angry.
   The people got really angry. I broke their window.

◇ PRACTICE 27, p. 261.

1. whose son was in an accident
2. James chose for his bedroom walls
3. I slept on at the hotel last night
4. that/which is used to carry boats with goods and/or
   passengers
5. whose children were doing poorly in her class
6. Ted bought for his wife on their anniversary
7. whose views I share
8. that/which had backbones
9. that/which disrupted the global climate and caused
   mass extinctions of animal life

◇ PRACTICE 29, p. 262.

1. who/that
2. that/which/Ø
3. who/that
4. whose
5. that/which
6. who(m)/that/Ø
7. that/which
8. whose

◇ PRACTICE 31, p. 264.

1. (Flowers) that bloom year after year are called
   perennials. (Flowers) that bloom only one season are
   called annuals.
2. B: Are you talking about the (boy) who's wearing the
   striped shirt or the (boy) who has on the T-shirt?
   A: I'm talking about the (boy) who just waved at us . . . .
   Do you see the kid (that) has the red baseball cap?
3. . . . . He stayed with a (family) who lived near Quito,
   Ecuador . . . . At first, all the (things) they did and
   said seemed strange to Hiroki . . . . He felt homesick
   for (people) who were like him in their customs and
   habits. But as time went on, he began to appreciate
   the way of (life) that his host family followed. Many of
   the (things) Hiroki did with his host family began to
   feel natural to him . . . . At the beginning of his stay
   in Ecuador, he had noticed only the (things) that were
   different between his host family and himself. At the

end, he understood how many (things) they had in
common as human beings despite their differences in
cultural background.
4. Many of the (problems) that exist today have existed
   since the beginning of recorded history. One of these
   problems is violent conflict between (people) who
   come from different geographical areas or cultural
   backgrounds. One group may distrust and fear
   another group of (people) who are different from
   themselves in language, customs, politics, religion,
   and/or appearance. These irrational fears are the
   source of much of the (violence) that has occurred
   throughout the history of the world.

◇ PRACTICE 34, p. 266.

1. up	7. over
2. out	8. out
3. in	9. up
4. out	10. out/in
5. over	11. out
6. down	12. up

◇ PRACTICE 35, p. 267.

1. out for
2. in on
3. up in
4. along with
5. around with
6. out of
7. through with
8. out for
9. back from
10. out of

Chapter 13: COMPARISONS

◇ PRACTICE 1, p. 268.

1. aren't as noisy as
2. is as lazy as
3. aren't as strong as
4. is as tall as
5. isn't as comfortable as
6. was as nervous as
7. isn't as big as
8. isn't as fresh and clean as
9. am not as ambitious as
10. are more interesting than

◇ PRACTICE 2, p. 269.

Part I:
1. almost as/not quite as
2. not nearly as
3. just as
4. almost as/not quite as

Part II:
5. just as
6. not nearly as
7. almost as/not quite as
8. almost as/not quite as

Part III:
9. just as
10. not nearly as
11. almost as/not quite as

Part IV:
12. just as
13. almost as/not quite as
14. just as
15. not nearly as
16. almost as/not quite as

◇ PRACTICE 4, p. 271.

1. E
2. C
3. D
4. G
5. B
6. H
7. F
8. A

◇ PRACTICE 5, p. 271.

1. stronger, strongest
2. more important, most important
3. softer, softest
4. lazier, laziest
5. more wonderful, most wonderful
6. calmer, calmest
7. tamer, tamest
8. dimmer, dimmest
9. more convenient, most convenient
10. cleverer, cleverest OR more clever, most clever
11. better, best
12. worse, worst
13. farther/further, farthest/furthest
14. slower, slowest
15. more slowly, most slowly

◇ PRACTICE 7, p. 273.

1. softer
2. colder
3. more expensive
4. cleaner
5. prettier
6. more careful
7. funnier
8. more confusing
9. more generous
10. worse
11. thinner
12. lazier

◇ PRACTICE 9, p. 275.

1. A, B
2. B
3. A, B
4. A, B
5. B
6. B
7. A, B
8. B
9. A, B
10. B

◇ PRACTICE 11, p. 276.

1. I did
2. she is
3. I do
4. she did
5. I was
6. he will
7. he does
8. he has
9. she did
10. he can

◇ PRACTICE 13, p. 277.

1. A
2. B, C, D
3. A
4. B, C, D
5. B, C, D
6. A
7. B, C, D
8. A

◇ PRACTICE 14, p. 277.

1. A, B
2. B
3. B
4. A, B
5. A, B
6. A, B
7. B
8. A, B

◇ PRACTICE 16, p. 278.

1. more slowly - ADV
2. slower - ADJ
3. more serious - ADJ
4. more seriously - ADV
5. more politely - ADV
6. more polite - ADJ
7. more careful - ADJ
8. more carefully - ADV
9. more clearly - ADV
10. clearer - ADJ

◇ PRACTICE 17, p. 279.

1. more newspapers - NOUN
2. more homework - NOUN
3. more snow - NOUN
4. more friends - NOUN
5. more pleasant - ADJ
6. more easily - ADV
7. more books - NOUN
8. more carefully - ADV
9. louder - ADJ

◇ PRACTICE 19, p. 280.

1. faster and faster
2. angrier and angrier
   [also possible: more and more angry]
3. bigger and bigger
4. colder and colder
5. better and better
6. harder and harder . . . wetter and wetter
7. weaker and weaker

◇ PRACTICE 20, p. 281.

1. The fresher . . . the better
2. The closer . . . the warmer
3. The sharper . . . the easier

4. The noisier . . . the angrier
5. The faster . . . the more confused

◇ PRACTICE 21, p. 282.

1. (D) Kangaroos are the most familiar Australian grassland animals.
2. (C) Giraffes have the longest necks of all animals.
3. (F) Apes and monkeys are the most intelligent animals that live on land (besides human beings).
4. (E) Bottle-nosed dolphins are the most intelligent animals that live in water.
5. (B) African elephants have the largest ears of all animals.
6. (A) Horses have the largest eyes of all four-legged land animals.

◇ PRACTICE 22, p. 282.

1. the deepest ocean
2. the cleanest air
3. The highest mountains on earth
4. the biggest bird
5. The two greatest natural dangers
6. the most popular forms of entertainment
7. The three most common street names
8. The longest river in South America
9. the largest living animal

◇ PRACTICE 23, p. 283.

1. the laziest . . . in
2. the most nervous of
3. the most beautiful . . . in
4. the worst . . . in
5. the farthest/furthest . . . in
6. the best . . . of
7. the biggest . . . in
8. the oldest . . . in
9. the most comfortable . . . in
10. the most exhausted of

◇ PRACTICE 24, p. 283.

1. the best . . . have ever had
2. the most responsible . . . have ever known
3. the nicest . . . have ever had
4. the most difficult . . . have ever taken
5. the best . . . have ever tasted
6. the worst . . . have ever made
7. the most beautiful . . . have ever seen
8. the easiest . . . have ever taken

7. I don't know when [the packages] [will arrive].
$$\overset{S}{\quad}\overset{V}{\quad}$$

8. Please tell me how far [it] [is] to the post office.
$$\overset{S}{\quad}\overset{V}{\quad}$$

9. I don't know [who] [knocked] on the door.
$$\overset{S}{\quad}\overset{V}{\quad}$$

10. I wonder [what] [happened] at the party last night.

Part II.
1. Where did Patty go last night?
2. Where do Joe's parents live?
3. Where does Joe live?
4. What time does the movie begin?
5. Where is Pine Street?
6. What did Estefan say?
7. When will the packages arrive?
8. How far is it to the post office?
9. Who knocked on the door?
10. What happened at the party last night?

◇ PRACTICE 3, p. 298.

1. where Jim goes
2. where Alex went
3. why Maria is laughing
4. why fire is
5. how much a new Honda costs
6. why Mike is always
7. how long birds live
8. when the first wheel was invented
9. how many hours a light bulb burns
10. where Emily bought
11. who lives
12. who(m) Julie talked

◇ PRACTICE 4, p. 299.

1. A: Jason works . . . does he work
2. A: did Susan eat   B: she ate
3. A: does that camera cost   B: this camera costs
4. A: can you run   B: I can run
5. A: did you see   B: I saw
6. A: Mr. Gow's office is . . . is Mr. Gow's office
7. A: did she get   B: she got
8. A: is it   B: it is
9. A: will you know   B: I will know
10. A: do you go   B: Do you mean . . . you want . . .
    I go   A: other people go
11. A: Who invented   B: who invented
12. A: did Toshi borrow   B: Toshi borrowed
13. A: does Rachel plan/is Rachel planning   B: she will
    return   A: was she   B: she was
14. A: did Tom go   B: you said   A: Tom went

38 ◇ *ANSWER KEY Chapter 14*

◇ PRACTICE 5, p. 301.

1. who [that man] [is]
$$\overset{S}{\quad}\overset{V}{\quad}$$

2. [who] [called]
$$\overset{S}{\quad}\overset{V}{\quad}$$

3. who [those people] [are]
$$\overset{S}{\quad}\overset{V}{\quad}$$

4. who [that person] [is]
$$\overset{S}{\quad}\overset{V}{\quad}$$

5. [who] [lives] next door to me
$$\overset{S}{\quad}\overset{V}{\quad}$$

6. who [my teacher] [will be] next semester
$$\overset{S}{\quad}\overset{V}{\quad}$$

7. [who] [will teach] us next semester
$$\overset{S}{\quad}\overset{V}{\quad}$$

8. what [a lizard] [is]
$$\overset{S}{\quad}\overset{V}{\quad}$$

9. [what] [happened] in class yesterday
$$\overset{S}{\quad}\overset{V}{\quad}$$

10. whose hat [this] [is]

11. [whose hat] [is] on the table

◇ PRACTICE 6, p. 301.

1. I don't know who that woman *is*.
2. I don't know who *is* on the phone.
3. I don't know what a crow *is*.
4. I don't know what *is* in that bag.
5. I don't know whose car *is* in the driveway.
6. I don't know whose car that *is*.
7. I don't know who Bob's doctor *is*.
8. I don't know who *is* in the doctor's office.

◇ PRACTICE 7, p. 301.

1. whose car that is
2. whose car is in front of Sam's house
3. who has the scissors
4. who the best students are
5. what a violin is
6. what causes earthquakes
7. what kind of fruit that is
8. whose hammer this is
9. who it is . . . where you are

◇ PRACTICE 26, p. 285.

1. the worst
2. worse
3. the best
4. better
5. the worst
6. worse
7. the worst
8. better

◇ PRACTICE 29, p. 287.

1. heavier than . . . the heaviest . . . of
2. friendlier than
3. the most famous . . . in
4. more wheels than
5. easier . . . than
6. larger than . . . darker . . . than
7. the safest
8. faster . . . than
9. bigger than
10. the loudest . . . in
11. the largest . . . in . . . the smallest . . . of
12. more important than . . . less important than
13. more information
14. kinder . . . more generous
15. more honest . . . than
16. the worst
17. The most important
18. more education than
19. the longest
20. the most delightful
21. The harder . . . the more impossible
22. the most common/commonest . . . in
23. faster than . . . the fastest . . . of
24. larger than
25. The greatest . . . in
26. safer . . . than
27. the largest . . . in

◇ PRACTICE 31, p. 291.

1. to
2. as
3. from
4. Ø . . . Ø
5. to
6. as
7. from
8. Ø . . . Ø
9. to . . . Ø . . . as . . . from
10. Ø . . . as . . . Ø . . . to . . . from

◇ PRACTICE 32, p. 292.

1. different
2. similar
3. the same
4. alike . . . alike . . . different
5. like
6. different
7. like
8. A: similar   B: like . . . alike
9. A: as   B: the same
10. A: alike   B: similar . . . the same

Chapter 14: NOUN CLAUSES

◇ PRACTICE 1, p. 296.

1. I don't know <u>where Jack bought his new boots</u>.
   NOUN CLAUSE
2. Where did Jack buy his new boots?   QUESTION
3. I don't understand <u>why Ann left</u>.   NOUN CLAUSE
4. Why did Ann leave?   QUESTION
5. I don't know <u>where your book is</u>.   NOUN CLAUSE
6. Where is your book?   QUESTION
7. When did Bob come?   QUESTION
8. I don't know <u>when Bob came</u>.   NOUN CLAUSE
9. What does "calm" mean?   QUESTION
10. Tarik knows <u>what "calm" means</u>.   NOUN CLAUSE
11. I don't know <u>how long the earth has existed</u>.
    NOUN CLAUSE
12. How long has the earth existed?   QUESTION

◇ PRACTICE 2, p. 296.

Part I:

1. I don't know <u>where [Patty] [went]</u> last night.
     S   V

2. Do you know <u>where [Joe's parents] [live]</u>?
          S   V

3. I know <u>where [Joe] [lives]</u>.
        S   V

4. Do you know <u>what time [the movie] [begins]</u>?
                 S   V

5. She explained <u>where [Brazil] [is]</u>.
                S   V

6. I don't believe <u>what [Estefan] [said]</u>.
                  S   V

◇ PRACTICE 10, p. 305.

1. if (whether) Tom is coming
2. if (whether) Jennifer can play the piano
3. if (whether) Paul went to work yesterday
4. if (whether) Susan is coming to work today
5. if (whether) Mr. Pips will be at the meeting
6. if (whether) Barcelona is a coastal town
7. if (whether) Carl would like to come with us
8. if (whether) I still have Yung Soo's address

◇ PRACTICE 15, p. 308.

1. I believe **that** we need to protect endangered species of animals.
2. Last night I dreamed **that** I was at my aunt's house.
3. I think **that** most people have kind hearts.
4. I know **that** Matt walks a long distance to school every day.
   I assume **that** he doesn't have a bicycle.
5. I heard **that** Sara dropped out of school.
6. Did you notice **that** Ji Ming wasn't in class yesterday?
   I hope **that** he's okay.
7. I believe **that** she told the truth.
8. A: Can Julia prove **that** her watch was stolen?
   B: I suppose **that** she can't, but she suspects **that** her roommate's friend took it.
9. A: Did you know **that** leopards sometimes keep their dead prey in trees?
   Yes, I understand **that** they save their food for later if they're not hungry.
10. A: Do you believe **that** a monster really exists in Loch Ness in Scotland?
    B: It says **that** some scientists have proved that the Loch Ness Monster exists.
    A: I think **that** the monster is purely fictional.

◇ PRACTICE 16, p. 309.

1. I'm sorry **that** you won't be here for Joe's party.
2. I'm glad **that** it's warm today.
3. I'm surprised **that** you bought a car.
4. Are you certain **that** Mr. McVay won't be here tomorrow?
5. John is pleased **that** Claudio will be here for the meeting.
6. Carmella was convinced **that** I was angry with her, but I wasn't.
7. Jason was angry **that** his father wouldn't let him use the family car.
8. Andy was fortunate **that** you could help him with his algebra.
   He was delighted **that** he got a good grade on the exam.

9. It's a fact **that** the Nile River flows north.
10. It's true **that** some dinosaurs could fly.
11. Are you aware **that** dinosaurs lived on earth for one hundred and twenty-five million (125,000,000) years?
12. Is it true **that** human beings have lived on earth for only four million (4,000,000) years?

◇ PRACTICE 20, p. 312.

1. I don't think that Alice has a car.
2. I think that Alex passed his French course.
3. I hope that Mr. Kozari is going to be at the meeting.
4. I think that cats can swim.
5. I don't think that gorillas have tails.
6. I suppose that Janet will be at Omar's wedding.

Chapter 15: QUOTED SPEECH AND REPORTED SPEECH

◇ PRACTICE 1, p. 314.

1. Alex said, "**D**o you smell smoke?"
2. He said, "**S**omething is burning."
3. He said, "**D**o you smell smoke? **S**omething is burning."
4. Rachel said, "**T**he game starts at seven."
5. She said, "**T**he game starts at seven. **W**e should leave here at six."
6. She said, "**T**he game starts at seven. **W**e should leave here at six. **C**an you be ready to leave then?"

◇ PRACTICE 2, p. 315.

1. "Do you smell smoke?" **A**lex said.
2. "Something is burning," he said.
3. "Do you smell smoke? **S**omething is burning," he said.
4. "The game starts at seven," Rachel said.
5. "The game stasrts at seven. **W**e should leave here at six," she said.
6. "Can you be ready to leave at six?" she asked.
7. "The game starts at seven. **W**e should leave here at six. **C**an you be ready to leave then?" she said.
8. "The game starts at seven," she said. "**W**e should leave here at six. **C**an you be ready to leave then?"

◇ PRACTICE 3, p. 315.

1. Mrs. Hill said, "**M**y children used to take the bus to school."
2. She said, "**W**e moved closer to the school."
3. "Now my children can walk to school," Mrs. Hill said.
4. "Do you live near the school?" she asked.
5. "Yes, we live two blocks away," I replied.
6. "How long have you lived here?" Mrs. Hill wanted to know.
7. I said, "**W**e've lived here for five years. **H**ow long have you lived here?"
8. "We've lived here for two years," Mrs. Hill said. "**H**ow do you like living here?"
9. "It's a nice community," I said. "**I**t's a good place to raise children."

◇ PRACTICE 4, p. 316.

CONVERSATION 1:

"Why weren't you in class yesterday?" Mr. Garcia asked me.

"I had to stay home and take care of my pet bird," I said. "He wasn't feeling well."

"What? Did you miss class because of your pet bird?" Mr. Garcia demanded to know.

I replied, "Yes, sir. That's correct. I couldn't leave him alone. He looked so miserable."

"Now I've heard every excuse in the world!" Mr. Garcia said. Then he threw his arms in the air and walked away.

CONVERSATION 2:

"Both of your parents are deaf, aren't they?" I asked Robert.

"Yes, they are," he replied.

"I'm looking for someone who knows sign language," I said. "Do you know sign language?" I asked.

"Of course I do. I've been using sign language with my parents since I was a baby," he said. "It's a beautiful and expressive language. I often prefer it to spoken language."

"Well, a deaf student is going to visit our class next Monday. Could you interpret for her?" I asked.

"That's great!" he answered immediately and enthusiastically. "I'd be delighted to. I'm looking forward to meeting her. Can you tell me why she is coming?"

"She's interested in seeing what we do in our English classes," I said.

◇ PRACTICE 7, p. 318.

1. he . . . his
2. I . . . my
3. she . . . her
4. he . . . me
5. she . . . my
6. they . . . their
7. he . . . his
8. he . . . me . . . him . . . his

◇ PRACTICE 8, p. 318.

1. needed
2. was meeting
3. had studied
4. had forgotten
5. was
6. would carry
7. could teach
8. had to attend
9. should leave
10. wanted

◇ PRACTICE 10, p. 320.

1. told
2. said
3. said
4. told
5. told
6. told
7. told
8. said
9. told
10. said

◇ PRACTICE 11, p. 321.

1. how old I was
2. if he was going to be
3. if I could hear
4. if he had ever seen
5. if she was passing her
6. if she had
7. when he would get back from his
8. if he had changed his

◇ PRACTICE 15, p. 324.

1. asked . . . to help
2. invited . . . to have
3. encouraged . . . to take
4. advised . . . to call . . . (to) apologize
5. permitted . . . to use
6. ordered . . . to sit
7. reminded . . . to order
8. warned . . . not to go

◇ PRACTICE 20, p. 329.

1. A
2. B
3. B
4. C
5. B
6. C
7. A
8. B
9. C
10. B
11. C
12. B

Chapter 16: USING WISH; USING IF

◇ PRACTICE 1, p. 333.

1. NO—She wishes she were safe at home.
2. YES—He wishes he had not come to the woods.
3. NO—Heidi wishes she could remember how to get back to town.
4. NO—Sara wishes she had listened to her mother.
5. NO—David wishes he had a flashlight.
6. YES—Heidi wishes they had not left the main path.

◇ PRACTICE 2, p. 334.

1. had
2. didn't have
3. taught
4. didn't snow
5. understood
6. could sing
7. didn't have . . . had
8. didn't have to study
9. were
10. were

◇ PRACTICE 3, p. 334.

1. don't . . . did
2. do . . . didn't
3. isn't . . . were
4. doesn't . . . did
5. am . . . weren't
6. can't . . . could

◇ PRACTICE 4, p. 335.

1. had had
2. hadn't had
3. had understood
4. hadn't lost
5. had been

◇ PRACTICE 5, p. 335.

1. did . . . hadn't
2. didn't . . . had
3. did . . . hadn't
4. don't . . . did
5. am . . . weren't

◇ PRACTICE 7, p. 336.

1. NO . . . NO—had . . . could build
2. NO . . . YES—were . . . would not be
3. NO . . . NO—had . . . could lead
4. NO . . . YES—had listened . . . would not have come
5. YES . . . YES—had not left . . . would not have gotten

◇ PRACTICE 8, p. 337.

1. were . . . could speak
2. didn't have . . . would ask
3. needed . . . would buy
4. weren't . . . would finish
5. had . . . could go
6. were . . . could paint
7. understood . . . could solve

◇ PRACTICE 10, p. 338.

1. need . . . will/can buy
2. needed . . . would/could buy
3. had needed . . . would have/could have bought
4. go . . . will/can see
5. went . . . would/could see

6. had gone . . . would have/could have seen
7. have . . . will/can write
8. had . . . would/could write
9. had had . . . would have/could have written

5. A
6. C
7. B
8. A
9. D
10. D

◇ PRACTICE 11, p. 339.

1. had gone . . . would have/could have finished
2. would have answered . . . had heard
3. had told . . . would have/could have helped
4. would have/could have seen . . . had come
5. had read . . . could have talked
6. had seen . . . would have/could have offered
7. had not had to get . . . would have/could have completed

◇ PRACTICE 15, p. 341.

1. hadn't been
2. wouldn't have found
3. hadn't yelled
4. had walked
5. wouldn't have heard
6. hadn't yelled
7. wouldn't have been found
8. hadn't known
9. would have had to spend
10. hadn't gone

◇ PRACTICE 12, p. 339.

1. you'd = you had
   I'd = I would
2. I'd = I would
3. I'd (known) = I had (known)
   I'd (have bought) = I would (have bought)
4. he'd = he would
5. I'd = I had
   They'd = They would

◇ PRACTICE 17, p. 342.

1. had . . . would take
2. were . . . would/could build
3. were . . . would look
4. watch
5. is/will be . . . would be
6. would rise
7. were . . . would the rainbow be . . . would be
8. A: stay/will stay   B: would stay
9. would you do . . . were . . . Would you run . . . Would you call . . . Would you use
10. would you do . . . were
11. A: had   B: had . . . could carry . . . (could) pick
12. would take

◇ PRACTICE 13, p. 340.

1. D
2. B
3. C
4. D